The Broad Scope of Psychoanalysis: Clinical, Theoretical and Applied

The Broad Scope of Psychoanalysis: Clinical, Theoretical and Applied

Francis Baudry

IPBOOKS.net
International Psychoanalytic Books

International Psychoanalytic Books
New York • http://www.IPBooks.net

The Broad Scope of Psychoanalysis: Clinical, Theoretical and Applied
Published by IPBooks, Queens, NY
IPBooks.net

ISBN: 978-1-956864-88-5

This book is dedicated to the memory of my son Alain who would have enjoyed its contents.

Contents

Introduction

    by Nathan Szajnberg..1

Clinical

1.   Remarks on Spoken Words in the Dream 9

2.   The Personal Dimension and Management of the Supervisory
Situation with a Special Note on the Parallel Process 37

3.   Kohut and Glover: The Role of Subjectivity in Psychoanalytic
Theory and Controversy...65

4.   Winnicott's 1968 Visit to the New York Psychoanalytic Society
and Institute: A Contextual View.......................................95

5.   The Problem of Change: Evolution of Theory and Technique........133

Character: Clinical and Theoretical

6.   The Evolution of the Concept of Character in Freud's Writings 149

7.   Character: A Concept in Search of an Identity.................181

8.   Character, Character Type, and Character Organization 205

9.   Character in Fiction and Fiction in Character.................241

10. The Relevance of the Analyst's Character and Attitudes
to his Work 271

Art Through the Psychoanalytic Lens

11. An Essay on Method in Applied Psychoanalysis 295

12. A Dream, a Sonnet, and a Ballad: The Path to Keats's
    La Belle Dame Sans Merci..327

13. Faulkner's *As I Lay Dying*: Issues of Method in Applied Analysis ..361

14. Flaubert and Madame Bovary: An Intimate Courtship 381

15. The Myths of the Virgin: A Psychoanalytic Review.........................399

16. Freud and Marie Bonaparte's Correspondence (1925–1939):
    An Intimate Relationship. 421

17. Montaigne: A Precursor to Freud..455

18. Pascal: Vacuum, Void, and Emptiness 487

Introduction by Nathan Szajnberg

This book is a quiet pleasure about inner life, clinical thought, how rich are the dynamics of our inner oceans, their currents and countercurrents, and the tectonic plates that lie beneath. The book also describes the ebbs and flows of how we touch others' shores and how they affect us.

Depths. To shift metaphors from ocean to cave (recalling Plato's cave of shadows), Dr. Baudry, like a spelunker, wears a bright head lamp to illuminate our passage through the tunnels, the twists and turns, the *cul de sacs* and continuations through the darkness of hidden life. Freud began his Dream book quoting Danté's beloved Virgil: *"Flectere si nequeo superos, Acheronta movebo."* If I cannot bend the heavens above, I will move Hell. (*Aeneid*; Book VII, Line 312). Baudry, at least, moves us, or rather guides us, through the darkness of hidden life.

This is, hence, a "guide book," a Baedeker's through the discipline of this thing many call psychoanalysis, the study of inner life.

It is divided into three: clinical, the nature of character, and how psychoanalysis can illuminate or art. This makes sense for the student of inner life: the clinical (or our interest in what goes on inside ourselves, and later, others) is what draws us to this discipline. "Character," as Wallerstein later showed, is mostly what psychoanalysis works with; and the arts are about what delights us but may originate from inner struggles.

A bit more on this tripartite division. Baudry starts with the clinical, such as dreams, specifically words embedded within them. The section on character is perhaps the best primer on this "thing" we all own, or

1

what makes us familiar to others (and ourselves). When Bob Wallerstein inquired of psychoanalysts, internationally, what their unique focus was, they responded: working on character. And Wallerstein—being Wallerstein, that is a thoughtful researcher—asked these analysts what the components of this thing called character are, they responded with what ultimately became seventeen aspects of "character," such as vivacity or lethargy, reliability/unreliability, optimism/pessimism, and so on. These were then incorporated into Shedler and Westen's assessment of character.

An introduction could go through each of the nineteen chapters of this book. Instead, I select a few that captured me, to give the reader a sense of the inner excitement that lies in wait for you. Let's begin with character, for it has become the focus of psychoanalysis, starting in the 1950's, and throughout the explorations of Borderline (Grinker, et al. 1968; Kernberg,1975), Narcissistic (Kohut, 1971), and general character neurosis (Giovacchini, 1989).

The chapters on character are necessary for studies for psychoanalysts. If there is consensus (God help us find *any* consensus today!) among international analysts, "character" is the primary subject of clinical work. Hence, a careful study of the character's nature is needed. Baudry gives this.

So, character work was the consensus in response to Bob Wallerstein's question, and the seventeen facets of character, now incorporated into the Shedler Westen scale (DeWitt, et al. 1999; Shedler, Westen, 2007) was the result. When I studied Wallerstein's scale with Kathy DeWitt, reading Baudry's three central essays on character was one of our first assignments. To read them in this book, is to have a primer on character.

Baudry begins with Freud's brief limning of "'character" ideas Freud developed when analyses were brief, before working through. Then, following Freud, the efflorescence of clinical studies of character, often precipitated by working with peripheral cases such as "borderline" or "narcissistic" (Knight, 1953).

Character is what is "etched within our bones," what makes us recognizable to many, what remains consistent from setting to setting, even if it is the predictably unpredictable "character" of the Borderline (Grinker et al., 1968). Study these few chapters, including the almost heretical paper on how the character of the psychoanalyst affects treatment, and you will have much of the clinical world in a grain of sand. Baudry is an honest scholar: he lifts the curtain on what happens in that quiet chamber where supervision of psychoanalytic work happens, and where, even there, the breezes of character ruffle the nature of the work.

The speech in dreams chapter is Baudry's first published paper (1974). It is not only a careful dissection of "heard" speech in dreams, but also with allusions to his teachers at NYPSI, such as Kris, Arlow and Isakower. In general, a sub theme in this book is how Baudry made rich use of the collegial community of NYPSI at its apogee. He begins with Isakower's pronouncement that heard speech in dreams are the superego's contribution. But this doesn't hold up to clinical experience. Dream speeches are rare, as Freud pointed out. And dream conversation is more subject to secondary revision (the fourth contribution to dream building). Baudry suggests that like Shapiro's neurotic styles, there may be dream styles. He opens a new scenario, dream styles, that I don't believe has been explored. In closing, he reminds us that the spoken word is the main route for acquiring culture. Speech has multiple roles in life and is reflected in its multiple meanings in dreams.

Baudry's report on Winnicott's 1968 presentation to NYPSI, and its excoriating reception by all three discussants is both an excellent summary of Winnicott's thought, and an anthropological account of the culture that was NYPSI at that moment. This paper was written in 2009, hence four decades have elapsed.

Baudry's access to the NYPSI archives enriches the account. Each of the NYPSI scientific meetings was an event, with formal attire expected—

tux and tails. Dinner with the speaker and a few important guests was *de rigour;* Winnicott declined. In my era, it was held at the restaurant next door, and, on one occasion, lamb was served from a colleague's Berkshire farm. Winnicott circulated his paper, "The Use of an Object," to the discussants, and they came prepared, knives out and sharpened. Ironically, as we will see, they "fell" for destroying the object—Donald Winnicott, which is the developmental stage before acceptance. The hall was filled, and the crowd overflowed to the library (in the basement, where I spent much time in the stacks).

Baudry starts with the culture of NYPSI: now the home of "ego psychology," imported by the HKL trio (Hartmann, Kris, and Loewenstein). There were also tensions that developed among the European Jewish refugee analysts versus the American Jewish analysts, such as Arlow and Brenner. (Today, we might consider these the narcissism of small differences, or almost irrelevant to whatever the styles of psychoanalysis are considered today.)

The three discussants appeared carefully selected. Edith Jacobson had recently competed her "Self and the Object World," but did so from drive theory: instincts were pleasure-seeking (not object-seeking); she criticized the Kleinians for not differentiating external objects from endopsychic representations. Ritvo (one of my teachers at Yale) was then considered a pre-eminent student of institutionalized deprived infants. He emphasized the object in development. Fine, while young, represented the NYPSI theory.

Next the paper. Winnicott flipped our understanding of "relating" to an object. He said that relating comes earlier; "using" implies that the baby now understands that the object (mother) is part of the external world. Today, after Dan Stern, we might say that "using" takes place after affect attunement (at about eight to ten months) when the baby "gets it" that the mother has a mind of her own, *which the baby can influence.*

Winnicott dissects this developmental sequence:

1. Subject relates to object
2. Object is "found" by the subject
3. Subject 'destroys" the object (the breast)
4. Object survives
5. Subject can use the object

Winnicott, a practicing pediatrician, knew from observation how ravenously the baby goes for the breast and sucks; he also saw how willingly the mother offers the breast. Brazelton (personal communication) described one mother as saying that when her baby sucked, she felt it from the tips of her toes. I will let you read the chapter for the almost ravenous consumption of Winnicott by the discussants. Having used up the discussion time, there was no time for responses from the audience (also my experience when I was a member of NYPSI), and little time for Winnicott to respond—except for him to quip that his concept had been torn to pieces and he would be happy to give it up!

But Winnicott's physical response the next day was to become so severely ill that he needed hospitalization: there is debate over whether this was influenza or exacerbation of his underlying heart ailment. But there should be little psychoanalytical debate over the toll taken on him by this onslaught.[1]

As I indicated earlier, Winnicott may have offered himself as the "breast" to be attacked (and destroyed) in order for his ideas to be used. If so, perhaps, we might assume, it was unconscious.

Now, Baudry gives us a gift at the end of the paper in which he offers Winnicott's three major postulates on self and place of aggression:

1. *The Role of Self:* Winnicott reverses Freud's sequence of mind's structural components. For Winnicott there is no id before ego, if we think

---

1 As Winnicott had no insurance in the US, a member of NYPSI paid for his medical care (personal communication).

of id as the *psychic* component of physiological processes, such as hunger or pain. And if we consider the latter, which is Freud's definition of id, then, in fact, Winnicott is closer to Freud's intent of id as a psychic structure (hence, needing some connection with an object).

2. *Role of the (Facilitating) Environment in Development:* Winnicott distinguishes maturation from development, although the two are necessarily interactive. Spitz's observations of institutionalized infants are tragic examples of how lacking a facilitating environment distorts maturation and development. Specifically, in 1945, Winnicott wrote that the baby has instinctual urges and predatory ideas. The mother, in turn, wants her breast "attacked." She must have tolerance and understanding. She is the first "object" external to the infant's self.

3. *Development of Aggression:* Primary nondestructive aggression (I prefer the term "assertion") is connected with appetite, assertion, motility, and life itself. Winnicott fundamentally disagreed with Klein that aggressive fantasies are directed at the depriving breast. He spoke of the ruthless infant at this stage. When concern for the whole object appears, we see something that Klein termed the depressive position. A tolerant mother helps the infant move from object relating to usage. Some borderlines appear fixated at this stage of true aggression. Another Winnicott difference with Klein: splitting is an adverse consequence of the mother's poor management of the baby's aggression.

Baudry reminds us that Freud (1915) speculated that *hate precedes love as a repudiation of the external world.* Hate is associated with self-preservative instincts. The hated object is a bundle of projections.

Let's leave this elegant discussion here, except to say this. Baudry paints a portrait of the '60s NYPSI scientific community, gives an honestly harsh view of the three discussants and Winnicott's near-death experience, and gives a brief, pithy review of Winnicott. A remarkable triple-play!

The final section is dessert: applying psychoanalysis to art.

Baudry touches on visual and written arts. I recall going to the Metropolitan Museum with Baudry (he lived down the street) to listen to him dissect the structure of a painting to bring out greater meaning. He will do this for you with Vermeer or "Bovary."

Here it is. A giant three-course feast on psychoanalysis, or as I prefer to call it, the study of inner life. Indulge and enjoy. A comparable culinary feast would be at *Brasserie Bofinger* in Paris, between Bastille and Place des Vosges. As Dr. Baudry is both French and American, he brings us the tastes of both cultures.

REFERENCES

DeWitt, K. N., Milbrath, C., & Wallerstein, R.S. (1999). "Scales of Psychological Capacities: Support for a Measure of Structural Change." *Psychoanalysis and Contemporary Thought* 22(3):453–480.

Freud, S. (1915). Instincts and their Vicissitudes. *S.E.* 14:109–140.

Giovacchini, P. L. (1989). *The Impact of Narcissism: The Errant Therapist on a Chaotic Quest.* Northvale, NJ: Jason Aronson.

Grinker, R. Drye, R. and Werbel, B. (1968). *The Borderline Syndrome.* New York: Basic Books.

Kernberg, O.F. (1975). *Borderline Conditions and Pathological Narcissism.* Northvale, NJ: Jason Aronson.

Knight, R. (1953). Borderline States. *Bulletin of the Menninger Clinic* 17:1–12.

Kohut, H. (1971). *The Analysis of the Self: A Systematic Approach to the Psychoanalytic Treatment of Narcissistic Personality Disorders.* Madison, CT: International Universities Press.

Shedler, J., & Westen, D. (2007). Personality diagnosis with the Shedler-Westen Assessment Procedure (SWAP): Integrating clinical and statistical measurement and prediction. *Journal of Abnormal Psychology* 116:810–822.

CHAPTER 1

Remarks on Spoken Words in the Dream
[(1974). *Psychoanal. Q.*, (43):581–605.]

I became interested in the problem of the spoken word in the dream as an outgrowth of a Kris Study Group on Validation of Psychoanalytic Hypotheses. Referring to the difficulties in validating psychoanalytic hypotheses, Arlow alluded to the concept, first stated by Isakower (1954), that spoken words in the dream *are a direct contribution from the superego to the manifest content of the dream* (p. 3). It was suggested that a 'simple' study be made to try to corroborate this idea. The present paper attempts such a study.

THEORETICAL ASPECTS

To bring together a number of dreams and see whether Isakower's hypothesis can be substantiated raised a number of complex procedural issues. In psychoanalysis substantiation refers to the issue of proof. In the case of lower levels of abstraction, it is possible to 'disprove' a hypothesis if available data contradicts the thesis under study. However, in the case of higher levels of abstraction, the concept of validation depends on the usefulness of the hypothesis—its serviceability in organizing and explaining less abstract clinical data. Isakower's formulation is, of course, at a relatively abstract level; its usefulness hinges on the following questions: Can we use the hypothesis to deepen our clinical grasp of the dream? Do more pieces fit together as a result of its application?

If we look closely at the wording—the spoken word is *"a direct contribution from the superego to the manifest content of the dream"*—we encounter an immediate stumbling block from the point of view of research. What clinical evidence would we need to confirm the *direct contribution of the superego*? The presence of a guilt conflict could not confirm it as it would not tell us about a direct contribution. In fact, there is really no clinical data that would do so. Therefore, the question arises whether it is an untestable hypothesis. An attempt is made here to set forth some of the meanings of Isakower's statement and to ascertain which of them can be supported by clinical evidence.

Intuitively it is appealing to think that the spoken word represents a crucial confrontation between the ego and the superego, i.e., that the patient has been confronted on some moral, critical ground even if this is not apparent on the surface. As the presence of the superego is ordinarily made evident during some conflict situation, in the absence of conflict there is usually no overt activity which betrays its presence. In *The Ego and the Mechanisms of Defence*, Anna Freud (1937) writes:

> Our picture of the superego always tends to become hazy when harmonious relations exist between it and the ego. We then say that the two coincide, i.e., at such moments the superego is not perceptible as a separate institution either to the subject himself or to an outside observer. Its outlines become clear only when it confronts the ego with hostility or at least with criticism. The superego like the id becomes perceptible in the state which it produces within the ego; for instance, when its criticism evokes a sense of guilt (pp. 5–6).

We might assume then, as Isakower implies, that the dream always arises out of some conflict situation and that at certain points in the dream the superego as an agency will make its voice heard.

My approach makes the following hypothesis: According to our clinical experience, self-observation in the dream often arises because some aspect of the dream becomes threatening to the sleeping ego and the censorship is roused to action. As self- observation is often associated with self-criticism, sometimes secondary to it, one would expect that if we follow Isakower's conception, whenever the superego is invoked at a specific point in the dream, clinical evidence might be found of some conflict situation involving the superego on the one hand and the ego on the other. I emphasize self-observation because at a manifest level spoken words in the dream often suggest descriptively one part of the self commenting on another part.

We know that clinically an important manifestation of conflict involving the superego is the affect of guilt, demonstrated either directly or indirectly (i.e., by way of a defense against it). Hence, is it possible to demonstrate in the manifest or latent content growing out of the spoken word a central and unique place for some conflicts involving guilt? The absence of such elements would not invalidate Isakower's thesis, but would make it clinically less useful.

In the present paper the focus is shifted from the demonstration of an abstract entity to the demonstration of the functions generally associated with that structure. I also imply that if there is a conflict situation which arouses the censor and forces the ego into an attitude of self-observation, it is likely that there is a conflict around the issue of guilt. This assumption is not clinically unsound. We know that genetically self-observation is tinged with criticism and that the child's reality testing is initially confused with moral right and wrong (as in the instance of the mother who scolds the child about to cross a street at a red light). Since the dream offers us examples of regressive functioning, this genetic connection may easily be revived.

Isakower's 1939 and 1954 papers reveal that his hypothesis is based on a special point of view concerning the nature of the superego and its relation to self-observation and the dream. According to Isakower (1972),[2] the superego affixes its stamp on the dream during the process of secondary revision, not before. A manifestation of this influence is the spoken word which represents descriptively the crossing of the language barrier, accompanied by partial awakening; structurally it signifies the re-establishment of the censorship. The phenomenon is dynamically a first attempt at interpretation of the dream. It is akin to the process of self-observation which Isakower allocates to the superego.

In nontechnical terms, the superego looks at the dream and in a hypnagogic state sees much more clearly the meaning of the dream than later, when it is reunited with the ego in the waking state. This accounts for the ambiguity almost always found in the spoken word in the dream. Other functions classically included under the superego, such as the punitive function, may also be in evidence, but not necessarily so.

According to this view, then, any spoken words, even those that do not manifestly imply a judgment or evaluation of the dream, are considered to be evidence of the functioning of the superego. The dream takes place on the optical level; the appearance of spoken words implies a shift in level of consciousness toward the waking state.

Isakower did not feel it appropriate to apply the principle of multiple function to the dream, and viewed what might be considered drive or defense contributions to the synthesis as simple extensions of superego activity. He believed that the superego could reflect on some aspect of the drive or defense, and saw the linguistic phenomenon as originating solely in the superego. He felt that dreams with apparent manifest content involving a story suggestive of punishment are probably fantasies taken over by the dream, but not created by it.

---

2 I had an opportunity to discuss the main theses of my paper with Dr. Isakower several years ago.

The crucial difference between Isakower's view and the one I shall elaborate here is that for him spoken words are *by definition* a superego contribution since they imply self-observation. However, as stated by Freud (1900–1901), the entire dream represents a projection, something observed, at times on a screen. It is thus of little heuristic value to single out the spoken word as having special significance unless other aspects associated with superego functioning can be demonstrated (themes of guilt, punishment, or self-criticism). Hence, this paper and my clinical examples deal primarily with the attempt to identify those elements that can be demonstrated in the analysis, and to show important contributions from other structures to the synthesis of the spoken word.

Contrary to Isakower, I find it helpful to differentiate the stamp of the superego on dream formation (the process) from that on the content of the dream. It seems to me that the superego is continually active and present, though in altered form, during the entire process, all the way from the formation of the unconscious wish (repression), to the dream work (censorship, distortion), secondary revision, and finally, the forgetting of dreams.

The presence of a conflict involving guilt, or defense against it, might be inferred in the manifest content of the following types of dreams: 1, dreams of punishment, being pursued; 2, dreams where figures ordinarily associated with crime or punishment are present (judge, police, jail, etc.); 3, dreams with inhibited motion; 4, examination dreams; 5, anxiety or distressing dreams; 6, dreams interrupted by sudden awakening; 7, dreams of observation (being watched or looked at).

I am aware the various categories of dreams listed do not have the same quotient of reliability as indicators of superego activity. For example, dreams of punishment or being pursued are certainly more suggestive than anxiety or distressing dreams. However, I have tried to make the list as inclusive as possible to indicate the type of manifest dream that might alert the analyst to the probability of some conflict involving the superego particularly.

In analyzing the manifest content of the dream, we generally depend on the patient's associations to reveal the precise meanings of those elements which pertain to the superego. If we are lucky, we uncover some particular conflict involving the superego and the affect of guilt or some defense against it. This classification of superego excludes the ego ideal. In the dreams of my patients which included spoken words, I found only infrequent participation of this aspect of the superego in a conflict situation.

If the analysis of the spoken word fails to reveal evidence of a conflict involving the superego, it is necessary to find the framework most useful in organizing our data. For this purpose, I suggest an extension to the analysis of dreams already implied by Waelder (1936) in a brief section of his paper on multiple function. If this view is correct, any element in the dream will, upon analysis, have multiple meaning and referents. That is to say, an element in the dream that primarily refers to superego functioning will on analysis have other referents—perhaps to a drive derivative or a defense or, more often, a combination of all three. The converse is also true; that is, any element in the dream could, if the analysis were pursued exhaustively enough, be shown to have some reference to superego activity. However, for purposes of clinical research what we are looking for is the valence or preponderance in the spoken word of the superego contribution, rather than its hypothetical presence being of no clinical significance.

The relation between spoken words and self-observation included in Isakower's views is at times strikingly demonstrated in the manifest content of certain dreams. The role of the superego in self-observation was the subject of a paper by Stein (1966) who states: "self-observation and self-evaluation are inextricably linked and are intimately involved with superego functions'" (p. 275). However, Stein also makes the point that reality testing and other manifest operations, including self-observation, may be understood best through the application of the principle of multiple function "… as resultants of components of the personality, rather than being treated as if they were a function of one alone" (p. 295).[3]

CLINICAL ASPECTS

I was confronted with a dilemma each time a dream with spoken words came up. My interest being aroused, I had to ask myself whether it was relevant and appropriate to the patient's analysis to inquire about the spoken words should no free association be spontaneously made to them (a common occurrence). All I can say is: I was aware of the problem and of the possible bias in selection. As an independent check, I noted that the incidence in my practice of dreams with spoken words did not significantly change after I became interested in the topic.

A basic procedural issue, limiting the size of the sample, is that for obvious reasons only dreams which have been associated to, or at least which are understandable, could be included; a difference had to be made between what one understands of a dream and what is interpreted.

The conflicting goals of therapeutic analysis and research were nowhere more emphasized than at this point. It was certainly possible in many instances to guess at the multiple meanings of the spoken words, especially with a patient whose main conflicts were already known. However, in the absence of definite associations, the scientific validity of such reconstructions is more open to question.

---

3 It may help the understanding of the mechanism of the function of self-observation if we break it down into a number of auxiliary mechanisms, such as reality testing, observation, and judgment. Cf., Grossman's (1967) Reflections on the Relationships of Introspection and Psychoanalysis.

Contrary to my expectations, except in very few instances, direct questioning of the patient concerning his associations to the spoken words was often disappointing. There were either no associations at all, or none that could be understood or traced back to the central theme of the dream. Only in one instance was a dream speech traced back to a speech spoken by the patient the day before. I am not sure what to make of this particular finding, especially in the light of Freud's initial statements concerning the day residue of spoken words. This was true even in instances where the dream as a whole could be understood. Hence this finding could not be attributed to a generally high level of resistance to the dream.

Because of the small number of dreams I could understand, I decided not to attempt a statistical survey on a large number of dreams, but rather to select from the many dreams available a few to illustrate the analysis of the various types of dreams with spoken words commonly encountered in my practice. I paid particular attention to dreams with spoken words whose manifest content did not show clear superego manifestations.

Classification of Dreams With Spoken Words

A problem arose in delimiting spoken words in the dream. Some dreams have direct speech. But what of dreams in which speech is alluded to indirectly—for example, dreams including telephone conversations, or dreams with thought content such as, "I said to myself" or indirect speech, "He reproached me for my timidity," or dreams where people were talking but no actual words were spoken?

In a passage in *The Interpretation of Dreams,* Freud (1900–1901) distinguishes between "... speeches in dreams as possess something of the sensory quality of speech, and which are described by the dreamer himself as being speeches" and "'other sorts of speeches, which are not... felt by [the dreamer] as having been heard or spoken (that is, which have no acoustic or motor accompaniments in the dream), [and] are merely thoughts such as occur in our waking thought-activity and are often carried over unmodified into our dreams" (pp. 419–420). Does a metapsychological difference underlie this descriptive difference?

In another passage discussing a brief dream, Freud states that a given thought, "'I can't bear the sight of it'... in the dream... failed to emerge as a speech" (p. 421), perhaps implying some sort of threshold, an intensity of cathexis which if sufficient will allow the element to be experienced as a speech rather than as a thought.

Communicative Speech and Spoken Words In Dreams

It is of interest to contrast the function of speech in the dream and in the waking state. With the patient in the recumbent position, in contact with the analyst mainly through speech, and with the regressive pull favoring the emergence of more archaic functioning in all three spheres of psychic structure, we have the ideal background for the study of primitive superego functioning. Even in the awake patient the analyst's voice, like the oracle, is endowed with all-powerful, all-knowing, critical attitudes. Projection, narcissism, and regression, together with temporary abandonment of reality testing, allow us to study more primitive manifestations. I suspect that the analytic situation itself is much more than is realized a day residue of the spoken word in the dream.

Loewenstein (1956) remarks on the three possible functions of speech described by Bühler as communicative between addressor and addressee: 1, speaking of objects and their relationships (i.e., of representations or cognition); 2, speech serving to express what is in oneself (i.e., the function of expression); and 3, speech serving as an appeal function (the speaker appeals to the addressee to respond in some way). The first aspect is, of course, most closely related to the mode of discharge characteristic of the secondary process, although it too can be used in the service of drive discharge; for example, by the patient who is using highly rational discourse to express very hostile, sarcastic attitudes toward the therapist.

In contrast to the waking state, spoken words in dreams do not have as their purpose *external communication* (though they may appear to do so in the manifest content) but rather *verbalization* expressed in regressive hallucinatory fashion; for instance, speech can be described as verbal imagery. This same process can be seen in the child and sometimes in the adult who will talk to himself instead of just thinking silently, a process of self-communication.

There is an important shift in content between Isakower's two papers which is relevant to the problem of multiple forms of speech in the dream. In his 1939 paper, Isakower alludes to the linguistic phenomenon connected with going to sleep and to the reverse phenomenon in awakening: "It often happens in this way that a word or short sentence still reaches a dreamer, while he is waking up, like a call, and this call has very often a super-ego tinge, sometimes threatening, sometimes criticizing—words for which the dreamer, as he wakes up, feels an inexplicable respect, although they are very often a quite unintelligible jargon" (p. 348). In his 1954 paper Isakower states: "*… speech elements in dreams are a direct contribution from the superego to the manifest content of the dream*" (p. 3).

In my clinical experience, words in the hypnagogic or hypnopompic phase are more likely to have a manifest superego tinge than those words safely tucked away in the beginning or middle part of the dream.

As a secondary issue, I wonder whether screams or grunts should be included under linguistic phenomenon. Such expressions would come under the second heading described by Loewenstein, i.e., speech as serving to express what is in oneself.

Certainly, from a genetic point of view, a young child will be quick to sense parental anger not so much from the content—which he may not be in a position to grasp either because it is beyond his intellectual understanding or because he is too anxious at the moment—as from the tone or even the facial expression of the angry or disapproving parent. (We see a similar reaction in analytic patients who constantly harp on their detection of disapproval by our *tone* of voice.) On the other hand, parental approval and loving is also displayed by tone: softness, cooing, caressing.

CLINICAL VIGNETTES

I now present some words in dreams. Since the emphasis of my investigation is on content rather than technique, associations are given; interpretations made to the patient are omitted. I have included as broad a meaning of the dream as possible rather than focusing on the main purpose of the dream. The latter, I found, might be only peripherally relevant to the spoken word. Further, more detailed material about the patient's analysis would be necessary to place the dream in its proper framework; this would unduly lengthen this paper.

My first example of a dream with speech that could be analyzed illustrates the application of the principle of multiple function.

The patient, Mrs. A, a young married woman in her early thirties, had come into treatment complaining that she felt "'lifeless." Her most pathognomonic relationships occurred in adolescence. She would make herself essential to a boy but when he showed he could not do without her, she would grow cold, distant, and, in the process of leaving him, would want to get pregnant—which resulted in one premarital abortion. In the third year of a tumultuous analysis, the patient wanted to terminate treatment. She asked, "What more do you have to give me?" She then said she had had a dream two days before, adding that her period had just come "quietly." In the dream she felt angry at her husband, and said, "Why don't you make me pregnant—it won't stick.".

Associating to the dream, she spontaneously spoke of pregnancy as making her feel whole. Part of her body is now missing but a baby is the opposite: it feeds on you, then leaves you as before. She then recalled a scene at age five. Her mother was telling her how to make babies: "You just want and want, and it comes." To her great disappointment, when nothing came, her mother said: "You didn't want hard enough." Her period, she continued, started at age ten. Her much older brother, to whom she had been very attached, had married when the patient was nine and his wife had become pregnant right away. Pregnancy gives her the feeling of power over a man.

The spoken words "it won't stick" embodied reproaches to the husband, the analyst, and herself. The baby, as substitute for a penis, always leaves her. The analyst, like the brother and the husband, disappoints her in the end and she remains as before. The patient also identifies with the intra-uterine/ suckling child and wants to repeat actively the passive narcissistic trauma she suffers at the hand of the analyst who, like her mother, blames her for her failures. (I might add that as a little girl she had had the fantasy that all children were born boys and that whether "it sticks" or not depended solely on the food mother gives—boy food or girl food.)

The dream speech can be conveniently divided into two fragments: 1, "Why don't you make me pregnant?" 2, "It won't stick!."

On a descriptive level the second statement is already a larval interpretation of the first. As Isakower sees it, "it won't stick" is a reflective statement, already a clear-cut indication of the process of secondary revision and manifestly sufficient to indicate evidence of superego activity. But this second statement, "it won't stick," is also a reproach to the analyst, as indicated by the day residue and the wish to leave analysis, and genetically is related to a reproach toward the mother who failed to give her the right food so "it" would stick.

On another level it is also a self-reproach related to the meaning of another part of the day residue—her period—symbolically referring to past abortions and, in her childhood, "not wanting it enough."

A substantial part of the analytic work had dealt with her wish to defeat me—meaningful to her on many levels, including a masochistic one. For the patient to have a successful analysis meant, among other things, to castrate me and drain me of my strength and then leave me, as she had done with the boys in her adolescence—a repetition of what she would have liked to have done with her brother. Hence the speech illustrates rather clearly components of the drives (aggressive, sexual), the superego (reproaches to self and analyst), the repetition compulsion (repetition of traumatic scenes and childhood failures of pregnancies), and finally, the ego (defensive aspect of the spoken word, i.e., displacement, condensation, and projection).

Likewise, the first statement, "Why don't you make me pregnant?" may be broken down into various components.

I should like now to explore a possible extension of the concept of the spoken word in the dream to the idea of verbalized communication. In this dream the acoustic motor hallucination was one of screaming, in the context of an open punishment motif.

The patient, Mrs. B, was a middle-aged married woman in the third year of analysis. Her character structure was basically narcissistic with masochistic features and a tendency toward paranoia. Around the time of the dream, she was struggling with highly ambivalent reactions to attempts at becoming pregnant, feeling very guilty because of her hostile attitude toward her husband, his sperm and "baby." She had recently expressed fear of secreting a chemical that could kill her husband's sperm. She also distorted her physician's remarks that her gynecologic disorder either would be cured by pregnancy, or might interfere with her becoming pregnant, to mean that she would either get pregnant or require an operation to remove the growing quasi-cancerous condition.

The day before the dream she reported a slip she had made confusing "cancer" with "dandruff," a conversation with her mother about "the baby" and her own fears that she must be doing something wrong to sabotage it, and fantasies of being in a hospital. She spoke of her dread of anesthesia, "having something over my face." The next day she reported a nightmare:

> This woman—I was watching her, also a young man—she had something in her head, he wanted it cut—he grabbed her—she screamed—he zipped open part of the head and took out a flesh disc—the screaming got weaker—I thought "she's losing her strength, going to die."

The patient awoke very upset. That morning, she had had intercourse with her husband. "There was a lot of pain—I started crying."

Her associations led to brain operations, someone doing something violent to her (like the treatment), nightmares, and then to a childhood operation on her sinuses. Later in the hour she spoke of fears that a layer of endometrium would prevent her husband from getting to the ovary, about hysterectomy, and of ideas of something growing inside unchecked. She said nightmares were "pushing into" her days and that she takes pills (a reference to occasional use of tranquilizers) to keep them under control. She is the opposite of her mother who was *dying* to have children and who, according to the story, risked her life to have the patient and was threatened by miscarriage. She continued to talk about ideas of being hurt by sex, and wondered how as a child she got these ideas since she was never raped. She needed to keep her aggressive, dominating side under control and force her husband (who has occasional premature ejaculation) to stay inside her longer. She went on to complain about the treatment: I should do something to force her to change—perhaps hypnosis to prove myself stronger than her.

Among other things, the dream represented graphic retaliatory fantasies for her active castrative wishes toward men, as evidenced by her fears of secreting a spermicidal chemical and related fantasies of her husband's and the therapist's impotence. Her associations to the dream were not differentiated from the complete dream, and in the context of the manifest content were in line with the dream story.

The scream in the manifest dream was followed by a reflective thought: "I thought she's losing her strength, going to die!." Then awakening intervened.

Following Bühler, the scream is an appeal and symbolizes strong emotions of terror. The reflection is the work of secondary revision and a commentary on the meaning of the dream. As Stein describes it, this quasi-traumatic dream could be for the purpose of saying to herself, "'This is only a dream,'" i.e., helping to deny the frightening reality of her fantastic world. The wish to be attacked was of course related to highly charged rape fantasies. The guilt is self-evident.

Many other elements are clear, especially with previous knowledge of the patient: the special emphasis on 'brains' as a compensation for her 'ugliness'; her competitive strivings with men, her sadomasochistic fantasies of intercourse, conception, and birth; the libidinization of anxiety as a defense against overwhelming, painful procedures on her sinuses as a little girl, associated with separation from the mother and rage at her for abandoning her; identification with a dead cousin who had been in the hospital, had been operated on, and had died as an aftermath; and her concept of hospitalization as allowing total regression and being taken care of by doctors who, in her childhood, also played the roles of the absent father and idealized mother. Finally, the patient was well known for her temper and outbursts during which she would scream and frighten those around her into submission.

The introduction of a dream with a scream leads to the topic of nightmares, recently studied by Fisher, et al. (1970). In the context of Fisher's work, the dream presented above is a REM anxiety dream. Thus, the scream can be thought of in the manifest content of the dream as susceptible to analysis, in contrast to a *pavor nocturnus* attack in Stage IV sleep which represents a "cataclysmic breakthrough of uncontrolled anxiety" (p. 778). The scream is a concomitant of that state and not generally subject to analysis.

The next example illustrates a type of dream with spoken words frequently met in practice; namely, speech that embodies a *manifest reproach*.

A few weeks after reporting her nightmare, the patient alluded to above (Mrs. B) was dealing with the worries of pregnancy and was in the midst of exploring fantasies around anal birth, loss of control, messiness, and her inability to be strong, self-sufficient, and at the same time get what she wanted from other people (generally referring to being loved, reassured of her perfection, etc.). The day before the dream she described her reaction to having met me with my wife on the street on New Year's Eve; she had thought that this was my girl friend, that I was not married, and that I looked bizarre and sick. She spoke of feeling ashamed to have been seen by me outside of analysis when she had such a nice appearance and was well dressed; she was afraid I would become envious, jealous, and would want to 'take it all away from her." She dreamed:

> I was defecating in the classroom on a toilet. Another person was telling me, "You should not let other people see you"—it was messy, all over the seat, but I couldn't help it—they were taking exam— husband too—the teacher asked me about the exam but I didn't know the questions.

Associations led to identification of analysis with classroom situations where she is bright and can demonstrate her brains, and views of analysis as defecation, messy like intercourse—terrified of pregnancy and there being no one to help—then the sexual stimulation of going to the bathroom, and finally a need to be reassured she is not terrible and weak because she feels ashamed and self-conscious that she has been here so long. Her problems are still here—she is embarrassed. This is like a classroom where she is failing.

The dream and its associations showed clearly though indirectly the multiple meaning of the spoken words. On the one hand, a reproach to herself and also to me—the projection of her bad self who was not confined to the office. The reproach over her enjoyment at having exhibited herself is clear, as is the wish to hide her weak, castrated self. Her main mechanism of defense is denial—the wish not to see. In this patient this is so pronounced in everyday life as to cause many minor accidents; she is always hurting herself by bumping into doors, cupboards, etc.

In the third example from the same patient, it is difficult not to confuse the manifest content of the dream with its latent content as the façade of the dream is so self-explanatory.

During an hour the patient reported a conversation on the phone with a woman friend, M, about not wanting to go to the funeral of the latter's father because she (the patient) would be so upset and frightened. That night she had the following dream:

> T was yelling at me, saying: "Everybody was upset and they are going to the funeral. Why shouldn't you?".

This dream at first glance seemed to require almost no interpretation. In real life T, a rather critical person, often stands for the patient's conscience by way of projection. During the hour the patient was so involved in berating herself that it was not possible to interpret the dream. Only later were other connections apparent between her own father's and stepfather's demise some years previously, and the secret satisfaction that it was happening to other people too.

The use of T as a displacement for her strong self-reproaches and the multiple meaning of berating herself, generally as a manipulative attempt to obtain reassurance from a benign external source, were dealt with analytically.

There is an interesting connection between spoken words in the dream and sleep-talking. The latter topic has been reviewed by Arkin (1966), who stated that 'There is general agreement that most sleep-talking occurs in association with non-REM sleep and that most sleep-talkers are "non-REM sleep-talkers"' (p. 121). From the genetic point of view, Arkin feels that sleep speech is the result of unresolved psychic conflict that originates in the developmental phase during which the main problem is the acquisition of mastery over sphincter control and motility.

In my own series, only in one instance did an analytic patient report a dream where the speech was actually spoken by her in her sleep, as corroborated by her husband. I quote the dream in full because of its relevance to our topic and because of its special interest, in that the spoken word in the manifest content of the dream coincided with the content of the sleep-talking. (I shall not debate here the issue of whether the spoken words are part of the dream or an appendage to it.)

The young married woman, Mrs. A, mentioned in the first example, had the following dream some nine or ten months after the birth of her second child, a boy:

> I dreamt of the baby falling out of bed and I shouted 'No! No!' as I grabbed onto his thigh. In reality I had grabbed on X's thigh [husband]. We both awoke suddenly. I said to X: "I thought you were E" [the child]. He told me he had been awakened by hearing me shout "No! No!."

The patient went on to state that E is very strong; he rolls over on his stomach so she cannot diaper him; he can stand up in the carriage, and she fears he might throw himself out. To "No! No!" the patient said, "That's when I'm overwhelmed or found fault with… sometimes when X approaches me to make love and I don't want to." The patient then went on to talk about her boasting about her children and how good a mother she feels she is, and finally, that she felt a bit annoyed at being tied down to the nursing situation and had recently toyed with the impulse to stop nursing.

In the recent past many fruitful comparisons had been made between making love, nursing, and the analytic situation where, depending on the state of the transference, she saw herself as either the child blissfully taking it all in, or the one who could never satisfy my needs as no matter how much she gave it was never enough. She also felt that in regard to her children, every need of theirs had to be fulfilled, otherwise she would think of herself as a bad mother. The "No! No!," strongly expressing a prohibition on several levels, broke through into both speech and motility, presumably because the content of the dream was too threatening and could no longer be tolerated by the sleeping ego. It also expressed a turning away from the husband and child: "I don't want to make love/nurse any more." In line with Isakower's earlier formulation, it is associated with awakening phenomenon, and implies a clear self-critical judgment dealing with the latent content of the dream.

In the context of sleep speech, the amusing dream of Anna Freud's infancy must be mentioned because of its historical interest. Freud (1900–1901) includes it as a dream, with the proviso, "if I may include words spoken by children in their sleep under the heading of dreams"' (p. 129). It occurred as an aftermath of a stomach upset blamed by her nurse on overeating strawberries. During the period of abstinence that followed, the child was heard to say in her sleep: 'Anna Fweud, Stwawbewwies, wild stwawbewwies, omblet, pudden!' (p. 130). The little girl was probably revenging herself in her sleep, defying her nurse. Although the dream speech is presented in the context of wish-fulfilment, the day residue includes certainly strong reproof (e.g., 'you naughty child who indulged yourself, and now look how you are punished'), and the dream is then a direct rebellion against this.

In the previously cited examples, the presence of superego influence on the spoken words could be easily demonstrated. I would like now to bring forward a number of dreams where it was not as easy in the context of the specific analytic situation to uncover the same predominant influence, at least of the punitive aspect of the superego, or to demonstrate the presence of a conflict involving guilt as the major contributing factor. The spoken word in these instances has, I believe, other functions to be described shortly.

In some patients (often with obsessional features) whose analytic behavior is marked by strong resistance to regression, I have encountered dreams which seem to consist almost entirely of *conversations*. Although, to be sure, such patients do carry their burden of guilt, I did not feel in such instances, even when the dream could be analyzed, that the superego's contribution was more remarkable than in any other of these patients' dreams lacking spoken words.

The first dream to be presented is mainly in the form of an extended conversation between the patient and several people. Though likely, it is not absolutely certain from the context that the many spoken words achieved hallucinatory intensity in the dream.

A young, unmarried, professional woman, late in her analysis had taken a step requiring considerable courage—giving up a cosmetic device which had protective magical qualities. She was also talking about termination. Her central conflict dealt with her feeling defective, flat chested, "brain damaged"—neither a woman nor a man. This was expressed in part through hypochondriacal complaints which, when analyzed, related to insatiable oral demands and extreme jealousy toward a three year older brother. She dreamt the following:

I went to see a specialist associated with the clinic to sign a form. When he saw me he said I had a cerebello-pontine angle tumor and should have mastoid studies. I went back and told a colleague I wanted studies that day—to change appointment times. I told the consultant I wanted tomograms. I made an appointment with a woman on the phone—she wasn't there; another technician was not interested in me; the radiologist came out and told me a joke; I went to get a consult on myself. I remember thinking, "No one else thinks I have a tumor, I have to make sure."

Relevant associations dealt with a conversation she had had with her father on the phone: that the last single cousin in the family was engaged and that the patient should visit her sister-in-law who was planning to enter the hospital soon for a major abdominal operation. The latter has two boys. The patient also associated to the specialist—someone impotent and nonthreatening like the analyst—and thought of a penis in connection with the tumor—something growing. She is working with two young boys suspected of having a tumor; X-ray studies are penetrating—reveal what's really inside— tomograms are three-dimensional-like—in depth. The patient also recalled being upset about her sister-in-law's operation—would she make it? She even had had a fantasy of taking care of the latter's children. In addition, other associations led to a reiteration of a longstanding transference complaint of not being taken seriously, i.e., my not going along with her concept of being defective and helpless, this, of course, being heightened by our recent discussion about termination. How can I leave her if she is still so defective, unmarried, etc.?

The dream's major themes—anxiety about being exposed, abandoned, and wishful identification with her sister-in-law, along with retaliatory punishment—are apparent. However, none of the spoken words had the cryptic, oracular quality of the injunctions typical of the single direct expression of superego influence as reported by Isakower.

Within the context of the analysis, the news that the last single cousin was engaged was another narcissistic blow. She had generally reacted in the past to news of this type by an increase in her passive dependent longings. These were often expressed through the wish to be ill or put in the hospital—to show me up, and at the same time to blackmail me and make me visit her, spend time with her away from patients. The news of the cousin's engagement, coupled with talk about possible termination, resulted in a dual reproach—toward the analyst and toward herself, i.e., she "can't do the analysis," she is to blame for being defective and the analyst is to blame for not doing more. But it seems to me that within the context of the associations, this last element is only a small part of the entire picture. This particular dream and the associations to it also illustrate the relative paucity of associations to the spoken words, and the rarity with which I am able to identify recent speeches as day residue.

It is my impression that certain dreams with spoken words have a structure similar to waking fantasies or daydreams. The lessened regressive quality might be due either to defensive maneuvers or to external circumstances, such as those prevailing in nap dreams and dreams following a period of wakening. The spoken words express not so much superego content but are closer to the structure of a daydream—a continuation of some pre-sleep preoccupation, with the mental apparatus not as yet being sufficiently regressed to allow visual imagery. An example follows.

The patient alluded to in the second vignette, Mrs. B, eventually became pregnant. One night she was kept half awake by her husband's insomnia and thrashing about. She was terrified when she suddenly felt his presence over her. He finally left for his office at nine o'clock. The patient then went back to sleep and had the following dream:

I was in a room with C, my cousin. He said, 'You're upset, I can tell'—We had a conversation—He said '|You're the only one I ever had feelings for;" suddenly I initiated making out with him on the floor. He said, 'What happens if we are discovered?' I said, 'Say we are looking for my contact lenses on the floor'.

The patient spoke about a big fight with her mother the day before, and a phone call from another cousin who is very attached to her and idolizes her. At this phase of the analysis she was going through a period of disappointment in her husband and the therapist. Historically she had generally turned to this cousin in the face of any disappointment as a child, primarily in the service of revenge. The story of the dream was a variation on a scene which actually had taken place years before but could not be carried to fruition because of severe guilt and anxiety. Many fantasies had evolved previously with this scene as a starting point.

To be sure, the words "What happens if we are discovered" could represent an allusion to some guilt feelings, but the predominant affective need around the time of the dream was a need for revenge and escape from the current reality. As a child, whenever she felt left out by her mother, she would in fantasy or in reality cuddle up to the cousin, imagine he belonged only to her and would rescue her and take her away with him. He represented a combined version of the ideal parent and a projection of her ideal self.

DISCUSSION

Starting from Isakower's premise that the speech content in the manifest dream is a direct contribution of the superego, I have sought to examine the role of the spoken word in the dream in the context of his views concerning the superego. In my clinical examples, the focus was on the presence or absence of conflicts involving guilt rather than on the aspect of self-observation. This approach was necessary because Isakower's hypothesis cannot be proven or disproven clinically as his conclusions are included in his premises by definition.

It seemed worthwhile to investigate clinically the spoken word in the dream based on the principle of multiple function (applied clinically in terms of multiple meanings). From my clinical samples, I concluded that conflicts involving the issue of guilt do not always occur in the analysis of spoken words, and that important elements of drive and defense also contribute to the meaning and form.

Particularly in patients who are not well able to tolerate regression, I noted dreams consisting of conversations as well as a tendency toward thinking without imagery. In such instances, the motive force resulting in speech seemed to be primarily defensive. Stated in the language of dream theory, one might say that dreams made up primarily of conversation are subject to secondary revision. Freud (1900–1901) wrote: 'We might put it simply by saying that this fourth factor ... [secondary revision] seeks to mould the material offered to it into something like a daydream' (p. 492).[4]

Although the entire dream is often a communication to the analyst—a comment or addendum to an interpretation given in the previous session—I was not impressed by any specialized communication expressed in dreams with verbal content in contrast to dreams without spoken words, particularly in the area of superego. The problem of indirect speech has been only partially elucidated. I suspect there may be a whole series of steps intermediary between a thought—a vivid thought with imagery—and spoken words with hallucinatory intensity. Hence, in my opinion it may be wiser at this time to

---

4 Isakower (1972) said that he did not view conversation dreams as true dreams, but rather as daydreams or fantasies. A dream, he stated, is by definition an optical phenomenon.

limit the investigation of superego functioning to words actually heard by the dreamer in the manifest content as reported in the analysis.

Direct speech is certainly what Isakower had in mind both from a descriptive and a structural point of view; otherwise, it is difficult to avoid the implication that what we are dealing with is not a dream but either a thought or a waking fantasy incorporated in the dream. However, such thoughts expressed as indirect speech are descriptively larval interpretations of the dream, comments on it, and indicate the process of secondary revision which is heavily influenced by the superego.

I had hoped to be able to contrast the "superego" element of the spoken word with other superego elements of the manifest dream. A colleague suggested that if one considers speech to be a relatively late contribution to superego precursors (being preceded by disapproving tone and angry or scowling face), one might conclude that spoken words in dreams deal more with Oedipal rather than preoedipal conflict. My series of dreams with spoken words do not confirm this.

Thus far I have considered only the content of the spoken word—both manifest and latent. I have not addressed myself to the analysis of the form. For instance, what does it mean that a particular reproach is expressed by speech rather than by a dream of being beaten? Following Waelder, we would expect some relationship between form and content. Thus, the format of speech could be associated with the wakening function, or, as suggested earlier, with the analyst as a projection of the patient's superego, or even as some vehicle or representation of an oral wish. Stone (1961) in *The Psychoanalytic Situation* has discussed the meaning of speech in the analytic situation and its peculiar importance. He sees speech as the psychosomatic vehicle for discharge of both libidinal and aggressive energies in addition to being a mode of communication and hence of object relations. Stone mentions Lewin's oral triad in this respect. Is speech in a dream related primarily to regressive mechanisms for expressing a thought in hallucinatory form—a means of representation related to peculiar states of psychic functioning of sleeping persons? I do not believe so since speech is not common in dreams; there are alternate means available to the dreamer for expressing the content (for example, a punishment dream in images).

I suspect that individual dream styles (in comparison with neurotic styles) are more significant as determining factors for both the presence of dream speeches and the use to which they are put. For example, the patient with severe guilt conflicts who had temper tantrums as a child, had an unusually high percentage of dreams with spoken words. I was struck by the extent to which her speech was involved in expressing her unconscious conflicts. She made continual slips both in and out of analysis, using one word for another. She confused the names of her husband and former boy friend, often said father instead of brother, referred to me as her obstetrician, and was constantly making further mistakes as she attempted to undo her verbal confusion. Finally, a statement about the validity of the application of the principle of multiple function to the clarification of dream speeches. I would say that developmentally, from the very start, the acquisition of speech in the young child has strong integrative and controlling functions, as well as magical qualities. The spoken word is, after all, the main vehicle for the acquisition of culture, and not only in its prohibitive aspect. It would seem only reasonable that this multiple role of speech be reflected in its multiple meaning in the dream.

REFERENCES

Arkin, A. M. (1966). Sleep-Talking: A Review. *J. Nervous Mental Disease* CXLIII pp. 101–122.

Fisher, C., Byrne, J., Edwards, A., Kahn, E. (1970). A Psychophysiological Study of Nightmares. *J. Am. Psychoanal. Assoc.* 19:747–782.

Freud, A. (1937). The *Ego and the Mechanisms of Defence.* London: The Hogarth Press and the Institute of Psycho-Analysis.

Freud, S. (1900–1901). The Interpretation of Dreams. *Standard Edition,* 4/5.

Grossman, W. (1967). Reflections on the Relationships of Introspection and Psycho-Analysis. *Int. J. Psychoanal.* 48:16–31.

Isakower, O. (1939). On the Exceptional Position of the Auditory Sphere. *Int. J. Psychoanal.* 20:340–348.

——— (1954). Spoken Words in Dreams. A Preliminary. Communication *Psychoanal. Q.* 23:1–6.

——— (1972). Personal communication.

Loewenstein, R. 1956 Some Remarks on the Role of Speech in Psycho-Analytic Technique. *Int. J. Psychoanal.* 37: 460–468.

Stein, M. (1966). Self Observation, Reality, and the Superego. In *Psychoanalysis A General Psychology. Essays in Honor of Heinz Hartmann,* Edited by R. Loewenstein, L. Newman, M. Schur, A. Solnit. New York: International Universities Press, Inc., pp. 275–313.

Stone, L. (1961).*The Psychoanalytic Situation. An Examination of Its Development and Essential Nature.* New York: International Universities Press, Inc.

Waelder, R. (1936). The Principle of Multiple Function: Observations on Over-Determination *Psychoanal. Q.* V:45–62.

CHAPTER 2

The Personal Dimension and Management of the Supervisory Situation with a Special Note on the Parallel Process

[(1993). *Psychoanal. Q.* (62):588–614.]

ABSTRACT: This paper focuses on the vicissitudes of the supervisor/ supervisee relationship and on the personal impact of supervision on the candidate. Conflicts within the supervisory situation and their potential intrusion into the learning process are discussed. The supervisee's character as a limiting factor and some of the dynamics of the parallel process are considered as well. A number of vignettes illustrate the problems involved and some possible remedies.

Supervision is an intense, emotionally charged experience for the developing psychoanalyst, yet the occasionally deleterious effects of the encounter on the learning process and its management have not received the detailed attention they deserve in our literature. The main thesis of this paper is that for supervision to function optimally, the supervisor must carefully monitor the state of the supervisor/supervisee relationship and the reactions of the candidate to being in supervision and to the necessity of exposing his or her work. I hope to demonstrate that problems in the relationship may originate from a multiplicity of sources and therefore that their management will be a function of the supervisor's understanding of the origins of the problems. This will include issues of the supervisee's character. I will present vignettes to illustrate possible interventions aimed at facilitating learning and confronting potential difficulties without intruding on the personal analysis of the candidate. Reference will be made to the so-called parallel process and its use and abuse in supervision. An introductory section will be devoted to some general remarks on the nature of supervision and to a brief review of the pertinent literature.

There is a remarkable lack of agreement about a theory of the supervisory process. How much attention should the supervisor give to problems in his or her relationship with the supervisee? My impression of the literature is that for the most part (e.g., Dewald, 1987); (Fleming and Benedek, 1966); (Wallerstein, 1981), the supervisor/supervisee relationship has not been given much attention except in instances of gross disturbance.

The main purpose of supervision is educational, namely, to teach a student how to analyze. My interest in the topic of the supervisor/supervisee relationship is solely to illuminate its relevance to this goal: how it helps or hinders the process of learning. Because of its neglect, I will somewhat exaggerate its importance in this presentation to make my point clear. I believe that the supervisory situation facilitates the manifestation of some of the most important unconscious aspects of the relation between the supervisee and his or her patient. These cannot be ignored for proper management of the treatment. Particularly in problem supervision, their neglect may have significant deleterious effects on the supervisory alliance and on the learning process (see the chapters contributed by Shevrin in Wallerstein [1981] for a dramatic demonstration of this point). In some instances, the warded-off aspects of the supervisor/supervisee relationship can intrude on the treatment itself.

For reasons of confidentiality, I find it a bit easier to write about examples taken from my work in psychotherapy supervision. This should not affect the points I wish to make, as my approach remains analytic even when supervising psychotherapists, regardless of the modality they employ, whether exploratory or supportive. Analytic candidates face the added complication of being in simultaneous training analysis. This situation allows for complicated displacements on the student's part—from supervisor to training analyst and vice versa.

General Remarks on the Nature of Supervision

There are no real boundaries around what constitutes "good enough" supervision. We would likewise be hard pressed to define "wild supervision" with any degree of precision. In contrast to clinical work, which is informed by a complex systematized theory and technique, supervision is essentially still an uncharted territory. This leaves much more room for the influence of the supervisor's style, character, and personal preferences (see the chapter by DeBell in Wallerstein [1981] for a review). The uncertainty is compounded by an almost total absence of guidelines about supervision in our analytic institutes. Once someone is appointed training analyst, supervisory duties are added on, and it is simply assumed that the analyst who is approved to train candidates is also qualified to supervise. In my own institute, there are no current study groups on supervision, and no guidelines are offered about what adequate reports on supervision should include. Yet with the absence of reporting by training analysts being the rule, supervision is the only real window afforded on the personality characteristics of the candidate as they affect his or her work. (For a good description of the content of a supervisory report, see Fleming and Benedek [1966, p. 231].)

How can we understand the mental life of an absent party when reported by a participant observer? In my review of the literature on supervision, one emerging trend is the attempt to draw analogies between the therapeutic process and the supervisory situation (Wallerstein, 1981). Arlow (1963) has outlined some of the more important similarities: the shifting of certain ego functions between experiencing and reporting, and between observation and identification. "The failure of the therapist to give a timely interpretation may be compared sometimes to the resistances which the patient experiences during treatment" (p. 582). Another feature noted by Arlow is the occasional community of defenses shared by patient and therapist. When doing supervision, the supervisor functions in multiple capacities: educator, observer, and psychoanalyst. Isakower alluded also to the possible interference in the supervisor who "in his main capacity is a therapist and not an educator, with a greater likelihood of slipping from a didactic mode to a therapeutic one" (New York Psychoanalytic Institute, 1963, p. 1). What are the limits on this latter function? Is Arlow correct in stating that although he takes pains to observe the identificatory phenomenon between supervisee and his or her patient, only rarely is it necessary to make the therapist aware of this identification, even when it is enacted right in front of the supervisor? I will discuss this issue further in the section on the parallel process.

In the same paper, Arlow (1963), quoting the 1955 Rainbow Report of the American Psychoanalytic Association's Committee of the Board on Professional Standards, described supervision as the "psychoanalysis of a psychoanalysis" (p. 583). I would add that in some respects it is more like the wild analysis of an analysis! This statement is meant to highlight the incompleteness, varied sources, and contaminated nature of the data given to us, in addition to the multiple ways of approaching it. First, what are usually termed the process notes of a session consist in reality of a heavily curtailed and edited version of a complex interchange, as interpreted by a participant through the mirror of his or her subjectivity. This edited version is enriched by the observations made by the supervisor about the supervisee's mode of delivery, accompanying affects (or their absence), behavior, attitudes, posture, slips, associations to the material, and comments about his or her patient's affects and nonverbal behavior. Additional input consists of the supervisor's own associations and reactions to the entire picture, including his or her own affects and shifts in focus as a consequence of evenly hovering attention. Yet in spite of the multiple sources of error and contamination, most students manage to learn a fair amount from their supervisory encounters.

Other writers have stressed the difference between analysis and supervision. For example, Solnit (1970), wrote: "The learning or educational supervisory situation promotes identification rather than transference and is not based on conditions that encourage or are likely to evoke regression. In analysis we offer ourselves as screen and in supervision, as teachers, we offer ourselves as figures with whom the students can identify" (p. 360).

Another approach in the literature focuses on the listening function of the therapist. This is the often quoted work of Otto Isakower, which was first presented in a series of meetings with the Faculty of the New York Psychoanalytic Institute in 1963. Isakower chose to focus almost exclusively on the workings of the analyzing instrument as an elaboration of some of Freud's remarks from Chapter VII of *The Interpretation of Dreams* and some hints in his technique papers of the middle period. Some of Isakower's points bear a close resemblance to the approach I will develop. This is hardly surprising, since I have been very much influenced in the development of my own style by the contact I had with him during my student days. Isakower favored hearing the digest of the material by the student rather than being subjected to detailed notes on the analytic sessions. He stressed the need for the supervisor to attempt to identify with the student analyst. He remarked at length on a clinical example cited by Arlow concerning the parallel process. In the material, a student began unconsciously to present the week's sessions in a manic-like fashion. Arlow confronted the student with his behavior and then asked him if his patient behaved that way. The student was caught by surprise and confirmed Arlow's shrewd guess. The supervisor then returned to the material of the patient. Isakower would have pursued this further with the student as an illustration of a failure of the analyzing instrument. I do recall that Isakower would often ask a student, "What made you say that?" Although this was sometimes heard as reproof, or worse, as an invitation to a shameful exposure, Isakower would clarify that he was not interested in the student's personal motives but rather in what it was about the patient that stimulated his or her particular response. No attempt was ever made by Isakower to analyze the student. In contrast to the interest in the process which is keenly evident in his approach, Isakower paid no attention to the ebb and flow of the supervisor/supervisee relationship, focusing instead on the functioning of what he defined as the student's "analyzing instrument" (New York Psychoanalytic Institute, 1963). Malcove (1975), developing some of these ideas, referred to the supervisor/supervisee relationship as "a very close one but on a spiritual level" (p. 11).

From a developmental perspective, learning takes place initially in the context of an interpersonal relationship. The mature individual can learn even from someone he or she does not like. I believe that useful comparisons can be made between the development of professional and of personal identity. The role of the supervisor is analogous to that of the parent for a young child. In an earlier version of this paper, I had written "father" instead of "parent," but the term is both sexist and limiting. It would be important to spell out the role of the mother in furnishing some building blocks for budding identifications (supervision might entail the wish to be fed). Initially, one can see idealization of the supervisor with magical thinking, and imitation rather than true identification. This can show up as regurgitation of the supervisor's interpretations in the analytic sessions immediately following supervision. Later on, one may encounter competitive oedipal conflicts with the supervisor. I recall a fantasy I had as a candidate that the supervisor kept the "really good stuff" for himself and gave me only second-rate suggestions. Attention must be paid to certain intrasystemic conflicts between some aspects of the supervisee's current self-image and his or her ideal self-image.

Before moving on to clinical vignettes, I must address one major stumbling block to this approach to the supervisory process: How can a clear boundary be preserved around the supervision so that it does not turn into some bastardized version of psychotherapy or wild analysis? For example, Dewald (1987) cited the case of a supervisee who repeatedly failed to acknowledge or manage his female patient's transference. The supervisee was eventually told that "he was sexually stimulated by the patient's erotic fantasies and was anxious about possible acting out but ashamed of such a response" (p. 22). Within the framework of my paper, I would consider such an interpretation to be an invasion of the supervisee's private space and more appropriate to the couch than to the supervisory encounter. That is, the supervisor does not address specifically the student's problem with the patient, and it is not clear to me how the above information would help the student work better with his patient. The comment by Dewald might stimulate associations in the student which he might feel tempted to reveal to his supervisor instead of keeping them for his analysis. Instances of splitting of the transference (either positive or negative) and direct displacements are common. Some supervisees may try to use supervision as an auxiliary psychotherapy or even as a preliminary to asking the supervisor to take them on as patients. If the supervisor accedes to the request, he or she will have to confront complicated transferences preformed as a result of the encounter, something which I believe is fraught with many difficulties.

As I just indicated, I believe that the dynamics or origins of the supervisee's conflicts are strictly off limits, no matter how obviously they might present themselves. The only area to be addressed includes the elements which directly interfere in an operational way with the candidate's work functioning (in this, I include the treatment and the supervisory alliance). Even with this proviso, such interventions as "Do you know what was going on between you and the patient that stopped you from addressing this issue?" or "What was it about the patient that got to you?" may be experienced as somewhat intrusive. I would rather take this risk than the opposite one of ignoring the stresses and strains of the situation and allowing them to fester and proliferate, with much more serious consequences for the work alliance and the treatment.

I believe some minimal personalization of the relationship helps decrease the mystique and excessive idealization commonly encountered; yet this should not go too far because of the possibility of interfering with the analysis by setting up too gratifying a counterpart. In some instances, the supervisee will allude to certain crises or external traumata in his or her outside life (losses, miscarriages, and the like). These events cannot be entirely ignored, particularly if they have some obvious impact on the supervisee's capacities or relate to the work with the patient in a more direct fashion. In one instance, one of my supervisees suffered a miscarriage. This affected her work for a few weeks, especially with a pregnant patient she was following at the time. In addition, her attention span was diminished because of her increased self-preoccupation and mourning. My recognition and acknowledgment of her plight was helpful to her.

In contrast to the approach I am developing, what might be described as a more "analytic" stance, in which the supervisor says very little in order not to "contaminate" the field, has the opposite, paradoxical effect, namely facilitating the supervisee's self-doubts, criticisms, and other regressive manifestations. This is analogous to the patient's reactions to the analyst's silence during an hour. I recall an early experience with one of my supervisors who clearly made some attempt to model the supervision on an analytic hour: he would simply open the session with a grunt and look up expectantly. This had the unintended effect of raising my level of anxiety several notches!

The supervisor provides, within the framework of supervision, an auxiliary observing ego and also a benign analytic superego. The above considerations govern my approach to the beginning of supervision, which I will now describe.

Setting Up the Supervisory Alliance: Practical Considerations

My experience in the course on character, during discussions on technique with advanced candidates, highlighted the fearful nature of the supervisory experience within an institute setting. Many candidates expressed reluctance to be really open about what went on in their work, and they searched for "what the supervisor was looking for." Other students expressed their concern about voicing disagreement with their supervisor for fear of hurting his or her feelings or damaging their own reputations or their proper progression within the organization. These candid revelations were all the more striking and troublesome because they were by no means limited to "problem" or difficult students who believed that they might have more to lose than to gain by being open, in contrast to their more fortunate colleagues who in theory could be more candid in their reporting without jeopardizing their student status (see Dewald [1987, p. 23] for a very clear example). Even more severe is the instance of a candidate who possesses a considerable number of blind spots and has to deal with both transference complications and reality dangers simultaneously.

Some supervisees are quick to pick up the supervisor's strongly held convictions and are reluctant to challenge them even when they have reasonably good grounds to do so. I have found this problem to be more acute in the case of some women students with male supervisors. Traditional gender role conflicts are superimposed on the other concerns. To be sure, not all the above problems originate in the arena of supervision; a substantial part derive from the displacement of ongoing powerful transferences to the training analyst.

In order to foster a relationship which minimizes the early inhibitions and frequent distortions candidates bring with them to the initial supervisory encounter, I have developed a number of principles which I have found personally helpful in getting supervision off to a good start.

1. I like to find out what the supervisee's experiences with supervision have been: what he or she found most helpful, least helpful; what his or her preferred mode of reporting is (presence or absence of notes).

2. I like to set up a supervisory contract that takes into account what a supervisee would particularly like to learn and what he or she thinks are his or her weak and strong points. This allows me to evaluate the supervisee's interests and capacity for self-observation. It also sets up specific goals that can later be evaluated jointly, and discourages a passive stance in the candidate, which is unfortunately all too common.

3. In some cases, I may occasionally say something about the problem of evaluation with the aim of decreasing what I will term the "superego factor." I indicate that there are very few situations in which there are clear-cut right or wrong answers, and I will say that I am more interested in finding out how the supervisee arrived at where he or she is than in whether he or she is right or wrong. I also try to foster an interest in stray thoughts. At the beginning of supervision, I will allow the supervisee to select the method of reporting, and suggest, in any case, that notes be brought so they can be referred to occasionally when it seems indicated.

Dynamics of Supervision

The relevance of the relationship aspects in supervision is supported by sound dynamic principles. The supervisory process requires on the part of the supervisee a considerable amount of personal involvement and degree of revelation of the workings of his or her mind and sharing of emotions. This process creates intimacy and is also quite threatening. In contrast to the analytic relationship in which patients are assured of an impartial, nonjudgmental reception, supervisees know all the time that they will be judged and evaluated by their supervisor and that to a greater or lesser degree advancement in their careers is dependent on the type of evaluation they receive. This is much more the case in analytic institutes than in residency training programs. Thus, the process of supervision is, by its very nature, fraught with potential paradoxes and built-in conflicts which must be faced by both participants.

From a systems point of view, conflicts that have not been resolved at one level are transferred to another level where they must be tackled. For example, if a candidate is unable to resolve a conflict experienced with a patient, the candidate is likely to bring this conflict to supervision in a different version. The conflict can best be overcome if it is confronted in the arena where it is dynamically active. A colleague recounted a brief vignette about a supervisee who complained that his patient refused all his interpretations; as he discussed the case in supervision the student began, without realizing it, to refute all of his supervisor's comments. In such a case, it is difficult to imagine how talking only about the patient and not including a reference to the parallel reenactment could possibly lead to a satisfactory resolution.

A note of caution has to be introduced. Problems in the supervisory situation or even in the treatment may not originate with the therapist-patient dyad. The candidate's conflicts in the transference to the training analyst may be displaced to the supervisor or enacted with the patient; therefore, the supervisor must exercise extreme caution in order to be sure that enactments in supervision actually come from the student-patient dyad rather than the student-training analyst dyad. A colleague reported the following incident. He canceled an hour with a candidate in order to attend a meeting. The candidate's reaction was to withdraw from his patients temporarily. The supervisor picked up this change and interpreted it as the supervisee's frustrated response to his patient's aggression. While this may have been correct in part, the training analyst, who was in possession of all the data, concluded that the chief dynamic rested in this candidate's reaction to the temporary absence of his analyst. Displacements are complex phenomena, and a supervisor possesses only limited information about the totality of a situation.

Just as a conflict enacted in the transference does not necessarily originate in the transference, so a conflict enacted with the supervisor or with the patient does not necessarily indicate either a problem with the supervision or with the patient. In one instance a conflictual situation with the supervisor, which had not been properly worked through, intruded itself on the therapist-patient dyad. During my early residency days, I had taken on for treatment (without discussing it with the ward chief beforehand) a young man afflicted with exhibitionism. This superior, who also happened to be my supervisor, became quite displeased with me, saying that I should have consulted her before agreeing to take the patient on. This could become a court case with untold complications for everybody. Within a few weeks I had managed to tell the patient that he was not really being open with me, so that treatment did not make sense at this time. Some time later I realized that, at the expense of the patient, I had been silently making "amends" by trying to undo what my supervisor felt was a gross blunder.

Another vignette will demonstrate a more subtle intrusion of the supervisor/ supervisee relationship into the treatment. A bright and sensitive psychology intern blurted out that he had made a terrible mistake with the patient we had been discussing together. The patient was a difficult young adult who suffered from an unusual syndrome (for a male) of anorexia and bulimia and was resistant to treatment. He spoke little and only superficially during the sessions, yet seemed quite invested in the process, always showing up on time and paying the bills promptly. Recently an appointment had been rescheduled, and the psychology intern had forgotten about it. He was quietly eating a sandwich and reading a book with his feet up on the desk when a knock on the door preceded by a few seconds the appearance of the head of the patient asking when the session was due to start. "Oh my God!" exclaimed the distraught intern. "Please give me a few minutes and I'll be right with you." He had just enough time to pull himself together and apologize profusely to the patient, so profusely that he later realized he was conveying the message that the issue need not be discussed any further in the hour. The patient, equally reluctant to tread on dangerous territory, said nothing more about the incident. When going over the whole sequence with me, the supervisee expressed his shame at not discussing the incident with the patient. I chose to focus on two issues: first, a remarkable congruence of themes of the hour and of the incident, and second, the understandable reason for the intern's omission, namely, a reluctance to confront delicate and painful issues and affects. Both the intern and I could see that his frustration with the patient was consistent with the slip he had made.

The incident remained with me, and for reasons I could not fathom at the time, I spoke about it to a colleague. I found myself describing some aspects of my relationship with this supervisee. Although very rewarding, this supervision case had its puzzles. The intern had canceled several hours at the last minute because of unavoidable reasons; almost every time this happened, he would say that he would call me next week to make another appointment, as though he believed that his regular hour would not be kept open for him. On one occasion (about three or four weeks before the incident in question) there had been a misunderstanding between us, and he had shown up at my office for a supervisory session which I believed he had canceled, and so I had scheduled it for someone else. I apologized at the time, and we spoke about it briefly the following week. One of us had made an unconscious slip. As I discussed this with my colleague, the exact fit of events seemed uncanny.

At the next supervisory session, I shared the above with the intern, and he responded, "This is extraordinary!" This afforded us an opportunity to explore his hurt feelings, which were more extensive than I had allowed myself to realize at the time. In reconstructing the events, it seemed that the supervisee's self-blame (a tendency I had been aware of previously) enabled him to avoid his annoyance with me. The suppressed nature of this feeling facilitated its discharge via the mechanism of turning passivity into activity.

Problems in Supervision and Their Management

There are, I believe, some indications for intervening in the supervisor/supervisee relationship. Here are some guidelines I have found useful; one should intervene:

1. If there are problems in the relationship.
2. If there are problems in the learning alliance.
3. If there is a high level of negative affects in the supervisee, such as anxiety, depression, hostility, or self-derogatory tendencies.

In many situations more than one guideline applies. It is my belief that the characterologic difficulties of the candidate—for example, compliance, inhibition, mistrust, fear, or sensitivity to criticism—will intrude on the learning process, leading to distortions in what is heard or to curtailment of free exchange. Such learning blocks are often blamed on the student's inexperience rather than being seen as the consequence of conflict, although both factors may be operative. I am particularly intent on spotting instances in which the supervisee says little (silently disagreeing) or agrees too readily with the supervisor. One can sometimes see this ready agreement in the supervisee's parroting of the supervisor's comments the very next session regardless of their relevance to the material. Naturally, the decision of the supervisor to comment on aspects of the supervisee's character has to be tempered by considerations of analytic tact and a sensitivity to the student's capacity to tolerate some narcissistic injury. In such a decision, the supervisor must also take into account the stage the supervision is in. In the beginning, before a good alliance is established, one should proceed with greater caution than at later periods. Likewise, one should proceed differently with a candidate's first case than with subsequent ones.

The following vignette will show how a mixture of clarification and support helped to diminish overwhelming affects of shame and anxiety in a beginning therapist who was not able to foster a therapeutic atmosphere. She seemed unable to depart from either a question-and-answer model or a supportive stance; she intervened continually and could not tolerate silence. I noted that when she reported her failure to achieve a more psychotherapeutic atmosphere, she became more troubled and anxious, particularly when describing her inability to follow up on her own desire to intervene less often. But she continued to voice supportive generalizations or reality-oriented questions which seemed unconsciously aimed at demonstrating to her patient how much she cared about and was interested in her.

During this period, I occasionally addressed her concerns in a supportive fashion, telling her that I could see that this was not an easy patient to work with, or giving her examples of times when I had been confronted with patients who made me anxious. I also indicated that I was aware that it was difficult to alter one's way of doing things and that it all takes time. These interventions were only moderately helpful. After continuing some time in this vein, I decided to intervene once more to express what I thought was her dilemma. I took cognizance of her greater awareness of her difficulties and suggested that I understood that it would not be easy for her to discontinue her supportive stance unless she had something else to substitute for it. To develop these other modalities would take time and effort. These interventions were made gradually over a couple of sessions, and the supervisee seemed somewhat relieved by them. At the end of the six-month period, in discussing our mutual reaction to the supervision she indicated that she had felt discouraged at times, since she experienced my remarks as pointing out to her what she did not do right rather than indicating the good things she did. This candid remark sensitized me to the danger of duplicating in a parallel process the problem in the treatment—that is, the temptation to adopt a supportive stance and not to confront the supervisee's difficulties in order to preserve a "good" learning alliance. I believe this vignette illustrates some of the multiple complexities of the supervisor/supervisee relationship. It is my belief that responding to one level of the therapist's anxiety within the framework of the cognitive aspect of the educational process lessened the degree of conscious distress that she experienced. I am also well aware that there must have been many more aspects to her anxiety, about which I had no knowledge, and which did not belong in the domain of supervision.

I believe that not addressing a supervisee's distress in such cases sets up a split and leads to greater alienation on a personal level between the supervisor and the supervisee, which can only have a deleterious effect on the educational process. It leads to a build-up of negative affects which can result in regression, mistrust, and withdrawal. Further, it presents a model of ignoring interpersonal relationships as a solution to certain conflicts. This is in direct opposition to the general principle we try to convey: conflicts and interpersonal difficulties gain by being verbalized and confronted.

Another vignette will illustrate how I introduce the therapist's own perspective and psychology even in an early stage of supervision. A novice trainee whom I had been seeing in supervision for about three months mentioned that a patient had not paid a recent bill. In answer to a query, the trainee indicated that he had not brought up the topic with his patient, as he feared appearing too greedy (even though he would not benefit from the money). I suggested that he might profitably take up the issue with his patient at the time of the next bill a few days hence. At our next supervision session, the trainee mentioned casually that when he handed the patient the bill, the patient apologized for the lateness of the previous month and explained that he intended to move some funds shortly and take care of the bill. The therapist acquiesced and asked the patient what he wanted to talk about that day. The patient then addressed some matters in the work area.

At the end of our session, I silently took note of the fact that the trainee had not followed through on our last discussion. I asked him how he had felt during the hour; he complained that it had been too intellectualized. When I questioned him about his not having pursued the delay in payment, he acknowledged that he had actually avoided addressing the troublesome fee area. Did he know what had motivated him? He replied that he felt very uneasy about his inexperience: he was afraid that if he brought up the question of the fee, the patient might point to the fact that the treatment was not worth very much because the therapist was a beginner. He would have no rejoinder. I then indicated that his inexperience, which was real, need not be a stumbling block. It could be admitted. But the issue for the patient was why he was alluding to it. What was he trying to accomplish by concentrating on his doctor's relative inexperience? At this point the supervisee breathed a sigh of relief, saying he now realized that he did not have to feel so defensive about his inexperience. In the supervision I did not address the personal meaning of this unease or its genetic origins or even other related dynamic constellations. I chose to address the resident's inhibition and its immediate antecedents only as they interfered with his conduct of the treatment.

Some of the issues touched upon in the preceding vignettes are related to character and will be discussed further in the following section.

The Impact of the Supervisee's Character

In a previous paper on the analyst's style and its influence on technique (Baudry, 1991), I mentioned that supervision during training might be the logical time for bringing to the analyst's attention the impact of his or her character on technique. However, we usually fail to touch on this vital issue for multiple reasons. (1) The supervisor is reluctant to tread on what he or she considers to be the domain of the analysis. (2) The supervisor may not conceptualize the problem in characterologic terms. (3) The supervisor may see the way the candidate's character intrudes on the treatment but may not be able to find a useful way to communicate this to the candidate. (4) The supervisee's character may intrude on the supervisor/supervisee relationship but, again, there may seem to be no clear way to deal with this.

Let me give a simple example drawn from our hospital psychotherapy seminar. A supervisee reported that just before a therapy session, a patient forcefully insisted that he accompany him to where he could show the supervisee a small notice posted on the bulletin board just outside the office. The therapist acceded to the patient's request, and the patient then followed him back into the office. The patient did not consider his behavior to be relevant to the treatment, and he resisted the therapist's attempt to bring it in. The inquiry did not get very far for several reasons. First, the acting out had probably discharged aggression or actualized some fantasy, but the therapist had meekly accepted the patient's rationalization. Previous knowledge of the supervisee indicated that he had reacted to an intimidating demand with his characteristic style of compliance. Although I made a number of suggestions about the technical handling of this situation in the ensuing discussion, which were clearly understood and appreciated by the therapist, I sensed that he felt mostly exposed and humiliated. It did not seem likely that he could behave much differently should a similar situation arise again: he had come up against a limitation of his character. Although he might try to behave differently, his basic fear of aggression and characteristic response to intimidation by compliance could not really be touched by the discussion.

There is no simple solution to this common dilemma. It is easier to describe what does not work in this situation: a repetitive confrontation of the supervisee's difficulties discussed only on the technical level is apt to be experienced as humiliating. A suggestion that he or she requires more analysis or should examine him/herself in this regard will probably seem intrusive, moralistic, or judgmental. It burdens the supervision with an additional layer—compliance with or intimidation by the supervisor. I believe that simply pointing out some aspect of the supervisee's style or identifying his or her dilemma with the patient or with the supervisor is the least damaging approach. For example, some reference could be made to the supervisee's being caught between an intimidating patient and the wish to carry out the treatment as he or she sees fit. The best timing for such an intervention is the moment the supervisor senses that he or she may be intimidating the supervisee. Then and only then may it be possible to demonstrate the attitudinal similarity between the two situations as an opening wedge to a broader discussion of the supervisor/ supervisee relationship.

The next example illustrates such an approach and a nearly ideal resolution. The vignette was communicated to me by a colleague. In her training she had been considered a model supervisee: she seemed to grasp the intent of her supervisor and carry it out with sensitivity. As a result, her cases progressed well, and both of her supervisors recommended discontinuation of supervision and graduation of the supervisee. Some years later, she experienced some difficulties in dealing with demanding patients. She felt an urge to be excessively accommodating, and she experienced anger when the patients, instead of being grateful, seemed to demand more. This time, however, she sought help from a supervisor who was particularly sensitive to the supervisor/ supervisee relationship. Instead of passively acquiescing in the repetition of the same pattern—the supervisee's compliance with his suggestions—he raised the question of whether the supervisee was always in total agreement with him, which was most unlikely. He also suggested an analogy between the problem presented by the supervisee in her work (her compliance with the patient) and in her relationship with him. Fortunately, the gifted supervisee was able to do some self-searching. She soon realized that she had been intimidated by the previous supervisors and had been inhibited in challenging their views and thinking for herself. She felt she had learned relatively little from her student experience—or at least less than she could have learned had her attitude been pointed out to her. Her compliance, she felt, had not raised a problem for the supervisor and hence had been ignored. It is of interest that this aspect of her character had not received adequate attention in her training analysis, perhaps for similar reasons. The supervisory situation is ideal for observing the effect of the analyst's character on his or her technique. Because character is so ego syntonic, these issues are apt to be overlooked in the analysis unless they impinge clearly on the transference, or become symptomatic.

Aspects of the Parallel Process

Arlow (1963) was one of the first to mention the parallel process in connection with the supervisory situation, although Searles in 1955 made brief mention of it. The first extensive study was done by Doehrman (1976). Sachs and Shapiro (1976) emphasized its occurrence in inexperienced therapists who have anxieties similar to those of their patients. Both members of the dyad attempt to meet impossible demands, and they share over-lapping vulnerabilities. I would extend the occurrence of the parallel process to experienced therapists as well, who have different narcissistic vulnerabilities and similar if not greater fears of exposure. Both Dewald (1987) and Schlesinger (in Wallerstein, 1981) commented openly on the stress of reporting on their supervisory work to a group of peers. Sachs and Shapiro (1976) raised the question of whether the parallel process is indicative of countertransference or of pathology. It is certainly evidence of conflict and displacement, which may lead to therapeutic difficulties.

It is important to differentiate those transitory identifications with the patient that are a necessary accompaniment to empathy from those identifications based on shared anxieties or defensive needs which impair the therapist's awareness of what is happening between him or her and the patient. The resulting enactments of these identifications are not in themselves productive of insight, although they have an important communicative value, which, if exploited with sensitivity by the supervisor, may lead to valuable insight. I agree with Sachs and Shapiro (1976) that the solution is appropriate clarification of the process in a supportive setting. I share their belief that "other teaching approaches, which ignore the therapist's emotional responses, have to rely on processing data about the patient on theoretical grounds. Here, the student is placed in the position of having to agree or disagree with the more informed view of the instructor whose authority stems from his superior ability. The validity of this teaching method rests on an assumption that the student can be objective in his approach to differences of opinion, that he can be open-minded, and that he can view dispassionately interpretations about the therapy which are at variance with his own. Our experience has demonstrated that this proposition is no more tenable in the conference than in psychotherapy" (p. 413). The most recent article on the topic (Gediman & Wolkenfeld, 1980), based in part on the work of a supervisory group led by the author in collaboration with William Grossman, stressed three common similarities between psychoanalysis and supervision that are responsible for some aspects of the parallel process: both are helping processes, both require involvement of the self, and both rely heavily for effectiveness on multiple identifications.

Here is a brief clinical illustration (taken from a supervisory seminar) of how the parallel process can help uncover problems in the treatment. I have been struck with the frequency with which a presenter re-enacts with the group certain aspects of the case which have given the presenter difficulty or which the presenter has not understood. These problems become apparent to the group when discussing some aspect of the group process with the presenter, and the problems require particularly tactful handling in order to avoid narcissistic injury. The group in this vignette was very cohesive, and there was considerable good will among its members. On one occasion a member, a rather critical person who was very sensitive to injuries to his self-esteem, presented an impasse in the treatment of a young woman. What emerged from the presentation and made an impression on the group was the patient's lack of reaction to certain interventions of the therapist which could have elicited some complaints from her. The group session ended with the group feeling at odds with the presenter, and not knowing how to deal with what seemed to be the presenter's blind spot.

At the next session the presenter brought in the patient's chart, opened it, and said he wanted to "set the record straight" and present the facts as he saw them. The members of this group were accustomed to responding to each other in an uninhibited fashion. One member commented that the presenter was acting like someone on the defensive, to which the presenter responded by saying that he had felt very much criticized by the group the previous week, but had been too inhibited to say anything. It was then pointed out that this seemed to mirror the group's sense of where the treatment was stuck. The presenter reluctantly agreed, and subsequent events in the case, in a follow-up session, confirmed the correctness of this intervention. The patient had indeed felt angry at the therapist, but because of her dependency needs, could not voice her criticism.

Such instances as the one given above are commonplace, yet it is difficult to describe the complex dynamics responsible for their occurrence. In this case the therapist's character traits made it difficult for him to deal effectively with his patient's inhibitions in expressing anger because he shared some of the same defenses. Attention to the parallel process then yielded a point of entry to the conflict of the therapist, the conflict of the patient, and a resolution of the impasse. It is clearly difficult to make hard and fast rules about the management of such occurrences, and so no generalizations can readily be offered.

The next vignette illustrates an instance in which the parallel process helped me to detect a covert but important reaction of my supervisee. A supervisee of long standing, with whom I had a very good learning alliance, presented a case in which his analysand complained that there were "bad vibes" between them. The patient had been in treatment for almost a year and had recently complained about his analyst to a senior person within the organization. The supervisee had attempted to interpret this issue by showing the patient the similarity between his complaints about him and the earlier relationship with his mother. In describing the interaction, the supervisee told me that the patient agreed only intellectually. This took the form of "so what you are telling me is so-and-so." He felt that through this statement the patient was simply rejecting and negating his work, and he did not know how to pursue it further. I then followed two lines of intervention. I could not be sure, from the statement "So what you are telling me is so-and-so," that the patient was simply rejecting his intervention. I felt that it also implied the patient could not allow himself to be a passive recipient but had to put his stamp on the interpretations before taking them in. I also felt that the patient was probably not ready to take the step of examining his complaint of "bad vibes" as a transference reaction but that more work had to be done in the here and now about these "bad vibes"—such as determining the patient's views about their origins and the difficulties they created for him. (He was a student in the training program and had previously expressed the fantasy of leaving.) As I completed my interventions, the supervisee, who had listened intently, said, "So what you are saying is …," and then he repeated my interventions. I laughed, and we both immediately understood the occurrence of a parallel process—a transient identification with his patient's mode of defense which seemingly required little further work. To clarify my hunch, I asked my supervisee if he was telling me that he felt about my interventions the same way that he reported the patient felt about his. This seemed to lighten the atmosphere, and he then explained that he thought my interventions implied some criticism of him; that if he had explained himself properly, I would have agreed with him. Interestingly enough, I had suggested to him previously that one reason his patient had failed to respond to his interpretations of "bad vibes" was that he felt his feelings were being negated and explained away rather than acknowledged.

There are, however, many problems with the concept of the parallel process. Like the term "character," the term "parallel process" is purely descriptive and *not* explanatory. It has become something of a fad, particularly among beginning therapists. In the course of my supervisory seminar, many supervisors proudly point out some phenomenon as an evidence of the parallel process and stop there as though they had actually explained some particular event. What is usually referred to is an apparent similarity between some incident in the treatment and its seeming re-enactment with the supervisor. The facts are, unfortunately, much more complicated. The parallel process is only a vague descriptive label applied to a multitude of phenomena, only a few of which would qualify as "true" parallel processes. In my view what is required, in addition to the surface similarity, is a dynamic and structural congruence between the two situations. This is often difficult to demonstrate, because so many of the crucial dynamics of the participants are unknown or can be inferred only with great caution. Thus, in cases which are in doubt I would refrain from commenting on what could be an instance of the parallel process, except to inquire cautiously about its context. Should the student have the same needs as the patient, a type of mirroring may be encountered. This does not necessarily qualify as an example of the parallel process. The following vignette will illustrate this point.

A supervisee reported that in almost every session his patient asked, in one form or another, for reassurance that she was doing the right thing. This behavior was therefore a characteristic of this patient. The same supervisee also happened to be quite insecure about his work, and in both verbal and nonverbal ways he sought to be reassured about the correctness of his interpretations and of his therapeutic stance. This occurred with all the patients he presented to me and did not seem to be specifically related to the dynamics of any particular patient. Hence, I would not consider this as evidence of the parallel process, and it would be inaccurate to relate the behavior of the patient to the behavior of the therapist during supervision.

A possible objection to my use of the parallel process is that the same or better results could be reached by other interventions. Further, I would need to show that there are no deleterious effects of this way of proceeding. A vignette will clarify this first point. A very reliable supervisee had difficulty in dealing with the termination of a very stormy treatment. The decision to terminate was complicated by multiple outside factors which combined both extrinsic and internal elements: the supervisee was considering relocating; he was leaving his current employment; and he was taking a leave of absence from his practice for personal reasons which aroused guilt and anxiety. He mentioned that in the last few weeks the treatment had gotten bogged down, and very little seemed to be happening. The patient emphasized how well his external life was going and that he was now taking some courses and felt less dependent on the therapist. The therapist accepted this change at face value, much preferring this type of session to the previous stormy ones, which were emotionally taxing. My suggestions that the patient was most likely avoiding painful feelings regarding the coming separation were understood by the therapist, agreed with, but led to no change in the nature of the sessions.

A couple of weeks later the supervisee called me on the day of our supervision, asking if he could cancel our meeting because an interesting conference was being held at the same time as our supervision. I said that I suspected something was going on and that I thought we had better meet. At the start of our hour I asked whether there was something between us that the supervisee wanted to avoid. My question unleashed a tearful outpouring of fears about our coming termination, which were reinforced by multiple other terminations occurring simultaneously. The supervisee then said that he now understood that he had not wanted to tackle his patient's fears of termination because he had needed to avoid his own. Subsequent hours with the patient became much richer and stormier as a result, and confirmed the correctness of this conclusion.

The supervisee later expressed gratitude at having been able to share his concerns with me. Although in this instance the results seemed positive, a question could be raised about whether the problem with the patient could have been handled without touching on the supervisor/supervisee relationship. Could I have said to this supervisee that he seemed reluctant to confront the patient's separation anxiety? To this, I would reply that I had pointed out to him the patient's difficulties without avail; true, I had not worded the problem in terms of his reluctance, but my preference was to deal with the problem where it seemed active at the moment, namely, in his wish to avoid meeting with me. This is in line with my earlier points. As to the question of negative effects, I have not found any overt problems when I have proceeded with appropriate tact and caution during the confrontations mentioned above.

REFERENCES

Arlow, J.A. (1963). The supervisory situation. *J. Am. Psychoanal. Assoc.* 11:576–594.

Baudry, F. 1(991). The relevance of the analyst's character and attitudes to his work. *J. Am. Psychoanal. Assoc.* 39:917–939.

Dewald, P.A. (1987). *Learning Process in Psychoanalytic Supervision: Complexities and Challenges. A Case Illustration.* Madison, CT: Int. Univ. Press.

Doehrman, M.J. G. (1976). Parallel processes in supervision and psychotherapy. *Bull. Menning. Clin.*409–104.

Fleming, J. Benedek, T. F. (1966). *Psychoanalytic Supervision. A Method of Clinical Teaching.* New York: Int. Univ. Press, 1983.

Gediman, H.K. & Wolkenfeld, F. (1980). The parallelism phenomenon in psychoanalysis and supervision: Its reconsideration as a triadic system. *Psychoanal. Q.*49:*234–255.*

Malcove, L. (1975). The analytic situation: Toward a view of the supervisory experience. *J. Phila. Assn. Psychoanal.*21–19.

New York Psychoanalytic Institute (1963). Minutes of the Faculty Meeting. Unpublished.

Sachs, D.M. & Shapiro, S. H. (1976). On parallel processes in therapy and teaching .*Psychoanal. Q.*45:*394–415.*

Searles, H.F. (1955). *The informational value of the supervisor's emotional experiences In Collected Papers on Schizophrenia and Related Subjects.* New York: Int. Univ. Press, 1965, pp. *157–177.*

Solnit, A.J. (1970). Learning from psychoanalytic supervision *Int. J. Psychoanal.*51:*359–415.*

Wallerstein, R.S., Editor (1981). *Becoming a Psychoanalyst. A Study of Psychoanalytic Supervision.* New York: Int. Univ. Press.

Wyman, H.M. Rittenberg, S. M. (1992). The analysing instrument of Otto Isakower, M.D. Evolution of a concept *J. Clin. Psychoanal.*1*165–316.*

CHAPTER 3

Kohut and Glover: The Role of Subjectivity in Psychoanalytic Theory and Controversy

[(1998). *Psychoanal. Study Child* (53):3–24.]

The role of conflictual elements in the genesis of a new theory and in relation to the use of theory in a psychoanalytic controversy will be explored in two "case" studies. In the first, a close reading of Kohut's "The Two Analyses of Mr. Z" and in the second, a detailed examination of Glover's shifting allegiances toward Kleinian theory will reflect the role of transference and of idealization as powerful motivating elements.

In our efforts to sustain a scientific discourse we often lose sight of the fact that theory, like all mental products, is a compromise formation. Although largely the product of secondary process, it is nevertheless inextricably interwoven with the subjective aspects of the personality. These include both the relatively "normal" factors present in any mental product and the more pathological conflict-ridden elements. It is the latter that I will examine here.

Like Rangell (1985) and Grossman (1995), I believe that theory is a very special type of mental object readily exploited by complicated transference and countertransference and easily entwined in conflicts around authority. Both the genesis of a theory and its subsequent use and misuse by the individual are influenced by unconscious components not generally spelled out in our scientific writings.

The role of intrapsychic conflict in the genesis of a new theory can be examined from the vantage point of the effect of infantile conflicts of the author. Each person has a private version of a theory of his own pathogenesis and a theory of cure (Arlow, 1981). Unavoidably, his infantile conflicts will affect, to a greater or lesser degree, the kind of theory he will construct and the clinical stance he will adopt. Such conflicts, encoded in the form of conscious and unconscious fantasies, are especially likely to press for discharge if the author has had a poor or incomplete analytic experience, including unresolved negative transference. In some cases, a fierce and implacable opposition to the basic tenets of analysis follows such failed analyses. In other cases, the outcome is a new theory.

In the first section of this paper, I will suggest some of the personal factors that I believe may have played a key role in the genesis of Kohut's theory about the self and at the same time limited its overall scope and explanatory power. I argue that in the case of Kohut, his relation to his primary object, his mother, then his transference to his analyst, and finally the role classical theory played in his mental life, all had the quality of authoritarian idealized objects requiring acceptance and submission. This particular dynamic, in my view, was a key motivating factor in his development of a new theory.

In the second section of the paper, I will examine some of the personal elements involved in the major psychoanalytic controversy between the Freudians and the Kleinians in Great Britain as they affected one of the principal protagonists, Edward Glover. I will focus particularly on Glover's dramatic shift in position toward Kleinian theory during the late 1930s and early 1940s. Within a relatively brief period of time, Glover, once one of Melanie Klein's most enthusiastic supporters, became one of her most implacable enemies. This had major consequences for the history of psychoanalysis in England. In both of my examples the problem arose in part from idealization of a theory and subsequent disillusionment.

Before addressing the dynamics of controversy, I wish to point out that there are some attributes of our field that promote ambiguity and differences of opinion without necessarily indicating the contribution of irrational factors, although these may become the seeds of controversy.

Freud did not always define concepts clearly or use them in the same ways throughout his career. Such was the case with the concept of fantasy. A second factor complicating the evaluation of a theory is the somewhat blurred relationship between data and theory. What constitutes "proof" and the nature of evidence have been hotly debated. Our inability to quantify and measure mental phenomena is also a problem. Finally, depending on one's preferences, it is possible to emphasize either the continuities or the discontinuities of development. As the debate between the Kleinians and the Freudians dealt largely with the reconstruction of the preverbal period, for which we have no direct analytic data, differences of opinion could not be settled by reference to clinical material.

Theory performs multiple functions for the individual and for the group. One is to organize data in the most parsimonious fashion; another is to bind its adherents together in a closely knit group. Any theory includes a series of postulates not based on clinical data but necessary to integrate these data into a meaningful whole. Participants in a controversy forget the hypothetical status of these postulates and attribute emotional truth to them, equating their being called into question with an act of disloyalty. The role of subjectivity is understandably increased during periods of controversy, and in an atmosphere of adversarial tension the irrational forces of group psychology become heightened.

It is almost tiresome to read "descriptions" of opposing systems presented by theorists who claim the superiority of one system over another. The "other" is either caricatured or oversimplified. A straw man is erected only to be slain triumphantly, and the "correct" version rises from the ashes of the prior system. This parody, by the way, applies as well to the classical analyst as it does to adherents of other schools. The reductionistic phenomenon is an aspect of group functioning, involving hostility toward outsiders and the familiar scapegoating pattern, plus the loss of perspective on the complexity of the opponent's point of view.

I do not mean to suggest that all theories have equal explanatory value or that it is not possible to discuss a particular theory on the basis of clinical material, evidence, internal consistency, logical flaws, contradictions, and the like. Clearly not all theories are created equal. Yet, even here subjective factors intervene. That is, there are no theory-free observations, and the very choice of data to illustrate a particular theory already entails a theoretical preference. A theory is never true or false; it is only more or less useful. This point easily gets lost in the heat of a controversy.

The Kohutian Revolution

Using as data the famous paper "The Two Analyses of Mr. Z," I will show how classical psychoanalytic theory functioned as a constricting, authoritarian mental object for Kohut[5] and how this "misuse" of theory interfered with his clinical work. I will then explore some of the subjective factors that I suspect may be related to this phenomenon and that led to Kohut's proposing a new theory about the self. My presentation does not address problems with our classical theory that Kohut tried to rectify in proposing his new concepts.

My ideas were sparked by recent suggestions about the veracity of the data in "The Two Analyses of Mr. Z" (Kohut, 1979). This article, one of the classics in our literature, recounts the improvements in technique that were a direct consequence of the introduction of a new theory. The case is written as a critical narrative of an analysis that took place in two distinct phases separated by a period of about five years. It includes a detailed description of the unfolding of insights and interpretations. There are scant data about the process itself, making an evaluation more difficult.

---

5 I am grateful particularly to Dr. William Grossman and other members of CAPS group VI for their contribution to some of my ideas in this section of the paper.

Kohut first analyzed Mr. Z in the late 1950s for a period of about four years, using what he felt was a correct application of the classical approach. Mr. Z was a graduate student in his mid-twenties living with his widowed mother. He had consulted Kohut for a variety of symptoms, including mild somatic ailments, anxiety, and frequent masturbation. He also complained of social isolation. The analysis first dealt with the patient's overly close attachment to his mother, which was interpreted along classical oedipal lines—that is, reflecting his victorious possession of her over his father, who had died a number of years previously. The analyst interpreted the patient's grandiosity and feelings of entitlement as due to his imaginary oedipal victory secondary to the father's hospitalization and subsequent affair with his nurse during the patient's third year. The father's estrangement left Mr. Z in sole possession of his mother. Most if not all manifestations of conflict were related to issues of sexuality and aggression, particularly castration anxiety and masochism.

In the first analysis, the patient opposed the analyst's interpretations with "intense resistances" (p. 5) and rages.[6] These rages were in part related to separations. The patient felt that his anger was justified because he was misunderstood by the analyst. After 18 months of continued work, his anger decreased, and the analyst commented approvingly on the change as "working through bearing fruit" (p. 5). In retrospect, the patient realized that he felt less angry temporarily because the analyst had behaved in a more empathic fashion—not because of any structural change. Thus, a fundamental difference existed between the analyst's and the patient's understandings about the origin of the improvement. When the narcissistic resistances returned in a late phase of the analysis, Kohut writes that he "consistently and with increasing firmness rejected the reactivation of his

---

6 In the following I will quote directly from the case report. The analyst is referred to in the first person and the patient is always quoted in the third person.

narcissistic attitudes, expectations, and demands by telling the patient that they were resistances against the confrontation of deeper and more intense fears connected with masculine assertiveness and competition with men" (p. 12).

The analysis lasted for about four years. Kohut became dissatisfied when some of the hoped-for gains proved to be short-lived, and difficulties for which the patient had first sought help recurred. The only clue to this incomplete resolution could be found in retrospect in a "shallow and unexciting termination phase." The patient returned for a second analysis after five years. In the interim, Kohut had introduced his new theory. As a direct consequence of the change, he modified his therapeutic stance and was able to correct the problems of the first analysis. The major difference concerned the understanding of the reasons behind the patient's narcissism.

My initial reaction to reading about the first analysis and the author's critique of it in the second part of his paper was to agree with Kohut about the limitations of the first treatment but to have a different version of the case. I thought that in the first analysis, Kohut was influenced by very strong opinions about what the patient should give up and was burdened by "goal-directed therapeutic ambitions" (p. 5). As a result, he behaved in a rather controlling manner toward his patient. Kohut wrote, "I expected that he [the patient] would with the help of analytic insights . . . relinquish his narcissistic demands and grow up" (p. 12). As I read the case, I thought that Kohut had failed to appreciate the complex entanglement with the mother that was being repeated in the transference. The clinical consequence of his new theory entailed a much greater sensitivity to the patient's narcissistic conflicts and the careful management of the narcissistic transference, both idealizing and mirroring. As Kohut writes, the new theory allowed him to "*perceive meanings or the significance of meanings he had not formerly consciously perceived*" (p. 12, italics added).

The key differences between analyst I and analyst II could not be stated more clearly: "I relinquished the health and maturity morality that had formerly motivated me, and restricted myself to the task of reconstructing the early stages of his experiences, particularly as they concerned his enmeshment with the pathological personality of the mother." As a result, the patient's opposition to the analyst's interpretations is no longer seen as rebellious behavior but rather as reflecting "the child's desperate and often hopeless struggle to disentangle itself from the noxious self object, to delimit itself, to grow to become independent" (p. 16).

When I first read the paper, I believed that the first analysis was stuck because of certain stylistic rigidities or countertransference reactions in the analyst. His solution was to develop a new theory as a requirement for him to become more sensitively attuned to the patient's needs and to abandon his therapeutic zeal. I did not think that increased sensitivity necessarily required the introduction of a new paradigm. To put it another way, the analyst blamed the unsatisfactory results of the first analysis on a shortcoming of the theory rather than on what seemed to me to be the misuse of theory or an inhibition in empathy possibly related to some preconceived ideas about the correct unfolding of an analytic process.

I did not think much more about the case until a startling suspicion was confirmed within the past few years in a book on Kohut's correspondence (Kohut, 1994). In an introductory chapter, Kohut's wife and son expressed their belief that Mr. Z was in fact none other than Kohut himself and that "the case reflected his unsatisfactory first analysis with Dr. Ruth Eissler in Chicago and his [subsequent] efforts at self-analysis in order to overcome remaining difficulties" (p. 10). If we accept this premise, a whole new vista becomes possible.[7]

---

7 According to Strozier (1996), the statement by Kohut's son is not based on direct evidence. According to Mrs. Kohut, Kohut never said anything directly during his lifetime about the identity of Mr. Z.; he had the habit of reading all his cases aloud to her before

For the purposes of this presentation, I will leave aside two troublesome issues: first, the ethical questions raised by the discovery of this massive deception, the distortions of the data, and some fabrications that were required to make it into a story about another person, particularly in the area of transference. For example, how can we evaluate references to the transference in the second analysis, including such items as the patient's curiosity about his analyst's private life? Second, on a scientific level, I had some doubts about the veracity of the data. As a piece of self-analysis, the work is remarkable in its depth, sensitivity, and detailed reconstructions. Certainly, the literature on self-analysis does not support the idea that self-scrutiny alone could yield this sort of result.

In line with my interest, I will demonstrate the congruence between Mr. Z's relation to his mother, his transference to his analyst, and Kohut's relation to classical theory.

If we were to accept for the moment the idea that Mr. Z was Kohut, then it is plausible to consider the narration of the first "failed analysis" as a somewhat fictionalized version of Kohut's unsatisfactory analysis with Dr. Eissler. This makes more sense than considering the entire paper as a report of a self-analysis. First, it does not seem plausible to assume that an analyst would be willing to expose, even after considerable disguise, a

---

publishing them. Mrs. Kohut claimed that after his death she came to the conclusion that the case was a disguised autobiography. The reason for this opinion was not stated. Kohut's son was said to have destroyed all his father's clinical notes without looking at the names of the patients; hence no written records remain. In any event, anyone familiar with the intimate details of Kohut's life would agree that the story of Mr. Z. is very self-referential; it fits in amazingly well with what is known about Kohut, his mother, her relation to him, her deterioration, and, perhaps most revealing, his lengthy homosexually tinged relationship with a camp counselor during adolescence. If the case is not autobiographical, it certainly includes many of the crucial episodes of Kohut's young life. I researched one additional fact. The case report mentions that Mr. Z's analyst heard from him on the occasion of his elevation to an important professional office. It turns out that in 1951, some time after the termination of Kohut's analysis, Dr. Ruth Eissler was elected to the post of Honorary Secretary of the International Psychoanalytical Society.

failed self-analysis. Second, the brief quote from the introduction to Kohut's correspondence is in harmony with this interpretation. ("The case reflected his unsatisfactory first analysis with Dr. Ruth Eissler in Chicago and his efforts at self-analysis in order to overcome remaining difficulties.") Third, by describing the first treatment and its relative failure, Kohut could feel much more justified in his clinical and theoretical innovations.

The portrait of Analyst I reflects Kohut's own ideas about what his analyst might have been thinking during the course of treatment and the alleged theoretical basis for her behavior. The first part of the report is to be seen more as a piece of fiction than as a true case history. We have to substitute "Dr. Eissler" for references to "the analyst," and "Kohut" for "the patient" whenever Mr. Z is mentioned.

If we assume that the report of the first analysis combines elements of fiction with a history of Kohut's analysis, we are in a better position to postulate some of the dynamic factors involved in the genesis of the new theory. What happened after termination of the "first analysis" can only be conjectured. Did Kohut actually return to see Dr. Eissler in consultation, as reading the report would suggest, or is it at this point that a new fiction is superimposed? Kohut describes receiving from Mr. Z "a Christmas card which, he wrote, he was sending me in order to congratulate me concerning a professional office I was currently holding (I later discovered that he had learned about this from a newspaper notice more than a half year earlier, without then writing to me.)" (p. 10). Are we to read this as a total fabrication or as an importation of a real event in which Kohut had written Dr. Eissler about an appointment of hers? In any case, after an initial consultation, Kohut writes that he suspected that "his [i.e., the patient's] experiencing an increase in well being after seeing me again was an aspect of the transference he had established" (p. 11). Are we dealing here with a fantasied object relation as a result of the initiation of self-analysis or with a resurgence of the transference after a real visit or even with a total fabrication required to make the "case" more lifelike? The analyst Kohut then "entertains the hypothesis that the patient [Mr. Z] was establishing an idealizing transference, a hypothesis that I had not entertained during the first analysis" (p. 11). Here we encounter the first real problem as we try to make sense of the emergence of a mirror transference. How can this occur in a self-analysis? When Kohut writes that "the patient became self-centered, insisting on perfect empathy, and inclined to react with rage at the slightest out-of-tuneness with his psychological states" we would have to assume that Kohut is importing at this point a fragment of the first analysis in order to show the difference in management that would result as a consequence of the new theory.

In the first part of the paper, the patient's mother is described as "holding intense unshakable convictions that were translated into attitudes and actions which emotionally enslaved those around her and stifled their independent existence" (p. 13). Mr. Z's need to please her was the best adaptation he was capable of under these trying circumstances. Reading the case, it seems that the first analyst may have missed the narcissistic aspect of the patient's need to please him (or her). Kohut writes: "What had been missing from his reports was the crucial fact that the mother's emotional gifts were bestowed on him under the unalterable and uncompromising condition that he submit to total domination by her, that he must not allow himself any independence, particularly as concerned significant relationships with others" (p. 13). It is not unreasonable to imagine that this crucial aspect was missing from the report because it was enacted in the transference instead of being made available in the verbal material. The description of the controlling attitude of analyst I is consistent with this hypothesis. One could imagine that too much of the first analysis was the unrecognized enactment of the following masturbation fantasy reported early: "fantasies of being the slave of a woman who unconditionally imposed her will on him and treated him like an inanimate object that had no will of its own" (p. 16).

The problems in the first analysis were particularly hard to detect precisely because the analyst and her theory were seen in the same light—powerful and idealized. This is illustrated in the following passage in which Kohut refers to his attitudes toward his work: "The logical cohesiveness of these reconstructions seemed impeccable, and in view of the fact that they were entirely in line with the precepts about the unfolding of an analysand's conflicts and about the ultimate resolution of these conflicts brought about in a well conducted analysis—*precepts that were then firmly established in me as almost unquestioned inner guidelines in conducting my therapeutic work* [italics added]—I had no doubt that Mr. Z's vast improvement was indeed based on the kind of structural change that comes about as a result of bringing formerly unconscious conflicts into consciousness" (p. 9). Seen in this light, similar dynamics governed Kohut's relation to his primary object, his mother, then to his analyst, and finally to psychoanalytic theory. The analyst and the theory as transference object were seen as authoritarian figures requiring total submission. Thus, Kohut's discarding of his version of classical theory could be seen as an attempt on a different terrain to accomplish what the first analysis had failed to do.

When a theory relies too heavily on a single pathogenic factor, I suspect that this factor has a very personal significance for the individual who constructs the theory. Such was the case for Rank, for Ferenczi, and to some degree to Wilhelm Reich. In self psychology, we also encounter a poverty in its theory of pathogenesis. The role of the unempathic mother is overemphasized, and other factors are hardly mentioned. Conflict is largely replaced by deficit. The emphasis on the boy's disappointment in his father during the latency period as a potent factor in narcissistic pathology also seems overly reductionistic. This state of affairs would be congruent with the hypothesis that Kohut's theoretical position was heavily influenced by the author's private theory about himself. It would be consistent with this to assume that Mr. Z/Kohut felt that his analyst was not sufficiently empathic with his mental state. The role of what has been criticized, perhaps unfairly, as the self psychologist's emphasis on corrective emotional experience would also be consistent with a complaint Kohut had toward his former analyst, regardless of whether one sees this as a problem in the transference or in the countertransference. If I am correct, then, a particular transference to the first analyst and to the theory she espoused limited the best possible application of the theory, interfered with the author's making maximal conflict-free use of his analyzing instrument, and led to a replacement of the classical views about the theory of drives and objects. Initially, the old language was retained, creating confusion about what the innovations really were, but eventually a new language replaced the earlier one.

The Glover Episode

I will now turn to a fascinating episode during the so-called Controversial Discussions held in the British Psychoanalytic Society during the Second World War. During the stormy scientific meetings held to discuss the place of the Kleinians within the traditional analytic society, Edward Glover changed dramatically from an ardent supporter of Melanie Klein to one of her bitterest opponents. The degree of animus, its persistence, and its unyielding nature suggest the intrusion of irrationality into very sound secondary-process thinking. In contrast to Kohut, whose new views created much debate, Glover had considerable influence on a pre-existing controversy. As I hope to show, Glover's about-face toward Klein's theory was partly a reaction to an idealizing transference to Abraham, who had analyzed both Klein and Glover. Glover's evident animus considerably weakened the effectiveness of his position concerning the incompatibility of the changes Klein introduced in the theoretical apparatus of psychoanalysis with the then prevailing classical viewpoint. I shall stress the more subjective and personal elements that may be teased out from a close reading of the text.

The positions taken by Glover, as one of the most respected leaders in the analytic community, were bound to have major repercussions on the field as a whole. His many contributions, including his brilliant textbook on analysis, display a keen understanding of the different parts of the analytic superstructure. They are written in a somewhat mordant and gently ironic style that makes them wonderful reading for readers at all levels of analytic sophistication.

In their scholarly and detailed minutes of these debates, King and Steiner (1991) give us an overall view. It is now possible to mine this rich work and begin to make detailed assessment of the key players and their influence on the course of events. As we read the record, we should not lose sight of the very human dimensions of the struggle. Here were very intelligent people caught up in cataclysmic events, including the bombing of their capital, uncertain about their very physical survival, suddenly confronted by a sizable number of very powerful immigrants, some with different views about their field, potentially weakening their economic position at a time of extreme stress. One can hardly blame them for behaving at times in an emotional, even irrational fashion.

The feud between Melanie Klein and Anna Freud has a long history, which has been exhaustively documented in our journals and reviewed in the King and Steiner volume. The British society was one of the three leading national organizations, along with Vienna and Berlin. Yet until the early 1930s, its members had not made any major discoveries. The most powerful member, Ernest Jones, was only beginning to differentiate himself from the Vienna school on the topic of preoedipal female sexuality. The views of Melanie Klein were more or less convergent with the British position, and after a preliminary trip to England, during which she gave a course of lectures that was enthusiastically received, she moved to London permanently in 1927.

Anna Freud and Melanie Klein were at opposite poles on such issues as whether and how soon children form transferences and when these transferences should be interpreted. They also differed on the role of pedagogic and didactic efforts in work with children, on the role of the so-called normal fears of childhood, and on the nature of fantasy life in the preverbal period. Yet, as far as adult work was concerned, the clinical differences between the Freudians and the Kleinians in the late 1920s were not so great as is commonly imagined. At the time lengthy analyses and the careful delineation of character defenses were not the rule. Analyses lasted only a few months, and the analyst's main effort was to demonstrate to the patient, especially if he was a trainee, the influence of his unconscious complexes. The concept of working through was very new, and the early Freud was quite ready to interpret "deep" unconscious material very quickly. Klein adhered to this early Freudian model and evolved a theory that allowed rapid and direct interpretation of the patient's "deep unconscious." It was because this way of working failed to achieve long-lasting results that Freud developed the concept of working through.[8]

In any event, when Melanie Klein moved to England, she brought with her an entirely new way of dealing with neurotic disturbances in infancy. Not only was she developing new theories, but her equation of the young child's playing with the adult's free associations opened new vistas for child analysis. Jones was so taken by her that he sent her his two children for analysis and a few months later his wife. Klein would often report back

---

8 Interestingly enough, some time later a number of the Kleinians came to the same conclusion, but their solution to the clinical dilemma was to focus almost exclusively on the transference and the moment-to-moment process in the session (see the current work of Betty Joseph as a good example of this tendency). Which came first—the theory or the clinical method—is not always clear. Either could be a justification for the other.

to Jones about the progress of Mrs. Jones's analysis and make references to meetings Mrs. Jones had attended that she believed threatened the continuation of the analysis.

Jones was a relatively passive leader who did not like to alienate people, and it is likely that he enjoyed the prospect of having a strong personality nearby to take the flak and shield him from open conflict with Freud. Matters became very stormy when Jones chose Edward Glover, another very strong and opinionated leader, to head the Society. Glover was a Scot, the younger of two brothers. His elder brother, James, was considered by the family the more promising of the two. James embarked on an analytic career and eventually convinced Edward to follow suit. The two brothers worked very well as a team until James's tragic death in 1928 from complications of diabetes. He barely had time to write two papers.

Very early on, Edward acquired a rebellious and obstinate streak. Like all proper analysts, Edward decided to go to the Continent for his analysis. He chose Abraham, and wrote of his Berlin days: "flushed with a new enthusiasm, I was ready despite training in independent thinking dating from my school and undergraduate days almost to swallow hook line and sinker any undisciplined extravagance and method." On a personal level, Glover had suffered some personal tragedies in addition to his brother's death. His first wife died of septicemia 18 months after their marriage in 1918. Two years after his second marriage in 1926 his wife gave birth to a mongoloid daughter, whom the family kept at home at considerable emotional cost.

Until 1933 Glover was one of Klein's most faithful admirers. In her correspondence with Jones prior to her move to England, Klein had made the point that for her to succeed in establishing herself in England, she would need the active support of Edward Glover. They both had had a course of analysis with Karl Abraham. Abraham had also recommended Klein to Glover shortly before his death.

The growing dissatisfaction within the British Society that came to a head a few years after the forced emigration of the Viennese wing to London, centered both on the increasing difficulty of accommodating two competing points of view and on Glover's leadership style. Further difficulties arose as a consequence of Klein's haughty manner. It is said that she was a matriarch who gave the impression that those who were not with her were against her. In consequence, discussions at scientific meetings often degenerated into the registration of allegiances.

Glover's position would be pivotal to the outcome of the disagreement. His growing disillusionment with Klein had both theoretical and personal grounds, the latter was suggested by the persistence and virulence of his attacks.

The earliest sign that Glover was beginning to rethink his adherence to Klein came in his famous paper "The Therapeutic Effect of Inexact Interpretations" (1930). In effect he was countering the Kleinians' argument that their good therapeutic results proved the validity of their theory by showing the role which suggestion could play in symptomatic relief. "It is probable that there is a type of inexact interpretation which, depending on an optimum degree of psychic remoteness from the true source of anxiety, may bring about improvement in the symptomatic sense at the cost of refractoriness to deeper analysis." Glover went on:

If we recall the familiar intrauterine phantasies which have been variously interpreted from being indications of birth trauma to being representations of pre-latency genital incest wishes; or the phantasies of attacking the father or his penis in the mother's womb or vagina to which special attention was drawn by Abraham; or again the more "abdominal" womb phantasies to which Melanie Klein has attached a special meaning or significance, it will be seen that we have ample material to illustrate the problem under discussion (p. 357).

Note the linking of Klein with Abraham, whose views Glover also questions, and the charge that the inexact interpretation of these fantasies, far from being deep analysis, have the opposite effect of making deep analysis more difficult. Most of his readers would know that "deep analysis" had become a code word to characterize the type of analysis the Kleinians thought they were practicing in contrast to the Freudian model.

In early 1932, Glover, assisted by Brierley, conducted a survey of the technical practices of the members of the Society, with the veiled intention of questioning Klein's approach. The partisan conclusions he drew made clear his intention to show that a much smaller number of members than was generally supposed supported Klein's technique.

Yet there was still some wavering in Glover's opposition. Some time in 1933 he reviewed Klein's book on the psychoanalysis of children and had this to say: "In two main respects her book is of fundamental importance for the future of psychoanalysis. It contains not only unique clinical material gathered from firsthand analytic observation of children, but lays down certain conclusions which are bound to influence both the theory and practice of analysis for some time to come.... It constitutes a landmark in analytic literature worthy to rank with some of Freud's own classical contributions" (Glover, 1993, p. 119). This was the last positive appraisal Glover would make. From that time on, he became relentless in his opposition.

If one event galvanized Glover's opposition it was the arrival in London of Klein's daughter, Melitta Schmideberg. She became an associate member of the British Society in 1932 and a full member in 1933. Melitta, like all Klein's children, had been originally analyzed by her mother (Klein had reported her case under the name "Lisa.") If Freud's daughter defended the theories of her father/analyst with passion, Melitta attacked her mother's theories with equal passion. She decided to enter analysis with Glover in 1933 after a brief period with Ella Freeman Sharpe. The reasons for the shift are unknown. Near the beginning of her analysis with Glover, she wrote her mother a very dramatic letter putting her on notice that their relationship was going to change irrevocably. She indicates (1971) that this letter was drafted for her by Glover! By 1934, subsequent to the suspicious death of her older brother Hans in a mountaineering accident, she became even more impassioned against her mother, when she blamed the mother for this event.

Melitta wrote in her 1971 memoir that in the course of the year 1935 Jones, sensing difficulties, took the unusual step of asking her and her husband to emigrate to the United States. When that effort failed, Jones asked her to discontinue her analysis with Glover! It is not clear from available sources just how long she remained "in analysis." It is hard to imagine that the vengeful alliance between patient and analyst left much room for any true analytic work, particularly in the area of transference. She writes simply: "Glover and I had agreed to ally and fight!" Melitta was clearly embarked on a path of vindictiveness and was out for blood. She was informed of everything that went on in the Training Committee by her analyst, who headed the committee until his resignation in 1944.

By the early 1940s, Glover felt that, with the arrival of Anna Freud and her Viennese colleagues, he would have the support he needed to finally expose Melanie Klein's heresy. He became convinced within a relatively short period of time that Klein was a deviationist like Adler and Jung and should have the same fate as her illustrious predecessors—total excommunication.

By spring 1941 the situation had become nearly untenable. Jones had virtually retired to the country, leaving Glover as director of the clinic and chairman of the Training Committee. To complicate matters further, Glover came under increasing criticism for his dictatorial ways of managing the Institute, which alienated many members. King and Steiner recount that Glover had silently chafed for years as Jones's second-in-command.

I will now move forward again to March 1942 to discuss the second Extraordinary Business meeting of the Society. Two thirds of the way through the gathering, Melitta, no longer in analysis, erupted in a shrill, paranoid sounding attack against the Kleinians. In it she detailed their efforts to persuade candidates to leave their Freudian analysts. She accused them of campaigns to defame reputations and of making scientific discourse impossible by attending lectures by non-Kleinians in order to attack them as a group in front of the candidates. According to King, what Melitta said was factually true and cut right to the economic and ethical questions underlying the debate. Eventually the more moderate members of the group, including Payne and Brierley, were able to reach an armistice, and the next several scientific meetings were devoted to a discussion of the Kleinian concept of Unconscious Phantasy as detailed in a paper by Susan Isaacs.

Though the discussion was centered around substantive issues, the tone of the meetings remained adversarial. The Kleinians were out to demonstrate their allegiance to Freud, and their opponents to show that Klein's system was incompatible with Freud's basic tenets.

Some of the best minds in the Kleinian group presented a number of papers that are still considered the foundation of the Kleinian system, particularly Isaacs' contribution on the "Nature and Function of Phantasy," which was to take up most of the next five scientific meetings. In his discussion of this paper Glover pulled no punches: "If Mrs. Isaacs' new metapsychology is right, then Freud is wrong, for the two are incompatible in a number of ways." And the next paragraph: "In my opinion, Mrs. Isaacs has failed in her attempt to build a new metapsychology. She has failed because she disregards, neglects or misunderstands precisely those parts of Freud's metapsychology which eliminate the very confusions into which she persistently falls. In particular, she is addicted to a sort of psychic anthropomorphism, which most of Mrs. Klein's adherents exhibit, namely of confusing concepts of the psychic apparatus with psychic mechanisms in active operation in the child's mind" (King and Steiner, 1991, p. 326). He accused the Kleinians of confusing "the relations of psychic reality to phantasy and to reality proving. And reality proving is after all concerned with the relation of gratification or frustration of instincts to the external objects of these instincts, not with snapshots of the Himalaya Mountains" (pp. 326–327).

Glover's piece reads like a brief by a prosecuting attorney. It is not that he is wrong; in fact, he put his finger on the key issue of incompatibility, which unfortunately was later lost sight of in the heat of the debate. But it is not easy to determine when his criticism is valid, when it is simply a matter of willful misunderstanding, and when there might be room for meaningful discussion. After all, Isaacs made it clear that her paper was a preliminary attempt to create a theoretical superstructure for some of Melanie Klein's ideas and that it was still quite tentative in its conclusions. Glover's piece was a total condemnation from which there was no recourse. He was not interested in addressing any of the problems of Freudian theory that may have prompted the Kleinians to develop their own system. In accusing them of introducing postulates and then treating them as axiomatic, he failed to mention that a theory of development cannot be based on proven observation and requires the introduction of postulates, which may be discarded should they prove unserviceable. Trying to decide whether a new idea was in line with Freud's thinking or a significant departure becomes a Talmudic exercise.

True to form, Melitta was even more dismissive. She did not attend the first scientific meeting, and her brief remarks were read in her absence: "As Dr. Isaacs' paper contains no clear statement of the controversy in question. I see no point in discussing her paper. Such a blatant omission is contrary to scientific tradition and spirit. It is the lack of these that makes it impossible to take Dr. Isaacs paper seriously" (King and Steiner, p. 340). She then goes on to accuse Isaacs of lumping her with Klein's group.

One can imagine Glover's consternation when, in the ensuing scientific discussions, Isaacs first dealt with every other speaker's intervention despite the fact that Glover, as head of the Training Committee, has spoken right

84

after Jones. She skillfully attempted to undermine his criticism by quoting extensively from his previous favorable comments on Klein.

The two opposing factions reached a compromise on training method and a split was avoided, although no one was convinced by the other side's arguments, and ill feelings persisted. The threetrack system which was put in operation still exists today. Glover resigned when he saw the tide turn against him within the organization. He had failed in his attempts to throw the Kleinians out of the Society. He joined both the Swiss and the Japanese Societies in order to retain his position in the International and totally withdrew from active participation in the British Society. Melitta abandoned all efforts to remain an analyst. She resigned after Glover and moved to the United States for a while.

Anna Freud resigned from the Training Committee. She felt that cooperation with the Kleinians could not be possible even though a Freudian "Independent Group" persisted within the British Psychoanalytic Society. With the encouragement of Dr. Kate Friedlander and of Dorothy Burlingham, Anna Freud sought to develop her own independent training program in child analysis. It took about eight years before the Hampstead Clinic formally opened its doors, eventually replacing the Hampstead War Nursery. By 1954 the clinic had won wide recognition within the London milieu. Because Anna Freud did not want to compete with the British Institute, she refrained from developing a training program in adult analysis. To some observers it looked as though the Kleinians had won the field by default. To this day they are by far the most intellectually active and successful group in England. I understand that their candidates account for 50–60 percent of the total.

DISCUSSION

What plausible hypothesis could we make about the dramatic change of heart of this talented analyst? The safest course I can follow is to identify some of the factors and offer some very tentative reconstructions. I will start with general factors. Least well understood because of their silent participation, but extremely powerful, are some aspects of group psychology such as the formation of cliques, with strong competitive feelings towards the "Other" and a reductionistic setting up of polarized alternatives: good guys versus bad guys. The "Other" deserves punishment and annihilation. There are also complicated transferences toward both the old theory and the new one (Rangell, 1985). The hostility to the Kleinians was probably enhanced by their positing themselves as the "true" followers of Freud. Their initial theories were greeted with much enthusiasm, and this may have intensified elements of transference. Pearl King suspects that a "turf" component was also involved here: The clinical contributions of Klein, as a lay analyst, centered more and more on the sicker patients, both children and adults. The psychoses had until then been the province of the psychiatrists.

Turning to the more personal aspects of Glover's attitudes, we are dealing with a complex admixture of internal and external factors. Some aspects of his personal drama were played out against the backdrop of the existing controversy within a particular psychoanalytic organization with its own rules, rigidities, and conflicts. It is not easy to delimit the part that each component contributed to the end result, including his dramatic switch in position.

Two elements seemed particularly relevant: first, Glover's statements concerning his over-idealization of Abraham, which led him to accept Abraham's recommendation of Melanie Klein rather uncritically. The manifest positive transference toward Abraham encompassed Klein and her theory. A later sober appraisal of Klein revealed many problems and was followed by a swing of the pendulum to the other extreme.

The second factor was Glover's accepting in analysis Klein's daughter, who was passionately fixated on opposing her mother and attempting to destroy her position of preeminence. Unfortunately, we do not know what Melitta Schmideberg told Glover about her mother during the treatment or precisely how the two combined forces to oppose Melanie Klein. There has been much speculation about Glover's motives for his increasingly bitter and relentless attacks on Klein and the role of Melitta in this change. Did Melitta seduce Glover into doing her dirty work? Melitta's very choice of Glover as an analyst was an enactment of sorts because he already had started to oppose Klein openly. But why did Glover so readily cooperate; was he using her for his own ends? There the picture clouds. The bond between Melitta and Glover, complicated as it was, may have been strengthened by the fact that each had recently lost a beloved brother. It is plausible that Melitta represented the daughter Glover longed for. In any case, during the course of treatment there were a number of boundary violations. Melitta was informed of the committee deliberations. Glover also showed questionable lapses in judgement, such as in helping Melitta write a vitriolic letter to her mother at the beginning of her analysis.

We also need to consider Glover's complex relation to a former analyst, Abraham, and to an analytic sibling, Melanie Klein. In a footnote to his polemical 1945 article in *The Psychoanalytic Study of the Child,* Glover commented on his efforts to reach a compromise and on his disillusionment: "But as is so often the case, these unsolicited attempts at compromise ended by wringing concessions from their own sponsor rather than from the opposing parties. Not recognizing that Klein's primary observations were speculative rather than clinical, I assumed that they were clinically valid. If this should seem to represent a deplorable slipshodness on my part I would remind the reader that at that time (1924–1929) most analysts were inclined to accept papers published in analytic journals at their face value" (p. 88). He had gullibly accepted too much uncritically, and he must have felt rather humiliated by this exposure. In a footnote to his diatribe against Klein, he wrote: "When Klein first adumbrated her theories, I found them stimulating.... Possibly the fact that like Melanie Klein, I had been a pupil of Abraham made me more readily responsive to her general line of thought which both then and later was considerably influenced by Abraham's work."

In his subsequent writings Glover continued his violent polemics against Klein. Perhaps the most characteristic and definitive statement is to be found in a 1956 commentary on his 1949 article "The Position of Psychoanalysis in Great Britain." "Since the death of Freud in 1939, no advances of importance have been made in the field of psychoanalysis in Great Britain." A clearer statement would be hard to find! With one stroke of the pen, he obliterated Klein, or at least the Klein after the enunciation of the key developmental concepts of the Depressive and Paranoid positions. Yet in 1933 he wrote about Klein's book on the psychoanalysis of children: "I have no hesitation in saying that it constitutes a landmark in analytical literature worthy to rank with some of Freud's own classical contributions."

Some Long-Range Consequences of the Freud/Klein Controversy

Although the organizational differences were papered over and a split was indeed avoided, I believe that the controversy had noxious consequences for our field as a whole. The debate hardened each side's position; instead of learning from each other and conducting a fertile dialogue, the opposing camps engaged for the most part in anything but a scientific discourse. Any compromise was seen as a sign of weakness. Any problem in a theory was eagerly seized upon as an excuse to vent personal animus and to disparage the adversary's entire approach. Glover's wholesale condemnation of the Kleinian approach prevented any useful exploration of the problems with the Freudian theory of early development. This was quite unfortunate, for this area had been largely neglected by Freud. Beyond the early reflex-arc model of the Dream book, there had been no over-all attempt to spell out clearly the development of the very young infant. As Compton (1985) writes, "the mental events ascribed to the baby at the breast are little more than a personification of Freud's theory about excitation." There were also rough spots in the formulation of how the earliest oral instincts could be represented in the mind, particularly in the first year of life. As the Freudians did not believe in the early existence of fantasy, they had difficulty making a place for the mental representation of these instincts. In the absence of an "idea," could a primitive drive be represented in the mind by an "affect"? Could there be another primitive imaginal or sensory component? It was just this void that the Isaacs paper tried to fill. The Freudian retort that the author was overextending the province of fantasy as defined by Freud was of course correct, but neither Glover nor Anna Freud inquired whether there was anything to be gained from such an extension and whether it would be possible to fashion it without doing violence to the core developmental theory as described by Glover.

The Kleinians were, with a few exceptions (for example, Ruth Mack-Brunswick), left alone for the next decade to explore the issue of early aggression and of inner life during the preverbal period. They could provide clinical data to buttress their arguments by miming the possibility of analytic treatment for very young children. Klein's proposal that the earliest conflicts of the child involve vicissitudes of anxiety over aggression rather than of anxiety over separation was also a major departure from accepted theory. The Freudians remained reluctant to accord aggression the central role in certain early pathological formations such as the paranoid states. Recent revisions in the pathogenesis of these conditions have de-emphasized the role of homosexuality and replaced it—correctly, as I see it—with vicissitudes of aggression.

The emphasis of the Freudians on the infant's fundamental narcissism and autoerotism hampered their exploration of the young child's inner life. To be sure, Ernst Kris organized a new periodical, *The Psychoanalytic Study of the Child*, to stimulate and present research into the psychology of the child. This was a good forum for Anna Freud to present her work from the Hampstead War Nursery. The detailed study of pathology in children would receive renewed impetus from the emergence of a number of women analysts including Edith Jacobson, Margaret Mahler, and Phyllis Greenacre. Another facet of early development, that of attachment, was gradually taken over by researchers such as Bowlby, who were discredited by the classical wing; attachment then became a favorite property of the so-called object relations group. Oedipal pathology acquired political overtones and became a rallying point for classical analysis in the 1940s and 1950s. Even later, it was espoused particularly by the analysts close to Brenner.

For her part, Anna Freud's stamp on the province of child analysis delayed the development of the understanding of transference phenomena. As Chused (1988) noted, the dispute with Klein seemed to have led Anna Freud to maintain that a transference neurosis did not occur in the child because he was still too close to his primary object. In order to differentiate herself clearly from the Kleinians, Anna Freud also emphasized the discontinuity between the preverbal and the verbal, thereby sacrificing the forging of links between the two periods.

In her early work, the child analyst Berta Bornstein remained very close to Anna Freud's position and vehemently opposed Klein's work. In a charming paper on sleep phobia in a two-year-old child, Bornstein (1932) demonstrated how a Freudian might work with a young infant. It is a pity that some of her suggestions about the way in which a young child's mind works were not followed up and properly exploited until the work of Piaget.

Would it have been possible to deal with the objections to classical theory formulated by some of the innovators without introducing a new paradigm? Kohut, for example, was confronted with a limitation in the therapeutic results of an analysis. Rather than seeing it as the result of a limitation in the analyst's understanding of the patient, possibly due to some countertransferential complication, he made the strategic decision to formulate the problem as a limitation of the theory. This solution then required an alteration in theory which allowed Kohut to behave differently. Some analysts, such as Annie Reich and Edith Jacobson, have developed the concept of self representations and narcissism while retaining the classical framework. In the case of the introduction of Kleinian theory, the issue is much more complex, but neither side made a concerted effort to identify clearly the problems of the old theory and to devise modifications within the old paradigm. Once the new system was more or less in place, there was no going back.

SUMMARY

I have emphasized the role of subjective factors in the development of theories and in the shift in positions by individual analysts. In our discussions we sometimes forget that we do not deal with theory but with each psychoanalyst's personal, idiosyncratic interpretation of theory. This is influenced by subtle subjective factors, which I have tried to point out in the above presentation. I have emphasized the role of transference and of idealization and subsequent disillusionment as particularly relevant.

REFERENCES

Arlow, J. (1981). Theories of pathogenesis. *Psychoanal. Quarterly* 50:488–514.

Bornstein, B. (1935). Phobia in a two-and-one-half year old child. *Psychoanal. Quarterly* 4:93–119.

Chused, J. (1988). The transference neurosis in child analysis. *Psychoanal. Study of Child.* 43:51–83.

Compton, A. (1985). The concept of identification in the work of Freud, Ferenczi and Abraham: A review and commentary. *Psychoanal. Quarterly* 54:200–234.

Dupont, J. (1994). Freud's analysis of Ferenczi as revealed by their correspondence. *Int. J. Psychoanal.*, 75, 2:301–321.

Glover, E. (1930). The therapeutic effect of inexact interpretation. *Int. J. Psychoanal.* 11:757.

——— (1933). Review of Klein's The Psychoanalysis of Children. *Int. J. Psychoanal.* 14:119.

——— (1945). The examination of the Klein system of psychology. *Psychoanal. Study of Child*, 1:2.

——— (1956). The position of psychoanalysis in Great Britain. *British Medical Journal* (1949). 6:27–31.

Grosskurth, P. (1986). *Melanie Klein: Her world and her work.* New York: Alfred A. Knopf.

Grossman, W. (1995). Psychological vicissitudes of theory in clinical work. *Int. J. Psychoanal.* 76:885–899.

Hoffer, A. (1991). The Freud-Ferenczi controversy: A living legacy. *Int. Rev. Psychoanal.* 18:465–472.

King, P. & Steiner, R. (1991). *The Freud-Klein controversies, 1941–1945.* The New Library of Psychoanalysis: Routledge.

Klein, M. (1927). The psychoanalysis of children: Symposium on child analysis. *Int. J. of Psychoanalysis.* 8:25–37.

Kohut, H. (1979). The two analyses of Mr. Z. *Int. J. Psychoanal.* 60:3–29.

——— (1994). *The curve of life. Correspondence of Heinz Kohut, 1923–1981.* Chicago: Chicago Univ. Press.

Rangell, L. (1985). On the theory of theory in psychoanalysis and the relation of theory to psychoanalytic therapy. *J. Amer. Psychoanal. Assoc.*33:59–89.

Schmideberg, M. (1971). A contribution to the history of the psychoanalytic movement in Great Britain. *British Journal of Psychiatry* (1971) 118:61–68.

Strozier, C. (1966). The question of Mr. Z.: Themes of sexuality and identity in Kohut's life and works. Lecture given on 3/29/96 at the New York Institute for Psychoanalytic Self Psychology.

CHAPTER 4

Winnicott's 1968 Visit to the New York Psychoanalytic Society and Institute: A Contextual View

[(2009). *Psychoanal. Q.* (78)(4):1059–1090.]

As a prelude to describing the form and content of Winnicott's 1968 (a) presentation to the New York Psychoanalytic Society and Institute, the author first outlines some crucial contextual background of that group and of the three psychoanalysts who discussed Winnicott's paper at that event. Summaries are presented of the paper itself and the discussants' responses. The author elaborates on Winnicott's highly idiosyncratic way of presenting his ideas, which may lead the unwary reader astray. In conclusion, some of Winnicott's most original contributions, both to theory and on their application to technique, are reviewed.

> *Just here one must allow obscurity to have a value that is superior to false clarification.—Winnicott 1968b, p. 240 ("Comments on My Paper 'The Use of an Object'")*

On November 12, 1968, Winnicott went up to the podium at the New York Psychoanalytic Society and Institute, preparing to deliver his paper "The Use of an Object" (1968a) in front of an audience that filled the space to capacity and overflowed into the library. This was a very exciting moment

95

for him. It was his second visit to the United States.[9] He had eagerly anticipated presenting his views to the group of classical ego psychologists at this prestigious institute, and was hoping his novel ideas would meet with an appreciative reception—particularly as his involvement in the British Psychoanalytical Society had met with a less than enthusiastic reaction from Kleinian analysts, and his ideas also differed in significant respects from those of the analyst often cast in opposition to her, Anna Freud.

Winnicott had very quietly presented another paper a few days earlier at New York's William Alanson White Institute, almost in secret, with no publicity. I assume he was concerned about possible negative reactions should the New York Institute learn that he had presented a paper at an institute that was not part of the American Psychoanalytic Association. Another paper was apparently given a day earlier at the Kings County Hospital, placing all three presentations within a four-day span. The topics of the other presentations, as far as I could ascertain, were much more limited in scope than the one at the New York Institute; they dealt with the squiggle game and Winnicott's ideas on infant development.

The way in which Winnicott approached the meeting—rather shyly and casually, yet making clear his demands and preferences with a certain arrogance—is well illustrated by a letter written to the New York Society's executive secretary on October 31, 1968, obviously in answer to a previous letter he had received:

I think I have no one that I wish to invite to the meeting. My idea is simply to be present at one of your meetings, although as it happens by your invitation I am reading a paper. I think I may be able to manage the black tie situation but I am glad that you are willing to

---

9 In the fall of 1962, Winnicott had presented papers in several major West Coast cities, as well as in Topeka and Boston.

let me off if necessary. Incidentally, I am grateful that I have not been asked out to dine before the meeting; so often meetings are spoiled in this way, although obviously the invitation is made with the best possible will in the world. In case you hear of suggestions along these lines I would like you to know from me that I would not be happy to accept a dinner invitation before the meeting, just as I would hate to seem rude by refusing.[10]

It is not clear why Winnicott did not want to attend a pre-meeting dinner, which was the rule rather than the exception, especially for a famous out-of-town guest. Did he fear informal contact? Did he witness a previous experience in which a presentation had been "spoiled" by a prior dinner? Was he shy or anxious about the coming presentation?

In any case, Winnicott would be hurt and sadly disappointed by the outcome of his presentation. The three discussants, Edith Jacobson, Samuel Ritvo, and Bernard Fine, had been carefully chosen to discuss the paper from a complex series of perspectives. Each took issue with it from a "classical" point of view, emphasizing the difficulty in integrating the author's ideas with the prevailing ideas and orientation in early childhood development. They also objected to Winnicott's new use of now-common terms, such as *object relating.* Finally, they tried to get him to clarify ambiguous aspects of his presentation and to expand on his novel and very different ideas about the early development of aggression.

I believe that the New York group's insufficient familiarity with Winnicott's way of conceptualizing the psychoanalytic encounter prevented them from appreciating his ideas. They were not able to see the real value in his formulations or to figure out how they could be incorporated, either

---

10 This previously unpublished letter is held in the New York Psychoanalytic Society and Institute's archives, and the author thanks the archival director, Nellie Thompson, for making it available to him

as additions to established theory or as promising a new approach to the treatment of borderline patients. The only contemporary local analyst who really understood Winnicott and might have contributed to a more positive tone was Phyllis Greenacre. Unfortunately, a last-minute problem prevented her from attending the meeting (Thompson 2009).

Some of the blame for this lack of communication rests with Winnicott himself. He was not a good explicator of his complex ideas; his language was at times quite obscure and hard to follow, and his case material frequently did not clearly illustrate his thesis.

The Culture of the New York Psychoanalytic Society and Institute

The New York Society and Institute spearheaded the branch of psychoanalysis known as ego psychology, but what did that represent, exactly, and what was the attitude of these analysts toward the British object relations theorists, including Winnicott and the Kleinians? Ego psychology had been created in the early 1950s, largely by three analysts: Hans Hartmann, Ernst Kris, and Rudoph Loewenstein. It was further developed by others, including Jacob Arlow and Charles Brenner, to mention only a few of its many contributors. These authors came to psychoanalysis from a perspective very different from that of Winnicott. Basing themselves on Freud's structural theory, they were devoted to developing a scientific psychology based on clear-cut definitions of the three structures of the mind and their connections with each other, believing these could be inferred from clinical work with adults that revealed probable childhood antecedents in early phases of development. Neither Hartmann nor Loewenstein had any clinical experience with children. Although they claimed that their entire theoretical corpus was inferred from clinical material, Hartmann, for one, never included any case histories in any of his papers.

Influenced by Anna Freud's (1937) ideas in her pioneering book on the ego and the mechanisms of defense, the ego psychology writers emphasized the scientific and intellectual nature of their approach. Yet, sensing limitations on some aspects of this view, Hartmann saw the value of differentiating the concept of self from that of the ego, in an effort to separate the more impersonal language (ego) from the more experiential level of personhood, thus obviating certain problematic references to structures as though they were people. These theoreticians also struggled with the ambiguous nature of the concept of the object in Freudian theory and the unclear relation between internal and external objects. Although as individuals they were much more flexible than might be thought (my own experiences in supervision at the time and the widely different styles of these analysts certainly attest to this), nevertheless, the group as a whole functioned quite differently from the individual practitioners who were part of it. This is probably true of any group that defines its identity through sharing certain theoretical ideas, and all the more so if these ideas are attacked from the outside.

I remember very well the way the institute's auditorium was set up for meetings: the front half of the hall was reserved for members only (not including students), and the first few rows were generally occupied by the institute's august and somewhat intimidating leaders: Hartmann, Loewenstein, Greenacre, Jacobson, Arlow, and Brenner, as previously mentioned, as well as Annie Reich, Margaret Mahler, Robert Bak, Victor Rosen, and Martin Stein. The meetings were a very formal and intimidating affair, with black tie and jacket being the norm for men until the late 1970s. They were generally very well attended by a largely members-only audience. Each presentation would be followed by two or three lengthy discussions, and the leaders would then make a few spontaneous comments from the floor before anyone else in the audience dared to speak.

The institute's students were taught the prevailing theoretical model with very little attention to alternative viewpoints. Discussing countertransference in supervision was not encouraged. Listening to associations, making appropriate interpretations, searching for the latent meaning behind manifest speech, following the patient's responses, understanding the evolution of defense mechanisms, and focusing on the transference when it was deemed to be present in the material—such was the stuff of psychoanalysis as it was taught in the 1960s. What the patient offered to the analyst, whether dream, symptom, or character trait, was viewed as an instance of manifest content whose unconscious or latent content would have to be decoded. Each piece of behavior was seen as a compromise formation, as described by Waelder (1930) in his classical paper on multiple function, later expanded upon by Brenner in a series of papers. Each component of the psyche was influenced by the four major contributors to ego synthesis: the drives, the superego, the repetition compulsion, and, finally, the demands of reality, which would (ideally) have to be understood before the working-through process could be completed.

Although some attention was paid by the leading analysts of this era to the preoedipal period, particularly in reference to the work of Jacobson, Mahler (in her observational studies on separation and individuation), and Rene Spitz, the oedipal constellation as the key concept in neurosis remained central. Earlier stages were often seen as only a preliminary way station on the road to the all-important oedipal phase of development, the core of all neurosis. Attention to the preverbal period and nonverbal communication was given minimal importance. Although Stone (1950) developed his view of a potentially widening scope of analysis, attempting to stretch its application beyond the usual limits to the treatment of some borderline conditions, he did not offer a major modification to the traditional theory or technique of analysis.

The leading child researchers in this country, Samuel Ritvo (one of Winnicott's discussants at his presentation) and Albert Solnit, were carrying out pioneering long-term child studies at the Yale Child Study

Center, contributing to the development of child analysis much along the lines suggested by Anna Freud. And since 1945, *The Psychoanalytic Study of the Child*—itself a journal having developed as a response to the growing influence of the Kleinians—had published the most advanced ideas on this developing new field.

The general attitude among New York analysts was one of intolerance and depreciation for other ways of thinking, such as that exemplified by Kleinian theory. This was particularly marked in the child analytic community, which included Mahler, Elizabeth Geleerd, and Berta Bornstein.[11] The ego psychologists took strong exception to the Kleinian concept of unconscious fantasy as elaborated in Isaacs's (1948) classic paper on the topic. In this they were not alone, as the very detailed volume on the *Controversial Discussions* confirms (King and Steiner 1991); the Kleinian group had been pitted against Anna Freud and Edward Glover (see also Reed and Baudry [1997] for a discussion of this controversy). Klein's ideas were poorly understood and heartily criticized as wild and unscientific. In fact, a number of faculty meetings that I attended at the New York Institute at the time were devoted to a demonstration of the heretical nature of Kleinian theory, particularly concerning the very early stages of development as elaborated in the concepts of the paranoid-schizoid and depressive phases and the first six months of a child's life.

---

11 I remember a story Bornstein told us as students in a class about an eight-year-old patient whom she had inherited from Klein. In an early session, the patient told Berta, "I want a piece of chocolate—I mean your breast!"—whereupon Bornstein replied indignantly, "You don't mean my breast, you mean a piece of chocolate!"

The New York Discussants in Context

The three discussants of Winnicott's paper had been carefully selected by the program committee of the New York Psychoanalytic Society and Institute. Edith Jacobson, the most senior discussant, was undoubtedly chosen because of her recently completed book, *The Self and the Object World* (1964), in which she elaborated the earliest stages of development of the concept of self and identity. Samuel Ritvo, from the Yale Child Study Center, represented the most sophisticated thinking of the time about early child development as derived from direct observation of children in institutions and in psychoanalytic treatment. Bernard Fine, a recently appointed training analyst, was the most classical ego psychologist of the three; I suspect he was asked to discuss this paper in recognition of his recent advancement, and with the expectation that he would present the current classical viewpoint in its best light.

Jacobson approached the early stages of childhood in a manner quite different from that of Winnicott. Her ideas were firmly rooted in drive theory. She saw instincts as pleasure-seeking rather than as object-seeking; she referred to the earliest mental structure as a psychophysiological self, thus emphasizing the connection of the mental apparatus to the biological apparatus. She criticized Kleinians for their failure to differentiate sufficiently "between external objects and their endopsychic representations, and worse.... [for failing] to differentiate those from introjects, a term Klein used improperly in describing the infantile superego" (1964, p. 46). According to Jacobson, self-images assume the characteristics of object images, and vice versa, as a result of the process of introjection.

In line with the tenets of classical ego psychology, Jacobson accorded a key role in the pleasure-unpleasure principle to the development of identifications and the gradual separation of wishful self-images and realistic self-representations. Yet she was also familiar with the transitional objects that "Winnicott has so magnificently described" (p. 48), and she shared some aspects of his general approach. For example, following Freud's suggestions, she broadened the concept of orality to include all the physical and emotional stimuli "of special importance with regard to the influence of maternal care on the growth of the infantile ego" (1964, p. 36). She also believed that "the earliest infantile stage is represented by the motherchild unit" (p. 38).

Ritvo, a leading researcher, had recently concluded a study on deprived infants in an institutional setting. He showed that infants deprived of proper maternal care demonstrate an overall delay and impairment in ego development, including acquisition of language skills, the capacity to play or to recover lost toys, and even the use of some instinctual activities, such as thumb sucking or finger sucking. Thus, his work demonstrated the interplay between maturational factors and the external environment. He concluded that the object is important in stimulating and mobilizing the energy with which the image or memory trace of the object, and all it entails, is cathected (Ritvo,1962).

As mentioned, Bernard Fine, the most junior discussant, could be expected to share the general theoretical view held by many New York Institute members. His publications included "Some Aspects of Psychoanalytic Methodology" (1964), in which he compared psychoanalysis to microphysics. For several years, he had provided reports of the New York Institute's meetings for publication in *The Psychoanalytic Quarterly.*

Winnicott's Advance Summary of his Presentation

Here is a summary of Winnicott's main themes in the paper, as prepared by him and distributed to the three discussants in advance of his presentation:

Object-relating can be described in terms of the experience of the subject. Description of object-usage involves consideration of the nature of the object. I am offering for discussion the reasons why, in my opinion, a capacity to use an object is more sophisticated than a capacity to relate to objects; and relating may be more to a subjective object, but usage implies that the object is part of external reality.

This sequence can be observed:
Subject relates to object.
Object is in process of being found instead of placed by the subject
in the world.
Subject destroys object.
Object survives destruction.
Subject can use object.

The object is always being destroyed. This destruction becomes the unconscious back cloth for love of a real object, that is, an object outside the area of the subject's omnipotent control.

Study of this problem involves a statement of the positive value of destructiveness. The destructiveness plus the object's survival of the destruction places the object outside the area in which projective mental mechanisms operate, so that a world of shared reality is created which the subject can use and which can feed back into the subject. How this usage develops naturally out of play with the object is the theme of this talk.[12]

---

12 This document is contained in the New York Psychoanalytic Society and Institute archives.

Sensing that his ideas might be difficult for an uninitiated audience to understand, Winnicott also suggested that attendees read a number of his seminal papers ahead of time.

The Formal Discussions of Winnicott's Presentation[13]

Jacobson gave the first response. She made it clear that this was a special occasion for her. She had been determined not to undertake any additional discussions of papers that year, but she could not resist the temptation to comment on this one, she said.

Jacobson's remarks might have been a disappointment for Winnicott, as he must have expected a warmer endorsement based on this senior colleague's interest in the early development of the self. She was critical of his term *use of an object* as distinct from the concept of *relating to an object.* She objected to Winnicott's view of relating, saying that in his conceptualization, a narcissistic, rather primitive type of object relations was described—quite the reverse of the use of the term in traditional ego psychology. She felt that his usage of *relating to an object* was thus a misuse of the concept.

She contrasted this perspective of Winnicott's with the idea that, in psychoanalysis as practiced in New York, *relating* was considered to be on a higher plane than *using.* Likewise, she disagreed with the idea that babies at the breast could be developmentally advanced enough to "use" the breast in Winnicott's terms. She then objected to his sequence of "the subject destroys

---

13 I am relying on the excellent summary of Winnicott's presentation and the accompanying commentaries that David Milrod prepared, and on my personal discussion with Milrod, as well as on my review of the full texts of Jacobson's and Fine's remarks. Ritvo did not keep a copy of his text; when I contacted him, he told me that the relative closeness of his own position to Winnicott's may have had to do with the fact that, of the three discussants, he was the only one with extensive experience with children. (Ritvo subsequently died in December 2008.)

the object," followed by the "object survives." She felt that he did not make it sufficiently clear whether he was also referring to the phenomenon of the patient who verbally attacks the therapist, and when the therapist survives, the patient subsequently experiences the lack of retaliation as a prelude to loving experiences. Jacobson contrasted Winnicott's position with her own experience with psychotic patients, some of whom, after a destructive attack on the therapist, did not seem to progress to a better place.

Jacobson was puzzled by Winnicott's central postulate that "whereas the subject does not destroy the subjective object, . . . destruction turns up and becomes a central feature in so far as the object is objectively perceived, has autonomy, and belongs to shared reality" (1969a, pp. 713–714). She also did not understand the difference between annihilation, anger, and destruction.[14] Finally, she felt that the case material (not included in the summary, but later published in *Psychoanalytic Explorations*) did not convincingly illustrate his theoretical position.[15]

Samuel Ritvo also tried to translate Winnicott's concepts in ego psychological terms, though somewhat less critically than the other two discussants. He suggested that Winnicott's idea that there is no real contact with the object until it survives destructive attack may "coincide with our understanding that the budding ego cathects the object with aggression when it experiences nonpleasure, and this in turn fosters differentiation of self from non-self." Furthermore, "[a] permanent object relationship is based on the capacity to tolerate frustration, a capacity which depends on the

---

14 My own opinion is that annihilation refers to the total destruction of the object image, with no trace remaining, while anger is the associated affect, and destruction refers to taking apart the object, but with traces of an object relation remaining.

15 Having read the lengthy clinical material that was distributed ahead of time to the discussants, I agree with Jacobson's critique on this point.

neutralization of aggression. This latter depends heavily on the facilitating environment."[16]

Bernard Fine, in the last and most searching critique, found Winnicott's presentation incomplete and wanting in several respects. He first made it clear that Winnicott's ideas were anything but simple. His perspective presented major reformulations concerning object relations, the theory of aggression, and problems of technique. Fine first posited himself as having taken the trouble to read "many of the author's past and present contributions so as to create a better context for his remarks" (from the text of Fine's remarks on file in the New York Psychoanalytic Society and Institute archives). This made his critique more significant, as he had clearly done his homework.

Fine objected that Winnicott seemed to leave out of the picture any reference to libidinal ties to the object as a crucial factor in the object's survival of attack. He felt that Winnicott underestimated the role of the ego, including its maturation, development, and relationship to the external object. Fine preferred to rely on such concepts as *ambivalence, fusion, defusion neutralization, and fantasies of merging*. He saw Winnicott's ideas of object destruction following separation as an unwarranted, far reaching, and unsubstantiated modification of existing theory. He understood Winnicott as reformulating the theory of aggression, with the placement of greater emphasis on environmental and experiential components.

In the last section of his commentary, Fine focused on Winnicott's concept of the transition from one phase to the next. He felt that neither the clinical material presented, nor Winnicott's experiences with borderline or psychotic patients, allowed for generalization to normal development. He also objected to Winnicott's clinical approach of waiting cautiously and letting the patient know the limitation of the analyst's understanding

---

16 These quotations are from Milrod's synopsis of Ritvo's comments, made available to me from the New York Psychoanalytic Society and Institute archives by Nellie Thompson.

(Winnicott 1969a, p. 711). Such an approach was applicable to borderline patients, in Fine's opinion, but made no real sense with more neurotic patients. Fine felt more comfortable with Mahler's more inclusive ideas about this phase of development; he saw these as a complex series involving the development of object relations, drive development, the maturing ego, and the individuation process that leads to differentiation between self and object. Fine also shared Jacobson's objection to Winnicott's concepts of *object relating* and *object usage.*

After Fine finished his discussion and sat down, no one from the audience asked any questions or made any comments, making Winnicott's task more delicate. After a long silence, he replied to his discussants in a charming and whimsical fashion, stating that his overall concept had been torn to pieces and that he would be happy to give it up! He had been trying to say something, but felt he had not succeeded. He returned to his clinical experience concerning patients for whom arriving at a point where they could use him as an analyst was more important than his interpretations to them. Such patients seem to need to protect the analyst from something— not merely anger, but destruction. Once they are able to take the risk of destroying the analyst, they are in a position to use him. Winnicott conceded that non-use can be fueled by hate and can lead to deterioration, but he was mostly concerned with non-usage based on the need to protect the object.[17]

Winnicott once ended another lecture by saying: "It is perhaps the greatest compliment we may receive if we are both found and used" (Winnicott et al. 1989, p. 233). He might have felt that the audience at his New York presentation related to him (i.e., listened to his ideas), but never used him (in the sense of having a real dialogue with a true external object).

---

17 What may be confusing for the unprepared reader is that Winnicott does not always make it clear whether he is referring to an internal object or to an external one. In the present instance, I believe that the object referred to is mostly internal—made up of projections, or at least poorly differentiated from the self.

Overall, Winnicott remained dissatisfied with the way he had expounded his ideas in this lecture, as his subsequent notes and writings suggest (see, for example, Winnicott 1968b). A number of audience members to whom I spoke were all struck by what seemed to be the primary speaker's extreme disappointment and dismay at the tenor of the meeting.

To further exacerbate matters, Winnicott was not well; he had a serious heart condition complicated by the development of a nearly fatal bout of influenza. He had to be hospitalized the day after the meeting, requiring several weeks' stay before he could recover sufficiently to return home to England in a weakened state and a somewhat despondent mood. Some maintain that he also suffered a heart attack, triggered by the stress of the evening, from which he nearly died and never completely recovered, but others dispute this and claim that he continued to lead a normal and fruitful life after returning to London.

In January 1969, Winnicott wrote to Anna Freud:

> If you were to ask me what about my paper "The Use of an Object," I would say that the answer is complex. I read the paper and got considerable personal benefit from the reaction of the three discussants so that I am now in process of rewriting it in a quite different language. The unfortunate thing was that the three said discussants occupied the whole of the time so that there could be no response from the very large audience which collected for some reason unspecified.... Actually I was already ill but I think this was not noticed [Kahr 1996, p. 120].

Was Winnicott being disingenuous when he wrote that the large audience had "collected for some reason unspecified"? Whether he actually revised his paper is questionable, since the published version (Winnicott 1969a) differs only in minor respects from his lecture in New York. In a contemporary letter, he writes: "I have just read a paper on this to the New York Psychoanalytic Society but my ideas are not well formulated in this paper" (Rodman 1987, p. 181).

Even some authors friendly to Winnicott (Reeves 2007) question his judgment in selecting this paper for presentation; why he chose an incompletely worked out paper and a diffuse case history for this special occasion remains a mystery. It may be that, at this stage, Winnicott was beginning to elaborate his disagreement with Freud about the concept of the death instinct, and that the reaction in New York stimulated him to spell this out in a subsequent paper: "The Use of an Object in the Context of *Moses and Monotheism*" (Winnicott 1969b) (Abram 2009).

Reeves (2007), writing on the New York presentation, suggests that

> Winnicott was deliberately, if unconsciously, setting himself the challenge of properly comprehending the issues himself. He could only let go of them once they were fully formed; yet he could only discover this by trying them out and observing the reaction [p. 367].

This seems consonant with what Winnicott himself wrote about his style of communicating.

Winnicott's letter to the New York Institute's administrative director shortly before the meeting (October 31, 1968), concerning his misgivings about the clinical material, is quite instructive:

> The point is that the case description must be long unless it is condensed by me and therefore distorted or possibly distorted to fit the theme. If one of the discussants should have time to read through this long description of a two-hour interview, then it may be possible to find something for discussion. It might be possible, for instance, for the discussants to claim that the material does not illustrate my

theme. I think that some of these difficulties are inherent. My hope is that the point that I am making may remind hearers of clinical material of their own.[18]

Posner et al. (2001) quote Winnicott as saying to his students: "What you get out of me you will have to pick out of chaos" (p. 172). What Winnicott meant was that he was "going to think and talk creatively, and if you hope to take anything in, you must listen creatively" (Walker quoted by Posner et al. 2001, p. 173).

The meeting stimulated Winnicott to refine and explain the ideas that his New York audience had such a hard time accepting. In "Comments on My Paper 'The Use of an Object,'" Winnicott returns to the New York presentation as if continuing an unfinished dialogue with his discussants. He starts out by stating that our theory about aggression needs some healthy rethinking. In accordance with Freud, he points out that aggressive drives are not related to hate or anger, but rather to muscle eroticism. Thus, in contrast to Klein, he did not posit an innate sadism; rather, he saw the young infant's biting of the breast as a spontaneous assertion of power—perhaps even as a pleasurable sensation in the service of primitive love.

Winnicott in Context: Formal Aspects

Winnicott felt strongly that the child's experience could not be described using secondary-process concepts without betraying its essential reality. To be sure, Winnicott did not make it easy for readers unfamiliar with his work or his style to follow him in his rather condensed way of presenting

---

18 This letter is in the archives of the New York Psychoanalytic Society and Institute and was made available to me by Nellie Thompson.

ideas, his idiosyncratic use of language,[19] or his delight in paradox. This is well explained in the following passage from an interesting chapter entitled "The Use of the Word 'Use,'" written in February 1968, six months before his presentation in New York. There Winnicott explained his strategy:

> We get so used to words through using them and become so dulled to their usage that we need from time to time to take each one and to look at it and to determine in so far as we are able not only how the word came into being through the poetry of etymology, but also the way in which we are using the word now [Winnicott et al. 1989, p. 233].

Winnicott thus spontaneously discovers a new idea arising as if by chance from his preconscious, and wants to play with it and discover its potential. By inverting the concepts of *relating* and *usage*, Winnicott acknowledges that *usage* in American psychoanalysis commonly has a pejorative meaning, whereas his revised concept of *relating* refers to the patient who "uses" the analyst (in the American analytic sense)—as, for example, a toilet, or as an audience for his products—and in so doing also relates to him, and this relationship is part of an overall developmental stage in the analysis.

Winnicott rejected a number of Freudian postulates that are basic to classical metapsychology (Fulgencio 2007). He was deeply suspicious of very abstract terms as applied to the individual's development. He disliked such concepts as the *life instinct* and *death instinct*, much preferring abstractions like *needs*, which he felt were closer to our experience of bodily functioning and the integration or satisfaction derived from bodily excitation, which for him was a primary building block of the sense of self. Winnicott expanded

---

19 Winnicott noted, "I have an irritating way of saying things in my own language instead of learning how to use the terms of psychoanalytic metapsychology" (Rodman 1987, p. 58).

on an idea first presented by Freud in "Instincts and Their Vicissitudes": "A better term for an instinctual stimulus is a need" (Freud 1915, pp. 118–119); such stimuli are the sign of an internal world. Winnicott also developed Freud's early ideas on ego drives and Nunberg's (1931) concept of an integrating or synthetic function.

Having treated many borderline and frankly psychotic patients, Winnicott felt, as did Klein, that Freudian theory needed revisions to account for the psychopathology and treatment technique of these sicker patients. He focused particularly on schizoid withdrawal, emptiness, despair, and the problem of making affective contact with such patients given their primitive transferences (they "related" to the analyst rather than "using" him).

Winnicott tried to link some of these phenomena to specific failures of the environment and developed a core set of ideas concerning the growing infant, including the birth of the object, the key role of play, and the development of aggression. These were buttressed by his rich mother-infant observations and his common-sense approach to early life. His ideas on these topics continued to evolve throughout his career. In fact, the paper he delivered in New York represented the culmination of thoughts he had first elaborated in his paper on primitive emotional development (1945) and then extended in a number of other papers, including his seminal one on transitional phenomena (1953).

Although, to be sure, any theory about development in the preverbal child is speculative in nature, Winnicott (1941) managed to devise ingenious interactive games involving a wooden spatula, which he placed on his desk within reach of the toddler, noting carefully what the child did with it (dropping it, ignoring it, handing it to him, playing with it, putting it in the mouth, etc.). This allowed Winnicott to probe the mind of the developing young child, somewhat along the lines adopted by Piaget in the early 1920s as he devised simple experiments with a ball and blanket to test his ideas on the development of object constancy in his young daughter, then age two.

Like any other writer on early childhood, Winnicott had to rely on a number of postulates about the developing mind. Although space constraints preclude my spelling out all these postulates here, I will discuss those that are most significant in terms of Winnicott's interaction with the New York group.

WINNICOTT'S FUNDAMENTAL POSTULATES: THE DEVELOPMENT OF THE SELF AND THE PLACE OF AGGRESSION

Postulate #I: The Role of the Self in Early Ego Development

In his considerations of early development, Winnicott reversed Freud's hypothesis about the order in which the mind's structural components develop:

> In the very early stages of the development of a human child, . . . ego-functioning needs to be taken as a concept that is inseparable from that of the existence of the infant as a person. What instinctual life there may be apart from ego functioning can be ignored because the infant is not yet an entity having experiences. There is no id before ego [Winnicott 1962, p. 56].

Although Freud referred to an undifferentiated matrix out of which both ego and id develop, he did not express the idea that there must first be a self to experience life before we can speak of the existence of instinct and of a structure called *ego*.[20] For Winnicott, the primary event is the child's

---

20 It is interesting to note that Freud's use of the word ego conflated two very different concepts: that of the ego as a structure, and that of the self as the nature of the subjective being. This conflation covered over a conceptual problem. Much confusion resulted, until Hartmann

development of the capacity to live an experience. One could say that he reversed the Cartesian motto *cogito ergo sum to sum ergo cogito.*

In contrast to the New York group, Winnicott assumed that a primitive self or being is present in rudimentary form almost from birth. In this he extended Freud's idea that an organism that functions only at the level of primary process could not exist. In this way of conceptualizing development, Winnicott fundamentally disagreed with Anna Freud, who believed that purely physiological needs and the absence of an object characterize the child's early period. For example, she stressed in the *Controversial Discussions* that the child must be aware of thirst and the need to satisfy it before he can conceive of water or of any external object satisfying that need.

In his paper on the transitional object (1953), Winnicott took his first step in describing the progression from the idea of a purely internal object to a transitional object.[21] In the paper presented in New York, he took the next step in attempting to describe the subsequent evolutionary process from an early transitional object to that of a truly external object.

Postulate #2: The Role of the Environment in Development

Winnicott believed that the child's development occurs on an interactive basis, depending heavily on the mother's receptiveness and responses to the child's communications (the *facilitating environment*, Winnicott 1965). In this he departed significantly from the theories of Klein. His emphasis on the mother-child unit opens up the issue of intersubjectivity in psychic

---

examined the concept of self from a metapsychological point of view (see Hartmann 1950). It was the development of the self as an entity that interested Winnicott.

21 The idea of a transitional space was already present in Freud's (1915) description of the transference as creating an intermediate region between illness and real life.

development, including unconscious communication between mother and infant.

The key passage in which Winnicott (1945) develops these novel ideas is as follows:

> In terms of baby and mother's breast (I am not claiming that the breast is essential as a vehicle of mother-love) the baby has instinctual urges and predatory ideas. The mother has a breast and the power to produce milk, and the idea that she would like to be attacked by a hungry baby. These two *phenomena do not come into relation with each other till the mother and child live an experience together.* The mother being mature and physically able has to be the one with tolerance and understanding so that it is she who produces a situation that may with luck result in the first tie that the infant makes with an external object, an object that is external to the self from the infant's point of view [p. 141, italics in original].

In commenting on this passage, Ogden (2001) points out the importance of the notion of complementarities between the inner states of the two participants, i.e., the fit between the two agents (the predatory baby and the mother who wants to be "attacked"), and the crucial role of the experience of living together, with an emphasis on being alive as a building block of the human psyche. "Human experience does not have life until we live it" (Ogden, p. 315). But there is another hidden idea in Winnicott's phrase, related to the earliest level of experiencing: "living an experience together" is still part of a quasi-fusional, undifferentiated state of the mother-child unit, a developmentally pretransitional phenomenon where outer and inner have no meaning.

Winnicott explains that the infant comes prepared with a (hardwired?) notion of a breast, which gradually becomes enriched and corrected by actual sensory experiences.[22] Winnicott's statement about the infant's "first tie... with an external object" was of course problematic if one assumed Winnicott meant that the infant would be in a position at this early stage to have a concept of an external object. Jacobson commented on this problem in her remarks. However, I believe that Winnicott was here condensing into one image the slow development of the concept of the object (an ideational approach that Jacobson found difficult to accept).

"The Use of an Object" can be seen as the author's attempt to spell out the transition from the earliest form of the object (the subjective object) to the first transitional object (which is poorly differentiated from the self), and then to the more advanced version, in which the object is clearly distinguished from the self and more objectively perceived. Winnicott is reconstructing the very early experiences of the infant from an object relations point of view—largely physiological, to be sure, but also indicating the contribution of these experiences to a primitive, developing sense of self. Early sensations occur at the limiting membranes, i.e., the skin, the seat of bodily phenomena, which are at first without meaning.[23] These sensations have to be experienced within a psychical apparatus in order to acquire meaning. Mechanisms of introjection and projection allow for the integration of good and bad experiences with the environment, leading to a sense of continuity, a feeling of existence that eventually allows for the development of a psychical apparatus and the growth of cognitive functions. This early

---

22 Here Winnicott's ideas are very close to those of Bion (1962): "Psychoanalytically, the theory that the infant has an inborn disposition corresponding to an expectation of a breast may be used to supply a model. When the preconception is brought into contact with a realization that approximates it, the mental outcome is a conception" (p. 306).

23 These ideas have been taken up by some French analysts who have been quite influenced by Winnicott (see, for example, Green 1975).

development precedes the differentiation into the tripartite structure of classical ego psychology.[24]

Postulate #3: The Development of Aggression

Winnicott's writings on aggression are amongst the most difficult parts of his theory, in part because the clinical basis for these ideas is less rich, especially given the limitations of exploring the mind of the newborn from the inside (see Posner et al. 2001; Samuels 2001). Nevertheless, an excellent discussion and explication of his formulations on this topic can be found in Abram and Hjulmand (2007).

Winnicott posited a primary nondestructive aggression, seen as a healthy development connected with appetite, assertion, motility, and life itself, although at some point cruel aggression intervenes. The mother may experience the baby's "aggression" as dangerous or destructive, leading to pathological consequences for the developing infant (a fear of the possibility of retaliation). In contrast to Klein, Winnicott believed that it is only by chance that early aggression is destructive or hurtful, not by intent, and that it is not directed at the object, as Klein believed. He fundamentally disagreed with Klein's view of primitive aggressive fantasies in the neonatal period as directed at the depriving breast.

Winnicott spoke of the "ruthless" infant—referring to infants during the first two years of life, roughly speaking, prior to the stage of concern for the whole object (see, for example, Winnicott 1945, p. 142). Concern for the whole object cannot arise if the child's ruthlessness has not been given free expression. The word *ruthless* could be confusing, however,

---

24 I am indebted to Anzieu (2009) for clarification about this aspect of Winnicott's ideas on early development.

because Winnicott does not make it clear from whose point(s) of view he is describing it as such—certainly, from the mother's or an outside observer's viewpoint, but also from the infant's? Winnicott does not assume that the baby can have a destructive intent or an awareness of the destructive aspects of his own behavior, let alone concern for the welfare of the other.

For Winnicott, the primitive destructive urge seen in ruthlessness belongs to an early stage of love. It is crucial for the mother to be able to tolerate this ruthless behavior without retaliating. The child is then able to progress from a purely subjective view of the internal object, one undifferentiated from the self to the perception of a truly external object. In Winnicott's terms, he moves from the stage of object relating to object usage that is dependent on the creation of an external object. The survival of the "real object" allows the child to locate the primitive internal object outside the subjective sphere, in the external world—that is, beyond the area of projection.

It is at this very early stage that some borderline patients may become fixated. In this view, a primitive violence toward the object is present in the earliest encounters, and it is this violence not specifically aimed at the destruction of the outside object that Winnicott calls *aggression*. This can be seen in the young child who appears to take pleasure in tearing his toys apart, which might be seen as a way station to his placing them outside the sphere of his omnipotent control. Interestingly, Milner extends these ideas to the realm of creativity, referring to

> ... the aggressive relation with the object required if the artist is to make it her own; she has to destroy the original, recompose it, transform it and thus enable it to be seen and experienced as it is in what it can offer and provide [Milner quoted in Caldwell 2007, p. 2].

The newborn chick destroying its shell in the process of birth might be an appropriate analogy for Winnicott's perspective. One could say that he focuses much more than others do on the healthy aspect of mental functioning. He is more optimistic than Klein. At times he has even been criticized for underestimating the role of aggression, both theoretically and clinically. This becomes evident from a reading of the clinical case material that he distributed to the three discussants at his New York presentation.

I believe that Winnicott's ideas on the dual role of aggression were influenced by Greenacre, who saw the role of aggression "both as a manifestation of biological growth and as an expression of destructive, cruel impulses" (Thompson 2008, p. 262). For Winnicott, there is a key difference between healthy destruction in fantasy that becomes integrated into the personality, and pathological destruction, which indicates an aggression that "has not been integrated into the personality and remains split off—this belongs to emotional immaturity" (Abram and Hjulmand 2007, p. 25). Although this view of early aggression as nonhostile and nonaggressive should have been familiar to the discussants, they did not seem to take it into consideration when commenting upon Winnicott's paper.

In contrast to Klein, Winnicott makes another assumption: namely, that splitting into good and bad objects is a consequence of the mother's poor management of, and inability to tolerate, her baby's expression of "healthy aggression"—rather than a necessary stage of development based on an inability to fuse good and bad aspects of objects for fear of the power of destructiveness. Winnicott's evolving ideas on aggression could be linked with Freud's opinions as expressed in "Instincts and Their Vicissitudes" (1915), in which he wrote a somewhat cryptic statement that puzzled me until I came to appreciate Winnicott's elaboration:

Hate, as a relation to objects, is older than love. It derives from the narcissistic ego's primordial repudiation of the external world with its outpouring of stimuli. As an expression of the reaction of unpleasure evoked by objects, it always remains in an intimate relation with the self preservative instincts [Freud 1915, p. 135].

Freud is here pointing out that love requires a more advanced stage of object relations than hate. Winnicott extends Freud's idea of initial hate related to unpleasure by emphasizing that, at this stage, the hated object is mostly a bundle of projections.

Clinical Consequences of Winnicott's Model

Somewhat like Loewald (who was implicitly influenced by him), Winnicott posited the role of the therapist as analogous to that of the competent mother, allowing the child to develop in his own fashion without a preconceived path. These ideas are particularly applicable in those instances where there has been a failure of the mother to provide a facilitating environment (Winnicott 1965). It is in this context that the role of regression in the analytic situation must be understood. When such issues are at play, interpretation takes second place to a sensitive attunement to the patient's regressed needs, particularly when the "as-if" quality of the transference no longer obtains, and the analyst finds himself having to engage with the patient as the person he is.

This view was further developed by Green (1975), who emphasized that in such situations, there is a "danger of overfilling the psychic space when one should be helping to form the positive cathexis of the empty space" (p. 17), and that the analyst must avoid the trap of a premature intrusion. The aim is not to transform primary process into secondary process (as in the classical view), but rather "to initiate play between primary and secondary processes" (Green, p. 17).

One of the analyst's most important functions is to enable the patient to freely play with thoughts and feelings. This is more important than the content of interpretations given by an all-knowing therapist, according to Winnicott. In "The Use of an Object," he points out that if all goes well, we can see a subtle shift in some patients who, after a certain point in treatment, begin to really *use* the analyst instead of merely *relating* to him. This change, usually noted by both participants, is gratifying (and in fact never occurs with some patients). Although Winnicott does not exactly define what he means by this shift, he assumes that experienced analysts will intuitively understand what he means without further clarification.

I believe that here Winnicott is referring to the intimate relationship that can develop with some patients and not with others. When this occurs, the patient can freely and flexibly use the analyst as a true transference object, rather than relating to him in a rigid and stereotypic way in which he remains fixed in either an idealized, compliant, or depreciative transference. For this shift to happen, the patient has to be able to express his aggression externally, to be sure, but we must also keep in mind that the main target of that aggression is that of the primitive, internal, probably idealized object. Also of importance is that the analyst must survive the attack without retaliation.

Winnicott gives few clues about how to create the optimal psychoanalytic atmosphere. Perhaps the closest approximation to this is his view that the analyst should have the capacity to offer himself as an object, allowing the creation of another—a means of permitting chaos to acquire meaning and representations to replace unformed, unsymbolized experiences.

Here I am reminded of one of my borderline patients, who clearly described with great sensitivity her two-year-old son's shift in relatedness as a developmental achievement. At first, the baby would have tantrums and throw food at her with his spoon, with no regard for what was happening. Then one day things changed dramatically: the little boy looked at her intently, then aimed his spoon at her face and fired his weapon. She immediately understood the important shift that had just taken place in her baby's relation to her. If I am right in seeing this as a transitional moment between relating and object use, then Winnicott would say that, if at this point the mother "survives" and does not retaliate, the toddler will gradually be able to place the object outside the self and initiate a relationship with a true external object. He will also be in a position to internalize this experience, and a more positive object relationship will ensue. The object that is really under attack is the external one, but what may be difficult to grasp is that, in my belief, a sequence like this one also involves the object representation of the mother in the process of being differentiated from the self-representation (to use Jacobson's language), or what Winnicott would term the *subjective object.*

In discussing "The Use of an Object," Fine clearly misunderstood Winnicott's new way of formulating the analytic process with certain borderline patients. At one point in this paper, Winnicott states in a semi whimsical fashion that, with his borderline patients, he interprets "mainly to let the patient know the limits of my understanding" (Winnicott 1969a, p. 711). Fine, rather taken aback, wonders "whether this method can be established as an approach or generalization concerning the work with neurotic or character neurotic patients? If it is relevant, it certainly suggests an important shift in technical procedure and orientation" (quoted from the text of Fine's comments in the New York Psychoanalytic Society and Institute archives).

I believe this very concrete reaction to Winnicott's point misses what the latter was trying to convey. First, Winnicott was mostly concerned with the sicker patient who often tries to establish a childlike dependency on the analyst as a magical cure for what ails him. Second, upon reading his clinical material, it becomes quite clear that Winnicott did not mean to be taken so literally. He certainly relied on free use of interpretations. He was most likely alluding to the idealization of the analyst by both the patient *and* the analyst, and warning that this idealization can stand in the way of a realistic assessment by the patient of his own potential, fostering an attitude of passive expectancy that is contrary to Winnicott's spirit, and that further impoverishes the use of the analyst by the patient.

Rather than laboriously describing all this in great detail, Winnicott pithily resorts to a humorous paradox, a bit of a joke. In contrast to the traditional view that accurate interpretations and the data supporting them are very much part and parcel of the teaching of psychoanalysis, Winnicott playfully turns the whole theoretical edifice upside down and makes us confront an unpleasant reality—namely, that we typically know much less about the patient than we think we do, and that interpretation can serve the useful function of dispelling unhealthy idealization of the analyst by both parties[25]

Thus, an important clinical consequence of Winnicott's thinking is a deemphasis of the role of interpretation, which is partly replaced by the fostering of a climate allowing the patient to creatively reappropriate his experiences—particularly those traumatic ones occurring very early in life that could not be represented by the immature psyche. This process helps undo for the patient what Winnicott refers to as a "lack of being" (the *false self*).

It is interesting that none of the New York discussants commented on the almost total absence of the father in Winnicott's theoretical presentations. In his writings, the analyst is often seen as maternal, especially in providing a holding environment. This lack would later be corrected in one of Winnicott's last papers, "The Use of an Object in the Context of *Moses and Monotheism*" (1969b).

---

25 At the time of my own psychoanalytic training, candidates were taught with almost scientific rigor about the extreme value and multiple appeal of a properly crafted interpretation—including identification of the data justifying it, how to follow it up by listening closely to ensuing associations for confirmation, and so on. Such traditional thinking was dear to the hearts of most analysts at the New York Institute in 1968.

Revisiting the Discussants' Remarks

In reading the critique of the three discussants, it is clear, first, that none could establish a meaningful exchange with Winnicott, nor incorporate any of his new ideas into their systems of thought or therapeutic outlooks. Yet on careful rereading, I sense that many of the objections were raised not so much to criticize as to try to address the very real problems in the paper that had not been adequately considered.

Jacobson understood that Winnicott's concept of object relating was in fact close to the primitive narcissistic level of development that she had written about in her own work, but the key developmental step leading to object use remained difficult to grasp, for good reasons. None of the discussants felt comfortable with Winnicott's reversal of the common meaning of the terms *relating* and *usage*. Neither could they relinquish their familiar terminology for the earliest stages of development, whether it was based on Mahler's ideas or on those of Hartmann, Kris, and Loewenstein, nor could they establish bridges with Winnicott's formulations.

All three had considerable difficulty appreciating Winnicott's original views on aggression, particularly when it came to the idea of "subject destroys object." Jacobson wondered whether he was referring to actual attacks on the therapist as an outside object, or whether the attack might be followed by an abandonment of magical thinking, thus bringing the phenomenon in line with more primitive thinking. Unfortunately, Winnicott did not make it sufficiently clear that, for him, it is the encounter with the object that gives rise to the imaginative elaboration or mentalization of the instinct, not the other way around. Ritvo came closest to seeing it this way. At this very early stage, one cannot really speak of a positive libidinal investment in the object, since there is no true external object to be invested with libido, a point that was not appreciated by Fine.

125

The issue of the destruction of the object as a developmental step is not entirely foreign to ego psychology; there is some literature on the fate of the oedipal complex, with different terms used to describe its demise: *waning* versus *destruction.* That is, when one phase supersedes another, do the earlier issues and conflicts disappear or remain? Perhaps, in the process of transformation, some issues clearly disappear or become no longer relevant. Winnicott went a step further and posited the element of destruction of a more primitive object representation. Some of Klein's ideas on the progression from the paranoid-schizoid phase to the depressive position are consistent with this perspective, as was explicated by Geleerd (1963) in a discussion of Klein's well-known case of Richard:

> The next period of development, according to Mrs. Klein, is the depressive position, when the mind of the child has to breach the gap between the internal frightening fantasies of the annihilated love object and the growing awareness that the love object is real.... The first attempt to reconcile the violent and destructive inner world with the reality of a loving mother is through the hypomanic defence of denial; the denial of guilt over the destroyed love object. According to her, intensive processes of restoration and reparation now lead to reconciliation of the inner world of destroyed love objects with the more reality-adapted introjected good whole love objects [p. 499].[26]

---

26 The similarities and differences among Freud, Klein, and Winnicott on early aggression deserve amplification, but would require a separate paper to do them justice.

CONCLUSIONS

In the paper presented at the New York Psychoanalytic Society and Institute, Winnicott offered three new ideas: first, he focused on a type of analytic impasse encountered with some borderline patients who are stuck in a type of primitive transference. Second, he defined the dynamics of that transference as related to a particular stage of child development—one concerned with the existence of a primitive object, mostly internal, made up of projections of the self. Third, Winnicott described those processes that in his view are necessary for the progression from this primitive stage to the stage of relating to a true external object, outside the sphere of omnipotence. Thus, with "The Use of an Object," he completed his description of theoretical development that had been initiated in "Transitional Objects and Transitional Phenomena" (Winnicott 1953).

As an offshoot of this process, Winnicott elaborated on an aspect of nondestructive aggression that is necessary for the creation of a true external object. He also described some important clinical consequences of his view, incorporating the developmental issues he had discussed into a modification of the classical view of the role of the analyst as the clarifier of unconscious fantasies. Rather than relying largely on the curative aspect of interpretations, he stressed the role of the analyst as facilitator of a process of the patient's self-discovery through the use of a type of playing. This new view shifted the focus of the analysis to earlier primitive ego states, often reached through regression.

Winnicott's approach can be seen as an offshoot of Ferenczi's, with his emphasis on the role and importance of the relationship with the analyst. One could say that this psychology, based as it was on object relations, was a refined elaboration of life as seen from the point of view of the self or "being," rather than from the point of view of the primacy of instincts. Winnicott was interested in those processes by which the psyche comes into being, and the way in which the child uses his lived experiences to create representations and symbols. These in turn help bring about identity formation, which is always evolving. Experiences that are too traumatic to achieve the status of representation remain in an unmetabolized, split-off state; their existence can be inferred through certain actions or somatic manifestations.

Winnicott has been enormously influential on current French psychoanalytic thinking. Green developed his ideas on the negative and problems of nonrepresentation based in large part on some of Winnicott's concepts of absence and decathexis (see Reed and Baudry 2005). Winnicott's ideas on the transitional phenomena also allow more refined formulations on the early stages of representation and symbolization.

Winnicott exerted considerable influence on a number of American analysts as well: Kohut, Loewald, and Greenacre (Thompson 2008), and Zetzel, to mention but a few. Winnicott spoke of the pathogenic role of a failure of mothering in the early years, whereas Kohut referred to the impact of the mother's failures of empathy and their presence in the transference. Loewald followed Winnicott's ideas on the role and function of the analyst as a new object.

Winnicott's novel ideas about the clinical encounter also extend to the role he assigns to his reader. His purpose in presenting his ideas is not so much to teach, but rather to create the right climate to allow the reader/listener to discover within himself a personal resonance with his ideas (Rousillon 1997). Hence Winnicott may hope to convince others of the correctness of his ideas in the same way that an analyst might hope the patient will appreciate the correctness of his interpretations.

To truly appreciate Winnicott, it becomes necessary to leave the safety of one's preconceived ideas and to look at the analytic encounter in a much more open and less prejudiced fashion. It is also necessary to sometimes poke fun at oneself, but at the same time to maintain a profound respect for the potential growth of the patient, which can be fostered by an atmosphere both playful and respectful. There is probably nothing intrinsic to this view that contradicted the tenets of ego psychology, but a certain flexibility on the part of the New York analysts would have been required to appreciate his humor and slightly self-denigrating attitude and humility, coupled with the considerable empathy so characteristic of his approach. It was unfortunate for all involved that a more felicitous meeting between Winnicott and the primarily traditional analysts in attendance at this lecture did not occur.

In concluding, I can do no better than to quote from an unfinished paper that Winnicott originally intended to present to the British Psychoanalytical Society in September 1968, titled "Roots of Aggression." There he writes:

In our Society here, although we serve science, we need to make an effort every time we attempt to reopen matters which seem to have been settled. It is not only the inertia which belongs to the fear of doubt; it is also that we have loyalties [Winnicott quoted in Abram and Hjulmand 2007, p. 17].

Acknowledgments: The author is indebted to Nellie Thompson, archival director of the New York Psychoanalytic Institute, for making available the transcripts of the New York Psycho analytic Society and Institute meeting discussed here, including the summary prepared by David Milrod, and for her helpful comments. The author also thanks his colleagues who read earlier drafts of this paper and made valuable suggestions: first and foremost, Jan Abram, as well as Nasir Ilahi, Robert Grayson, and Peter Mezan.

REFERENCES

Abram, J. (2009). Personal communication.

Abram, J. & Hjulmand, K. (2007). *The Language of Winnicott: A Dictionary of Winnicott's Use of Words*. London: Karnac.

Anzieu, C. (2009). Personal communication.

Bion, W.R. (1962). The psycho-analytic study of thinking. *Int. J. Psycho-Anal.*, 43:306–310.

Caldwell, L. (2007). *Winnicott and the psychoanalytic tradition*. London: Karnac.

Fine, B.D. (1964). Some aspects of psychoanalytic methodology. *J. Amer. Psychoanal. Assn.*, 12:610–619.

Freud, A. (1937). *The Ego and the Mechanisms of Defence*. London: Hogarth.

Freud, S. (1915). Instincts and their vicissitudes. *Standard Edition, 14*.

Fulgencio, L. (2007). Winnicott's rejection of the basic concepts of Freud's metapsychology. *Int. J. Psycho-Anal.*, 88:443–463.

Geleerd, E. (1963). Evaluation of Melanie Klein's "Narrative of a Child Analysis." *Int. J. Psycho-Anal.*, 44:493–506.

Green, A. (1975). The analyst, symbolization and absence in the analytic setting. *Int. J. Psycho-Anal.*, 56:1–22.

Hartmann, H. (1950). Comments on the psychoanalytic theory of the ego. *Psychoanal. St. Child*, 5:74–96.

Isaacs, S. (1948). The nature and function of phantasy. *Int. J. Psycho-Anal.*, 29:73–97.

Jacobson, E. (1964). *The Self and the Object World*. Madison, CT: Int. Univ. Press.

Kahr, B. (1996). *D. W. Winnicott: A Biographical Portrait*. London: Karnac.

King, P.H.M. & Steiner, R., eds. (1991). *The Freud-Klein Controversies, 1941–1945*. London/New York: Tavistock.

Nunberg, H. (1931). The synthetic function of the ego. *Int. J. Psycho-Anal.*, 12:123–140.

Ogden, T. (2001). Reading Winnicott. *Psychoanal. Q.*, 60:299–325.

Posner, B. M., Glickman, R. W., Taylor, E. C., Canfield, J. & Cyr, F. (2001). In search of Winnicott's aggression. *Psychoanal. St. Child*, 56:171–190.

Reed, G. & Baudry, F. (1997). Susan Isaacs and Anna Freud on fantasy. *J. Amer. Psychoanal. Assn.*, 45:465–491.

——— & ——— (2005). Conflict, structure and absence: André Green on borderline and narcissistic pathologies. *Psychoanal. Q.*, 74:121–155.

Reeves, C. (2007). The mantle of Freud: was "The Use of an Object" Winnicott's todestrieb? *Brit. J. Psychother.*, 23:365–382.

Ritvo, S. (1962). Report on panel on object relations. *J. Amer. Psychoanal. Assn.*, 10:102–118.

Rodman, F. (1987). *The Spontaneous Gesture: Selected Letters of D. W. Winnicott. Cambridge*, MA/London: Harvard Univ. Press.

Rousillon, R. (1997). La fonction symbolisante de l'objet. *Rev. Franç Psychanal*, 61:399–413.

Samuels, L. (2001). The paradox of destruction and survival in D. W. Winnicott's "The Use of the Object." *Fort Da*, 7:38–53.

Stone, L. (1950). The widening scope of indications for psychoanalysis. *J. Amer. Psychoanal. Assn.*, 2:561–594.

Thompson, N. (2008). A measure of agreement: an exploration of the relationship of D. W. Winnicott and Phyllis Greenacre. *Psychoanal. Q.*, 77:251–281.

——— (2009). Personal communication.

Waelder, R. (1930). The principle of multiple function: observations on overdetermination. In *Psychoanalysis: Observation, Theory, Application*, ed. S. A. Guttman. New York: Int. Univ. Press, 1976, pp. 68–83.

Winnicott, D. W. (1941). The observation of infants in a set situation. *Int. J. Psycho-Anal.*, 22:229–249.

——— (1945). Primitive emotional development. *Int. J. Psycho–Anal.*, 26:137–143.

——— (1953). Transitional objects and transitional phenomena—a study of the first not-me possession. *Int. J. Psycho-Anal.*, 34:89–97.

——— (1962). Ego integration in child development. In *The Maturational Processes and the Facilitating Environment.* London: Hogarth, 1965, pp. 56–63.

——— (1965). *The Maturational Processes and the Facilitating Environment.* London: Hogarth.

——— (1968a). The use of an object. Paper presented at the New York Psychoanalytic Institute, November.

——— (1968b). Comments on my paper "The Use of an Object." In *Psychoanalytic Explorations,* ed. D. W. Winnicott, C. Winnicott, R. Shepherd & M. Davis. Cambridge, MA: Harvard Univ. Press, 1989, pp. 238–240.

——— (1969a). The use of an object. *Int. J. Psycho-Anal.*, 50:711–716.

——— (1969b). The use of an object in the context of Moses and Monotheism. In *Psychoanalytic Explorations*, ed. D. W. Winnicott, C. Winnicott, R. Shepherd & M. Davis. Cambridge, MA: Harvard Univ. Press, 1989, pp. 240–246.

——— Winnicott, C., Shepherd, R. & Davis, M., eds. (1989). *Psychoanalytic Explorations.*

CHAPTER 5

The Problem of Change:
Evolution of Theory and Technique
[previously unpublished.]

INTRODUCTION

This chapter will explore the disconnect between the theory of change as it evolved since Freud's discoveries, and what actually happens in the clinical situation and how difficult it is to pin down and explain the nature of change, what fosters it, and what impedes it.

My answer, after working on the topic of how change actually works in the clinical setting, is a disappointing "I don't really know." One major reason is that often when positive changes occur, we do not try to figure out the complex dynamics with the patient. It can occur suddenly, during an hour or some time afterwards, quickly, or periodically, as a result of some understanding which sinks in after working through. As an example, one of my patients was suffering from some GI symptoms which we assumed were at least in part psychosomatic. During a recent session in which he complained about their recurrence, we were able to deal with some aspects connected with a profound grief coupled with anxiety which, until then, had been only partially put into words. For the following two days, my patient's symptoms all but disappeared. Then they slowly came back. I have no way of ascertaining whether the improvement was coincidental, or whether it was related to beginning to master the sense of loss, or whether just the idea itself—that we were hitting pay dirt—was sufficient to bring temporary relief to this very insightful individual.

Definition of Change

What we mean by change has to be clarified. I will limit myself in this paper to positive change, although one could also explore what leads to negative change. There can be transient change due to external circumstances, for example, a lessening of anxiety after the patient is promoted in his or her job. There can also be a temporary dramatic change, for example, when a patient enters treatment with magical expectations of cure related to the emergence of an idealized transference. In this paper, however, I will focus on the process of change which results from an increase in effective understanding as a result of lengthy therapeutic work.

The change can lead to lessening of painful moods or affects such as anxiety, depression, or mourning, or in a decrease of particular symptoms. The most reluctant and slow aspect of change, if not resistance to change, however, is rooted in the dynamics of a person's character. I have written a number of papers on this particular topic (Baudry,1987, 1990). Our character is part of our personal identity. By nature, quite stable and also rigid, It is heavily invested with narcissism and, in general, it is that part of a person which is most resistant to change, particularly in training analysis which may impose an additional burden on the candidate fearful of raising too many controversial issues. As an example, I remember supervising many years ago a rather narcissistic and angry candidate who could not tolerate disagreement and was quite fixed in her views. One day she brought a session in which she identified some changes which she attributed to her good work. There was very little she would tolerate except my reluctant agreement that her work seemed to be progressing at this time.

An aspect which has changed over time is the nature of what can be defined as a complete interpretation. During my training in the 1960s, I was taught that, following Waelder's system, for an interpretation to be complete and effective required an ego part, a superego part, a drive aspect, and a reference to reality. My supervisors did not seem to adhere to this model as far as I can remember.

Freud's Views

Freud's initial views were related to the bringing into consciousness deeply repressed unconscious fantasies, often based on early trauma. Repeated interpretations with working through would lead to insight, the pathway to change. Defenses and resistances would be brought to consciousness and interpreted. The understanding of dreams as the pathway to the unconscious occupied an important role in the process of cure as dreams occurred during a partially normal state of regression during sleep, and thus opened a window into an aspect of the unconscious not previously available. Later in his work, he pointed out the crucial role of transference and the need to interpret it as a key component of treatment.

The superego was seen as an internal object filled with projections of pathological parental objects. In the process of cure the pathologic object will be analyzed. These pathologic objects can be seen sometimes as the only available link with an important, sometimes deficient, early childhood parent. Hopefully, the superego would come under the control of the rational ego. "Where superego was, ego shall be."

From a related point of view, the ego was seen as the precipitate of abandoned object cathexes; if ego syntonic, these cathexes contribute to growth; if ego-alien, they lead to conflicts and pathology.

The nature of the process can be described as including a number of steps: first the analyst has to listen to the patient's associations, second, he would infer unconscious meaning, third, he would share these with him, and finally (very importantly), he would draw inferences from the patient's responses. Beginning students often fail to follow up and listen to the patient's responses to their interpretations, thinking erroneously that once an interpretation is given, the analyst can move on to the next issue. I sometimes use the analogy of a tennis game to describe the back-and-forth interaction of the analytic process.

The increasing role of transference with new stages in our evolving theory should not be underestimated, and it opens a window on the subtle influence of hidden object relationships that govern all human interactions, not just those limited to the treatment setting.

Obstacles to Change

In my clinical work in supervision, I sometimes note that my supervisees are often not connected with the patient, talking at the wrong level, sometimes because of their inexperience. They are either too intellectual or unable to understand the level at which the patient is functioning at the moment. They may also be caught in an enactment of a pathologic object relationship.

The same thing happened to me a number of years ago. I was treating, in an analysis, a borderline patient, and to my dismay he was becoming angrier and angrier with me, making me feel very uncomfortable, and leading me to suggest that he might take some medication. Some time after, he interrupted the treatment. A few years later, he came back and confronted me with the issue of his increasing anger. He told me that I had completely misunderstood him, and that I had not realized that his anger was a desperate reaction to his feeling that he could not reach me emotionally at the time. I did not realize then that he was repeating, with me, his pathologic reaction to a distant father. My so-called neutrality was seen as an abandonment.

To avoid this not uncommon pitfall, I try to pay attention in the treatment setting to what unconscious object relationships are being repeated during the session. This may change during the course of an hour, and can be initiated by either party. The therapist may be totally unaware of this fact, and of his possible role in the pathologic interaction.

To manage these difficulties, the role of countertransference, initially downplayed, becomes central. It has a dual origin, both as a projection from the patient of unmanageable issues (more important in borderline or psychotic patients), and second, as related to the therapist's own unresolved conflicts. It needs to be explored in some detail. This is a thorny issue from a historical point of view, as the approach to this topic dramatically altered during the course of the history of psychoanalysis.

As the rules of proper behavior for the analyst slowly emerged, in the early 1920's, some genuine differences of opinion had to be gradually confronted and clarified.

Early in the days of analysis, some Hungarian analysts felt it would make sense for the same person to both treat and supervise the candidate, as it was deemed he was the person who knew his supervisee best and, therefore, could understand his countertransference best. Freud did this with some of his early patients. On the opposite end, some other early analysts felt that this dual role interfered with the proper management of the transference. Even further, some supervisors felt reluctant to address a countertransference issue which they saw as part of the supervisee's analysis.

To complicate matters further, most institutes have no seminar to discuss the management of supervision or its method or structure. They assume that training analysts could be left on their own to decide on their model of supervision. As a result, the individual style of each training analyst will influence the manner in which he conducts supervision.

One of my more challenging supervisors treated supervision like an analysis. As I came into his office, he would nod his head and give a short grunt, and wait for me to begin. I do remember, during my training, expressing my dismay at the wide variety of my supervisors' styles. "This can't all be supervision!" I exclaimed to my analyst one day! I must have felt at the time that there must be just one proper way of conducting supervision!

One of my early supervisors, discussing with me a very volatile and impulsive patient I was trying to treat analytically, told me one day, "The patient has you on the ropes!" Of course, I knew this already, but besides making me both anxious and a bit ashamed, this statement was totally unhelpful. Perhaps my supervisor thought I would discuss my issue with my analyst. Neither of us realized at the time that it might have been more helpful to help me figure out the dynamics of the situation which led me to feel quite helpless. Another of my early supervisors used the material I presented as an entry to describe the dynamics of the patient within the system of ego psychology. I learned a great deal from this interaction but a crucial piece of my relationship with the patient was never discussed. Still another supervisor, sitting very far from me in her living room, would conduct supervision by imagining or reconstructing (or constructing?) the story and fantasies she derived from my patient's associations, creating deeper and new meaning from the more disorganized material I presented. I felt better after each supervision, thinking I had gained new insight into this patient. As this patient was very astute, she usually could tell when I had my supervision, as the following hour with her would be richer. I would sometimes anxiously disgorge the understanding I had gained in my recent supervision, not always realizing that the reconstructions we had arrived at applied very nicely to the Friday hour, but did not always fit in with the material of the following Monday hour! I don't think that, at the time, I was aware that the urge to disgorge the supervisor's interpretations had more to do with my anxiety about missing some crucial connections arrived at by my supervisor than with what was happening during the session with my patient. The supervisor did not necessarily ask about my subjective experience, so I was surprised and a bit dismayed when she suddenly told me one day that she thought we could end our supervision as she felt I understood the patient well enough. I remember telling my analyst, the next session, that I did not share my supervisor's opinion. He urged me to discuss it with my supervisor. I think I was reluctant to challenge her view. I also recall that I found another early supervisor rather empty and just mouthing theoretical banalities. In order to deal with this issue, I asked another training analyst to periodically discuss the case with him. I was fearful of confronting the supervisor. What a relief it turned out to be to hear the fresh human views of this other supervisor!

What was missing during all my supervisory experience was the nature of the process during supervision, the nature of my relation to the supervisor, and any attention to my countertransference. I have written a paper to address just those issues (Baudry, 1993). This should not obscure the fact that, for the most part, I valued the many supervisions I had during my training, and learned a great deal from the majority.

Another obstacle to change is the patient's expectations that as long as he is in treatment, he can take his time and not rush the boat. Patients can give as a reason that, after all, they cannot control their feelings. I will then point out that indeed what they say is true, but they can control their behavior. This is very important with dysfunctional couples where each partner is locked into repeating toxic object relationships, often with a sadomasochistic tint, or remaining withdrawn to avoid being hurt.

Process of Change

Not all patients are able to change. There are certain basic requirements for change to be possible. This includes three components: (1) being curious about oneself, (2) being able to observe oneself, and (3) to be able to communicate, mostly verbally, one's inner life. Related to this last issue is the role of the trust the patient experiences towards the therapist. Monitoring its change during the course of time, and its management in the transference, is crucial to progress. The capacity for change also requires the ability to confront guilt and shame.

One of my favorite teachers, Rudolph Loewenstein, said that there are patients who both want to work and to change. A second group wants to change without working; a third group wants to work without changing; and a final group wants neither to work nor to change. In order to find out to which group a patient belongs, it is essential to find out first why the patient came to treatment and, second, how he imagines it will work. Often one encounters patients who imagine treatment is like bringing your car to the garage to be fixed; you leave it and pick it up once the work is done. The patient has to realize he is the one in charge of change, the therapist is only giving him tools to do so.

Somewhat related is the role of masochism as a resistance. There are some patients who seem to derive pleasure in exposing their suffering to the analyst (or parent) as a sadistic attempt to regain power and make the recipient suffer. This can also be an act of revenge against the parent who is unconsciously blamed for some defect, bodily or otherwise. For example, it was true of Marie Bonaparte who almost consciously blamed her father for depriving her of the masculine organ she so coveted.

Even though I seem to suggest that change is at the bottom of most good therapy, nothing could be further from the truth. There is a difference between how we think we can make a difference analytically, and by non-analytic means. The former is generally based on interpretations, the latter by a type of subtle caring and acceptance of the patient as he/she is.

For example, I have had patients whose mate gradually deteriorates due to an irreversible disease. In these cases, it is most helpful for me to validate their feelings of frustration, anger, and helplessness mixed with anxiety. Occasionally, I may point out some hidden unconscious component, but I feel I am more in the role of a good friend to whom they can reveal all their issues. Such modes of treatment might fit into the "supportive mode," sometimes with a subtle implication that this is second-class therapy. Nothing could be further from the truth. As a result, these patients change subtly, become more accepting of a bad reality, and are very gratified they can share their guilty thoughts without reproof. Another option is for the patient to be able to differentiate between guilt and responsibility. The former leads to conflict and symptoms; the latter is a view of reality which must be accepted. There are also other types of intervention outside of what is strictly considered analytic behavior, for example, the role of humor, which can lighten the atmosphere, introduce a human element, or even help to resolve a situation where the analyst feels stuck.

However, a final note on so-called supportive interventions: one must be aware that, on occasion, the patient may clamor for support as a way of avoiding more in-depth work which he is very capable of undertaking.

Changes in Theory

With the emergence of new theories, three aspects drew attention, each centered on an object relation previously minimized: first, the role of the analyst as a new object, i.e., one who does not behave like the pathologic parent. Second, following the emergence of object relation theories, therapists began to focus on the crucial importance of the relationship, including the role of love and caring.

Third, different theories paid attention to differing data. For example, the Kleinian theory emphasizes early aggression. Kohut's theory looks for failures in empathy and behaviors as damaging to the self. Laplanche looks for projections of unconscious fantasies onto the child by the mother as the cause of problems.

The role of the analyst as a new object has been studied by Loewald (1980). However, it is important to state that this new relationship is not an end in itself, but rather the first step in a long road. It is a bit like the softening of a crust to allow some removal or change. It occurs as part of the transference neurosis which remobilizes frozen pathological earlier object relations. As a result of the new relationship, it is hoped that the patient can also begin to identify with the analyst, and develop more neutral ways of observing himself.

Loewald compares the analytic relationship with that of the parent-child relationship. Because of his experience, the parent is not distracted by temporary obstacles but holds in his mind the capacities of the child, his assets and talents leading to growth in the future. This could be seen as an aspect of benevolent caring and love.

The problem of the match between therapist and patient is very crucial and has been the focus of study in recent years. This would also include aspects of the therapist's character which clash with the patient's personality characteristics. For example, a therapist who was brought up by submitting to parental authority and behaving according to rules might have trouble dealing with a narcissistic demanding patient, or a patient with anger issues.

Decreasing Focus on Defenses

There is another change in my clinical work which renders the patient-therapist relationship less adversarial. Instead of focusing on defenses, I focus on the adaptational approach. For example, I have a patient who needs to be in total control, with a wife who is very loving, gentle, and totally devoted to his welfare. With the passage of time and aging, my patient has become more vulnerable and, in reaction to his increasing weakness, he has become more controlling, leading to some arguments and difficulties in the marriage. In response to his behavioral change, I said to my patient, "Of course I can understand why you need to do this; because during all of your childhood you were faced by a difficult, controlling, and castrating mother, so it makes sense that, in spite of differences, you cannot take a chance and become vulnerable. You are still struggling with an internal mother, and you are afraid your wife could become like her."

In another case, one of my patients dealing with massive anger problems, expresses massive rage towards a very critical and controlling sibling, and seems to want to justify his behavior, but is a bit overwhelmed with his feelings. I told him that we have to differentiate two aspects of his reaction: "First, your sibling's behavior is unacceptable. There is no problem with this, but can you see that because of the massive anger you are struggling with, you also use this opportunity to discharge some of the anger which has nothing to do with the problem with your sibling?" To my relief, the patient agreed with my distinction and our work could proceed.

The Issue of the Relationship

Unfortunately, the theoretical role of the relationship is not easy to examine in a neutral fashion as it has occasionally been used by a group of object relations theorists who want to make it the central core of their theoretical edifice instead of seeing it as only one aspect of a very complicated situation.

There are two components which need to be distinguished: first, the therapeutic relationship, and second, the admixture of the real relationship, theoretically independent from the therapeutic one. A bit like ivy growing on a tree, the so-called real relationship may silently lead to enactments, particularly if either patient or analyst are not aware of its corrosive potential, because on the surface it seems so benign and acceptable. Freud himself allowed the personal relationship to intrude on the professional. An extreme example can be found in the 1000-page book of his correspondence with Marie Bonaparte who sought analysis with him. Her wealth allowed her to ply Freud with many gifts from Greece, including rare vases, honey, and later, an urn to contain his ashes. Marie also developed a close relationship with Freud's daughter, Anna, and Mrs. Freud often brought her strawberries in a basket as she boarded the Orient Express back from Vienna to Paris. Freud also allowed Marie to send her daughter Eugenie to Freud for analysis, and he was willing to have the latter's potential husband come to Vienna so he could judge his appropriateness as a mate.

In one of his letters to Marie Bonaparte, Freud commented that he was aware that the so-called real relationship would not have existed apart from the transference, and that it could also be used as a resistance but, in the end, he said that he thought the two could coexist.

Therapeutic Relationship

I will first deal with the problem of the therapeutic relationship. First, in order for the treatment to take hold, there must be a combination of hope, optimism including an expectation of gain, and a minimal amount of trust. This often makes it difficult for patients with major trust issues as part of their character, such as paranoid personalities, to develop a workable relationship with their therapist. Even if this develops, the suspicious patient may see it as phony because the relationship is not genuine; it is bought or, even further, care is given not spontaneously but in response to the patient's pleas, demands, or complaints. What the patient does not realize is that, independent of the pure therapeutic part, the therapist may genuinely care about his patient.

Recently, Celenza (2022) put together a very thoughtful book of short essays entitled *Transference, Love, Being*. Perusing the book, I note the great difficulty in exactly stating what we mean when we use the word love, and we sometimes connect it with surrounding sexuality.

The limits of what the therapeutic relationship can include have evolved considerably over the course of the history of the theoretical foundations of our field. It has altered from the initial view of the analyst as a reflecting mirror to a slowly growing involvement without clear limits. I do remember, during my training analysis, that I was completely surprised when, one day, I entered my analyst's office with a limp, having hurt my ankle, and my analyst questioned me about what had happened.

In a recent lecture, I heard David Tuckett present various models illustrating different types of possible interactions during the course of an analysis. The first was asymmetric, described as the theater where two people watch a live play where the patient casts the analyst in various unconscious picture roles. The second model was "cinema" with two people watching a film projected on a screen. The third model (symmetric) was that of immersive theater with audience and players, and both patient and analyst cast each other in a different role. Each model would modify the interaction between patient and analyst.

The role of neutrality can be confusing as the analyst has to have the capacity to observe in a scientific fashion what is going on, but also has to experience and allow human interactions with feelings in both directions, which he then needs to observe and utilize, as appropriate.

The Real Relationship

We do know that, as I detailed earlier in this paper, Freud was comfortable in having a real relationship with many of his patients. He gave food to some of them, or even gave them money.

This is a very complex topic to address. I will start with the question of self-revelation. As a student, if a patient asked me where I was going on vacation, I was taught rather mechanically to say back: "Why do you ask?" In my view, this is a toxic unhelpful response. If I am puzzled and not sure how to respond, I might say: "How would it help if you knew?" With sicker patients, I err on the side of revealing rather than hiding. I am supervising a candidate whose patient cannot hold the image of the analyst in his absence. If such a patient asked me where I was going on vacation, I might offer an interpretation: "Would it make me more real when we are separated if there were a place you could connect with me?" I would also be more likely to simply say where I was going without needing to interpret the meaning or request the patient to associate. The latter could be seen as intrusive, rather than a reasonable demand, within the confines of analytic work.

Another aspect of the real relationship is the question of whether and when to accept gifts from a patient. Again, there is no clear answer, and the therapist must anticipate whether the patient could tolerate a refusal without being badly hurt. In my early days, a patient who was about to terminate an analysis (which was only partially satisfactory because of what I thought was the appropriate emotional distance) said she intended to give me a genuine letter signed by Freud—which was quite rare, and, I assume, quite expensive.

Reluctantly, I thanked her for her care but said that I did not think it was right for me to accept such a gift.

With increasing experience, rules, which in my early days were to be followed, have become principles to guide me, but not to *force* me, to adhere to them. As a result, my work is much looser, less rigid, and much more spontaneous. I see this as a gain rather than a loss.

REFERENCES

Baudry, F. (1987). Character, Character Type and Character Organization. *J. American. Psa. Assn* 37:655–686.

——— (1990). The Relevance of the analyst's Character and Attitudes to his Work. *J. American Psychoanal. Assn* 39:917–938.

——— (1993) The Personal Dimension and Management of the Supervisory Situation. *Psa. Q.* 62:588–614.

Celenza, A. (2022). *Transference, Love, Being.* Routledge London and New York.

Loewald, H., (1980). Psychoanalytic theory and the psychoanalytic process. In *Papers on Psychoanalysis.* New Haven: Yale Univ. Press, 1980, pp. 277–301.

CHAPTER 6

The Evolution of the Concept of Character in Freud's Writings
[(1983). *JAPA* (31):3–31.]

Among the few papers written by Freud (1908a), (1916), (1931) specifically devoted to the topic of character, there exists a rather rich weaving and slow development of the concept. In this section, I shall spell out the unfolding of Freud's thinking and show how the major strides in his clinical and metapsychological works made possible the evolution of character theory, or at least of some of its components, since an overall conceptual framework is lacking. In a subsequent section, I shall attempt to summarize the evolution of the concept and its shifting emphasis and definition in the course of Freud's work. I shall purposely delay an overall formulation, as I believe it might detract from my description of the unfolding of Freud's thinking.

A problem in proceeding through isolation of the term "character" in the index and following up on the text references is that some short passages including the term may be difficult to evaluate unless placed in context. In addition, certain papers dealing indirectly with issues related to character but not under that label could be left out entirely—a consequence of the rather mechanical aspect of retrieval. This will be remedied by occasional reference to other papers that seem relevant to the topic. I shall, somewhat arbitrarily, divide the material of Freud's work into three sections: (1) works preceding the paper on anal character (Freud, 1908a); (2) papers leading up to the paper on the three character types (Freud, 1916); and (3) later writings, including the libidinal types classification (Freud, 1931). In what follows, I shall omit obvious repetitions and dwell only on those references indicating a change—either progress or regression in the use of the term.

Early Development and Usage (1895–1907)

Early in the development of the theory and technique of analysis, character plays essentially no role. The reasons for this are several. (1) The main interest was focused on symptoms—what stood out—rather than on character—the matrix. (2) The concept of resistance and transference central to the manifestation of character in the analytic situation had not yet burgeoned. (3) Freud was more concerned initially with the sexual drives *per se* and their multiple manifestations than with adaptation and reality. (4) Psychoanalysis was first concerned with the unconscious rather than with exploration of the conscious.

Until the *Three Essays* (Freud, 1905b), all references to character are incidental and may be omitted from this survey, except for a brief allusion (Freud, 1904) which makes a connection between character and resistance. This is not the only instance of a major discovery that is buried and unearthed some years later as in Freud's (1916) paper on character types. Here is the 1904 passage: "if the physician has to deal with a worthless character, he soon loses the interest which makes it possible for him to enter profoundly into the patient's mental life. Deep-rooted malformations of character, traits of an actually degenerate constitution, show themselves during treatment as sources of a resistance that can scarcely be overcome" (p. 254). This formulation recalls the then prevalent theory of personality disorders of 19th-century German psychiatry which included theories of hereditary determinism of human behavior. It may be recalled that in the early formulations, the socially deviant aberrations received the greatest attention; hence, the distinctive judgmental quality which emerges at this time. The contamination of the lay usage of the term and its moral connotations are apparent. This passage also suggests the operation within the analyst of countertransference resistance—that is, the reaction of dislike to the patient, rather than being seen as a source of data, is conceptualized as a source of resistance "that can scarcely be overcome"—the theory at this point then serves a protective function for the analyst.

The first major development is to be found in the *Three Essays* (Freud, 1905b) in the section on sublimation, in the summary. It anticipates the paper on anal character by showing how instincts and impulses that have been transformed by processes of reaction formation and sublimation fuel and contribute to the person's character traits. Freud also hints that in an artist one may find a mixture of perversion, efficiency, and neurosis—presumably according to the formula in usage at the time, equating perversion with the direct expression of impulse, the neurosis with its negative, and the efficiency with reaction formation or sublimation.

> What we describe as a person's "character" is built up to a considerable extent from the material of sexual excitations and is composed of instincts that have been fixed since childhood, of constructions achieved by means of sublimation, and of other constructions, employed for effectively holding in check perverse impulses which have been recognized as unutilizable. The multifariously perverse sexual disposition of childhood can accordingly be regarded as the source of a number of our virtues, in so far as through reaction-formation it stimulates their development [pp. 238–239].

One gains the impression that by "constructions," Freud had in mind some stable structure, anticipating the ego. This passage also foreshadows the future division of character traits into reactive and sublimatory. Freud assumed at this time that efficiency (presumably referring to socially acceptable instinctual derivatives such as character traits), perversion, and neurosis were equivalent potential outcomes of the transformation of instincts.

A note of caution is necessary in placing Freud's emphasis on drive manifestations in the context of the overall development of his theory. Freud's portrayal of character as originating in the transformation of drives should not be taken to mean that character is nothing but transformed instinctual derivatives; rather, Freud approached all of mental functioning from this viewpoint at that particular time. The implication of the historical approach, particularly for a term as inclusive as character, is that the evolution of the concept recapitulates the history of the development of psychoanalysis itself.

In another passage, Freud briefly introduces the role of masturbation during the oedipal phase; referring to this second phase of infantile sexual activity, Freud (1905b) writes: "But all its details leave behind the deepest (unconscious) impressions in the subject's memory, determine the development of his character, if he is to remain healthy, and the symptomatology of his neurosis, if he is to fall ill after puberty" (p. 189). Freud seems to imply that the person's character is a healthy development in contrast to the symptoms of a neurosis. This idea will be rapidly modified in the next few years.

The last theoretical formulation before Freud's (1908a) paper on anal character is to be found in 1907. Freud stated, at a meeting of the Vienna Psychoanalytic Society, "In general, the human being cannot tolerate contrasting ideas and feelings in juxtaposition. It is this striving for unification that we call character" (Nunberg & Federn, 1962, p. 236). Thus, Freud introduced the synthetic function of character formation, the problem-solving aspect, later developed by Nunberg (1931).

As Stein (1969) reminds us, by 1908 Freud had the elements of a fairly complete theory of symptom formation as elaborated in the remarkable paper "Hysterical Phantasies and Their Relation to Bisexuality" (1908c). The paper on anal character (1908a) does not present the same concision and depth of understanding of the processes of character formation. I shall summarize, through a few formulas, Freud's theory in 1908 as it applied to patients with anal character.

1. On a descriptive level, this category includes orderliness, parsimony, and obstinacy (the three character traits).
2. These patients had unusual difficulty in controlling direct expression of instinct in childhood (i.e., they were born with unusually strong constitutional anal propensities).
3. During the period of latency, strong reaction formations formed "at the expense of the excitations proceeding from the erotogenic zones," opposing "like dams" direct expression of instincts (p. 171).
4. The traits mentioned above are direct results of the sublimation of the instincts—defined as a deflection of excitation from sexual aims to other aims.
5. Character is formed out of the constituent instincts—either as unchanged prolongation or as sublimations or reaction formations against them.
6. Other component instincts such as the urethral instinct can undergo a similar fate. The theory described so far comprises (a) clinical description and isolation of recurring grouping; (b) constitutional predisposition and factors in early history; (c) some hints of a developmental process occurring during latency; (d) an attempt to describe the process by which the transformation occurs and to generalize from this clinical instance.

It is tempting to speculate why the obsessional character was the first to be described. On the clinical level, obsessional patients have a great propensity to verbalize. It may be that a clear organizational structure is the formal counterpart of the clinical manifestations, and thus was easier to isolate.

We may wonder about the reasons for the more simplistic theory of character development as contrasted to the theory of symptom formation. It is due in part to the relative neglect of character in clinical work at this stage of development of psychoanalysis. Although it is possible to describe some of the disagreeable character traits that colored Dora's treatment (Freud, 1905a)—her wish for revenge, her manipulativeness—these are not related by Freud to other manifestations of her pathology and, of course, not yet to the course of the transference which has a close relationship to character. Character traits being experienced as self-syntonic are not brought by the patient as something to be analyzed. It is left to the analyst to bring them up for consideration. Freud did not do this in the case of Dora because he did not realize that her character attitudes would serve the purpose of resistance and would bring a premature end to his efforts.

Second Period of Development (1908–1916)

Excessive masturbation was given a role in weakening character. Initially masturbation was understood to represent a close derivative of the sexual drives. However, Freud (1908b) was beginning to depart from his previous mechanistic emphasis, as this passage suggests:

> The sexual behavior of a human being often lays down the pattern for all his other modes of reacting to life. If a man is energetic in winning the object of his love, we are confident that he will pursue his other aims with an equally unswerving energy; but if, for all sorts of reasons, he refrains from satisfying his strong sexual instincts, his behavior will be conciliatory and resigned rather than vigorous in other spheres of life as well [p. 198].

There follows a passage relating the inhibition of women in intellectual matters to the taboo against their interest in sexual issues. This finding expressed in clinical terms the primacy of the sexual instincts in determining patterns of behavior—this at a time when the theory of the ego had not yet been developed.

A brief sentence in the Leonardo paper (1910a) alludes to the constitutional aspect of character—its roots in the organic matrix. "We are obliged to look for the source of the tendency to repression and the capacity for sublimation in the organic foundations of character on which the mental structure is only afterwards erected" (p. 136). This is one of the very few references Freud makes to the inborn biological roots of character.

Freud's paper on object choice (1910b) is a good example of the papers that deal indirectly with the concept of character and yet do not mention the word *per se*. He isolates a clinical picture, describing certain men with consistent characteristics in their conditions for loving: the presence of an injured third party, the selection of a woman of ill repute, the high value the man sets on her, and finally the urge to rescue the woman who is loved. Freud is able to unite these apparently diverse and puzzling attributes as derivatives of the psychic constellations connected with the mother. Freud's explanation remains at a clinical level. He refers to the Oedipus complex and the position of the boy looking for revenge. At the end of the paper, he alludes to his method of classification:

> I have in the first place aimed at singling out from the observational material extreme and sharply defined types. In both cases we find a far greater number of individuals in whom only a few features of the type can be recognized, or only features which are not distinctly marked, and it is obvious that a proper appreciation of these types will not be possible until the whole context to which they belong has been explored [pp. 174–175].

This paper is the first to introduce the term "types" as a classification concept referring to some aspect of object relations. The term will recur again in his (1931) paper, "Libidinal Types." This paper enriches the concept of character by broaching the important topic of object relations—novel at the time. It deals in clinical fashion with the outcome of the Oedipus complex and with character in other than instinctual vicissitudes. It also illustrates the shaping influence of unconscious fantasies on the character and behavior of the mature individual.

In this relatively brief review, I can mention only in passing two metapsychological papers whose concepts lay the groundwork for much of the theory of character formation: the paper on "Two Principles of Mental Functioning" (1911) and the paper on "Instincts and Their Vicissitudes" (1915a). The former paper, by clearly identifying the reality principle, foreshadows the adaptive point of view and spells out the development of critical ego functions—memory, judgment, attention, and thought. The latter paper, concerning the processes of change in the aims of instincts—reversal into the opposite, turning around on the subject, repression, and sublimation—lays down broad principles which will play a role in determining the shape of character traits.

From 1914 on, we find rather precipitous and momentous developments following each other. Probably the key concepts determining such an explosion of discoveries include the elaboration of narcissism and the formulations of the concept of transference in the paper "Remembering, Repeating and Working Through." The key passage introducing the concept of repetition compulsion (in the clinical sense) is as follows:

> We have learnt that the patient repeats instead of remembering, and repeats under the conditions of resistance. We may now ask what it is that he in fact repeats or acts out. The answer is that he repeats everything that has already made its may from the sources

of the repressed into his manifest personality—his inhibitions and unserviceable attitudes and his pathological character-traits. He also repeats all his symptoms in the course of the treatment [Freud, 1914, p. 151].

The central issue of repetition was already hinted at in his previous paper, "The Dynamics of the Transference," in which Freud refers to the individual's acquisition of

a specific method ... in his conduct of his erotic life—that is, in the preconditions to falling in love which he lays down, in the instincts he satisfies and the aims he sets himself in the course of it. This produces what might be described as a stereotype plate (or several such), which is constantly repeated—constantly reprinted afresh—in the course of the person's life, so far as external circumstances and the nature of the love-objects accessible to him permit, and which is certainly not entirely insusceptible to change in the face of recent experiences [Freud, 1912, pp. 99–100].

Although the process of repetition is first related to the strength and tendency of the unsatisfied instincts which are repressed and dominate the object-seeking behavior, the next step involves the discovery of resistance to the analytic process, as it manifests itself in the transference.

The second major discovery concerns the substitution of action for memory; behavior (or character trait) is a communication—in another language—about the individual's past which needs to be analyzed and becomes, via the transference, the most useful tool and the source of the strongest resistance; the struggle at this point is dynamically active and, therefore, subject to interpretation.

The concept of the "stereotype plate reprinted afresh" seems to apply a metaphor drawn from the original literal meaning of the term character. This term does not appear anywhere else. Since character is ego-syntonic, the patient will not bring it up. The analyst, however, cannot afford to do the same; he is forced to pay attention to resistances anchored in the patient's character. He is also confronted with the clinical fact of repetition of "unserviceable attitudes and pathological character traits."

A subsequent paper, "The Disposition to Obsessional Neurosis" (1913), allows Freud to stand back and contrast the process in character formation and symptom formation.

> In the field of development of character, we are bound to meet with the same instinctual forces which we have found at work in the neuroses. But a sharp theoretical distinction between the two is necessitated by the single fact that the failure of repression and the return of the repressed—which are peculiar to the mechanism of neurosis—are absent in the formation of character. In the latter, repression either does not come into action or smoothly achieves its aim of replacing the repressed by reaction formations and sublimations. Hence, the processes of the formation of character are more obscure and less accessible to analysis than neurotic ones [p. 323].

Thus, reasons for the difficulty in understanding character formation emerge—some practical, some theoretical. The process is silent, ego-syntonic and not obviously involved in conflict with various signposts indicative of the struggle. In his theory building, Freud had attempted until then to apply the same model for the formation of character trait and symptom. This could lead only to confusion, as each obviously arose from different exigencies, i.e., a neurotic symptom is always a pathological process, whereas character formation is a normal developmental process which, though involved in conflict, is not necessarily pathological.

Yet another reason complicating the comparison between symptom and character (pointed out by Rosen [Panel] 1957) lies in the dichotomy apparent in early analytic writings: symptom formation is understood in terms of regression from oedipal conflicts whereas, character at least in its instinctual components, is seen in terms of pregenital fixations. This oversimplification was not to be rectified until the 1930's, with the interest in female sexuality. By then analysts became sensitized to the distorting effects of the pregenital phases on the oedipal one.

There is no question that a character trait is not as clear-cut an entity as a symptom. Hence, it is more difficult to delineate and to study. There remained to develop the concept of the ego before new advances could be made in the field. In the paper on repression, Freud (1915b) describes the evolution of a character trait from the transformation of a repressed hostile impulse.

It is this hostile impulsion against someone who is loved which is subjected to repression. The effect at an early stage of the work of repression is quite different from what it is at a later one. At first the repression is completely successful; the ideational content is rejected and the affect made to disappear. As a substitutive formation there arises an alteration in the ego in the shape of an increased conscientiousness, and this can hardly be called a symptom. Here... repression has brought about a withdrawal of libido; but here it has made use of reaction-formation for this purpose, by intensifying an opposite... Here substitute and symptom do not coincide [pp. 156–157].

In this passage dealing with obsessional neurosis, Freud is probably referring to the formation of a character trait, should the alteration in the ego persist. The same impulse whose transformation gives rise to symptoms according to the classical formulations can also give rise to another type of substitute formation, namely, an alteration in the ego. As the role of aggression in human development becomes better understood, its key role in character formation will emerge.

"Mourning and Melancholia" (1917), though not directly referring to character formation, alludes to those processes through which an object cathexis under the influence of loss is replaced by an identification. The role of identification will, of course, be elaborated in 1923 in *The Ego and Id*, as will be described later. The setting up of the superego as a critical agency split off from the ego is also hinted at.

In "Thoughts for the Times on War and Death," Freud (1915c) tackles the issues of the prerequisite leading up to a completed character formation. In a section describing reaction formation and the presence in the unconscious of opposite impulses which are eventually synthesized in the personality, Freud writes:

> Psycho-analysis adds that the two opposed feelings not infrequently have the same person for their object. It is not until... these "instinctual vicissitudes" have been surmounted that what we call a person's character is formed, and this, as we know, can only very inadequately be classified as "good" or "bad";... most of our sentimentalists, friends of humanity and protectors of animals have been evolved from little sadists and animal tormentors [pp. 281–282].

Freud's concern with good and bad has to be placed in context of the timing of this paper and its subject matter—disillusionment and war. He again takes up an idea first quoted in 1907—the synthetic aspect of character formation. As the most common mode of transformation was reaction formation (in theory), Freud deals mostly with obsessional neurosis. The allusion to surmounting instinctual vicissitudes as a prelude to character formation is an important early step in indicating the way-stations to completion of character formation.

The last paper in this period is the second major paper of Freud's (1916) devoted entirely to our topic, "Some Character-Types Met with in Psycho Analytic Work." The classification of character is unsatisfactory to this day. Often a literary allusion (Don Juan character) or a brief description (the exceptions) may capture the flavor of certain individuals and encapsulate the essence of their make-up better than a more scientific term. Of the three categories described by Freud, only the "exceptions" could describe a general type of character; the other two, "those wrecked by success" and "criminals from a sense of guilt" do not easily lend themselves to translation into character traits. The former deals more with onset of illness, the latter with antecedents of a particular behavior. Both describe patterns of a very general order. All three are in one way or another related to issues of guilt. Freud makes the following specific points: (1) Analysts are forced to pay attention to character because some major resistance to analytic work is a manifestation of character—a reemergence of a point first made in passing in 1904. (2) The character traits that show up in the analytic situation as resistance are not necessarily the ones that are outstanding outside the analysis. This latter point highlights the difficulty confronting analysts in evaluating the observations they may make about their patient's character in the office. This paper illustrates the problems of a classification scheme. Freud suggested one approach for the practitioner—the evaluation of character from the point of view of resistance.

Third Period of Development (1916–1939)

We now come to the last period in Freud's work on character. With the shift in clinical work toward more detailed analysis of resistance and its subtle manifestations, interest in character was bound to increase. This third period saw the evolution of the structural theory, the understanding of masochism and increased interest in the general role of aggression, and finally the delineating of the functions of the superego and ego ideal. Increased clinical experience led to the delineation of certain clinical syndromes and the influence of key fantasies (e.g., beating fantasies) on character and behavior, and also the beginnings of the theoretical relation between character and neurosis. Many of the clinical examples given by Freud will be drawn from the obsessional neurosis (really character manifestations of these patients).

In his lecture dealing with transference resistance, we find the following passage:

> It may... be said that what is being mobilized for fighting against the alterations we are striving for [in the analysis] are character-traits, attitudes of the ego. In this connection we discover that these character-traits were formed in the relation to the determinants of the neurosis and in reaction against its demands, and we come upon traits which cannot normally emerge... which may be described as latent [Freud, 1916–1917, p. 291].

A later section implies that an essential function of analysis lies in bringing these resistances to light and overcoming them.

Emphasis is laid on the latent aspect of some of these traits. A point made previously is that the traits which contribute most heavily to the resistances are not necessarily the most obvious or manifest in the person's functioning outside the analysis.

The relation between character and transference neurosis deserves a longer discussion than can be given here. There are complicated connections between the view of the analyst in the transference (e.g., punitive father, seductive mother), the character traits that arose as solutions to conflicts with the original objects, and compromise formations arising out of the current transference neurosis with an analyst who represents all these images in conflict with the adult personality and its character rigidities.

In another section, speaking of the form the castration complex takes in the little boy, Freud states that it "plays a great part in the construction of his character if he remains normal, in his neurosis if he falls ill, and in his resistance if he comes into analytic treatment" (1916–1917, p. 318).

From a developmental point of view, the solution to the Oedipus complex is the last infantile watershed. From it emerges a new structure, the superego, which will give character its own stamp.

The paper "A Child Is Being Beaten" afforded one illustration of the effect of an unconscious fantasy on character formation, specifically the second, unconscious masochistic phase.

> ...we can also detect effects upon the character, which are directly derived from its unconscious form. People who harbor phantasies of this kind develop a specific sensitiveness and irritability towards anyone whom they can include in the class of fathers. They are easily offended by a person of this kind, and in that way (to their own sorrow and cost) bring about the realization of the imagined situation of being beaten by their father [Freud, 1919, p. 195].

The structural theory allowed Freud to formulate more stringently the mechanisms of character formation, specifically the role of identification in both ego and superego formation. It also allowed for a more thorough understanding and description of the dynamic relations in the mind. This was developed in *The Ego and the Id* (1923). An entire chapter, "The Ego and the Superego (Ego Ideal)," deals with this topic—the view of the ego as the precipitate of object cathexis replaced by identifications.

The main points relevant to our topic are: (1) The replacement of object cathexis by identifications "has a great share in determining the form taken by the ego and that it makes an essential contribution towards building up what is called its 'character'" (p. 28). (2) The character of the ego is a precipitate of abandoned object cathexis and contains the history of those object choices. (3) There are various degrees of capacity for resistance which decide the extent to which a person's character fends off or accepts the influence of the history of his erotic object choices. (4) In some cases, the alteration in character may precede the loss of the object. (5) "The transformation of object-libido into narcissistic libido which takes place obviously implies an abandonment of sexual aims, a desexualization—a kind of sublimation" (p. 30). (6) If the various identifications are incompatible with each other, a pathological outcome may occur. (7) The effect of the first identification made in childhood will be general and lasting. (8) The ego ideal (in the boy) is derived from identification with the father. (9) Identifications are influenced by two major organizers—the Oedipus complex and the constitutional bisexuality. (10) The dissolution of the Oedipus complex consolidates the masculinity of the boy's character. (11) The superego is not simply a residue of the earliest object choices of the id; it also represents an energetic reaction formation against those choices.

Freud stresses the motives for the formation of psychic structure as an attempt to deal with object loss (negative) and also loving, admiring feelings (positive). Both may lead to identification. In this process, energy is desexualized—an issue pursued by Hartmann, among others. The crucial role of identifications (or struggles against identifications), both ego and superego, the greater influence of the earliest identification, and the timetable of character formation, including the necessary resolution of the Oedipus complex before the identifications are sufficiently stabilized, explain the clinical facts.

The introduction of the structural theory presages much of the contemporary view of character and the development of ego psychology. It lays much of the groundwork for the clarification of the key role of identification and inter- and intrasystemic conflicts. It also presents some hints of a developmental line that can be contrasted with the early version (Freud, 1908a) and its primary emphasis on vicissitudes of the libido as a prime organizer. In contrast, the structural theory presents largely an object-relations model.

Although dealing with other topics, *Beyond the Pleasure Principle* (Freud, 1920) elaborates in greater detail than the paper on "Remembering, Repeating and Working Through" (Freud, 1914) the concept of repetition compulsion as it applies to character.

> What psycho-analysis reveals in the transference phenomena of neurotics can also be observed in the lives of some normal people... The compulsion which is here in evidence differs in no way from the compulsion to repeat which we have found in neurotics, even though the people we are now considering have never shown any signs of dealing with a neurotic conflict by producing symptoms. Thus, we have come across people all of whose human relationships have the same outcome: such as the benefactor who is abandoned in anger after a time by each of his protégés, however much they may otherwise differ from one another, and who thus seems doomed to taste all the bitterness of ingratitude... or, again, the lover each of whose love affairs with a woman passes through the same phases and reaches the same conclusion [Freud, 1920, pp. 21–22].

This description was to be elaborated later in Alexander's concept of the fate neurosis. Although it purports to demonstrate the strength of the repetition compulsion as it applies to pathological character traits—particularly those involving some unpleasure—there is no fundamental reason to assume that other phenomena in mental life are not directed by repetitive strivings, character being such a phenomenon.

In *Group Psychology*, Freud (1921) stresses the unifying or synthetic aspect of character formation—an idea that had first arisen in 1900 and then been lost sight of, though the later version is more complicated than the former. Freud compares those processes in the formation of the ego with the coordination of all the sexual instincts into a definitive genital organization. He states further that the unification of the ego is liable to the same interferences as that of the libido. Freud takes pains to show that unless there is a special situation, such as the increase in cathexis of an unconscious fantasy, the unconscious will tolerate conflicting tendencies without production of a pathological outcome—an important point in considering the relation between character and normality.

An important passage in *Inhibitions, Symptoms and Anxiety* clarifies the relation between character and neurosis. Freud contrasts the end results of reaction formations in obsessional neurosis with those in hysteria. In the former, one may speak of widespread effect, having the universality of a character trait, whereas in the latter, the reaction formations are confined to particular relationships. "A hysterical woman, for instance, may be specially affectionate with her own children whom at bottom she hates; but she will not on that account be more loving in general than other women or even more affectionate with other children" (Freud, 1926, p. 158). Freud then deals with the obvious question—what then are the characteristics of the hysterical personality? He refers to their tendency to scotomize as the particular way the anticathexis operates. Though this mechanism is described in general terms, it is possible to derive a number of character traits from it.

At this time, the model for character formation was still derived from analogies made with the processes in obsessional neurosis. This has obvious important consequences. "These reaction-formations of the obsessional neurosis are essentially exaggerations of normal traits of character formation..." (p. 157). They should be regarded, according to Freud, as yet another mechanism of defense and placed alongside regression and repression. The reasons for this choice lie in the greater clarity with which it is possible to observe the fate of some of the ideational representatives of the forbidden instincts: "the ego is... much more... the scene of action of symptom formation in obsessional neurosis than it is in hysteria..." (p. 119).

As Freud examines in greater detail some of the common defense mechanisms in obsessional neurosis, he anticipates the principle of multiple function as he realizes that the behaviors of undoing and isolation also express the very instincts they are attempting to avoid. As the mechanisms of defense are thus described and broadened, their distinction from character traits blurs; one may say that they are a slightly more abstract way of describing a person's behavior and that, on a more directly observational level, it would be possible to infer the operation of a number of character traits derived from them. A careful reading of Freud's use of the term obsessional neurosis suggests that what he has in mind is more the total personality organization of such individuals than just the symptoms.

At this time in his life, Freud's illness made it almost impossible for him to participate in scientific discussions. Nevertheless, he held irregular meetings in the waiting room of his office. Waelder quotes the following anecdote from one of these sessions held some time in 1926 or 1927. Schilder had just presented a multidimensional system of characterology:

As was customary on these occasions, Freud opened the discussion, and in the course of his comments said that he felt like the skipper of a barge who had always hugged the coast and who now learned that others, more adventurous, had set out for the open sea. He wished them well but could no longer participate in their endeavor: "But I am an old hand in the coastal run and I will remain faithful to my blue inlets" [Waelder, 1958, pp. 245–246].

In the last phase of his thinking on character, Freud became concerned with broader issues involving adaptation to one's fate and happiness. A very beautiful passage in *Civilization and Its Discontents* aptly describes this aspect of his work.

> Happiness, in the reduced sense in which we recognize it as possible, is a problem of the economics of the individual's libido. There is no golden rule which applies to everyone.... All kinds of different factors will operate to direct his choice. It is a question of how much real satisfaction he can expect to get from the external world, how far he is led to make himself independent of it, and, finally, how much strength he feels he has for altering the world to suit his wishes. In this his psychical constitution will play a decisive part, irrespectively of the external circumstances. The man who is predominately erotic will give first preference to his emotional relationships to other people; the narcissistic man, who inclines to be self-sufficient, will seek his main satisfactions in his internal mental processes; the man of action will never give up the external world on which he can try out his strength.... Any choice that is pushed to an extreme will be penalized by exposing the individual to the dangers which arise if a technique of living that has been chosen as an exclusive one should prove inadequate [Freud, 1930, pp. 83–84].

The word constitution as used by Freud is a bit misleading. I originally believed it referred to the biological inborn element, but the passage, then, would make no sense—the man of action is not inborn. In this paragraph, Freud uses the word constitution as synonymous with make-up. It includes both biological inborn factors and experiential ones. This is taken up later in his paper on libidinal types (1931), wherein Freud makes a significant contribution in spelling out the requirements for a classification: (1) It "should not merely be deduced from our knowledge or our hypotheses about the libido..."; (2) "it should be easily confirmed in actual experience..."; (3) "it should contribute to the classification of the mass of our observations and help us to grasp them"; (4) the types should "not coincide with clinical pictures [but] must comprehend all the variations which ... fall within the limits of the normal" (p. 217).

The rest of the paper dealing with the attempted working out of a classification based primarily on libidinal types has largely fallen into oblivion. The concept of libidinal types refers mostly to a combination of object relations and innate predisposition. Freud was trying to arrive at a character make-up independent of pathology. The paper's main drawback is its lack of dynamic framework and its distance from more clearly observable character traits. We are fortunate in that Freud saw fit to attempt to summarize some of his more important views in a passage in the *New Introductory Lectures*:

> You yourselves have no doubt assumed that what is known as "character," a thing so hard to define, is to be ascribed entirely to the ego. We have already made out a little of what it is that creates character. First and foremost, there is the incorporation of the former parental agency as a super-ego, which is no doubt its most important and decisive portion, and, further, identifications with the two parents of the later period and with other influential figures, and similar identifications formed as precipitates of abandoned object-relations. And we may now add as contributions to the construction

169

of character which are never absent, the reaction-formations which the ego acquires—to begin with in making its repressions and later, by a more normal method, when it rejects unwished-for instinctual impulses [Freud, 1933, p. 91].

The important aspects of this section are the relegation of character as an aspect of the ego, the primary importance attributed to the role of the superego, and the role of identification as shaping external influences. The internal aspects relate to the defense of reaction formation as the most important mechanism—both in terms of form and content (the incorporation of unwished-for instinctual impulses). This last defense, derived from the early days of analysis and its study of obsessional neurosis, thus remained a cardinal point in Freudian theory. Fenichel, much later (1941, p. 91), classifies character traits into reactive and sublimatory, still attesting to this point of view. I could not be entirely sure of what Freud had in mind when he wrote about the ego's "normal" methods of rejecting unwished-for instinctual impulses. Was Freud alluding to conscious repudiation on the basis of established reaction formation or had he some other mechanism in mind—suppression? Secondary repression? Beyond this passage there are only scant references in Freud that add anything to the above.

In the last few papers, Freud was preoccupied with two themes. (1) The role of trauma in character—in the sense of the overcoming of trauma as playing a role in shaping character and the fixation to trauma which "may be taken up into what passes as a normal ego and, as permanent trends in it, may lend it unalterable character-traits, although, or rather precisely because, their true basis and historical origin are forgotten" (Freud, 1937b, p. 75). This passage describes the working of the repetition compulsion but in a new way, i.e., character as remnants of forgotten events. (2) The last major paper, "Analysis Terminable and Interminable," deals with therapeutic impasses and indirectly with some of the dynamics of unalterable ego states which can take the form of character resistances. Freud hovers between consideration of traumatic versus constitutional factors as limiting factors to the therapeutic effect of analysis. he considers the fixations of defense mechanisms "regular modes of reaction of [a person's] character, which are repeated throughout his life whenever a situation occurs that is similar to the original one" (Freud, 1937a, p. 237).

The constitutional factors described such as adhesiveness of libido, psychical inertia or, in case of women, insoluble penis envy, are open to question as explanatory statements. As Grossman and Stewart (1976) have shown, the so-called resistance of penis envy is capable of further analysis in its pregenital roots of narcissistic hurts. It is not necessarily the bedrock of analytic resistance Freud considered it to be in 1937, when analysis was devoted largely to the understanding of neurotic disorders viewed as regressions from an oedipal situation. In terms of the process of theory building, it may be that when a gap exists in our clinical understanding of a condition, it becomes useful to fall back on "explanations" of a higher degree of generalization. Freud, when faced with certain intractable resistances in analysis, introduced into his theory the concept of psychic inertia, adhesiveness of libido, excessive mobility of libido, and the need to hold on to illness or suffering. Freud hypothesized that these are attributes of the ego, either innate distinguishing characteristics, dispositions, or trends early in life which will, in part, determine the choice of defense mechanisms. This brings us back to the question of temperament—in contrast to that of character.

By this time, Freud had applied many aspects of the theory of neurosis to the form and content of character traits (early trauma, defense, latency, outbreak of neurotic illness, partial return of repressed via character traits either expressing or avoiding trauma, and identification with parents). The major difference would seem to lie in whether pathological outcome, alterations, take place in the ego itself or whether they confront it as alien to it.

In the *Outline of Psychoanalysis*, Freud (1940) added to the above list of traumas "Derivatives and modified products of... early masturbatory phantasies [which] make their way into his later ego and play a part in the formation of his character" (p. 190).

We are fortunate in possessing a brief case history of Freud's, cited as an example of a neurosis including character traits resulting from the combination of several traumas. It is presented in a brief section in *Moses and Monotheism* (Freud, 1937b, pp. 79–80). Briefly, the illustration (which I assume to be the Wolf Man), deals with a little boy witness to the primal scene at an age when he had scarcely learned to speak. Following his first spontaneous emission, neurotic symptoms consisting of insomnia and sensitivity to noises developed; in addition, the little boy's identification with his father aroused his aggressive masculinity; he masturbated frequently and attempted to attack his mother sexually. Following a castration threat, the boy "gave up his sexual activity and altered his character." He became passive and provocative toward the father; he also clung to his mother and became an exemplary boy in school. In puberty, the manifest neurosis emerged with sexual impotence, avoidance of women, sadomasochistic fantasies and, secondary to the pubertal intensification of masculinity, there emerged "furious hatred of his father and insubordination to him... reckless to the pitch of self-destruction. He must be a failure in his profession because his father had forced him into it. [He made no] friends and he was never on good terms with his superiors." After his father's death, he married and "developed a completely egoistic, despotic, and brutal personality, which clearly felt a need to suppress and insult other people. It was a faithful copy of his father as he had formed a picture of him in his memory: that is to say, a revival of the identification with his father which in the past he had taken on as a little boy from sexual motives." Freud considered this last fact an example of the return of the repressed.

172

Can we refer to the traditional view of neurosis: early trauma—defense, latency, outbreak of neurotic illness, partial return of repressed—and see where the concept of character fit in Freud's view? The first reference to character modification—the substitution of passivity for activity and the development of a masochistic provocative attitude during the latency period is a consequence of the castration threat, experienced as a narcissistic mortification. In this context, Freud described a behavioral change as a result of the activation of certain unconscious fantasies. These fantasies could also be described as secondary to new identifications with the boy's view of the mother and abandonment of the identification with the father followed by its replacement by an object tie. The alteration in behavior could also be understood as a negative reaction to the threat, an avoidance. Freud (1937b) states, "These negative reactions too make the most powerful contribution to the stamping of character" (p. 76). He also refers to the compulsive quality of the symptoms, the inhibitions, and the stable character changes (implying, of course, that some changes, as in the case cited, are not stable) to be replaced by others when new conditions (e.g., puberty) prevail.

This compulsive quality refers to the great psychical intensity of the trait and its far-reaching independence of the organization of the other mental processes adjusted to the demands of the real world. When Freud refers to the "inhibition upon the life of those who are dominated by a neurosis" (p. 78), it is clear that he has in mind a global concept combining symptoms, inhibitions, and ego alterations or character traits. As Freud conceptualizes it, the emergence of the character traits of egoism, despotism, and brutality is clearly a consequence of the reappearance of an aspect of identification with the father under the sway of increasing masculine strivings at puberty. One could say that the sadistic coloring reflected an identification with the punitive father and the child's misunderstanding of the primal scene.

Freud also implied that the character traits were a solution to the previous neurotic adjustment (failure in life and in a profession forced on him by the father). The character trait, then, has a more complicated origin than the symptom, representing the result of certain identifications and the attempt of the ego to adjust to previous neurotic illness. The opposite may also be true, that is, "defensive mechanisms, by bringing about an ever more extensive alienation from the external world and a permanent weakening of the ego, pave the way for, and encourage, the outbreak of neurosis" (Freud, 1937a, p. 238). It is important to dwell on this last point because, until then, Freud thought that neurotic character was a consequence and not a causative factor in neurosis. This argument formed the basis of his disagreement with Adler. Freud considered that unconscious sexual conflicts forcing themselves on a relatively weak ego were more fundamental than the ego's attempt to compensate for inferiority as a causative factor. The last passage quoted suggests that a chronic fixity in defense mechanisms, something close to character traits, could, by weakening the ego, encourage the outbreak of neurosis. This, toward the end of his career, represents a considerable enrichment in Freud's views.

SUMMARY

There now remains the task of recapitulating the route that has been followed. As many of the references to character in Freud's work are minor statements interspersed among other current preoccupations, it is unavoidable that the preceding survey leaves one with the impression of a patchwork quilt. Any attempt to synthesize may thus stem more from the writer's need for closure than from any valid description of the evolution of Freud's theory. However, I believe there is some purpose to be served in recalling some of the main way stations previously covered.

The early usage of the term character was nearly synonymous with its lay origin, not being clearly distinguished from behavior. Aside from a few minor references, we find the first serious effort to delineate a truly psychoanalytic concept of character in the section on sublimation in the *Three Essays* (Freud, 1905b). It introduces the concept of transformation of instincts and their relation to individual character traits. As the concept of ego was not developed fully, it was pretty much used interchangeably with that of character. Beyond minor references to the role of masturbation and synthetic aspects of a person's character, we find little until the key paper on anal character (Freud, 1908a). It is hard to appreciate the breakthrough of this short paper—the concept of character as an organization of character traits, belonging together because of certain common origins. A process of development and its timetable were introduced. That much has been added since to our understanding of anal character should not detract from the audacity of the concepts and Freud's idea of establishing a relation between a superficial attribute (a trait) and an underlying organization (the drives). I consider "A Special Type of Object Choice" (Freud, 1910b) an important landmark; it was the first time that a clinical constellation of repetitive behavior was explained on the basis of unconscious fantasies derived from the Oedipus complex. While not clearly characterological, the paper introduces the concept of object relations and types. The next decade witnessed one major advance after another. The cornerstone of this edifice is the paper on "Remembering, Repeating and Working Through" (Freud, 1913). Until that time, Freud had not found it necessary to make this differentiation as long as character traits were thought to be largely determined by instinctual vicissitudes. Additional data on the role of aggression and its fate and the key paper, "Mourning and Melancholia," offered a formulation liking identification, object loss and thereby hints of a developmental process of the ego (Freud, 1917). This was finally clarified with the emergence of the structural theory. Freud (1923) indicated that the character of the ego was a precipitate of abandoned object cathexis and contained the history of those object choices. This view was later to be altered in that it was not deemed necessary to have an abandoned object cathexis as a precondition for identification. The development of the concept of ego ideal and superego allowed more precise formulations, showing the combination of identifications with parental objects and reaction formations to the child's own aggressive strivings. The increasing focus on aggressive drive manifestation led Freud (1920) to a sobering outlook concerning the limits of analysis: *Beyond the Pleasure Principle* introduces the repetition-compulsion. This same caution is again highlighted in the final paper, "Analysis Terminable and Interminable" (Freud, 1937a), with such concepts as psychical inertia and adhesiveness of the libido. Another limiting factor is the impact and effect of trauma. We see offshoots of this in the current controversy between conflict and developmental defect.

As a way of summarizing, I shall list the major determinants of character as they were developed by Freud, more or less historically. These comprise character as (1) a derivative of libidinal drives; (2) reflecting the influence on behavior of certain unconscious fantasies, often masturbatory in nature; (3) an outgrowth of identifications with significant parents; (4) the outgrowth of certain solutions to critical complexes (castration and Oedipus); (5) influenced by constitution; (6) an expression of certain mechanisms of mental functioning—denial, projection, reaction formation, introjection, displacement; (7) a reaction to trauma (positive and negative); (8) a derivative of a conflict involving the superego; (9) a result of an attempt to deal with a neurosis or an ego distortion, or representing the equivalent of well-recognized neurotic symptom formation.

Although we are lacking an overall theory of character, it is possible to organize the above list into a primitive schema. If we conceive of character as an amalgam—an attempted compromise between inner and outer—then a natural ordering presents itself. Constitution and the libidinal drives would be the bedrock. On the most primitive level, these would be influenced by interaction with significant adults, largely through mechanisms of identification. This interaction could be described along several different axes—one would be the organization of unconscious fantasies; another, more complex and implying a developmental thrust, would be the major complexes (Oedipus, castration); still another would be the selection of certain preferred mental mechanisms as methods of solution (denial, reaction formation, projection, and the like). The latest factor, from a developmental point of view, would be the superego. Trauma combines the accidental factor and an economic point of view. Finally, as preferred solutions lead to neurosis or ego distortions, character formation has to deal with these disturbances as further raw material.

Many of the above elements are found in combination; they do not operate in isolation. Nevertheless, some character traits are more easily related to one factor. Thus, obstinacy is certainly clearly an outgrowth of drive transformation and the character type. The exceptions reflect the pressure of the superego.

I believe it is a tribute to Freud that, without meaning to, he outlined the basic elements contributing to character formation. Although the forty years since his death have seen many refinements in his formulations, the core remains as valid today as when it was first described.

REFERENCES

Fenichel, O. (1941). *Psychoanalysis of character Collected Papers Second Series.*
    New York: Norton, 1954.
Freud, S. (1904). Freud's psychoanalytic procedure *S.E. 7.*
——— (1905a). Fragment of an analysis of a case of hysteria *S.E. 7.*
——— (1905b). Three essays on the theory of sexuality *S.E. 7.*
——— (1908a). Character and anal erotism *S.E. 9.*

——— (1908b). 'Civilized' sexual morality and modern nervous illness *S.E.* .9.

——— (1908c). Hysterical phantasies and their relation to bisexuality *S.E.* 9.

——— (1910a). Leonardo da Vinci and a memory of his childhood *S.E.* 11.

——— (1910b). A special type of object choice made by man *S.E.* 11.

——— (1911). Two principles of mental functioning *S.E.* 12.

——— (1912). The dynamics of the transference *S.E.* 12.

——— (1913). The disposition to obsessional neurosis *S.E.* 12

——— (1914). Remembering, repeating and working through *S.E.* 12.

——— (1915a). Instincts and their vicissitudes *S.E.* 14.

——— (1915b). Repression *S.E.* 14.

——— (1915c). Thoughts for the times on war and death *S.E.* 14.

——— (1916). Some character types met with in psychoanalytic work *S.E.* 14.

——— (1916-1917). Introductory lectures on psychoanalysis. Lecture 19, resistance and repression *S.E.* 16.

——— (1917). Mourning and melancholia *S.E.* 14.

——— (1919). A child is being beaten *S.E.* 17.

——— (1920). Beyond the pleasure principle *S.E.* 18.

——— (1921). Group psychology and the analysis of the ego *S.E.* 18.

——— (1923). The ego and the id *S.E.* 19.

——— (1926). Inhibitions, symptoms and anxiety *S.E.* 20.

——— (1930). Civilization and its discontents *S.E.* 21.

——— (1931). Libidinal types *S.E.* 21.

——— (1933). New introductory lectures *S.E.* 22.

——— (1937a Analysis terminable and interminable *S.E.* 23.

——— (1937b). Moses and monotheism *S.E.* 23.

——— (1940 An outline of psychoanalysis *S.E.* 23.

Grossman, W. & Stewart, W. (1976). Penis envy: From childhood wish to developmental metaphor. *J. Am. Psychoanal. Assoc.* 24(Suppl.) 193–213.

Nunberg, H. (1931). The synthetic function of the ego. *In Practice and Theory of Psychoanalysis* New York: Int. Univ. Press, (1948). pp. 120–136

——— & Federn, E., Eds. (1962). *Minutes of the Vienna Psychoanalytic* Society Vol. 1. New York: Int. Univ. Press.

Panel (1957). Preoedipal factors in neurosogenesis. V. H. Rosen, reporter. *J. Am. Psychoanal. Assoc.* 5:146–157.

Stein, M.H. (1969). Problems of character theory. *J. Am. Psychoanal. Assoc.* 17: 675–701.

Waelder, R. (1958). Neurotic ego distortion: opening remarks to the panel discussion. In *Psychoanalysis: Observation, Theory, Application,* ed. S.A. Guttman. New York: Int. Univ. Press, pp. 244–247.

CHAPTER 7

Character: A Concept in Search of an Identity[27]
[(1984). *J. Amer. Psychoanal. Assn.* (32):455–477.]

It is hard to imagine a concept of more everyday concern to our work than character. It is essential in formulating a character diagnosis, and occupies the bulk of our time, particularly in the process of so-called "working through." The majority of patients who come to consult us nowadays hardly ever complain of symptoms. The presenting picture is generally one of vague dissatisfactions in their professional or personal life, or various inhibitions, or an inability to "find themselves." All these are manifestations of character pathology.

In spite of its common appearance, scant reference is made to problems of character and character theory in the current psychoanalytic literature. What we may be witnessing is a process similar to what Sandler (1961), writing about the superego, refers to as the dissolution of an analytic concept.

Introduction of Character in Psychoanalysis

Freud (1908) was able to identify a common clinical picture with three outstanding character traits, dynamically related to one another. He could also identify the origin of these traits as particular vicissitudes of the anal

---

27 I am indebted to the colleagues with whom I have shared early versions of this paper and whose comments have been invaluable: Drs. Robert Grayson, William Grossman, Vann Spruiell, the later Herbert Waldhorn, and Herbert Weiner.

drive and make some guesses about constitutional factors and certain early life experiences which were possibly involved. There is, unfortunately, no other clear-cut easily identifiable clinical picture based on a drive vicissitude that matches the elegance of the one described by Freud.

Freud's paper illustrates very well the double contribution of the psychoanalytic concept of character—first the clinical observation of certain traits as a stable cluster, second the establishment of a relation between a superficial piece of behavior and a deep structure, in this case, an instinctual drive. Thus, character shares in common with many other psychoanalytic concepts the quality of being a bridge or relational structure. Looking at character from this vantage point will be very helpful when we examine the problem of classification.

Freud's interest in 1908 was clearly the clarification of drive theory; hence the deep structure to which behavior was related turned out to be a derivative of a drive. As psychoanalysis progressed new structures of the personality and of its functioning were gradually isolated—certain defense mechanisms (identification, reaction formation) or broader structures (superego). The development of these concepts allowed connections to be established between behavior and some deeper structure other than a drive derivative.

Conceptual Ambiguities in the Definition of Character

Unlike some other terms, character has been afflicted by an unusual degree of ambiguity: there is doubt about its data base and its relation to behavior; what is or is not included under its heading is often ill-defined. The descriptive terms applying to it are taken over from lay language, lacking precision. Character also overlaps a number of other concepts (symptoms, mood, style). Not surprisingly, this confusion is reflected in the different ways psychoanalysts have written about it. In this section, I shall examine some of these problems in greater detail.

Character has in common with many other psychoanalytic terms two levels, a clinical level close to data of observation (character traits) and a more abstract one (character organization).[28] The latter will be dealt with in another paper. On the clinical level, character traits require the isolation and identification of relatively stable patterns of behavior specific to a given individual; from these it is possible to infer character traits. The concept is close to, but not identical with the data of observation. I use the term behavior in its broadest possible context. This includes such concepts as attitudes. Jacobson (1964) has introduced the term "ego attitudes" as defined by "characteristic features which become manifest in the most general way in all mental areas: in a person's ideals and ideas, his feelings, and his behavior" (p. 97). It is necessary to interpret the term ego as referring to the individual as a whole. It would make little sense to attribute attitudes (i.e., a subjective, introspective term) to a structure. Fenichel (1945), likewise, refers to character attitudes and ego attitudes pretty much interchangeably.

A given piece of behavior can be the concrete expression of many different character traits. A person who on the surface appears to say just the right thing might be tactful, hypocritical, adaptable, sensitive to the feelings of others, frightened of offending people, polite, chameleonlike, deceitful. This depends on the situation and on the reconstruction of the motives of the person and some aspects of his inner experience at the time. A character trait is not directly observable; it is inferred. In fact, what is observable in the adult are certain stable, repetitive behavior patterns. Description, often more successfully carried out by a good novelist than by a clinician, has then to be organized along dynamic, structural, and genetic

---

28 I have used the term character to apply to both levels. In general, the context will make it clear whether I am referring to the concrete or to the abstract level.

lines to become truly psychoanalytic. This requires extensive use of clinical observations and inferences. The subjective element in the identification of character traits has been well spelled out by Stein (1969) who alludes to the moralizing tendency, the ill-defined placement on the scale of adaptive versus nonadaptive, the confusing role of reality. A man who fails to respond to some external provocation might be described as cowardly or cool, depending on a complicated combination of external circumstances and inner motivations; a friendly person would be tempted to evaluate him differently from an unfriendly person; a value judgment is involved here as well as some appreciation of the socio-cultural context of the moment. The assessment of character requires that we build into the system the attitude of the person who is placed in the role of the observer. What is special about analysis is not the absence of such biases in evaluation but rather that the analyst is more aware of their existence and their role in shaping his evaluative judgment.

Part of the confusion associated with the concept of character arises from unclarity about its data base. Some authors use behavior (in the sense of activity), others use attitudes, still others refer to traits or even modes of reaction or style, even further adding to the confusion; the range of possible data from which one could infer character is very great indeed—body language, mannerisms of speech, the entire range of expressive movements, posture, gait, dress, to name but a few (see Feldman for a descriptive survey).

I will illustrate the historical aspects of the ambiguity of character through examples of how various authors have approached the descriptive aspect of character. Though Reich (1949) does not give a concise definition of character, he alludes to his conception of the "character of the ego" as the external manifestation of the latter, "also the sum total of the modes of reaction which are specific of this or that personality—that is, a factor which is essentially functionally determined and expresses itself in the characteristic ways of walking, facial expression, posture, manner of speaking—this character of the ego consists of various elements of the outer world of prohibitions, instinct inhibitions and identifications of different kinds" (p. 160). Reich's examples are drawn mostly from the bodily manifestations of behavior in line with his biophysiological approach to psychic energy. Alexander (1923) states, "by a character trait we mean a certain stereotyped attitude in life; those people whom we call neurotic characters show this stereotyped attitude in the whole rhythm of their lives at the most decisive moment and most important turning points" (p. 15). Fenichel writes, "The term character stresses the habitual form of a given reaction—its relative constancy" (p. 467). More recently, Greenson (1967), following Reich, wrote, "The neurotic character refers to the generally ego-syntonic, habitual attitudes and modes of behavior of the patient which serve as an armor against external stimuli and against instinctual uprisings from within" (p. 76).

The ambiguity concerning the definition of "character" has been amply demonstrated by the frequently confusing use of the term by various authors. As an example, Waelder in the paper on "Multiple Function" (1930) writes, "Identification is an attempt to solve tasks in a certain problem situation. It can be designated a character trait, when an individual, in a certain combination of instincts, superego demands, and difficulties with the outer world, regularly finds his way out through identification, as his specific method of solution in a diversity of problem situations" (p. 78). In Waelder's usage, a character trait can be an abstract complicated mental mechanism such as identification as long as this device is stable, repeated, and predictable in a given individual. Rosen (1961) writes, "The term *character* is meant to convey the sense of an over-all expressive style which determines, in ways that frequently can be predicted, how an individual will react to situations or cope with given tasks." In contrast to character, style is not a dynamic concept. It is not a bridging term. It describes broad areas of the person's functioning—more general than traits, and more abstract than observable behavior. Rosen defines it as "a progressing synthesis of form and content in an individually typical manner and according to the individual's sense of 'appropriateness'" (p. 447). There will naturally be a relation between an individual's style and character (Shapiro, 1965). Because of his special interest in style, Rosen chose to express character through that term. Other authors might choose a different emphasis. However, the basic core remains: character on the most descriptive superficial level refers to recurrent, identifiable, stable patterns of the person's functioning.

The ambiguity surrounding character and its delimitations extends to its demarcation from symptoms and moods. For example, the statement "X. is an anxious person" can refer to the person's proneness to develop anxiety reactions with minimal external justification, emphasizing both a symptom and a trait. However, this statement need not imply the presence of actual symptoms, but could refer to a chronic state of being on guard, expecting the worst, which would constitute a character trait. I have alluded above to the distinction between symptom and character trait. Although this distinction may at times be blurred, there is, to my mind, some value in distinguishing between ego-alien disruptive aspects of behavior (symptoms) and generally self-syntonic patterns (character). An individual is able to rationalize a character trait, whereas he will complain of a symptom or be embarrassed by it. There are exceptions to this.

There are other stable characteristics which are generally grouped under the rubric of mood rather than character. The reasons for distinguishing moods from character on a superficial level are clear; moods are primarily affective discharge patterns in contrast to character, which is much more inclusive and nonspecific. Whether to consider mood as an aspect of character or to grant it specific independent status is a secondary question. A statement such as, "He is an angry person" or a "sad person" and other terms of purely affective nature describe the person's basic mood. There is very little psychoanalytic literature devoted specifically to moods. Jacobson

(1964) describes "generalized modifications of all discharge patterns lending to our thoughts, actions and feelings a characteristic color which finds expression in what we call our mood" (p. 133). Weinshel's (1971) description of moods as "complicated psychological configurations, organized structures which encompass behavioral and cognitive elements as well as affective ones," emphasizes the similarity of mood to character. He also remarks that descriptions of character or character traits are often related to the mood of the individual concerned—boredom, bitterness, enthusiasm, smugness, and the like (p. 313). He distinguishes certain moods referred to as cast of mind or temperament which could be included under character specifically because of a "more enduring tendency and their syntonicity with the sense of self" (p. 314). I am in general agreement with Weinshel that certain moods so infuse the personality structure that they give character its stamp. The relation between mood and character is a complex one. If the mood disturbance is pronounced and chronic, it may color whole aspects of the person's functioning. We refer to depressive, hypomanic, or cyclothymic characters. On a less abstract level, we encounter chronic optimists or chronic pessimists. Mood has to be differentiated also from affective disturbances. There may be chronic pessimists who do not suffer from a clinical depression. It is in the nature of moods to "color, or at least overstate one aspect of reality and understate or blot out differing or opposing aspects; they involve, to some extent, mechanisms of denial and distortion of reality" (Jacobson, 1971, p. 87).

Perhaps we could say that mood is an aspect of character. Certain character traits (e.g., passivity) may predispose to certain moods (e.g., boredom). The tendency to moods can be a characteristic either of individuals, as in the expression, "he is a moody person," or of certain phases, particularly adolescence. Mahler (1966) has described the greater tendency for women to have depressive moods as a reaction to certain conflicts of the separation-individuation phase. Aggression and its vicissitudes play key roles in moods, and both self- and object representations are altered.

The Ingredients of Character

Having explored the conceptual ambiguities of the term character, it is now time to spell out what I believe can heuristically be included under its label.

The breadth of attributes included under the descriptive heading of character traits is very great: generous, dishonest, kind, haughty, hostile, impulsive, cold, cheerful, brave, inhibited, superstitious, are all commonly cited traits. They describe generally either ways of relating to people or reacting to situations, or ways of being (attitudes). A character trait will include or be heavily influenced by defenses, but it is more than a defense. It combines references to the person's moral system (dishonest, cheat, liar), to his instinctual makeup (impulsive), to his basic temperament (cheerful, pessimistic), to complex ego functions (humorous, perceptive, brilliant, superstitious), and finally to basic attitudes toward the world (kind, trustful) and himself (hesitant).

The breadth of character is enormous, as the whole of an individual's stable functioning is included under its heading. Character traits then represent an amalgam—a synthesis that expresses under one heading a combination including derivatives of drive, defense, identifications, superego aspects, though certain traits will be more directly determined by one factor. In listing the theoretical points of view from which it is possible to examine character, I shall draw largely from Waelder's (1930) remarks in his seminal paper on the principle of multiple function. The libidinal level has to be considered the prime factor; a close second would be the major mechanisms of defense; a third would be the nature of the person's object relations; next would follow the major fashions in which the person's self-esteem is regulated; other elements would include description of the person's major identifications and an assessment of the person's moral code and values; finally, character implies an adaptive function which has a genetic aspect. The latter refers to the dilemma confronting the child for whom the character trait represents the chosen solution. The concept of character is then a way of relating in a dynamic sense many different aspects of the person's functioning. It falls just a bit short of a complete metapsychological profile.

Here we come to the first major critique of the term. We can apply to it what Glover (1966) wrote about the concept of identity. "It either means little or nothing or comprises the whole of psychoanalytic psychology—the influence of instincts, the development of ego and of object relations, the part played by a sequence of mental mechanisms and finally constitutional and environmental factors. No term that involves such a complicated interaction of factors and phases of development can lay claim to the status of a basic mental concept" (p. 188).

Although I agree with Glover's overall critique, there are certain ways of organizing character that relate it to both current and past objects and have considerable clinical value. Character often includes as one of its components certain fantasies involving the person and an outside agent. The patient's behavior is determined by these fantasies, often unconscious, which the person holds about himself (this includes his past history of object choices), the world at large, and his expectations of how he will or should be treated. The task of analysis is to uncover these fantasies and trace their origins. Seen from the point of view of object relations, the behavior of the patient involves the playing out of a scenario; for example, the patient may play the part of the rebellious child, casting the analyst in the role of controlling mother. The patient is stuck in this repetition because unconscious conflict, in this instance, generally around passivity, allows for no other solution. There is, however, another crucial reason for the maintenance of such character attitudes—their adaptive value at the time of formation of the trait in question. The selection by the child of a particular attitude is often the only way for him to maintain an object tie or is seen as a precondition to being loved or paid attention to.

There is still another way of integrating the interpersonal relation with the intrapersonal or intrapsychic conflict. Character, to the degree it involves another person, can be defined as the development of interpersonal strategies to avoid internal conflict (Glover, 1926).

Problem of Classification

It must be kept in mind that no individual will ever be adequately described by a classificatory label. No two people assigned to the hysterical character category will be alike, nor is it possible to synthesize the complexity of any given character under the label. These terms are only approximate; they convey in shorthand fashion certain major aspects of a person's functioning conveniently grouped under certain headings.

Taken in broad historical perspective, the problems of classification have not altered significantly in form. Character as a concept was not invented by psychoanalysts. In the prepsychoanalytic era, it was variously shared by writers, philosophers, moralists, phrenologists, sociologists, alienists, and physiologists. The classifications adopted were as varied as they were fanciful, influenced by biases, preconceptions, nationalistic views, and class-bound prejudices. Two divergent trends appear very early—one leading to the description of a large number of characters organized around one mode of behavior. This is the so-called literary method. Some of its exponents include Theophrastus, Ben Jonson, La Bruyère, Addison, Steele, and Butler. The second route followed is that of temperament—bound up with the aim of explaining and relating each basic type to bodily humors (the sanguine, melancholic, choleric, and phlegmatic) or bodily types (Sheldon and Kretschmer are more recent examples of this trend). This same trend may be found in our current classification.

On the most concrete level, a number of classifications of traits have been suggested. Fenichel (1945) refers to traits which are all pervasive versus those traits which arise only in certain situations. In the former, the attitudes are nonspecific and indiscriminately maintained toward everybody. Another approach also described by Fenichel is to classify character traits depending on whether the person avoids (phobic attitude) or opposes (reaction formation) the original impulse. Complications arise as there may be reaction formation against reaction formation, and combinations of the two types. On a more general level, Fenichel refers to pathological behavior resulting from the ego's conflict with the id, with the superego, and with reality. More general character types are derived from this last model. Of these three possible classifications, the first is based on purely a descriptive level of observation, the second is based on a mechanism which is inferred (i.e., a dynamic level), the third is clearly a structural classification. Fenichel was dissatisfied with all his efforts. As character is such a global concept, a unilinear classification is bound to rob it of its richness.

Because character does not occupy a well-defined place on the line between health and pathology, classification becomes more complicated. Character is an aspect of the individual's functioning which implies neither health nor pathology. There is no person without a character. Ideally, one would want to develop a classification of character *types* some of which would be pathological, others not. As classical psychiatry and clinical analysis start with pathology, our classification has tended to evolve from our work with character disorders; these clearly imply a pathology of character. On the clinical level, however, the normality or abnormality of a character trait are important issues. There are several vantage points from which one evaluates this: descriptive, dynamic, functional, adaptational, and structural to name the common ones. There may be no good correlation between these approaches. Certain character traits of a narcissistic nature indicative of severe pathology may not interfere with the individual's adaptation, whereas certain traits of shyness or feelings of inferiority based on much higher-level conflicts may cripple the person afflicted with them. Abnormality is a much more ambiguous concept when it comes to character traits as it requires a consideration of the sociocultural setting in which the given behavior occurs. Both internal factors (for example, flexibility of the trait) and external ones need be considered; adaptation is not identical with conforming behavior. In certain situations, rebellion may be a sign of overall strength and autonomy.

The term character disorder has generally been applied to chronic maladaptive patterns, inflexible in nature and generally experienced as ego-syntonic. From a psychoanalytic viewpoint, it should be apparent that a descriptive nosology is insufficient. Criteria for defining what will be considered a disorder are obviously lacking, since there is no easy clear-cut differentiation between pathology and normality in the field of character. This contrasts with neurosis in which the presence of a symptom is always pathological. Character disorders represent malformations of the ego resulting from attempted compromise formation to accommodate conflicting demands impinging on the individual from the four agencies cited by Waelder (1930)—reality, superego, the drives, and the repetition compulsion.

Another term related to character disorder is character neurosis. Waelder (1960) defines this as either the avoidance of an impending neurosis through character changes or the integration of a developing or developed neurosis into the personality by neurotic ego distortion. The term character neurosis is simply a dynamic way of referring to certain types of character disorder which have a particularly close relation to neurosis. A common example would be the integration of an obsessive neurosis into an obsessional character structure.

What do we expect from an overall classification and what are its requirements? In the neglected paper on libidinal types, Freud (1931) spells out the requirements for a psychoanalytic classification:

> It may fairly be demanded that this classification should not merely be deduced from our knowledge or hypotheses about the libido, but that it should be easily confirmed in actual experience, and that it should contribute to the clarification of the mass of our observations and help us to grasp them. It may at once be admitted that these libidinal types... shall not coincide with clinical pictures. On the contrary, they must comprehend all the variations which... fall within the limits of normal [p. 217].

The multiple points of view contributed by psychoanalysis to the study of character is reflected in the confused classification of character according to libidinal type (e.g., anal), neurotic organization (e.g., phobic, hysterical), or mode of relating (e.g., passive, feminine character). Study of the superego indirectly led to the description of certain types, but with no attempt at setting up a classification—e.g., the "exceptions" or "those wrecked by success" (Freud, 1916); The "fate neuroses" belongs here. Interest in the partial instincts also contributed its own nomenclature, e.g., sadistic or masochistic character. Concern with affects and object relations led to further types—the depressive character and the "as-if" character. Clearly not all of these "types" are on the same level of abstraction. Phobic character is a more general category than the "exceptions."

An early attempt to integrate the findings of ego psychology into a classification of character is that by Waelder (1930). Some of the points he made bear repetition. The principle of multiple function allows for a deeper understanding of the relation between the major drive organization and the person's major preferred solution to conflict (generally a defense). Waelder demonstrates convincingly that the form chosen must in some way also allow for the satisfaction of the drive: Identification, when analyzed, has in it a form of oral drive satisfaction; projection allows for a homosexual gratification. Waelder views the drives as primary, fueling all behavior which is then secondarily contained and directed by the ego. The advantage of Waelder's approach is the undoing of the fragmentation characteristic of most other attempts at classification. His work has not been exploited fully. Yet an attempt by Glover (1932) to combine all aspects of an individual's functioning in a systematic ordering dynamically relating character, symptoms, and sexual orientation became so cumbersome and unwieldly as to lose its usefulness. This is a function of the wide scope of character.

Two facts stand out: first, almost any neurosis or syndrome or even affect disturbance of a symptomatic nature can be found to have some underlying characterological formation, dealing with similar conflicts, justifying the use of the same label; second, certain character organizations stand out from a descriptive point of view because of one outstanding feature, or again represent a fit with a well-known literary or fairy-tale figure which encompasses many of the features. More scientific precision could dislodge some of these latter types and reduce them to other terms in our nomenclature. The Don Juan type is most likely a variation on narcissistic disturbances, the Cinderella type, a form of masochistic character. Yet there is something to be said for retaining the vividness and coloring of the literary labels.

Character and the Analytic Situation

Having examined some of the problems, ambiguities, and conceptual issues of the term character trait, it is time to turn to its clinical application. How does it come up in our work? What obstacles are there to its usefulness? What role does it play in our formulations?

Observation and Evaluation

Stein (1969) has described the obstacles to approaching character in our daily work. The first arises from the difficulty in observing character in the analytic situation. The regression induced by the process complicates the task. It is well known that a patient's behavior in the waiting room or after he leaves our office may be markedly different from what we see on the couch. Not all character traits can be readily observed. Some may be quite hidden or defended against, whereas others may be more on the surface. Certain individuals may be more secretive about their character, others more open.

The data we have as analysts derives from our own observations, particularly about the way the patient handles the "real" transactions with us (time, money, cancellation) and the way the patient reacts to us and to our interpretations. We also have as data (more biased) the patient's observations of his own behavior with others or reports about other people's comments about him. Finally, we have the so-called transference resistances, perhaps the most important leverage in bringing character into the analytic situation.

On the clinical level, character traits represent the way an outside observer (the analyst) classifies and organizes repetitive aspects of the behavior of the person under observation. As such, character traits are observable by others, but not easily liable to introspection. Confronting a person with some aspect of his character often arouses anxiety or anger. Patients will often hear our comments about their behavior as veiled or not so veiled criticism, implying they should change. Why should there be such a reluctance to confront one's own character? What is the dynamic significance of this fact? Do we need to postulate a resistance against becoming aware of this aspect of oneself, or is it in the nature of the beast—that is, one cannot be both inside and outside oneself? Does the traditional reluctance to see ourselves as others see us emanate from a narcissistic investment in maintaining an ideal self-image, so that comments about ourselves are heard as criticism to be shunned or praise to be embarrassed about? One aspect of the resistance to facing one's character is related to the tendency to moralize about character or to hear references to one's character as critical; this can be understood from the developmental point of view. There is an intimate connection between the process of character formation and the formation of the superego. Character traits are formed in large part in relation to parental standards and as a solution to external pressures (via submission or rebellion); character formation is not completed until a firm superego (and ego) become established. A second aspect of the difficulty patients experience in facing their character is related to the different language of inner and outer experience. Behavior is, after all, a complicated compromise—the end result of conflicting tendencies only some of which are capable of entering consciousness. The person who is stingy does not experience himself that way. His inner sense may be that he should be careful and save his money, for he is uncertain what future catastrophe might befall him—though he may be conflicted about his behavior and react with guilt or shame when it is pointed out to him. When seen from the inside, behavior is no longer character but is a reflection of self-image or self-representation. Character then would represent the behavioral aspects of self-representations. Only a small portion of the latter are capable of introspection, depending on their relation to conflict and the individual's ability to tolerate facing less desirable aspects of himself. Yet, after a successful analysis, we expect that a patient will have gained a good bit of insight into his behavior and will be more aware than before about his character, its rigidities, its limitations and hopefully will have been able to modify certain pathological traits.

Character Resistance and Character Analysis

Glover (1926) remarked that subjecting the seemingly banal routine of everyday life to detailed scrutiny is the best prescription for the conduct of an analysis of character. This is as true now as it was then!

Reich (1949, p. 47) introduced the term character resistance to refer to certain stereotypic, formal aspects of general behavior "the manner of talking, of the gait, facial expression and typical attitudes such as smiling, deriding haughtiness, overcorrectness, the manner of the politeness or of the aggression." These resistances "remain the same no matter what the material is against which it is directed." The distinction between character resistance and transference resistance which Reich introduced is a valuable one. In contrast to transference reactions to the analyst, the character resistances are general, diffuse responses of the patient to people at large and to dangers emanating from his inner world of conflict. In this type of reaction, people are treated in indiscriminate fashion, as though they were all the same. These resistances to be sure, also arise in reaction to earlier experience with significant persons. In one case, a patient had to maintain considerable emotional distance from all persons regardless of sex, age, or character type. This emotional isolation arose as a consequence of certain disturbances in early mothering. The patient's mother, a narcissistic individual, became, in addition, quite depressed following the unexpected death of a child for which the patient was unconsciously blamed. Such so-called generalized transference reactions, as Greenson (1967) coins them, are "characteristic of the patient's object relations in general" (p. 257). They represent frozen residues of past conflicts.

There is an important area of character and behavior not dealt with by Reich because of his focus on character as a frozen final solution—an armor plating as it were. I have in mind aspects of character and behavior that are the resultant of currently active conflicts often dating from childhood.

The classical definition of character as "a once-and-for-all resolution" would seem to disqualify them from being considered a part of character; yet in every other respect, such as stability and repetitiveness, such conflict-related traits must be included. These traits may be closer to symptoms or inhibitions. Examples might include shyness or withdrawal from competitive situations as a result of exhibitionistic conflicts which are unresolved, painfully experienced, and dynamically active in the present. Greenson (1967), in his volume on technique, writes extensively about transference and resistance without any allusion to the concept of character save in a brief passage. He agrees to the necessity of tackling the patient's character traits but does not indicate how and when. This is where the art rather than the science of our discipline enters. There are clearly no hard and fast rules, and each practitioner will develop his personal style and approach. The most difficult character traits to deal with are related to the hidden or latent resistances described by Glover (1955). The patient will very subtly distort the analytic process, or the analyst will become numbed to the destructive effect of certain chronic attitudes. A patient of mine, behind a compliant attitude, would offhandedly refer to the fact that bosses in his institution were heavy-handed in their use of authority. He did not trust people to have his interest at heart, and played his cards close to the chest. It was very difficult for me to demonstrate the same pervasive attitude in the treatment toward me, particularly as he seemed to listen very closely to what I said yet subtly ignored the substance of my communications. This patient's reaction was almost always the same—he would feel hurt, criticized, and would desperately try to modify his behavior so as to conform to what he believed I expected of him. This trait of conforming outwardly while maintaining his inner attitudes unchanged was iron-clad. Analysis of its antecedents, its adaptive value, made little impression on this patient. In this case, severe early trauma and defective mothering had seriously impaired the flexibility of the patient's character and limited the development of nondefensive self-observation.

It is possible to describe the more obvious obstacles to analysis either in terms of traits (impulsivity, tendency to act out, inability to tolerate frustration, unreliability, excessive passivity, dishonesty) or in terms of various ego and superego functions. The former are closer to clinical observation and hence easier to validate. There are certain global qualities, such as psychological mindedness or motivation, which depend in part on the presence of certain character traits (curiosity, willingness to wait, tolerance). There are also certain attitudes such as inability to tolerate shame, embarrassment, or criticism which vastly complicate our task.

Beyond the initial screening, many pitfalls await us during the course of treatment. It may not be possible to detect early which character attitudes will make or break an analysis. In one instance, a severely traumatized professional person whose life was in shambles made a dramatic recovery aided by an unusual capacity to observe himself with a wry sense of humor. He was able to take distance from his behavior. He had an unusual degree of motivation and determination to succeed—identifying with his mother who had had to overcome severe odds in her own life.

The opposite problem is illustrated by a young woman referred to analysis because of what looked like a masochistic character disturbance and difficulties in relating to men. Attractive, bright, and apparently motivated for change, she seemed an ideal analytic case. This impression remained for the first few months as she presented many dreams—too many, it seemed. Her daily life all but disappeared from the sessions. A gentle comment to this effect was greeted by shock, silence, and heralded severe narcissistic character resistances. The patient had to control the sessions, would only talk about what she wanted. Any new interpretation dealing with material she decided was inappropriate would be greeted with rage or stony silence.

In spite of fairly severe symptomatology and impaired object relations which caused her pain, the treatment could not really overcome what looked like a wall of narcissistic resistances. Eventually, the treatment was terminated by mutual consent. She was then seen in psychotherapy by another analyst; a similar impasse was reached. This patient had certainly developed very intense negative transference attitudes that could not be analyzed. She often compared the task of associating to being asked to walk unaided into the cage of a tiger.

Character Change in Analysis

There is a wide range of opinion concerning the possibility of character change in analysis ranging from those analysts who feel that structural change is not possible to those who are quite optimistic about character analysis producing more than behavioral adjustments. My own view is cautious optimism. I have no question that the basic core and organization of an individual remains relatively fixed; that is, an obsessional individual will never become a hysteric no matter how long he remains, but if successful, the treatment will alter considerably the degree of his obsessionalism, enable him to make more appropriate object choices, be happier, and so on. Pathogenic fantasies will lose their grip on his behavior which should become less automatic as certain infantile danger situations lose their threatening quality. Competition does not have to entail the elimination of the rival; activity does not have to have a hostile tinge.

Often we understand something about the structure of a given pathological entity after a successful piece of analytic work leads to modification of that structure. What do we find in the domain of character analysis? First of all, it is much more difficult to pinpoint change in a given character trait. The patient may comment on it in passing, or the analyst may conclude that the patient's behavior has changed, for example, that he is less passive. The therapist might be tempted to account for the change in theoretical terms—the working through of conflicts around passivity. Such a formulation tells us very little about the actual process leading to change. Can we discover with the patient what has made a difference from the experiential point of view? Is this a stable or a temporary result dependent on some vicissitudes of the transference? Just as there is a multiplicity of influences that determine the choice of a given character trait which our theory can never fully account for, we are faced with the same problem in accounting for change. This is the problem of determinism—studied particularly by Waelder. Our explanations are shorthand ways of referring to factors influencing a given behavior or change rather than causing it. Can we say anything about the types of traits that remain imperious to analysis? I would imagine that traits which are firmly rooted in the person's constitution or basic instinctual make-up (i.e., belong to a pre-conflict period) are more resistant to change than those based on identifications with early parental figures. Freud observed that masochistic character had a better prognosis in those instances in which the masochism was itself the result of an identification with a masochistic parent. Characteristics related to a person's temperament are probably more fixed than those which are the outcome of conflicts. A slow-to-warm-up child may turn into a somewhat distant, aloof adult with limited capacity to change this basic orientation. We also know that certain character types are more flexible than others. Rigidity is a trait more commonly encountered in obsessionals than in true hysterics. A trait that arises in reaction to a specific situation is more readily changed than a trait that encompasses broader issues. Conflicts around ambition are often difficult to resolve. Pathology rooted in early conflicts and trauma is generally considered more resistive to structural change, yet there are obvious exceptions to this rule. Certain oral characters who need to be needed often respond well to analysis, better than certain anally rooted traits, thus contradicting the hypothesis that traits deriving from earlier phases in life are more stubbornly rooted and, therefore, resistive to change. There is an unavoidable gap then between our theoretical expectations and our clinical findings. This gap exists in other aspects of our work—not only character analysis. However, the relative vagueness of a character trait in contrast to the specificity of a symptom heightens the difficulty.

CONCLUSION

In spite of its confused status as a term, I hope the preceding has demonstrated the need and relevance of character for our theory and our practice. In addition to the role of character in the diagnostic assessment and evaluation of analyzability, character continually confronts us in our daily work as a resistance and also in its intricate relation with neurotic symptoms. From a developmental point of view, we are interested in studying antecedents of both symptoms and character traits. In the treatment, analysis of character traits often leads to states of anxiety and transient symptom formation as the rigid conflict is remobilized. Character formation and neurotic symptoms are both possible paths of conflict resolution, i.e., compromise formations. Even descriptively, the borderline between symptoms and neurotic character traits is blurred. Both are also liable to the same type of analysis—descriptive, economic, dynamic, and adaptive. Character allows certain issues to be redefined by relating a superficial aspect of behavior to a deep structure derived from our theory of mind. It highlights the way in which defense, identifications, and instincts mold stable behavior. It provides the most clinical way we have of pinpointing, in clear and communicable fashion, stable attributes of the individual. It presents us with a clinical language through which we can define structure and the role of fantasy.

SUMMARY

I have attempted to clarify the clinical usage of the concept of character. I have examined such terms as character trait, character, and character disorder. I have described various schemes of classification, and have proposed key definitions for the above terms. I have described the unique aspect of character, that is, its capacity to establish a relation between a superficial attribute and a deep structure. Finally, I have suggested that character represents the core of the individual from a particular point of view—a precipitate of a person's relations to the outside world.

REFERENCES

Alexander, F. (1923). The castration complex in the formation of character. *Int. J. Psychoanal.*4:11–42.

Fenichel, O. (1945). *Psychoanalytic Theory of Neurosis.* New York: Norton.

Freud, S. (1908). Character and anal erotism.. *S.E.* 9.

——— (1916). Some character types met with in psychoanalytic work .*S.E.*14.

——— (1931). Libidinal types. *S.E.* 21.

Glover, E. 1926 The neurotic character. *Int. J. Psychoanal.* 7:11–30.

——— (1932). A psychoanalytic approach to the classification of mental disorders. In *On the Early Development of Mind.* New York: Int. Univ. Press, 1956 pp. 161–186.

——— (1955). Counter-resistance and counter-transference. In *The Technique of Psychoanalysis.* New York: Int. Univ. Press, pp. 88–107.

——— (1966). Metapsychology or metaphysics. *Psychoanal. Q.*35:177–19.

Greenson, R. (1967). *Technique and Practice of Psychoanalysis.* New York: Int. Univ. Press.

Jacobson, E. (1964). *The Self and the Object World.* New York: Int. Univ. Press.

——— (1971). *Depression.* New York: Int. Univ. Press.

Mahler, M. (1966) Notes on the development of basic moods: the depression affect. In *Psychoanalysis: A General Psychology, ed.* R.M. Loewenstein et al. New York: Int. Univ. Press, pp. 152–168.

Reich, W. (1949). *Character Analysis.* New York: Orgone Institute Press.

Rosen, V. (1961). The relevance of "style" to certain aspects of defence and the synthetic function of the ego. *Int. J. Psychoanal.* 42:447–457.

Sandler, J. (1961). On the concept of the superego. *Psychoanal. Study Child* 15:128–162.

Shapiro, D. (1965). *Neurotic Style.* New York: Basic Books.

Stein, M.H. (1969). The problem of character theory. *J. Am. Psychoanal. Assoc.* 17:675–701.

Waelder, R. (1930). The principle of multiple function. In *Psychoanalysis: Observation, Theory, Application,* ed. S.A. Guttman. New York: Int. Univ. Press, 1976 pp. 68–83.

——— (1960). *Basic Theory of Psychoanalysis.* New York: Int. Univ. Press.

Weinshel, E. (1970). Some psychoanalytic considerations in moods *J. Am. Psychoanal. Assoc.* 51:313–320.

CHAPTER 8

Character, Character Type, and Character Organization

[(1989). *J. Amer. Psychoanal. Assn.* (37):655–686.]

ABSTRACT: This paper explores the relevance of the concept of character organization for psychoanalysis and argues for its usefulness in preserving what is specific to character. Character organization is viewed as a bridge concept between the observable and the structural, the role of fantasy and object relations in development, and as a convenient way of describing certain global phenomena not easily encompassed by the structural theory or compromise formation.

In a previous paper (1984), I outlined two levels of the concept of character—a clinical one concerned with character traits, and a more theoretical one dealing with the general organization of character. It is to this second level that this paper addressed itself. By and large, this aspect of character has been neglected in the literature.

I take the position that both character traits and character organization make important contributions to psychoanalytic theory: (1) character serves as a bridge concept between the observable (behavior or attitudes) and a deep structure; (2) character offers a way of conceptualizing nonconflictual elements in personality organization; (3) character allows for a convenient way of integrating the role of object relations and of fantasy in structure; and (4) character enables us to talk in a nonreductionistic fashion about certain global issues relating to self, style, identity, and family interactions. I will show that it is possible to relate some aspects of character to the structural theory without doing violence to either. I take a position against reducing all mental products to compromise formation, and also emphasize the profound differences between character and symptom, both clinically and developmentally. Finally, I shall argue for the relevance of character structure in adaptation.

I shall define the terms *character, character type*, and *character organization*, and briefly review Freud's views, using the anal character as a model. I shall examine (1) the relation between character and the structural theory; (2) the relation between character and symptom; and (3) the development of character; (4) the adaptive nature of character.

By character, I mean the broadest grouping of stable, typical traits and attitudes by which we recognize a particular person. Our concept of character is made necessary by the fact that we find in individuals recurrent clusters of traits with a degree of consistency suggesting that some underlying principles govern the selection, ordering, and relations of these traits to one another. Psychoanalytic theory attempts to explain and justify which attributes are selected and why they are selected. It also tries to explain in terms of basic psychoanalytic concepts why certain clusters of traits occur together with a greater than chance frequency. How are the various levels of character related to each other? From observable behavior, we isolate recurrent stable modes of reactions and attitudes from which we infer character traits.29 This term is close to the data of observations, requires minimal inference, and can serve as a useful marker for the development of identifications

---

29 To arrive at a character trait, we have to take into account intentionality. Consider a child who frequently behaves in a manner that provokes his parents. The effect of such behavior is that the parents become angry; but, is that the child's intent or motive? In fact, several different intents may underlie the behavior—one may be to provoke punishment, another might be to gain (through a beating) reassurance from an absent, abandoning, punitive mother. Although the behavior may be superficially the same in various individuals, the character and underlying motives may be quite different.

and object relations within a broad context of adaptation. This concept of trait also serves as a signpost of resistance within the analytic situation, and its alterations give valuable indicators of therapeutic progress. Once we arrive at the identification of a number of traits, we attempt to infer the simplest organizers to account for their grouping. If the organizer is inclusive enough, it may be found in the nomenclature as a classificatory label for the individual. We refer to this label as *character type*. From our study of character types, we attempt to arrive at principles on a general level which account for the *origins, existence*, and *structure of character* as a whole. I shall refer to these principles as *character organization*. In order to make of character a psychoanalytic concept, we need to relate the clinically observed traits to our traditional metapsychological points of view (dynamic, structural, economic, adaptive, and genetic), and to the accepted concepts that characterize our approach: the drives, conflict, defense, resistance, the dynamic unconscious, and the principle of multiple function. Without these underlying concepts, a descriptive organization would not be psychoanalytic; rather, it would revert to the worst nosological confusion, characteristic of the current *DSM III* (American Psychiatric Association, 1982) classification and its mechanistic orientation.

The Anal Character as Model

My purpose in considering the anal character from a historical point of view is to demonstrate how a relatively simple organization of three traits, first described in 1908, grew in complexity and came to include many of the core concepts in analysis related to character—instinct, defense, identification, aggression, superego, perception, memory, autonomous functions, narcissism, and trauma.

Freud (1908) in his classic paper, "Character and Anal Erotism," remarked, "our attention is drawn to the behaviour in his childhood of one of his bodily functions and the organ concerned in it" (p. 169). Appropriately enough, Freud coined the term "anal character." The related term "obsessive-compulsive" highlights the presence of clinical symptomatology—obsessions or compulsions.

A careful reading of the paper on anal character reveals the many embryonic elements of a theory of the mind including aspects of development, etiology, mental mechanisms (dynamics), and economics. Based as it is on Freud's topographic model and instinct theory, it is very much an economic model derived from hydrodynamic concepts such as "damming up" and "alternate pathways of discharge." The anal character was the first character type to be described by psychoanalysis. Freud clearly established a relation between the three traits of obstinacy, parsimony, and orderliness and the anal instinctual level. It is not emphasized enough that, from a historical point of view, the concept of anal character is the first character type that is truly analytic. In contrast to the Don Juan type or "the exceptions," which can be described without recourse to analytic concepts, the anal character requires the instinct theory to account for the grouping of the three classic traits. Moving on to the description of the defensive organization in anal character, Freud (1926) showed in *Inhibitions, Symptom and Anxiety* that the behavioral attitudes from which the typical defense mechanisms are inferred (isolation, reaction formation, undoing) also include drive manifestations. In addition, the patients' cognitive style (memory—attention to detail) is consonant with the interplay of drive and defense. We also anticipate a highly developed self-critical attitude and difficulties with direct expression of aggression.

These widely different aspects of functioning are related to one another in dynamic and economic fashion. In the case of obstinacy, the basic ingredients include vicissitudes of aggression toward an object resolved via internalization of an early conflicted object relation, incorporating both drive and defense aspects. Parsimony also includes both a vicissitude of the anal drive and a self-image. As the theory grew in complexity, the concept of anal character was expanded to include other layers of instinctual organization, both libidinal and aggressive, and many other mechanisms and aspects, such as narcissistic issues, identifications, and the overcoming of traumas. However, as the contributions of K. Abraham and E. Jones have amplified, there remains a particularly compelling connection between the anal phase of development and many related behavior manifestations in these individuals.

Character and Ego: Structural and Functional Relations

In this section I shall address (1) the relation of character to the tripartite model, (2) the question of the autonomy of character, and (3) the relation of fantasy and of object relations to character.

When we speak of anal character, we have a descriptive entity, that is, a cluster of traits whose grouping requires some explanation. It is not an agency in the sense of the ego, i.e., having energy at its disposal. One cannot ascribe causal effects to it, and it has no explanatory value *per se* in accounting for behavior. It is tautological to state that a person behaves stingily because he is an anal character. Although character is related to the ego, it is on a level of abstraction different from that applicable to the tripartite model.

Character and the Tripartite Model

I take the position that it makes the most sense to describe the development of character to the ego as the seat of the synthetic and integrative function of the personality. This position has been well elaborated by Reich (1933), and Fenichel (1945) who writes:

> The dynamic and economic organization of its [i.e., the ego's] positive actions and the ways in which the ego combines its various tasks in order to find a satisfactory solution, all of this goes to make up character [p. 467].

Fenichel is thereby describing character as an aspect of the synthetic function of the ego, perhaps its best example.

Although it is customary to stress the synthetic or unifying aspect of character, we are all aware in our everyday experience of the degree of contradiction and incompatibility tolerated by the ego. A substantial part of our work consists in confronting patients with these glaring inconsistencies, which, through a combination of denial, rationalization, splitting, and disavowal are so blithely tolerated.

It is not easy to relate global concepts such as character, self, or identity to such terms as the ego. Freud uses "ego" in various ways in his writings, resulting in ambiguity and confusion. As Hartmann (1952) observes, Freud sometimes uses the term ego in a descriptive sense, as referring to the person as a whole; sometimes as a differentiated organ on the surface of the body, as in the first topographic model; and, finally, as one of the three structures of the mental apparatus.

We find a similar ambiguity permeating the concept of character. It is sometimes used in the sense of a loose descriptive entity—little more than an attempt to group together under some heading a cluster of traits which occur frequently in clinical practice. Sometimes character is used in a more rigorous sense as referring to a structure at a level of abstraction different from that applicable to the tripartite model. At times, character is seen as a resultant of certain functions of the ego, and at other times as giving form to the ego, determining and causing behavior. Schafer (1979) clearly spells out the inconsistency of these last two positions. Part of the confusion is that in psychoanalytic writings, function, genesis, properties, and results or end products are not always clearly differentiated. Character trait as a clinical term is sometimes confused with character organization or with character formation.

Character traits are compromise formations which are the end product of the operation of many ego functions (synthetic, defensive, adaptive). Character is not the synthesis, but is the end result of the synthesis. Once character is formed, we speak of the ego as rigidified, altered, or hardened. This is obviously a metaphor to allude to the clinical fact that a person's patterns of reaction, once laid down, remain relatively fixed. We then apply the same adjective to the structure.

As is not atypical for Freud, there is some ambiguity in the relationship he sees between ego and character. [30] In a paragraph describing the crucial role of identification as a substitution for object cathexis in the formation of the ego, he writes:

> ...we have come to understand that this kind of substitution has a great share in determining the form taken by the ego and that it makes an essential contribution towards building up what is called its "character" [Freud, 1923, p. 28].

---

30 If we disregard the Project (1895), the concept of character functioned as Freud's first structural theory, coming some sixteen years before The Ego and the Id (1923). There are kernels of ideas related to character to be found earlier, however, in his concept of "alteration of the ego." This concept was developed as early as Draft K (1896a), and amplified in "Further Remarks on the Neuropsychoses of Defence" (1896b). Freud makes further occasional reference to this term in the 1915 paper, "Repression," and finally in his last paper on splitting in the process of defense (1940).

In this sentence, does Freud mean that character is a substructure of the ego or does he use the word character to refer to a specific attribute which would distinguish the workings of the ego in one person from those in another?[31] If the latter, then one could, in theory, also refer to the character of the superego or of the id. In practice this is not done. We may refer to the superego as harsh or corruptible, but this is a shorthand way of describing in a metaphorical sense the workings of a structure. There is no direct behavioral counterpart since, by definition, all behavior is channeled through the ego, as the executive agency of the total personality. We think of the superego as influencing the nature of a person's character by its effect on the ego. We do not refer to the form of superego functioning as its character. We think of such traits as honesty, lying, and cheating as reflecting particularly the influence of the superego. Behavior, action, and attitudes, however, are the province of the ego, though influenced by the other systems.

Stating that character is a resultant of functions of the ego tells us nothing new either about the ego or about character—rather it flows from the way we have defined our terms. The issue of definition traps us in that we can arrive at statements which only restate our terms. In this case, as the relation between ego and character is confusing, let us instead turn to what is meant when we apply the term structure to character.

By definition, the concept of structure implies stability. In contrast to symptoms, which are transient, character achieves a fairly permanent, fixed solution to a conflict. Character can be described as a limitation of the

---

31 For a different interpretation of the same issue, see Boesky (1983) who tackles some problems relevant to my paper. Boesky takes the position that character is influenced by all psychic structures and therefore not only relegated to the ego. He also feels that the concept of character organization is widely unnecessary and should be deleted from our vocabulary. I believe Boesky is combining two different ideas: first, that character is propelled by drives and superego and influenced by constitution; second, that character cannot be reduced to the ego because of that fact. I do not see any logical difficulty in having an aspect of the ego influenced by other mental structures. This is clearly stated in Waelder's (1930) paper on multiple function.

freedom of choice available to an individual. It functions as switch points, favoring certain directions in the person's behavior or attitudes. For example, being given an order by a boss is understood only in terms of an invitation to submit. The fixity of character traits in no way relates to the presence or absence of current conflict, a point not stressed sufficiently by Wilhelm Reich. In adults, character is resistant to change and capable of "influencing" a wide variety of attitudes and behaviors.

This position might seem to contradict my earlier statement that character is a purely descriptive entity, but a clinical example will illustrate my point. A person who is stingy will, if called upon to be generous, develop anger or anxiety, or will rationalize and flee from the situation altogether. Except in rare circumstances, he will not be able to avoid acting on his customary beliefs and attitudes. Else, he is said to act "out of character," exhibiting behavior that requires explanation, since character implies a degree of predictability in behavior. It is possible that the person may at some point be ashamed of his stinginess and attempt to hide it through reactive generosity, or he may develop guilty reactions or self-punitive attitudes or even a compulsive symptom.

Character and Autonomy

In general, character attributes are quite stable even in situations of stress or danger. This stability can be thought of along several axes; one would be rigidity or flexibility—superordinate to the recognizable character traits; another is autonomy. Rigidity refers to the person's inability to alter his behavior even when internal or external circumstances would make such a change appropriate or adaptive. It may be related to stubbornness and is different from persistence, though the differentiation may well include a subjective element! The secondary autonomy of character, which can also be described as relative stability or instability, refers both to the end stage of a developmental process leading to relative independence from conflict and to the protection of character against instinctualization and regression. This protection is relative and not absolute. Some patients have a tendency to regress considerably under states of stress, fatigue, or illness. Should we think of this regression as behavior change or character change? To avoid confusion, I prefer to view the regression as a behavior change which reflects certain aspects of character makeup. For a given behavior to reflect true character change, we require a modification of some deeper structure, such as an unconscious fantasy. This is certainly true in analytic work when we refer to structural change (see Schafer, 1979).

Issues of autonomy also refer, in a more personal sense, to the subjective feeling we have of acting as more or less independent and free-willed agents. Such issues of overall functioning cannot really be accounted for by reducing them to structural components which refer to functions rather than to personal experience. This is where such concepts as self and identity, although retaining some imprecision in their boundaries and status, make an important contribution to psychoanalytic theory. Indeed, character and self share certain common areas. Stable attitudes held by a person can be seen as either part of the self or part of character. It should not come as a surprise to find that similar problems in relating the descriptive to the structural plague the concept of self, well described by Meissner (1986). To wit, is the self to be regarded as representational or structural? Meissner sees the self as "an intrapsychic entity which serves as a frame of reference or an organizing principle for integration of the interactions of other psychic structures" (p. 384). This interaction often mirrors early infantile object relations.

Character, Fantasy, and Object Relations

Can we describe the way in which a mental content leads to or becomes part of a structure? What is the internal structure that reflects the constraints of character? On a clinical level it can be described as a set of fantasies which, as Grossman (1984) points out, are both mental content and organization or structure. It is fantasies that determine the form behavior will take. Fantasies are compromise formations which, once formed, become part of the mental organization affecting a wide variety of behaviors. A particular fantasy can influence more than one trait—in fact, it can color an entire character. The converse relation is also varied. A particular trait may be the outcome of more than one unconscious fantasy. Examining character from the point of view of object relations is, to my mind, quite congenial to the concept of character. I suggested in my earlier paper (1984) that many character traits or attitudes can be seen as the enactment of certain unconscious expectations the person has about himself, the world at large, and the relation between the two. These fantasies often reproduce some past crucial relationship. It is also possible to include the contribution and influence of the superego under this heading—the superego being a prime example of the internalization of a very specialized relation to the parents' values and expectations. Fenichel alludes to it as the best example of the formation of sublimatory character traits. The central role of identification with positive attributes of the parents fosters development of the nondefensive aspect of character.

The concept of character as seen particularly from the viewpoint of internalized object relations has been most extensively developed by Kernberg (1976), who takes the position that character can be seen as structured object relations, although he does not clearly spell out the way in which object relations, a representational concept, becomes structured.

215

The character structure is also under the influence of intrapsychic and actual relations with others, the activation of self and/or object aspects by means of character traits in interaction with others implies the attribution of reciprocal roles to such persons. In more general terms, the internal world not only shapes the perception of the external one but influences by means of the character structure the individual's interpersonal field. Some people have the capacity to bring out the best in others; other people bring out the worst [pp. 74–75].

Character, as Kernberg sees it, is a manifestation of the organization of basic units which he views as including affective state, object representation, and self-representation. It is the outcome of identificatory processes which lead to internalized object relations. These are then stabilized and become character patterns.

We may summarize the relation between character and structural theory as follows: As character encompasses most of the functioning of individuals, there are many different ways of describing its component parts from a structural point of view. In my previous summary of Freud's work (Baudry, 1983), I listed a number of them. The list, which is quite comprehensive, includes such items as defenses, instincts, identification, reactions to trauma, and the like. Each can be seen as a component and could, in theory, serve as an organizer.

We define the ego by its functions; the end products of the operation of these functions are a set of compromise formations, such as unconscious fantasies. These reflect themselves in the person's behavior; some are enduring, others are transient. The organized, enduring, stable traits we choose to call character. We observe these traits and allied behaviors and derive from them a character type. Our theory tries to account for their origins and interrelations according to psychoanalytic assumptions and hypotheses about the mental apparatus. Because of their stability and slow rate of change, these traits can be considered as a type of microstructure. Various authors have struggled with the attempt to reconcile character with the structural theory. Boesky (1983) comes to a solution which discards the concept of character organization altogether. Although he accepts as clinically useful the concept of character traits, he reduces character to concepts of multiple function and compromise formation achieving a dissolution of character. To my mind, this does away with what are the specific attributes of character, particularly the complex nature of the relation of the individual to the outside, including the important people in the past, and the way these relations have been internalized. Kernberg modifies the structural theory by adopting a different organizer—that of object relations—which is more congenial to the concept of character organization. My own work is in the direction of retaining both character organization and structural theory in our conceptual apparatus, as each has specific contributions to make.

Dynamic Point of View: Character, Symptom, Conflict, and Defense

In this section, I shall argue against the recent position most eloquently stated by Brenner (1982) which tends to reduce all mental products to compromise formation and also blurs the boundaries between symptom and character. I shall do this historically, descriptively, and developmentally. I shall also suggest a role for affects other than anxiety and depression in character formation.

In the early days of analysis, a symptom, defined as an ego-alien manifestation, was seen as a relatively simple structure—a compromise between a drive and a defense, primarily a regressive manifestation of some conflict, usually around the oedipal phase. In contrast, a character trait, seen as an ego-syntonic manifestation, was understood as a vicissitude of a pregenital drive, a fixation as a result of conflict which was less defined than was the case in symptom formation. Regression, as Arlow (1963) spells out in a lucid article, is a keynote of most symptom formation in adults but does not occur as frequently in character formation. Freud originally thought that sublimation and reaction formation, the key mechanisms responsible for character formation, acted primarily against pregenital drives, particularly sadism and anality. He developed this point of view because his ideas about character represented little more than an extension of his understanding of obsessional neurosis and its characterologic underpinnings.

Freud's first anxiety theory was based on economic considerations. Pathological conflict resulted from the increased quantity of drive energy which the individual could not discharge or master, necessitating some defensive measure. Such considerations crept into the character model and remained a permanent fixture in the writings of Wilhelm Reich, who stressed the timing and frustration of drives as a key element in character pathology. Even though the focus of interest has shifted to the workings of the ego, we have kept an economic model, as when we speak of the strength of the integrative and synthetic capacity of the ego and the regulatory principles of mental functioning.

Continuing the comparison with symptom, I shall now focus more critically on the role of conflict (whether intrasystemic, intersystemic, or with an external agent) in the formation of character. Conflict will influence the content, the quality, and the nature of the resulting traits, but character formation itself is a normal outcome of maturation and development, of which conflict is only a component. As analysis observes human behavior from the perspective of conflict, it can say relatively little about the formation of character outside this sphere. I shall pursue this issue in greater detail in the sections on development and on adaptation.

Character formation and symptom formation have different degrees of efficiency of conflict resolution. Freud wrote in 1913 that what distinguishes character development from the mechanism of neurosis is the absence of any miscarriage of repression or "return of the repressed" in the former. "In the latter, repression either does not come into action or smoothly achieves its aim of replacing the repressed by means of reaction-formations and sublimations" (p. 323). This statement does not imply the absence of conflict, but rather that the eventual compromise is reached via a different route—an alteration of the ego—a transformation which is difficult to conceptualize, particularly as it is a process that generally requires considerable time, in contrast to circumstances associated with symptom formation.

Freud's (1913) statement shows the influence of an early phase of his thinking, when he conceived of character traits primarily in terms of vicissitudes of instincts (reaction formation, sublimation). At that time, a symptom was seen as a compromise formation resulting from a failure of defense; it signified the return of the repressed. This was largely an economic view. As the transformation of drive derivative into character trait was thought to take place directly, there was no need to postulate a repressive mechanism. Freud never referred directly to this process again, but in all likelihood he altered his view as the complexities of character formation became clearer to him. In 1915 he wrote about repression in obsessional neurosis:

> The effect at an early stage of the work of repression is quite different from what it is at a later one. At first the repression is completely successful; the ideational content is rejected and the affect made to disappear. As a substitutive formation there arises an alteration in the ego in the shape of an increased conscientiousness, and this can

hardly be called a symptom. Here, substitute and symptom do not coincide [pp. 156–157].[32]

Although Freud goes on to discuss the return of the repressed, there is little doubt that this alteration in the ego is in fact the precursor of what later turns out to be a character trait. Our clinical experience certainly suggests that the conflicts which are resolved through the formation of character traits are for the most part totally outside the realm of consciousness. As Reich (1933) writes,

> The establishment of a character trait, therefore, indicates the solution of a repression problem, a tendency of the ego to bring about unification of different psychic strivings. These facts explain why it is so much more difficult to eliminate repressions which have led to the formation of well-established character traits than repressions which led to a symptom [p. 161].

It could be said that character depends on the development of interpersonal strategies in order to avoid or minimize internal conflict, both inter- and intrasystemic. This has considerable adaptive value. Tampering with this equilibrium naturally arouses considerable opposition.

Once established, the formation of character makes repression less necessary, particularly in those instances in which the conflict is no longer active. This might result from the ego's abandoning certain pursuits. For example, a man with a passive-feminine character might resign himself to not trying to establish a relationship with a woman. The energy of the warded-off instinctual impulses is used in the maintenance of the anticathexis—

---

32 It is of historical interest that Freud retains here an old idea which first appeared in the 1896 paper on defense neuropsychoses.

the defense that becomes rigidified in the character trait. In the process of character formation, certain impulses may be intensified in the service of defense. For example, certain individuals with a phallic-narcissistic character will demonstrate masculine, active strivings as a defense against feminine, passive wishes associated with fantasies of anal penetration.

In other instances, the picture may shift from character to symptom under the pressure of anxiety or other distressing affects. A symptom may represent the inability of a character structure to master a particular conflict. An example occurred in a young student who had an unusual need to do everything perfectly, a significant character trait, based in part on the wish to compete with her siblings who were outwardly more successful, and replace her mother with her father. These wishes had been accompanied by considerable guilt which showed itself in bouts of self-destructive behavior. In her second year of college, her lack of success in her social life led to considerable turmoil in her ability to concentrate on her work. She noticed that she began to recopy her class notes, allegedly to help her study better. Eventually, the need to recopy the notes began to take over her life—if the letters were poorly spaced or if a word was crossed out, she would recopy the whole page, spending many hours on this project and sacrificing time she needed to study for tests.

Although I have been emphasizing the differences between character and symptom, mention must be made that certain traits are structurally similar to symptoms. That is, they perform similar functions and, most important, are less pervasive of the entire mental apparatus than is true for other character traits. A trait such as excessive cleanliness is closer to neurosis; i.e., it is anchored in similar fixation points and serves to ward off more limited conflicts—for example—around the wish to soil. In contrast, other traits such as frankness or smugness are more difficult to relate to limited conflict resolution and seem to pervade the entire mental apparatus—something less clumsily described in character terms than in id, ego, superego ones.

Character and Defense

The relation between character and defense is a particularly intimate one, both descriptively and genetically. This point is well made throughout Freud's writing as early as Draft K. (1896a), and as late as *Analysis Terminable and Interminable* (1937). Referring to defense mechanisms, Freud (1940) writes in his last paper:

> It sometimes turns out that the ego has paid too high a price for the services they render it. The dynamic expenditure necessary for maintaining them, and the restrictions of the ego which they almost invariably entail, prove a heavy burden on the psychical economy. Moreover, these mechanisms are not relinquished after they have assisted the ego during the difficult years of its development.... But these [i.e., mechanisms of defense] become fixated in his ego. They become regular modes of reaction of his character, which are repeated throughout his life whenever a situation occurs that is similar to the original one [p. 237].

The establishment of fixed defensive modes is a major contributor to the form of the emerging character trait, and it is possible to show how one leads to the other. Thus, a patient who relies heavily on the mechanism of projection can develop several behavior patterns, allowing one to infer different character traits. His readiness to blame the other person may lead him to be suspicious, snoopy, pugnacious, hostile, vindictive or inquisitive, analytic, or curious, depending on many factors including the fate of instinctual vicissitudes and the underlying fantasy that is expressed.

When we refer to defense, we traditionally think of anxiety as a stimulus. However, we should consider the contribution of other affects as stimuli for defense. Following Brenner (1982), I agree that the role of other painful affects such as anger, shame, depression (including reaction to loss) in motivating character defenses has been underplayed, the key role in development having until recently been attributed to anxiety. In light of our increasing understanding of the narcissistic aspect of character and what has been termed narcissistic defenses around issues of shame, embarrassment, and self-esteem maintenance, one cannot stress enough the crucial impact of experiences of humiliation to which the child is continually subject because of his immaturity, small size, and vulnerability. How he deals with such experiences and the resulting affects must have a major influence on his evolving sense of self and on his character formation. In order to master these traumas, he is prodded to adopt a variety of coping styles, some more successful than others.

The lack of development of a theory of aggression and of its various stages hampers efforts at construction of a theory of character. It would be important to sketch a developmental framework of defenses against aggression and its attendant danger situations. Many defenses, such as denial, displacement, reaction formation, projection, identification with the aggressor, undoing, turning on the self, are particularly prominent. In fact, the list includes most, if not all, of the mechanisms listed by Anna Freud (1936)! Could it be that the topic of aggression was very much a latent content of the clinical work, initially hidden behind the interest in the vicissitudes of sexuality? It came into its own along with the development of character analysis and the pioneering work of Abraham (1949) and Reich (1933). The latter has emphasized the binding of aggression in the formation of "character armor." The formation of psychic structure is heavily dependent on vicissitudes of aggression. Hartmann (1952) has stressed the role of neutralization of aggression in structure building. The same writer (1948), in another observation, recalls a late observation of Freud to the effect that there may exist an individually varying tendency toward conflict—independent of the conflict itself—which could be correlated with the amount of free aggression.

Character: Development and Genesis

There are two requirements for the development of character: an external one—the evolution of stable traits observable by another person, and an internal one—the acquisition of persistent unconscious fantasies which become organized in increasingly complex fashion and shape these traits. I shall argue for the value of distinguishing "pre-stages" from stages of character formation in analogy with terms used in describing superego development.

As a child develops, when does it make sense to talk about character, or to put it another way, when may we consider characteristics (found in every newborn) as equivalent to character? Infant observation reveals that a newborn infant will quickly show certain patterns of behavior that clearly differentiate him from every other newborn. The infant's gaze has a degree of primitive organization, but its intent and meaning cannot be evaluated. The same holds true for early imitative behavior; such schema are prestructural. Unfortunately, the literature on child analysis does not offer studies on child development from the point of view of character. This leaves the theory of character formation largely in the hands of analysts working with adult patients. These analysts have to work retrospectively, trying to reconstruct the various components that enter into psychic conflict and their timetables, using the shifts in transference and resistance as data.

From a developmental point of view, we are uncertain at which point it makes sense to talk about character formation. Where does the concept of character belong in our developmental model? Is it more useful to say that character formation begins at birth or even in utero with very slow increments (the first view), or to adopt the position that character formation is a specific developmental step which has its onset some time during latency and, in normal circumstances, is more or less completed in late adolescence (the second view).

I believe clarity is introduced in our conceptual apparatus if we distinguish "prestages" from "stages" of character formation. We do this in the case of superego formation with considerable advantage. Evidence shows that a considerable level of ego development, including the capacity for neutralization, identification, internalization, self-object differentiation, and ideal formation, is necessary before the final formation of a stable, well defined character trait. The above could represent a structural definition of character formation. The establishment and integration of these capacities does not occur before the resolution of the Oedipus complex, in early latency. Yet, even at this point, character development is by no means complete, since some reworking takes place during adolescence.

Two exceptions have to be mentioned to this structural definition. These represent diametrically opposite conditions: (1) Individuals with chaotic character structure who never achieve the degree of stability implied in my definition. It does not follow that such individuals have no character, but rather that their character is unstable, shifting, or chaotic. Yet even impulsive or chaotic individuals have a certain degree of predictability in their impulsivity or lack of reliability. (2) Children who develop very early stable reactions leading to rigid patterning which becomes an integral part of character structure, uninfluenced by later developmental stages. Certain rigid obsessional adults develop out of fearful rigid obsessional children. Yet not all obsessional children go on to become obsessional adults, and not all obsessional adults emerge from similar childhood neurosis.

The patterning of drive and defense which is first stabilized during the latency period is influenced by the vicissitudes of the preoedipal phase. Silverman et al. (1975) argue that it is possible to define a stable central psychic constellation observable during the phallic preoedipal period. This constellation includes "the pattern of phase progression, drive balance and discharge patterns, the impact of early variations in ego equipment and organization, the self and object representations, and the modes of regulating self-esteem, with which the latter are associated" (p. 130). Their view minimizes the accretions due to the resolution of the Oedipus complex. Only detailed longitudinal observations of children can demonstrate its validity.

The more traditional view, which I favor, states that normal character formation follows the resolution of the Oedipus complex; this process bears a close relation in time to the setting up of the infantile repression. Jacobson (1969) points out that "the period of infantile repression succeeds in excluding a considerable sector of memories from the preconscious and conscious mind. Consequently, the object and self representations emerging with the subsiding of the infantile psychosexual conflicts bear the imprint of this exclusion as well as of the countercathectic ego formations which safeguard the results of infantile repression" (p. 135). This is another way of talking about character formation.

The time of completion of the process of character formation is also uncertain. There is some general agreement that character formation cannot be said to be completed before the conflict resolution of the adolescent period. The process of this resolution has only been sketchily described (Blos, 1968). What can be said about the impact of subsequent life events on the continuing evolution of character? Life experiences, both good and bad, certainly contribute to change of lesser degree in some aspects of character structure, though the basic makeup remains the same.

As this paper is not meant to be an encyclopedic survey of the field, vast areas of importance cannot be included. One such area which I have left out of my discussion is the topic of masculinity and femininity, and sexual identity. How a little boy becomes masculine and a little girl feminine are questions that bear close relation to character. Masculinity and femininity become stable components of personality organization, clearly the outcome of conflict influenced by biological, psychological, and social forces. In recent years the Freudian concept of the development of the female has been closely reexamined, challenged, and amplified.

Character and Infantile Neurosis

The relation between character and infantile neurosis is complicated. If a neurosis in childhood is not resolved satisfactorily, pathological character traits may develop. We can ask: (1) What is the relation between neurotic symptoms and character in the adult, and how does neurotic character emerge as a solution to a childhood neurosis? (2) What processes favor a clinical picture in which symptoms predominate versus one in which character disturbances are in the forefront? (3) How do we understand character formation in adults who had no clear-cut infantile neurosis?

In the child beyond the second or third year, the immature ego will have to take certain defensive measures against anxiety. If the immediate measures fail, a symptom may develop. If a chronically stressful situation persists (such as the child being presented with incompatible demands over a long period of time), a compromise of a different order will result—a permanent ego deformation, a second line of defense, as it were, which we term a character trait. For example, the boy's fear of the father and severe castration anxiety might be dealt with first by an animal phobia and secondarily through the development of a submissive attitude to authority, with the fantasy, "There is no need to castrate me. I shall behave as though I am already castrated." Other outcomes, involving different traits or other types of psychopathology, such as acting out, are also possible. In this developmental schema, the formation of a character trait in childhood is an attempt to deal with a conflict which was imperfectly resolved through symptom formation.

The presence of symptoms is not necessarily indicative of a poor prognosis. In fact, quite the opposite may be the case—a point made by Glover (1926). It can be demonstrated clinically that the analysis of a character trait may lead either to anxiety or to some other affect, or to symptom formation, again suggesting alternating means of attempting to deal with conflict.

Our understanding is limited about conditions that favor the emergence of symptoms in contrast to character traits. The predominance of certain defense mechanisms such as reaction formation and rationalization favor the development of character. Others, such as reversal, undoing, and again reaction formation, are involved in both (Lustman, 1962). From a developmental point of view, earlier events are more likely to influence the form of experience (i.e., lead to character deformations) whereas later events are more likely to influence the content (i.e., lead to symptoms). Freud (1937) refers to this issue indirectly in *Analysis Terminable and Interminable* with such concepts as "adhesiveness of the libido" (p. 241) and "psychical inertia" (p. 242). Loewald (1978) suggests that if a behavior in the child is disapproved of by the parent, it is more likely to give rise to a symptom. This idea is based on the assumption that what is considered wrong by the parent will not be directly integrated into the child's evolving mental apparatus without considerable conflict, and hence will result in the formation of a symptom—that is, an ego-alien structure. Loewald states further that, if conflicts in a family are brought out in the open and confronted, symptoms are more likely to emerge, in contrast to situations in which resolution is nonverbal, which favor the development of character traits. More research in child development is needed to demonstrate the validity of these views.

Sometimes a trait that arose originally as an attempt to resolve a conflict may at some later time acquire a different function and be harnessed in the service of adaptation. For example, one of my patients developed aggressive behavior in the service of a hypermasculine façade erected largely as a defense against passive longings. This trait was initially maladaptive but later proved a valuable asset in practicing a profession in which, when properly channeled, aggressivity and activity were essential.

An increasing number of patients with primary character pathology seems to have gone through a disturbed childhood without the clinical manifestations of a clear-cut infantile neurosis—that is, without overt symptoms of anxiety, obsessions, phobias, or somatic manifestations. It is not certain whether such symptoms did occur and were either transient or thoroughly repressed, or whether developmental disturbances took the form of fixations, pathological relations to parents and school, and various types of acting out. Another patient, who developed an obsessional character structure in adult life, was sent for treatment as a child of six because his parents had considerable difficulty managing his rebellious behavior. He would refuse to do most routine chores, such as cleaning his room or raking the garden and helping his mother. His refrain was, "why do I have to, it's not *fair*." He was (and is still) a procrastinator, ran away from home a number of times, and managed to perform quite dangerous feats partly out of an insatiable curiosity to see how things worked. At an amusement park, he pressed a button marked "start" and climbed into a car which started running faster and faster. His screams for help quickly brought his angry and distraught parents to the rescue. He remembers the incident with a mixture of secret pride and smugness at his unmanageability and inventiveness.

Genesis of Character

In Arlow's (1960) summary of the genesis of character, the substrate includes the biological endowments (inborn tendencies) and the infant's earliest experiences of gratification of instinctual needs. These influence the ways in which the child learns to master his primitive sexual and aggressive impulses, and finally the tempering effects of experiences, especially of sorrow (including loss) and humiliation. Because of the difficulty of differentiating the development of character proper from that of the individual as a whole, I shall touch on only some of the more problematic areas of controversy in the categories mentioned by Arlow. The innate factors include such elements as constitution, strength of drives, and stimulus barrier. These elements have to be inferred. On a less abstract level, one would include temperament and natural endowment, anatomy, sex, appearance (including height), beauty, race, and the like. After the neonatal period, the role of temperament becomes more difficult to isolate, as the child's behavior is influenced more and more by the parents' dynamics and responses.

It is nearly impossible to adduce evidence to prove the existence of any character traits not influenced by the instincts. Some researchers maintain that the only feature that has predictive value is the amount of activity (Fries et al., 1935). Of interest is Emde's (1988) work on the developmental line of emotions. He postulates emotions as constituting the basic core of the self, the "patterns" of emotionality remaining fairly stable from early on, influenced, to be sure, by the environment.

The developmental factors include the normal unfolding of maturational sequences along with possible developmental lags or out-of-phase advances (e.g., premature intellectual development in obsessional character). They also include fixations and regression.

Our theory has attempted to describe the impact of very early rigid patterning through the concept of the repetition compulsion. This refers to a slightly different concept from the traditional term of fixation. As used by Freud, this latter term includes both clinical aspects—the compulsion to repeat, characteristic of the transference, the play of children, traumatic dreams, and the fate neurosis—and a more abstract aspect, the repetition compulsion proper.

This aspect is described in unclear fashion in *Beyond the Pleasure Principle* (Freud, 1920). Grossman (personal communication) suggests that Freud may have been attempting to take into account the imprint on the child of prestructural traumata damaging the child in the preverbal stages. It may be that Freud (1937) was referring to this second aspect of the repetition compulsion when he used terms like "adhesiveness of the libido," or its opposite, "mobile libido" (p. 241). Freud does not exclude the possibility of constitutional givens, but makes room for the possibility that these characteristics of the libido could result from influences on very early stages of development. Such effects of the repetition compulsion would then both impose certain limitations on the range of possible character types and influence the content of certain basic attitudes. Such residues are probably beyond analytic resolution, because they are preconflictual. Other techniques may have to be developed to heal the damage. Heinz Kohut has addressed himself to these issues in his theory and method of treatment of narcissistic personalities. Even in non-narcissistic individuals, one can encounter certain basic personality attributes, such as extreme passivity or basic mistrust, which respond minimally to conflict interpretation.

I shall now turn briefly to so-called autonomous ego development. Hartmann, (1952), explores in detail the nonconflictual, autonomous factors that play a role in shaping the outcome of conflicts and the development of certain defense mechanisms. He also calls attention to our grossly oversimplified way of observing and conceptualizing development. We are so accustomed in our work to relating development to conflict and instinctual transformation that it is necessary to point out that certain character traits may develop independently of conflicts or be minimally influenced by them. Child development studies by Mahler and her co-workers (1979) delineate phases in the separation-individuation process from a perspective outside the domain of conflict.

The reconstruction of the role of environmental factors is part of our everyday analytic practice and will not be dealt with here except for one element, the influence of the family group on character development. Because the analytic approach tends to favor intense investigation of the one-to-one relationship, analysis has lagged behind in studying the relevance and detailed influence of family (group) processes on character formation. Because of his immaturity and normal dependency needs, the child may easily fall prey to certain typical group phenomena—e.g., the casting of the child in the role of the scapegoat or as the carrier of the parents' unconscious inferiority feelings. The effect on the child's character depends on whether he accepts the role assigned to him, rebels against it, or is able to form alliances with one parent against the other. Another approach to the understanding of the influence of the family has been to study the family's general or preferred type of conflict resolution, which then becomes a model for the child. Richter (1975) refers to a dissociative type of family interaction in which one part of the family can remain strong as long as another part is weak or sickly. Denial and masochistic formation are employed in another type. In the so-called paranoid type, inner dangers and tensions are avoided by common use of projection and focusing on an outside enemy. In the phobic type, the whole family adopts a defensive style of avoidance, disavowal and retreat, with all risks painted in exaggerated fashion. In all of these instances, the group exerts pressure toward maintenance of a particular defensive style. The selection of defensive style by a child is influenced by compromises he reaches as the conflicting identifications are reconciled, under pressure of the group style, and the influence of other siblings and their identifications. In the literature such identifications are often described solely on the intrapsychic level, and the influence of the group process is underestimated. Such global phenomena can best be understood by reference to the individual's overall relations to others.

232

In addition to describing the development of character in general, it is important to describe the genesis of specific traits. This is very much the bulk of our day-to-day analytic work. We are in a position to describe retrospectively the meanings of the choice of a particular solution by tracing the history of the transformation of the drive processes, the defenses chosen, and the principal existing identifications and traumas dealt with at the time of emergence of the trait in question. Yet we cannot easily explain why a person chooses to identify with certain traits in the parents, and not others. To understand the process of such identifications, the meaning of the behaviors of the parent at the time the identification took place has to be reconstructed. Superficially similar traits will have different functions and meanings in parent and child; certain meanings, however, may be shared. A given trait, e.g., being overly willing to do one's share of work, may be ideally suited to handling guilty feelings or discharging aggression on the self, for both parent and child. The process of character formation, the backbone of the theory, is ill-understood. We can describe certain mechanisms (e.g., ego and superego identifications, reaction formation, sublimation) as well as certain requirements, antecedents, and influences which will modify the end result—constitution, trauma, early experiences with the mother—e.g., the way a misfit between mother and child will warp or influence the budding processes. However, we still lack a basic overall organizational scheme and timetable except as an extrapolation from the abnormal.

Character and Adaptation

Until now I have focused primarily on the relation between character and symptoms. This emphasizes the role of intrapsychic conflicts. To round out the picture of character, note must be made of its role in interpersonal relations and adaptation to reality. This concept is largely alien to the world of symptoms. One of the functions of character is to develop strategies to deal with the demands of external reality which confront the child and minimize conflict with others. This usually means the parents, then siblings, other children and adults, and the school. By external reality I do not mean only the "objective" reality as seen by an outside observer, but more significantly the perception of reality as colored and distorted by the child's own internal world.

The child perceives and responds to the mother's unconscious affective tone and latent message which he may emphasize or distort because of who he is. There is room for considerable maladaptive potential when a child molds himself in semi-symbiotic fashion to live out certain unconscious fantasies about his or her role held by the mother. In one of my patients, the mother saw herself as all-powerful and capable, and allotted to the child the role of passive bystander. Accepting the role assigned to him allowed my patient to maintain a submissive relationship to a controlling, willful mother, but at the cost of sacrificing his own independence and creativity. In his adult life he was full of self-doubts and inhibitions.

The childhood of another patient was devoted largely to adapting to what he perceived as his father's angry, bullying rages, persistent criticisms, and futile attempts to transform him into the sort of a man the father would have wanted to be. A slightly older sibling faced with the same situation chose the path of identifying with the father, having temper tantrums, being chronically dissatisfied, and making a general nuisance of herself by getting everyone to pay close attention to her in an attempt to appease her endless demands and loud complaints. My patient developed what seemed to be the opposite tack. He retreated to his room, quiet as a mouse, built countless models, and developed artistic talents in the performing arts. However, he would manage in his own subtle way to provoke his father by exhibiting unobtrusive habits which he knew would exasperate the latter—for example, quietly sucking his thumb while watching television with the father, or eating just a bit too noisily, something the father was very sensitive to. The boy hardly ever complained, and made no demands on adults. This earned him the mother's admiration. His overt response to his father's tantrums appeared to be total indifference "like water off a duck's back." Inwardly, his rage and fury knew no bounds. His sadistic fantasies were largely displaced to women. On a preconscious level, he hoped the appearance of independence and self-sufficiency would earn him the position of favorite sibling. In adult life, he developed multiple inhibitions, masochistic tendencies, and feelings of inferiority. His characterologic solutions in childhood (which were repeated in the transference, particularly in the form of emotional withdrawal and inertia) could be examined from the point of view of adaptation; that is, his choice of characterologic solution as a child attempted to reconcile his views of the father, his views of the sister's coping style, and the reactions of the adults around him. It also accommodated his own inner conflicts. Only late in the analysis did certain positive attributes of the father emerge as the patient's own sadistic tendencies were reconstructed. I have left out of this brief description the complicated role of the relation to the mother.

In general, a behavior that appears maladaptive to an outside observer will often turn out to be the best available solution for the person under the given circumstances. Much of analytic work deals in part with the reconstruction of the setting in which certain characterologic choices were made. In the case of my patient, mentioned above, the emotional withdrawal, blunting, and severe inhibition of any aggression was his way of protecting himself and others from murderous feelings and subsequently maintaining the image of the father as a strong powerful person. It also allowed the development of a self-image of independence and detachment which helped control his inner turmoil and suppress his great dependency needs. This adaptive quality of character gives it a much broader range and function than symptom, an idea that is disputed by analysts such as Brenner (1982) who deny that there are any major structural or dynamic differences between symptom and character trait, stressing instead their nature as compromise formations.

Note must be made of the attempt by individuals with varying degree of character pathology to select an occupation or life style that is congruent with their fundamental attitudes and aptitudes. It does not surprise us to hear that an obsessional individual selects accounting as a profession, that a schizoid patient works the night shift in a post office, or that a phobic patient who was enuretic as a child becomes a fireman.

I have omitted from consideration in this section on adaptation the role of character in successful achievements in work and in harmonious relationships. This is not because its importance is minimal—quite the contrary; rather, our concerns and energies are more geared to the pathological and maladaptive side of the personality. Identification that plays a major role in character development has an adaptive component as well. Identification with positive attributes of the parents' personalities becomes a source of pride and cements parent-child relationships. Certain qualities, such as persistence, hard work, optimism, warmth, openness, can be aspects of character makeup in part derived from similar positive attributes in the parents, and contribute enormously to the achievement of a happy and contented life. The very stability of character contributes to one's sense of identity, continuity in time, and selfhood.

REFERENCES

Abraham, K. (1949). Psychoanalytic contributions to character formation. In *Selected Papers,* New York: Basic Books, 1953, pp. 370–418.

American Psychiatric Association (1982). *Diagnostic and Statistical Manual of Mental Disorders (DSM III)* Washington, DC: Amer. Psychiat. Assn.

Arlow, J.A. (1960). Character and conflict. *J. Hillside Ho*sp. 15:140–150.

———— (1963). Conflict, regression and symptom formation. *Int. J. Psychoanal.*

44:*12–23.*

Baudry, F. (1983). The evolution of the concept of character in Freud's work. *J. Am. Psychoanal. Assoc.* 31:1–31.

———— (1984). Character: a concept in search of an identity J. *Am. Psychoanal. Assoc.* 32:*955–979.*

Blos, P. (1968). Character formation in adolescence. *Psychoanal. Study Child* 23: 245–263.

Boesky, D. (1983). Resistance and character theory: a reconsideration of the concept of character resistance. *J. Am. Psychoanal. Assoc.* 31(Suppl.) 227–247.

Brenner, C. (1982). The Mind in Conflict. New York: Int. Univ. Press.

Emde, R.N. (1988). Development terminable and interminable: 1. Innate and motivational factors from infancy. *Int. J. Psychoanal.*69:23–42.

Fenichel, O. (1945). *The Psychoanalytic Theory of Neurosis.* New York: Norton.

Freud, A. (1936).*The Ego and the Mechanisms of Defense. Writings 2.* New York: Int. Univ. Press, 1966.

Freud, S. 1895 Project for a scientific psychology. *S.E.* 1.

———— (1896a). Draft K. The neuroses of defence. *S.E.* 1.

———— (1896b). Further remarks on the neuropsychoses of defence. *S.E.* 3.

———— (1908) Character and anal erotism. *S.E.* 9.

———— (1913). The disposition to obsessional neurosis. *S.E.* 12.

———— (1915). Repression. *S.E.* 14.

———— (1920). Beyond the pleasure principle. *S.E.* 18.

———— (1923). The ego and the id. *S.E.* 19.

———— (1926). Inhibitions, symptoms and anxiety. *S.E.* 20

———— (1937). Analysis terminable and interminable. *S.E.* 23

———— (1940 Splitting of the ego in the process of defence. *S.E.* 23.

Fries, M.E., Brokaw, K. Murray, V.F. (1935). The formation of character as observed in the well baby clinic. *Amer. J. Dis. Child.* 49:28–42.

Glover, E. (1926). The neurotic character *Int. J. Psychoanal* .1:11–20.

Grossman, W.I. (1967). Introspection and psychoanalysis *Int. J. Psychoanal.* 48:16–31.

——— (1984). The self as fantasy: fantasy as theory. *J. Am. Psychoanal. Assoc. 30:919–939.*

Hartmann, H. (1948) Comments on the psychoanalytic theory of instinctual drives In *Essays on Ego Psychology.* New York: Int. Univ. Press, 1964, pp. 69–89.

——— (1952). The mutual influences in the development of the ego and id In *Essays on Ego Psychology.* New York: Int. Univ. Press, 1964, pp. 155–181.

Jacobson, E. (1969). *The Self and the Object World.* New York: Int. Univ. Press.

Kernberg, O. (1976). *Object Relations Theory and Clinical Psychoanalysis.* New York: Aronson.

Loewald, H. (1978). Instinct theory, object relations, and psychic structure formation J. Am. Psychoanal. Assoc. 26:493–506.

Lustman, S. (1962). Defense, symptom, and character *Psychoanal. Study Child* 17:216–244.

Mahler, M.S. (1979). *Selected Papers. Vol. 2: Separation-Individuation* New York: Aronson.

Meissner, W.W. (1986). Can psychoanalysis find its self *J. Am. Psychoanal. Assoc.* 34:379–401.

Reich, W. (1933). *Character Analysis.* New York Orgone Inst. Press, 1949.

Richter, H. (1975). Role of family life in child development *Int. J. Psychoanal.* 57: 385–395.

Schafer, R. (1976). *A New Language for Psychoanalysis.* New Haven Conn.: Yale Univ. Press.

———— (1979). Character, ego syntonicity, and character change. *J. Am. Psychoanal. Assoc.* 27:867–891.

Silverman, M.A., Rees, K. & Neubauer, P.B. (1975.) On a central psychic constellation *Psychoanal. Study Child.* 30:127–161.

Waelder, R. (1930). The principle of multiple function: observations on overdetermination In *Psychoanalysis: Observation, Theory, Application, ed.* S. A. Guttman. New York: Int. Univ. Press, 1976, pp. 68–83.

CHAPTER 9

Character in Fiction and Fiction in Character[33]
[(1990). *Psychoanal. Q.* (59):370–397.]

ABSTRACT: This paper examines the concept of fictional character from a psychoanalytic point of view, including its synthesis and the role of reader response. A second section takes up the role of fiction in the development of character.

> *That fiction is a lady, and a lady who has somehow got herself into trouble, is a thought that must often have struck her admirers.*
> —Virginia Woolf (1927)

INTRODUCTION

Students in analytic institutes are often advised to read great nineteenth century novels by such authors as Flaubert, Dickens, and Dostoevsky to learn about character. What, in fact, do such works as *Madame Bovary* or *Crime and Punishment* have to teach us about character? I will approach this topic by comparing character in the literary sense with character in real life. I will illustrate key points by examples taken from well-known literary works, and will explore the relation between fiction and character from diametrically

---

33 I am indebted to Dr. Donald Kaplan for his assistance in discussing with me core ideas in this paper.

opposed points of view. After stressing the different realities of fiction and of real life, I will show how much of our character is determined by certain fictive elements which we unconsciously create in order to achieve continuity and to deal with frightening or intolerable aspects of reality.

The main section of my paper will deal with character as it is portrayed in the nineteenth century romantic novel. The romantic emphasis on the individual and on emotional life, and the questioning of the accepted social order, created a perfect spawning ground for the parallel development of the realistic novel and of psychoanalysis. Auerbach (1946) defined the nature of realism as consisting in "the serious treatment of everyday reality, the rise of more extensive and socially inferior human groups to the position of subject matter for problematic-existential representation, on the one hand; on the other, the embedding of random persons and events in the general course of contemporary history—these, we believe, are the foundation of modern realism" (p. 491). Zola, for example, devoted many hours to the scientific observation of the social milieu of his novels—the fishermen of a small village in Brittany, the railway workers, the miners. By this means he hoped to achieve an accurate and realistic depiction of the life of his characters.

Several questions come to mind. How is a literary character different from an individual in real life? How is the illusion of three dimensions achieved? What goes into the creation of a literary character? The best introduction to these questions will be through the examination of the nature and structure of the genre in which literary characters live: the novel and its frame, the fictional space.

The Novel and Fictional Space

A novelist, according to Kundera (1986), is a person who is committed only to the discovery of truth through the fusion of reality and the dream. The novel combines two elements that enable the reader to enter and enjoy the fictional world: first, an image of life—a story which is believable at least as long as we are reading the work; second is an imaginative construction which organizes this story and creates a coherent artistic whole. These two elements can be compared to the two components of psychic reality as suggested by Arlow (1969) in his two-projector model: first, external reality and, second, unconscious fantasies. What great authors strive to achieve, then, is a portrayal of *psychic* reality, not just external reality.

The novel portrays life, but life is not a "given" existing out there; rather it is a construct. Each artist, depending upon a combination of personal factors, the values of the time, and esthetic concerns, will have a different view of what "life" consists of. As Auerbach (1946) so well explored in his *Mimesis*, the representation of reality and what constitutes reality evolved gradually, from Homer to the Bible, on to the contemporary view. Even within the narrow span I am considering—the period of the nineteenth century novel which gave birth to modern realism—different authors constructed very different realities.

Henry James (1884), one of the most influential theoreticians of his time, wrote in his "The Art of Fiction" that the appearance of reality is the supreme virtue of a novel. Creating the illusion of life is the beginning and end of the art of the novelist. James's belief raises the issue of the nature of the fictional space in which the novel unfolds. Part of the skill of certain novelists rests in the ways in which they try to make us forget that the characters are *not* real. But the question of what is meant by "real" within the fictional world needs further examination. Put in this way, the question of "real" is reduced to one of skill in making believe or dissembling. That is, a novel is never true or false—it only suggests appearances of reality or of the imaginary. It must appear plausible to the reader who is willing to enter the fictional realm and "willingly suspend disbelief," as Coleridge put it.

Literary critics such as Genette (1969) have emphasized that the novelist or playwright in the French classical tradition strives for verisimilitude (that is, to give the appearance of reality) rather than an accurate portrayal of reality. This was certainly true in the classical era. One has only to read Corneille's introduction to his 1637 play, *Le Cid*, and the critical debates of the period to realize that the key question was usually one of plausibility. Corneille's play was severely criticized by Georges de Scudéry, a literary critic, because the heroine, Chimène, a girl of noble origins, was going to marry Rodrigue, the killer of her father (compare Shakespeare's *Richard III*).

The criteria for verisimilitude were usually based on unstated, implied values and beliefs applicable to a given period. Hence it was a relative concept. The idea of verisimilitude goes back to Aristotle, who wrote that the subject of theater, and by extension of all fiction, is neither the true nor the possible but the plausible; the latter tends more and more to be identified with some ideal realm, with what should be. The concept of verisimilitude seems to imply the existence of a fixed external reality with which some other reality is compared, whereas plausibility refers primarily to our subjective reaction to something we feel is believable or at least does not violate our inner sense of what constitutes the boundaries of reality. In fact, the implausible is a privilege of the real world, not of the fictive one, at least according to the classical point of view. This attitude toward verisimilitude, which reached its pinnacle in the schools of Realism and Naturalism in the nineteenth century novel, began to break down toward the second half of the nineteenth century, with the growing indifference of the novelists toward pleasing the public, the revolt against norms of any kind, and the desire to reach certain fundamental truths by routes other than realism.

The "reality" of the novel, more accurately its plausibility, is an illusion which readers must accept if they are to enjoy the work and immerse themselves in it.

Freud (1927) drew our attention to the characteristics of illusion: ". . . we call a belief an illusion when a wish-fulfilment is a prominent factor . . . and in doing so we disregard its relations to reality, just as the illusion itself sets no store by verification" (p. 31). These characteristics describe very well the nature of the novel. What is the relationship between make-believe and reality, and what is the relationship of truth and illusion within the fictional realm? Is the relation between external reality and fictional reality one of analogy, identity, or resemblance?

This is the well-known problem of the relation between "art" and "life." Shiff (1979) studied the metaphoric relationship between them. Art is a construction of a fixed external public world, perfected but bounded and restrictive; life refers to immediate personal experience, never adequately captured in a reflected artistic image. The representation of private experience must depend on a medium or metaphor. "As the medium which separates art from life is perfected it becomes transparent. We see through it as though it were not there" (p. 114).

Strictly speaking, a novel, being the creation of its author, is all make-believe in its ordering and unfolding, even if the novel is based on some actual event, as in the case of *Madame Bovary*. Fictional reality is fictional, a fact forgotten by those who treat the characters in a novel as though they were real. An analogy may be drawn to the attitudes of certain patients who concretely ascribe to characters in their dreams the same autonomy and capacity to initiate motivated behavior as their real life counterparts. "I know why my mother behaved as she did in this dream," said a patient. "She felt guilty!" From one perspective, we would label this behavior as resistant, or naïve, because it ignores the fact that characters in dreams generally (there are exceptions) do not represent themselves or only themselves.

Let us examine how the novel represents inner life and makes us believe people in it are real. One device is to introduce characters who have existed in real life and whose existence cannot be questioned. Tolstoy's *War and Peace* has Napoleon as one of its protagonists, although the presence of Napoleon is by no means a guarantee of historical accuracy. Victor Hugo also introduced a Napoleon in his novel, *Les Misérables*, but Hugo's Napoleon bears no resemblance to the character portrayed in *War and Peace*. Authors are free to introduce in their characters some aspects of people whom they have known in the past or know in the present. Authors can also simulate mental life by creating a character with "motives" which can be retrieved from the text or reasonably inferred. This can be facilitated by giving the character an identity, including persistent traits, and having him or her interact with others and evolve as a result of the action. Mental life may be simulated by the character's giving the appearance of being more than is described, having a certain ambiguity, and acting as a consequence of motives which are or are not clarified by the author. This may all be revealed through a character's speeches, gestures, actions, and thoughts or through comments made by other characters. For the purpose of my argument, I am vastly oversimplifying the concept of the reality which is portrayed in a novel. In general, this refers to psychic reality, not external reality. The representation of reality in Western literature has slowly evolved through the years, undergoing many changes as a result of various biases, beliefs, and theories about what was appropriate to include in the fictional work.

Having now explored some of the means by which illusion is created (that is, the similarity between literary characters and real-life persons), it is now time to explore the opposite issue—the many differences between literary characters and character as we encounter it in real life. Although most of the differences are self-evident, their enumeration will facilitate further discussions concerning the treatment of fictional characters as if they were real. I will start by mentioning some of the differences between fictional reality and external reality.

Hochman (1985) reminded us that in a novel we know all we need to know according to the purposes of the author, in contrast to the obscurity and at times unreliability of information we have about real life.[34] A novel has a coherence always lacking in real life—it is prepackaged. Characters in fiction are part of a whole which intrinsically means something. They are part of a configuration of meaning which the work as a whole articulates, however obscurely.

A novel focuses on portraying a character's mental life. Love, misery, suffering, and death occupy an inordinate amount of space, in addition to most other feeling states except happiness. Certain bodily functions (eating, excretory processes, and sleeping) are largely absent. There are, to be sure, exceptions to each of the above statement. Proust spends the first fifty pages of À la recherche du temps perdu on recounting the details of the narrator's falling asleep. An appreciable segment of contemporary literature dwells on the scatologic functions. The management of time in a novel is clearly different from what is applicable to life. A character may be introduced at a certain age and may mention parts of her or his earlier life, while certain developmental phases that would be crucial to an analyst's reconstruction of the past may be altogether missing or briefly summarized. Flashbacks are common. In contrast to slices of life, which in large segments are continuous, a novel has to have a beginning, a middle, and an end. Fairy tales often end with the stereotyped "and they lived happily ever after." This is to satisfy what adults interpret as the child's need for a happy ending. Adult readers may feel cheated if a novel trails off without a sense of closure. This is clearly a departure from verisimilitude and becomes an issue of expectation about the genre. Closure is clearly a falsification of reality.

---

34 Occasionally, a novel, such as What Maisie Knew by Henry James, may incorporate an unreliable narrator, but this is part of the author's plan.

Novels, finally, express the author's theories about what character consists of and how it evolves. This theory is sometimes expressed directly. For example, Balzac's writings are full of explanations to account for his characters' actions through generalizations about social groups or classes of individuals. In other instances, the theory has to be inferred from the work. Such theories are usually derived from the author's personal views, assumptions, and attitudes which reflect his or her character. Proust writes mostly about the greater intensity of feelings generated by a fantasied love object whom one does not possess, in contrast to a real one. This was a characteristic of his personal love life as well.

Classification

From a literary point of view, how have characters been classified? The simplest division is the one proposed by E. M. Forster (1927) between the round characters—those who are fully sketched, replete with conflicts, and are central to the work—and the flat characters—who play a secondary or flanking role and are described in a very limited, stereotyped fashion. They do not exist outside of their function and do not evolve with the course of the narrative.

Another classification somewhat related to the above divides the characters into those who represent reality, i.e., copy or mirror some aspect of it closely, versus those who illustrate it. Illustration differs from representation in narrative art, in that it does not seek to reproduce actuality but rather to present selected aspects of the actual—essences referable for their meaning not to historical, psychological, or sociological truth, but to ethical or metaphysical truth. Thus, we are not called upon to understand their motivation as if they were whole human beings, but to understand the principles they illustrate through their actions in a narrative framework.

Dickens was particularly adept at giving us caricatures of people. He tended to overload his personages to portray in a condensed fashion a particular view of reality found in the lower classes.

Description

Freud commented that his case histories read more like short stories than like scientific studies (Breuer and Freud, 1893–1895, p. 160). An analysis begins with a description of surface behavior. One might expect that description, organization, and classification of literary characters could be identical to those of characters in real life. Do we not use certain types drawn from the literary to describe our patients—Don Juan, Don Quixote, and Cinderella being the most obvious examples? However, in the case of a novel all we have is a text which has been constructed, an artifact of the human mind; a literary character does not exist per se unless it is retrieved from the text and reconstructed from bits and pieces. It has no life of its own save that projected onto it by the reader.

Hochman has developed a comprehensive taxonomy for literary characters. His categories include stylization, coherence, wholeness, literalness, complexity, transparency, dynamism, and closure. I will comment on some of these categories. Said Hochman (1985):

The skilled author gives us only part of imaginable life, yet we respond as though we had a complete image. This is so much the case that we are sometimes tempted to extrapolate beyond the boundaries of the time or space of the novel! Wholeness in the fictional world is different from that in real life. The illusion of wholeness may be created by an author with limited presentation, particularly in certain characters tightly woven around a small number of themes or preoccupations (p. 70).

Such characters as Shylock or Molière's invalid (*Le Malade Imaginaire*) are examples of this trend.

Literalness is an interesting category: should the character be taken literally or does the character suggest some symbolic representation or function? This relates to the breakdown of character previously mentioned: representation versus illustration. Freud's (1916, pp. 318–324) discussion of Lady Macbeth illustrates the symbolic function of a character. He found that he could not account for that lady's breakdown within the text of the play, and he adopted Ludwig Jekel's solution to consider her as one half of a single character, with Macbeth the other half; she was thus the carrier of some of the guilt feelings of Macbeth. Whether one agrees with this solution or not, it does illustrate the arbitrary nature of motivation in literature.

On the surface this capacity of literary characters to symbolize someone other than themselves would not seem to apply to a live person. Yet consider the psychotic individual who lives out the fantasy that he is Napoleon or Jesus Christ. What about instances of borrowed guilt or the cases of depressive patients who identify with a part or all of a departed loved one? In fact, much of our clinical work involves the reconstruction of what I would call the overloading of the self concept by such symbolic objects.

Transparency refers to the availability to the reader of the character's inner life. This concept could apply to both literary and real persons. Whether authors choose to convey their characters' motives and in what detail is a complex question. The flat characters are generally more opaque than the round ones, as their scope and complexity is not relevant to the artistic purpose. Ambiguity may be maintained to sustain interest. Such characters as Hamlet, although described in great detail, are sufficiently obscure as to provide food for endless debate. Shakespeare's Antonio in *The Merchant of*

Venice suffers from a profound melancholy which is clearly shown in the opening lines of the play.

> *In sooth, I know not why I am so sad:*
> *It wearies me; you say it wearies you;*
> *But how I caught it, found it, or cam by it,*
> *What stuff 'tis made of, whereof it is born,*
> *I am to learn . . . (I, i, 1–5).*

Yet it is never clearly explicated during the course of the play, and the audience is allowed to conjecture whether, in fact, Antonio's sadness is related to his anticipation of Bassanio's departure even before the latter's suit to Portia runs its course.

Motives

The nature of motives in fiction is central to the theory of novels and the understanding of character, both literary and real. In a novel the reader may be taken in by the "as if" nature of the interactions and believe that characters are more than puppets in the hands of the hidden author. To speak of the unconscious of a literary character is, as I see it, to introduce one's own fictions on top of the author's and to attribute to an artificial creation an aspect of real life—as the character, Nathanael, did in E. T. A. Hoffmann's novel, *The Sandman*. A character is only the agent of the author's purposes and aims.

The comparison between motivation in a novel and motivation in real life is crucial to the clarification of the nature of fiction. A novel is a closed vessel. The author is all powerful. Anecdotally, certain authors claim that while composing, they have lost control over the characters, who acquire a life of their own and determine the course of events in the narrative. How true this can be in practice is hard to say. The ending of a book is often already present in the author's mind before she or he begins the work. The order of writing does not always follow the chronological unfolding of the narrative. The author is free to ascribe any motive to a character to justify any action. Dickens has been criticized for inconsistency in the motivation of his characters and was well known to change them in midcourse under pressure from his editor, who felt that the public would prefer some other direction. The end of *Great Expectations* was changed on the advice of Lord Lytton. Dickens had actually intended to write a sad ending; Lytton suggested he adopt an optimistic conclusion which would please the public, and Dickens bowed to this advice.

It would be better to use the term justification, explanation, or pseudodetermination to accurately portray the essentially arbitrary nature of motivation in artistic productions. The clinical analogue of this justification would be the mechanism of rationalization. Certain events may occur because the author needs them for the unfolding of the plot or the effect he or she wants to have on the audience, such as arousing pity or anger. Motivation is often introduced as a screen for the more pressing determinants of the work, which include its formal structure and governing design. Sometimes there is a breakdown between the two, and the author abandons the attempt to justify certain behaviors; such is the case in the famous monologue of the lists of aphorisms by Polonius in *Hamlet*. This creates a problem for the actor who plays this role. As Genette (1969) puts it, from the point of view of the elegance of a narrative, there is a diametrical opposition between the function of a passage and its motivation. If its function is (roughly speaking) its purpose, then its motivation is what is necessary to hide its function.

It is, of course, possible to write a novel or a play with an apparent lack of conscious motivation as a form. *Waiting for Godot*, for example, thrives on apparent senselessness and lack of narrative development. This does not prevent it from being powerfully evocative of certain primitive fragmentary affects, such as loneliness and anxiety. It even has a certain degree of plausibility! How can we understand this paradox? I suspect that what determines our sense of the plausible is not primarily a comparison we make with a fixed external reality but rather the evocation of some obscure inner subjective reality, which can range from the most advanced to the most archaic —as in the case of Beckett's work. This may explain the very powerful appeal of such characters as Don Quixote who have the most implausible series of adventures.

The French poet, Paul Valéry, once wrote, "Perhaps it would be interesting to compose a work which would show, at each of its switch points, the multiplicity of possibilities which present themselves and out of which the author selects the one that will be given in the text. This would substitute for the common illusion of a sole determinant imitating reality that of the 'possible' at each moment, which seems more plausible. It has even happened to me to publish different texts of the same poem—some versions were even contradictory to each other, and I have been criticized for this. But no one has yet told me why I should have abstained from writing these variations" (see Genette, 1969, p. 85). This passage is reminiscent of the problem of determinism in clinical work, with one major difference. We would not say that behavior in a real person is arbitrary, though we may not be in a position to predict future actions. Perhaps the arbitrary unfolding of a plot could result from the interaction of multiple determinants too complex to isolate; its arbitrary nature is only apparent.

Let us briefly compare the two sets of determinants in clinical work and in a literary work. How do we account for a bit of behavior in analysis? We are careful not to refer to causes or determinants but rather more modestly to meanings, which we conveniently break down according to agencies— instinct reality, superego, and possibly the repetition compulsion. Each of these agencies can, of course, be broken down further. Could we set up a similar set of agencies or determinants in the case of a behavior of a character in a novel?

One could proceed either synthetically or analytically. One can try to reconstruct the way a novel was written and the choices made, by a close examination of the early drafts and the correspondence of the author—staying within the framework of the text. One could also broaden the net and examine earlier examples in the same genre and the authors who influenced the writer. Moving closer to the sphere of individual psychology, one could study the author's previous works, detect similar patterns or characters, and attempt to explain their existence in terms of the author's earlier life experiences. For example, Dickens often tended to include in his novels a childlike man who is incorrigible, good natured, unable to handle money matters, a pathological optimist, totally unadapted to reality. Mr. Micawber in *David Copperfield* and Mr. Skimpole in *Bleak House* are two such characters. It turns out that their traits mirror rather closely those of John Dickens, Charles's father, who landed himself in a debtor's prison and was totally unable to manage financial matters, always saying that "something would turn up." In the case of Flaubert's *Madame Bovary*, a great deal is known about the composition, events, and determinants of Emma's character. The end result is a complex combination: a compromise formation in the sense in which we use the term in analysis; a composite in the sense of a conscious and preconscious amalgam by the author of things seen, heard, experienced, and imagined; and some autobiographical projections of aspects of his self. Finally, there are also some determinants derived from the function of Emma within the novel and other esthetic requirements of narrative and plot.

Although the final package as seen from the outside is a fictional character, the elements which synthesize it are clearly very different from those resulting in the character of a live person (for example, temperament, trauma, early life experiences, and the like). The critic who proceeds to do an analysis of Emma as though she were a real person, without being cognizant of the synthesis mentioned above, runs the risk of methodologically unsound practices. I believe that a proper explication of the text and of the characters it contains is immeasurably facilitated by some appreciation of the structure of the text, the motives of the author (to the degree that they can be reconstructed), and a knowledge of the rules of the genre to which the text belongs. It is possible to undertake a textual analysis of a character within the framework of a novel without concerning oneself with the above (see Wangh, 1950); (Simon, 1988). However, what constitutes evidence and how one proceeds with interpretations requires great skill and sensitivity. In the absence of dynamic interplay and the process of the clinical situation, it becomes necessary to make certain assumptions about relationships, textual sequences, symbolic meanings, commonly shared definitions, and connotations of imagery and metaphor. I have tried a clinical exercise of this nature on a short passage from *Madame Bovary* (Baudry, 1979). It is essential to avoid the temptation of drawing conclusions beyond what the text can effectively support.

Theories of Literary Criticism and Character

How have critics, both analytic and literary, struggled with the immense task of interpretation of character? Two divergent approaches present themselves. Advocates of the first group treat the characters in fiction as though they were real and had motives, and as though their interactions could be analyzed in analogy with persons in real life. Although their papers are interesting, critics who use this first approach rarely teach us much that is new about the text as literature. Some exceptions include Wangh's (1950) paper on *Othello* and Simon's (1988, pp. 177–212) work. To be successful, the author of such a paper must devise a question which analysis is in a position to answer, using the text as data (see Baudry, 1984). Wangh started with unexplained factors in the relationship of Iago and Othello. He focused on an analysis of jealousy and rage in Iago, and traced subtle defense mechanisms in Iago's awareness of his feminine identification and in his unconscious homosexual bond with Othello. Wangh's observations are well documented by quotations from the play. Was Shakespeare aware of these subtleties? In all likelihood not. It is conceivable that the playwright either portrayed some personal attitudes which he projected onto Iago or possessed an uncanny intuitive grasp of such dynamics in other people. The discovery of these elements in the play had to await the elaboration of the mechanism of homosexuality by Freud in the Schreber case, and related papers on jealousy.

The second group of critics, which includes the structuralists and the deconstructionists, treat character as a textual effect. The structuralists wish to avoid description of character that uses psychological concepts. Instead, they refer to participants as agents and to sequences of actions proper to them (e.g., fraud, seduction). The contemporary structuralists, such as Barthes or Hamon, stress the illusory nature of the reader's construction of literary characters. They attempt to analyze in textual terms how character can be understood—whether in terms of action, discourse, functions, point of view, or themes.

Molière's theater can be profitably examined from the point of view of roles defined not through psychology but through the cohesion of actions given to them by the narrative, e.g., the young lovers, the faithful servant, the foolish husband, the coquette, the seducer, the evil one, etc. Molière's characters, like dancers in a minuet, carry out the actions of the plot and structure as defined by the author, and their behavior is fairly predictable from play to play.

Has analysis anything interesting to say about the view of character as the analogue of a person versus character as a textual function? Are they mutually exclusive, and does the structuralist approach invalidate the analytic one? My answer would be a cautious, "It depends on what uses one wants to put a literary text to." I continue to maintain that an understanding of the textual function of character will enable the analyst to avoid asking methodologically inappropriate questions. Neither approach is sufficient in itself. As Frow (1986) pointed out, the structuralist theory fails to account for "the activity of the reader in the constitution of these represented subjects; it fails to explain the affective force of the imaginary unities of character" (p. 232). It does not integrate into a consideration of character the role of unconscious fantasy which we analysts consider pivotal. The structuralist view deals more with the meticulous organization of texts and can provide us with important clues about themes and relationships. However, in dealing with the formal aspects of a text, it neglects the role of dynamics, which constitutes an essential element of character.

Retrieval

How do we retrieve a character in a novel? From the many indications given by the author about behavior and attitudes, both direct and indirect, the reader reconstructs a fictional persona to explain a sequence of actions, attitudes, or feelings. I have written elsewhere (Baudry, 1983) that the concept of character establishes a relationship between a superficially observable trait and a deep structure (a drive, a defense) whose existence we infer from a multiplicity of manifestations. Is there a similar relationship in a literary work? The author describes for us, both directly and indirectly, a number of traits which we extract from the text. So far, there is a similarity to the clinical situation of a candidate reporting to a supervisor, or of an intake interview with a new patient. However, there is no deep structure in the text to which we can relate the described traits unless we posit a fictional person through a process combining identification and projection. The fictive mind we posit may have no relation to what the author had in mind and may be quite different from fictive minds other readers would create. One of the vexing problems of applied analysis is the lack of rigorous criteria to evaluate the validity of these multiple and at times contradictory constructions.

As an example, Frattaroli (1987) started with the observation that Shakespeare's characters are often inconsistent; he then went on to conclude that this is based on "Shakespeare's consistency in portraying his characters as unconsciously motivated" (p. 427). To my mind, this conclusion, even though plausible, is not warranted, unless one could consider other possible causes for the inconsistency and evaluate these critically. Charney, in a passage quoted by Frattaroli, pointed out that "Shakespeare's characters are not developed novelistically by accumulating details that lead one to irresistible conclusions. Rather the characters respond to various dramatic contexts, and therefore they may seem discontinuous or even inconsistent in different parts of the play.... Many speeches are the product of the occasion rather than the personal mood of the speaker ... the speaker is speaking not in his own behalf but the needs of his subject, theme or plot before those of his dramatic persona" (p. 426).

This sobering view, with which I am in full agreement, suggests that the understanding of the psychology of a character cannot be done outside of the dramatic context. To return to a point made earlier by Genette, the function of a character has to be understood properly before one can tackle the thorny issue of motivation. Thus, if Shakespeare endowed his characters with inconsistency, we could not assume a priori that in a given scene the inconsistency requires a psychological explanation. It could reflect an indifference in Shakespeare to making his character consistent and an overriding interest in the development of plot.

The nature and type of text will determine how far one can pursue the analysis of character. The play, *Macbeth*, with its admixture of fantasy and reality and the absence of reference to any character's past (except for the comment on Macduff's being untimely ripped from his mother's womb) presents a different challenge from that of the character of Shakespeare's Coriolanus, who is presented in a more realistic fashion, with lengthy exchanges between himself, his wife, and his mother. It would make no sense to pursue the individual motivation of a character in a fairy tale because fables do not concern themselves with individuals per se or with the development of character, being focused only on story and plot. Certain characters may have a secondary or flanking function within the plot which determines their existence. The role of *confidentes* in French classical tragedy is to present to the audience some aspect of the conflict of the major character. They have no other role and have to be seen as externalizations of one part of a key character and nothing else.

In contrast with the multiple ways of reading character in the literary field, the clinical situation has far less ambiguity and more clearcut goals. In the latter, the purpose of isolating and confronting character is both hermeneutic and therapeutic. In contrast, the literary search has only a hermeneutic aim, the search for meaning and explanation.

Reader Response

Much has been written about reader response to a literary work. Holland (1975) sees the literary work as presenting little more than a foil for the individual reader's projection of his or her inner world. This leads to a totally subjective view of interpretation. Other critics see the reader and author as establishing a close object relationship with characters. Flaubert wrote about losing his sense of self when he composed, merging with his characters, and treating them as though they were real. He referred affectionately to Madame Bovary, who was giving him a lot of trouble.

Works of fiction can arouse affective reactions in the reader as strong as or stronger than those elicited by a live person. The sharply etched character can allow displacement, ventilation, and multiple identifications in the reader, whether admiring, sympathetic, cathartic, or ironic (Frow, 1986). These identifications can have powerful lasting effects. A patient who had difficulty in experiencing closeness and grief after his mother's death cries openly when reminiscing about certain movie scenes involving the death of a character.

A very detailed description of a "love affair" between a gifted author and a fictional character may be found in Vargas Llosa's *The Perpetual Orgy* (1986). In this work Vargas Llosa detailed his "unrequited passion" for Madame Bovary. He pointed out that, in contrast to a real person, "a fictional character can be brought to life indefinitely merely by opening the pages of the book and stopping at the right lines" (p. 8). For him, the book becomes part of his life helping him in a difficult period. Reading about Emma's suicide curtailed his own suicidal wishes. Vargas Llosa "each time found consolation and a sense of proportion, a revulsion against chaos, a taste for life in those heart-rending pages. The fictional suffering neutralized the suffering I was experiencing in real life" (p. 16).

Readers of a novel bring to the work the full strength of their unsatisfied longings and the wish to succumb momentarily to the illusion created by the writer. There arises a mutual collusion between the writer who creates a fictive world and the readers who wish to be taken in and to suspend reality testing momentarily for the purpose of gratification. Copying reality closely is not a requirement for a novel to have a powerful effect. Kundera (1986) reminded us that a character is not a simulation of a living being, but rather an imaginary one, "an experimental self." "Don Quixote is practically unthinkable as a living being. And yet in our memory, what character is more alive?" (p. 34) When an analyst treats a character as though it were a real person, does he not fall prey, to some degree, to the same realistic illusion as the unwary reader? The analyst's position becomes analogous to that of the therapist who acts on the patient's requests rather than analyzing them. The willingness to enter the fictional universe has a developmental line starting with early identifications with a playing adult (see Loewenstein's [1957] description of seduction of the aggressor) transitional phenomena, and the capacity to play.

That novels have a profound impact on people has been taken for granted by governments which have banned the publication of such works as *Madame Bovary* and *Ulysses*. What is the basis for the fear that public morality can be so profoundly corrupted? Do the governing officials understand the power of the dream of the novelist to touch and influence the hidden reality within each of us? Flaubert once wrote that the successful novel would be "*un qui ferait rever*"—"one which would cause the reader to dream." Madame Bovary is dangerous to the degree that the readers find her real and believable, and might, through identification, be aroused to live out their own fantasies and to emulate her actions, thus undermining the very fabric of social institutions. At one point Flaubert wrote that "*en ce moment ma Bovary pleure dans vingt villages de France*" ("as of this moment my Bovary is crying in twenty villages of France"), suggesting that his fictional creation was in fact mirrored by real women whose plight had been unrecognized.

There is another factor which may account for the intensity of reader reactions to a novel: an unexplored similarity between a fictional character and the makeup of one's own character.

Fiction In Character And Self

The role of illusion in the sense of a belief distorted by wish fulfillment is certainly not limited to pathological mental products but accompanies normal development as well. Illusion is a part of infantile omnipotence. It plays a role in idealization, in falling in love, and is often necessary for maintaining our equilibrium and self-esteem in times of trauma or reverses, and in dealing with severe illness or death. But illusion is also part and parcel of our everyday self. Grossman (1982, p. 929) quoted Stone: "'... the adult organism' can 'preserve the subjective illusion' of reacting as a whole '... only with the aid of an elaborate unconscious system [and] various compromise formations (ranging from dreams to well-marked symptoms or pathological character traits)... ' In short, 'the self' is a 'personal myth'..., a myth of which everyone has his own more or less original version."

Auerbach (1946) made a related point when he wrote that

> there is always going on within us a process of formulation and interpretation whose subject matter is our own self. We are constantly endeavoring to give meaning and order to our lives in the past, the present, and the future, to our surroundings, the world in which we live; with the result that our lives appear in our own conception as total entities—which to be sure are always changing, more or less radically, more or less rapidly, depending on the extent to which we are obliged, inclined, and able to assimilate the onrush of new experience [p. 549].

The process of interpretation and synthesis to which Auerbach referred has all the hallmarks of a work of fiction—not in the sense of being untrue, but in the sense of a complex combination of real events, their inner meaning, and the overriding influence of unconscious fantasies. The imaginative production which we call our self has its origins in childhood.

Its derivatives—the amalgam of unconscious fantasies which organize mental life—occasionally coalesce to form condensed discrete "imaginative" works. The French for family romance is *roman des origines*, literally translated as "novel of the origins." The term stresses the fictional nature of this group of unconscious fantasies.[35] No great distance separates these imaginative productions from the plots of fairy tales. At times, other imaginative products determine in unusually clear fashion the behavior or lifestyle of certain individuals. Such is the case of impostors who live out a life which could be described as fictional. For example, some pretend to be doctors and for a long time may be able to fool the establishment. Such impostors have been known to treat patients successfully and skillfully without ever having gone to medical school or having a license. They are often caught because of some trivial mistake which exposes the hoax. Greenacre (1958) described some of the characteristics of impostors, including their need to enact family romances, disturbances in their sense of identity and sense of reality, and malformation of the superego.

A related group includes those patients who have accomplished a great deal in their lives and yet who believe themselves to be impostors; in these, we find different pathology. In one patient the feeling of being an impostor was based on an identification with a father who repeatedly exposed himself to shame and humiliation by trying to pass himself off as an expert in a field in which he had only moderate knowledge. The father would elaborate ingenious theories based on imaginative reconstructions, which he would present as facts. As a result, he would be ridiculed by the true experts. In his grandiosity, which bordered on imposture, he would claim that he was far ahead of his time and that his adversaries "resisted" his findings because they could not tolerate his revolutionary ideas. The patient's feelings of being an impostor also originated in his retreat from the oedipal struggle. The disturbances in the sense of identity and sense of reality described by Greenacre were also present. Chasseguet-Smirgel (1984) has studied a particular type of imposture related to certain perverse structures.

---

35 In an early paper, Anna Freud (1922) traced the evolution from beating fantasies to a piece of creative writing.

To return to the classical analytic situation, the view analysands have of themselves, and of their character, changes as treatment proceeds. The distortions introduced into the narrative of one's life—its fictions one might say—are understood in terms of defenses, adaptation, and re-enactment. A screen memory is like a very brief work of fiction, a story unconsciously created by its author to retain a complicated amalgam of real events, fantasies, and wishes. Time is distorted and episodes have to be interpreted symbolically and analyzed as one would analyze a dream whose latent meaning has been altered by the processes of condensation and displacement. New reconstructions are elaborated. Such constructions need not portray actual events, but rather can be seen as fictions—in the sense of imaginative narratives combining some bits of historical truths with plausible reconstructions of earlier psychic states for which we may or may not have complete evidence. This is how we speak of a patient's infantile neurosis. We have to fill in missing pieces, and the analysis does not always allow us to confirm the validity of our hypotheses with the emergence of new memories.

Related to this question of "real" versus "fantasy" in the makeup of psychic structure is a vast literature, including such authors as Laplanche and Pontalis (1968) and Spence (1982). Loewald (1975), in a paper comparing transference neurosis and a play, wrote:

In the promotion and development of the transference neurosis, analyst and patient conspire in the creation of an illusion, a play. The patient takes the lead in furnishing the material and the action of this fantasy creation, while the analyst takes the lead in coalescing, articulating, and explicating the action and in revealing and highlighting it as an illusion (note that the word illusion derives from the Latin ludere, to play). The patient experiences and acts without knowing at first that he is creating a play (pp. 279–280).

Substantial aspects of our character are based on such symbolic re-enactments of conflicted early object relations encoded in the mind as unconscious fantasies.

These early object relations do not represent the relation of the child to the actual parent but to the imagined parent. This imagined parent is a fictive creation of the child's mind, presenting an amalgam of the real object colored and distorted by the child's projections, identifications, idealization, or depreciation in accordance with the child's unconscious fantasies. There will often be a close relationship between the unconscious fantasies and the type of fiction individuals will write should they be creative. The same relationship will apply to the genre of autobiography. DeMan (1984) wrote:

> We assume that life produces the autobiography as an act produces its consequences, but can we not suggest, with equal justice, that the autobiographical project may itself produce and determine the life and that whatever the writer does is in fact governed by the technical demands of self-portraiture and thus determined, in all its aspects, by the resources of his medium? [p. 69].
>
> Autobiography then, is not a genre or a mode but a figure of reading or of understanding that occurs to some degree in all texts [p. 70].

DISCUSSION

To return to my original question, what do great works of literature have to teach us about character? The answer would have to be both relatively little and a great deal! If we are interested in finding case histories, we will be disappointed. In a few instances, a type may afford a label in our diagnostic category. When it comes to etiology or dynamics, the novel, being less interested than we are in development or unconscious fantasy or the relation between trait and symptom, will have little to teach us. It can teach us a great deal, however, in the sense that poets or creative writers can have very insightful glimpses into the unconscious; they may be able to convey in a condensed fashion something that we struggle to articulate in much more cumbersome fashion. We can sharpen our clinical acumen and appreciate the finesse of the description of the inner life—whether in a play by Shakespeare or in the detailed introspection of Marcel in Proust's À la recherche. I occasionally find myself associating to a character in a novel while listening to a patient, and, by following the trend of my own thoughts, I discover something unexpected about the patient which first came to my mind via the literary association.

For example, while listening to a patient describing how he had stopped living—was letting his house go uncared for and was no longer productive—I found myself thinking of Miss Havisham, the character of the eccentric lady in *Great Expectations* who was abandoned by her suitor shortly before her wedding and secluded herself in her house, stopping the clocks and allowing her wedding dress to disintegrate. This picture suddenly allowed me to discover the profound erotic bond between the patient and his father whom he had lost in childhood. This bond had not been apparent in the clinical material until then.

It is possible that a reading of Sophocles' *Oedipus Rex* during Freud's adolescence resurfaced many years later and allowed him to crystallize his own oedipal conflicts. This discovery then allowed him to appreciate the gripping power of the play. In the October 15, 1897, letter to Fliess, Freud mentioned the discovery in his self-analysis of his love for his mother and jealousy of his father. He then added, "If this is so, we can understand the gripping power of *Oedipus Rex*, in spite of all the objections that reason raises against the presupposition of fate..." (Masson, 1985, p. 272).

I would like to conclude my discussion by alluding to a real danger in the application of analysis to works of art. It resides in the problem of boundary and the use of analogy, which has been studied by Kaplan (1988) and Ricoeur (1970). If a heart is like a pump, it is also more than a pump, and the "more than" cannot be expressed by any of the properties of the pump. This is the well-known issue of reductionism. Analysis will tend to see in the novel the components of its systems of the mind—that is, a complex combination of instinctual derivatives, defenses, identifications, projections, and the like. While these elements do play a role, their addition leaves something essential out of the picture. Ricoeur writes about the Janus-like quality of symbols, their two faces: one looks toward the regressive or infantile, and the other is the creative forward looking innovative side. Likewise, a work of art or a character in real life is more than an intricate combination of mechanisms and infantile elements. In the same vein, art is more than a form of instinctual renunciation, and a novel is more than a substitute for life. Psychoanalysts have tended to talk about art as a substitute for symptom formation. This leaves out an irreducible element of the new or the "novel." Reading a great work is an enriching experience. I have suggested that some of the associated excitement is the identification with the experience of the author who creates other selves. This enriching process may allow us to give new meanings and new interpretations to our own lives and, even further, to gain new understanding about our own prize fictions—ourselves!

We have now come full circle. Although I initially started to write a paper about the differences between literary characters and character in real life, and the dangers of treating a literary character as though it were real, the second part of my paper on fiction in character seemed to blur some of the distinctions between the two entities. However, I would like to end by restating that the motives for creating fictions within ourselves are very different from those which apply to a work of literature. Fictions are created within ourselves for defensive, synthetic, and adaptive ends. The novelist writes, as I have indicated earlier, primarily to please, to guide, and to offer new insights into human nature and the world at large.

REFERENCES

Arlow, J.A. (1969). Fantasy, memory, and reality testing. *Psychoanal. Q.* 38:28–51.

Auerbach, E. (1946). *Mimesis. The Representation of Reality in Western Literature* Translated by W. R. Trask. Princeton: Princeton Univ. Press, 1953.

Baudry, F. (1979). On the problem of inference in applied psychoanalysis: Flaubert's "Madame Bovary." *Psychoanal. Study Society* 8:331–358.

——— (1983). The evolution of the concept of character in Freud's writing. *J. Am. Psychoanal. Assoc.* 31:3–31.

——— (1984). An essay on method in applied psychoanalysis. *Psychoanal. Q.* 53:551–581.

Breuer, J. & Freud, S. (1893–1895). Studies on hysteria. *S.E.* 2.

Chasseguet-Smirgel, J. (1984). *A psychoanalytic study of falsehood In Creativity and Perversion* New York: Norton, pp. 66–79.

De Man, P. (1984). *The Rhetoric of Romanticism* New York: Columbia Univ. Press.

Forster, E.M. (1927). *Aspects of the Novel* New York: Harcourt, Brace World.

Frattaroli, E. (1987). On the validity of treating Shakespeare's characters as if they were real people. *Psychoanal. Contemp. Thought* 10:407–437.

Freud, A. (1923). The relations of beating fantasies to a daydream. *Int. J. Psychoanal.* 4 89–102.

Freud, S. (1916). Some character-types met with in psycho-analytic work. *S.E.* 14.

——— (1927). The future of an illusion. *S.E.* 21.

Frow, J. (1986). Spectacle binding. *Poetics Today* 7:227–250.

Genette, G. (1969). Vraisemblance et motivation. *Figures* 2:1–99.

Greenacre, P. (1958). The impostor. *Psychoanal. Q.*27:359–382.

Grossman, W.I. (1982). The self as fantasy: fantasy as theory. *J. Am. Psychoanal. Assoc.* 30:919–937.

Hochman, B. (1985). *Character in Literature.* Ithaca, NY/London: Cornell Univ. Press.

Holland, N.N. (1975). *5 Readers Reading.* New Haven/London: Yale Univ. Press.

James, H. (188). The art of fiction In: *Partial Portraits.*. New York: Haskell House Publ., pp. 375–408, 1968.Kaplan, D.M. (1988). The psychoanalysis of art: some ends, some means. *J. Am. Psychoanal. Assoc.* 36:259–293.

Kundera, M. (1986). *The Art of the Novel.* Translated by L. Asher. New York: Grove Press, 1988.

Laplanche, J. & Pontalis, J.-B. (1968). Fantasy and the origins of sexuality. *Int. J. Psychoanal.* 49:1–18.

Loewald, H.W. (1975). Psychoanalysis as an art and the fantasy character of the psychoanalytic situation. *J. Am. Psychoanal. Assoc.* 23:277–299.

Loewenstein, R.M. (1957). A contribution to the psychoanalytic theory of masochism. *J. Am. Psychoanal. Assoc.* 5:197–234.

Masson, J.M., Translator and Editor (1985). *The Complete Letters of Sigmund Freud and Wilhelm Fliess 1887–1909.* Cambridge/London: Harvard Univ. Press.

Ricoeur, P. (1970). *Freud and Philosophy. An Essay on Interpretation.* New Haven: Yale Univ. Press.

Shiff, R. (1979). Art and life: a metaphoric relationship. In *On Metaphor* ed. S. Sachs. Chicago: Univ. of Chicago Press, pp. 105–121.

Simon, B. (1988). *Tragic Drama and the Family. Psychoanalytic Studies from Aeschylus to Beckett.* New Haven, CT: Yale Univ. Press.

Spence, D.P. (1982). *Narrative Truth and Historical Truth: Meaning and*

Interpretation in Psychoanalysis. New York/London: Norton.

Vargas Llosa, M. (1975). *The Perpetual Orgy: Flaubert and Madame Bovary.* Translated by H. Lane. New York: Farrar, Straus Giroux, 1986.

Wangh, M. (1950). Othello: the tragedy of Iago. *Psychoanal. Q.* 19:202–212.

Woolf, V. (1927). The art of fiction In *The Moment and Other Essays.* New York/London: Harcourt Brace Jovanovich, 1948, pp. 106–112.

CHAPTER 10

The Relevance of the Analyst's Character and Attitudes to his Work

[(1991). *J. Amer. Psychoanal. Assn.* (39):917–938.]

ABSTRACT: This paper is intended to sensitize analysts to the role of their character in analytic technique. The relation of character to countertransference, its role in analytic style, in the introduction of parameters, and in transference neurosis, will be elaborated. The problem of matching and of accounting for our failures will illustrate the complex meshing of character with more traditional factors.

The personality of the analyst has a far greater impact on the course of treatment than our theory allows. This is in part because a theory, due to its general nature, cannot take into account individual differences. Normally one does not think of the character of the analyst as a component of analytic technique. Perhaps it is relegated to the "art" part of psychoanalysis, those subtle, unfathomable, intuitive aspects of the professional behavior of an analyst that provide much of the frame and background of the analytic relationship. Its relevance to the analytic situation was noted as early as 1935 by Balint: "The character of the analyst is an integral factor in the analytic situation and with the best of will in the world it cannot be eliminated." My hope in writing this paper is to sensitize therapists to look at this neglected area in our technique.

In what follows, I shall divide the structuring effects of character into two overlapping areas: (1) general character attitudes, (2) analytic style. I shall then show the relevance of the analyst's character on four aspects of our work—countertransference and then transference neurosis, the introduction of parameters, and the problem of accounting for our failures. Each topic listed could be studied in depth, but my purpose here is simply to underline the importance of the analyst's character in these areas.

In the title of this paper, I have purposely used the terms "character and attitudes." By the analyst's character I mean the complex organization of stable recurrent traits, behaviors, and attitudes which define him. The term "attitude" is closer to the level of observation; it refers to ego-syntonic mind sets which lend form to the analyst's perception and shape his view of the world and therefore his responses to other people. Character responses seen from the inside are, for the most part, forced choices of an automatic nature, not open to question. They are like a pair of colored glasses one is not free to remove. It is possible to describe these general attitudes as mind sets—predilections for certain reactions or sensitivity to certain constellations and the readiness of their being evoked in the analyst. This includes both cognitive and affective reactions. The concept of character allows for deductive processes, that is, the analyst's character can be shown to influence a wide array of behavior, professional and personal.

There is no easy way of classifying character responses. For the purpose of this paper, certain categories suggest themselves as primitive organizers: some character responses are self-initiated, others are responsive; some are verbal, others are nonverbal; some are general, others are more specific. In contrast to some writers on the topic, I believe that not all character responses are syntonic—some may be experienced as dystonic or symptom like. I shall allude to most of these categories. The term "style" is drawn from lay language and is purely descriptive in nature. It is slightly more abstract than behavior, but is not organized in dynamic fashion. Though relating more to other disciplines, such as esthetics or sociology, style can usefully convey in nontechnical language the way an analyst conducts himself professionally. Style has the advantage of isolating direct observations about the analyst's behavior with minimal generalization and without commitment to diagnostic or genetic considerations or even inferences to a specific character structure. In contrast to character, which is here used deductively, the concept of style allows us to proceed inductively. Style also delineates more sharply than character the behavioral components of the analyst's professional identity.

There are a number of methodological issues relevant to the way I have chosen to proceed. The description of traits and attitudes by another bypasses the subjectivity of the observer. This large topic has been addressed in the psychological literature. Deaux (1984) writes that the "eye of the beholder does not affect perception alone but can affect behavior as well" (p. 114). She quotes Darley and Fazio (1980) who have reviewed the evidence for self-fulfilling prophecies and have detailed steps by which expectancies are confirmed in social interaction.

It is possible to write about character from different vantage points. My point of entry has been traits and attitudes which are close to the data of observation. Reich (1951), (1973) refers to *conflicts* of analysts which interfere with their work. This latter term has the advantage of being within a dynamic framework of reference. It also allows for a much greater latitude: a given conflict may be manifest in a multitude of ways, depending on modes of expression chosen and mechanisms of defense. However, I have preferred in this paper to select more surface manifestations of character. A second problem resides in the topic itself. Our character will be revealed not only in the way we conduct our practices but in the subject matter we write about and in the way we write about it. Because of the ego-syntonic nature of character, I can only be very partially aware of the extent of what I am disclosing about myself in this paper or of its impact on others. There is a danger that the reader might focus on revelations about my character or try to identify who the analysts I refer to are, rather than appreciate the more general points I am trying to make. If such were the case, the purpose of the paper would be lost.

Effect of the Analyst's Character on Technique

Relatively little has been written specifically about the influence of the analyst's character on the therapeutic effect of psychoanalysis and on technique. Ticho (1966) studies the relevance of personality attitudes to the analyst's work. His net is broader than the one I am considering here. He includes such elements as professional competence, commitment, values, range of education, ideals, language, customs, interests, physique, and residues of life experiences. He raises questions similar to those I shall take up here, and shares my belief in the role of supervision as a proper forum for the demonstration of the analyst's attitudes. He draws a sharper distinction than I would between intrusion of the analyst's traits and development of the transference neurosis. He raises questions about the extent to which both participants react to personality traits in the other that do not become part of the analytic work proper. Finally, he notes that the treatment of the sicker and more regressed patients is more likely to be influenced by personality variables of the analyst.

It is very instructive to read the early cases in the analytic literature and see the correlation between the absence of a well developed technique and the greater flourishing of more personal (i.e., nontechnical) reactions on the part of the analyst. The principle of neutrality (abstinence) is a safeguard for the analyst against too personal an intrusion. I have found that the analyst's character is more likely to be a factor in those ambiguous situations in which there are no obvious ways of proceeding. I do not believe I am overstating the case in seeing the purpose of technique and its structure as an effort to tame the personality of the analyst so as to allow psychoanalytic work to be done.

That is, the rule of abstinence limits the development of a real relationship between the patient and the analyst. It can also be used in the service of the analyst's neurotic tendencies—for example, the need to keep one's emotional distance or uninvolvement.

By real relationship I mean one in which the analyst interacts with the patient outside the boundaries of what is commonly defined as the therapeutic role—for example, gives advice, acts as a friend, socializes with the patient, tells him about himself and his own life, freely responds directly to questions. Different therapists will do some or all of the above with alleged therapeutic aims, justifying their stance on the basis of the patient's needs. Lipton (1977) elaborates on what he defines as the personal relationship, "a relationship which is outside technique and subject to individual variation" (p. 268). Taking his lead from Freud who by and large excluded his personal relationship with the patient from the treatment, Lipton sees this personal relationship as necessary to analytic work proper by allowing irrational elements of the transference to find a foothold in a real or nonimaginary space. I hope to show that the character of the analyst plays a pivotal, silent role in the structuring of this personal relationship but that contrary to what Lipton says, it cannot safely be excluded from the treatment without a significant loss. Stein (1981), in a paper on the unobjectionable transference, writes about the need to regard the "unobjectionable component"... not only as a welcome manifestation of certain conflict-free psychic elements, but also as the manifest resultant of a complex web of unconscious conflicts which must be, and are capable of being, sought for and described" (p. 891). In addition to the so-called "real" relationship, there may be other aspects of the analyst's reality which have an impact on the treatment and are often deleted by mutual collusion. A colleague was in treatment with an older therapist who was afflicted with chronic bronchitis. The sessions were often interrupted by episodes of coughing and wheezing yet the patient felt far too embarrassed to mention his reaction to this disturbance. He would fall silent and count the coughs waiting for the episode to run its course.

Gill (1982) has written on the value of paying close attention to resisted aspects of the transference. Our own taking for granted certain ego-syntonic aspects of our style and behavior requires constant vigilance on our part not to miss the patient's reactions to it. The critical question is how such stylistic differences affect the process (even if the patient's reaction to them is taken up) and whether they significantly affect the end result? Clearly, there is no either-or. I shall return to this important issue a bit later when I discuss the problem of matching, which includes the influence of the sex of the analyst.

How does the analyst's character affect his technique? I shall select from the myriad possible avenues three components: (1) general self-syntonic beliefs and attitudes which permeate all aspects of the analyst's functioning both personal and professional: pessimism/optimism, degree of permissiveness, activity vs. passivity, degree of warmth vs. distance, rigidity/flexibility, authoritarian tendencies, and so forth; (2) aspects of the style of the given analyst: tone, manner, verbosity, use of humor, degree of irony; (3) the analyst's characteristic reactions to various affects of the patient or to problems in the treatment, such as stalemated situations.

General Attitudes and Traits

There are personal qualities of the analyst that form a backdrop to the conduct of the analysis. Day (1988) lists some of the more relevant ones: charm, the way one shows interest or concern, degree of relatedness, tolerance of affects, frankness, tolerance of a misfit in matching, capacity for enthusiasm, the tendency to see oneself as an authority. How much of the analyst's character will be perceived and identified correctly by the patient is very much a function of the particular patient's capacity to observe, in addition to the nature of the transference. Each of these attitudes will affect the patient depending on his sensitivity to these traits. For example, a schizoid patient might work better with a more emotionally restrained analyst. A patient recently seen in consultation had sustained major losses in the recent past. She had decided not to work with a previous analyst because of her sensitivity to his neutrality and emotional reticence. There is another set of attitudes in the narcissistic sector which deserve mention. An analyst may have more than his share of therapeutic omnipotence or zeal to rescue his patients. This can lead to overactivity or the wish to influence the patient's life. This wish to cure is often found in young therapists who have a need to prove their adequacy and have their patients improve. If the patient senses this, he may retaliate and try to defeat the analyst who is too invested in his getting better. This combination can cause particular difficulty in institute candidates under supervision. These young analysts may have a hard time distinguishing between the "reality" of the situation and the transference component. Their wish to graduate is seen as depending on the patient getting better—rather than through analysis of the patient's transference patterns which are repeated in these battles, including turning aggression on the self and injuring the self as the way to hurt another person.

There are other qualities, such as overall mood, which affect the atmosphere of the treatment. A depressed patient may react to subtle nuances in tone and be only marginally aware of his analyst's depressed mood, because it is so pervasive. Unfortunately, it is very difficult to research this topic. We only possess anecdotal information from our observations of our supervisees or about patients who come for a second or third analysis, or finally from our own patients who confront us at one time or another with some aspect of our character.

Each analyst, however, acquires (whether justly or not) a certain reputation—Dr. A. is talkative; Dr. B. is a silent type. Greenson (1967), in his textbook on analysis, clearly labels himself as overtalkative! It is very difficult to disentangle an analyst's professional behavior (and style) from his character. Although, technically speaking, his behavior as an analyst reflects his professional therapeutic stances, it is subtly infiltrated by his character. For example, it might not surprise us to hear that an analyst with obsessional traits is a bit more of a stickler for rules, a bit more rigid in his expectations and less compromising on certain therapeutic issues, e.g., whether to charge for all missed sessions. He might also be more persistent in questioning the patient about every instance of lateness. Because of the ego-syntonic quality of such attitudes, some of the more relevant personal origins still rooted in conflict may remain unexplored and rationalized behind therapeutic or theoretical rationales. Furthermore, the patients' reactions to the analyst's stance may not be taken up in the treatment.

In discussing various motives for particular behaviors of the analyst, I am purposely focusing on the personal and, therefore, leaving out the more conflict-free, conscious and preconscious components: the learning the analyst has acquired during his training, the identifications he may have made with his supervisors, and the thoughtful integration of the above into what will eventually turn out to be his personal style. I am also leaving out the major impact of the identification with the training analyst—his values and attitudes and the degree to which the analysand accepts or rejects them and works through this aspect of his professional identification. These last purposive acquisitions may themselves be involved in conflict. Finally, it is common knowledge that as an analyst gains more experience, his professional attitudes change. He often can become less rigid, less concerned about rules and their infractions, and more willing to reveal personal attitudes. With the process of aging, still other changes may occur in the direction of inflexibility and irritability.

The Problem of Analytic Style

As I have defined it analytic style is the final common pathway, the melting pot as it were, including conscious understanding and integration of technique and its acquisition through learning as it is filtered through the analyst's overall personality organization. Style is a descriptive concept drawn from lay language.

What are some components of analytic style, the subtle formal matrix in which interpretations are imbedded? Many variables exist, such as intonation (degree of uniformity), manner, humor, intensity, verbosity vs. pithiness, conviction vs. tentativeness, use of authority. Such elements are the counterpart of the patient's style. It is important for the analyst to be aware of their presence and potential impact.

There are important differences in the degree of activity of different analysts, not explained by rules. I have heard the humorous epithets of hunters vs. trappers in describing two extremes of stylistic approach! Is the trapper more likely to be a passive analyst? A colleague who had had two analyses confided that his second analyst's more loquacious manner had allowed him to take distance from and realize the impact of his first analyst's scant verbal pronouncements—clearly a stylistic difference that had a major effect on the course of the treatment. He realized in retrospect that he had silently interpreted the paucity of his first analyst's interventions as a reflection of the poverty of his productions; it was not until his second analysis that he came to realize the degree to which he had silently blamed myself for what was an aspect of his first analyst's style. Although his own concern about being a good patient had often been interpreted, the pervasive demoralizing aspect of his first analyst's silence was never picked up by him nor connected with his reaction to his style.[36]

I have not ceased to be amazed by both stories and vignettes of what well known teachers and respected analysts could do within the limits of their style without apparent major difficulties. A now deceased senior analyst was well known to touch certain depressed patients during the course of therapy, apparently intending to convey concretely warmth and caring. I could imagine a student copying this approach and getting disastrous results. The results would be disastrous because an analyst's behavior only makes sense within a particular context, which includes the state of the relationship with a given patient and the integration of the behavior with the analyst's mental life so that it appears appropriate and self-syntonic. Another analyst who used to share a suite with a fellow therapist confided how often he would hear his colleague yell at his patients through the soundproof door. To him, this did not sound like anger but rather like a demonstration of loving concern.

The problem with such issues of style is that they are hardly, if ever, analyzed, and because they are so ego-syntonic, the patient's responses to them are often misunderstood or glossed over, i.e., understood within the distorting prism of the style.

One patient revealed that he had felt very sustained and excited by his former therapist's enthusiastic and slightly manic tone. This apparently minor aspect of the analyst's style fed an extremely stubborn transference gratification which had not been analyzed; it required some time to uncover the roots of this in certain games played with a parent in childhood. Another patient's angry resentment at his analyst was not properly brought out

---

36 Naturally these observations of style are both subjective and retrospective. Like any other mental products, they are compromise formations subject to error and distortion.

because the latter's charm and verbal agility quickly disarmed and seduced the patient into a mutual enjoyment of the dialogue.

As my personal experience as an analysand amply demonstrates, patients are often intimidated by aspects of our style and behavior which they sense is invested with a certain sense of pride and is not open to question; this is often conveyed in nonverbal ways. A generally straightforward patient once told me he was unable to express his thoughts freely about what he considered to be certain unacceptable habits of his former analyst. The latter would never get up to greet his patients, but simply left his door ajar as a signal to the patient in the waiting room that he was ready. The patient sensed a no-trespass sign and was fearful of attacking the analyst in too personal a manner, particularly in an area in which he felt the analyst was simply rude.

Specific Situations

This category—the analyst's reaction to specific situations—is dealt with in most writings on countertransference. However, I shall examine it from the characterological point of view. A good point of entry into the topic is the relation between character and countertransference.

Character and Countertransference. Reich (1951) defines counter-transference as "the effects of the analyst's own unconscious needs and conflicts on his understanding or technique" (p. 138). She differentiates between the more transitory or acute manifestations from what she terms permanent or chronic countertransference. By the latter, she understands those manifestations that reflect permanent neurotic difficulties of the analyst—at times an expression of a general character problem of the analyst. She gives as examples "unconscious aggression which may cause the analyst to be over conciliatory, hesitant and unable to be firm when necessary; unconscious guilt feelings which may express themselves in boredom or therapeutic overeagerness" (p. 142). She further believes that most countertransference difficulties are of the permanent type. In a final paper (1973) she reverses somewhat her previous stance and states that chronic attitudes not stirred up by something specific to the case represent neurotic behavior patterns not solved in the previous analysis. They occur not only when analyzing, but also in many life situations and *should not be considered countertransference.*

The ambiguity in the definition of countertransference hinges on its relation to character. The broad definition includes the totality of the analyst's unconscious reactions to his patient. According to Fine and Moore (1988) countertransference "refers to the attitudes and feelings, only partly conscious, of the analyst toward the patient" (p. 29). A narrower definition limits countertransference to those unconscious attitudes of the analyst which interfere with the analysis. This more pragmatic definition limits countertransference to the symptomatic; it excludes those ego-syntonic characterological difficulties of the analyst which silently or not so silently affect the course of treatment in a deleterious fashion. It is the latter with which I am concerned. Since character includes both the adaptive and the maladaptive, it will be a factor in both definitions.

Character and Transference Neurosis. There is perhaps no greater test of the analyst's sensitivity and character than the proper clinical management of the transference neurosis. In this section I would like to show by a clinical example the special importance the analyst's character traits play in the development, dynamics, and resolution of the transference neurosis. I believe that the analyst's real character traits serve as hooks on which patients can hang their transference reactions and give them a measure of plausibility. It is important for the analyst to be in touch with his characteristic responses so as to be able to monitor his own contributions and see how the patient uses them.

In the heat of engagement in certain negative transferences, I transiently often experience a certain helplessness, as though I were caught up in the patient's way of subtly distorting the situation between us. When I examine myself further, I often find the kernel of truth in the patient's accusations which lead me to be caught up in his subjectivity ever so briefly. An example follows, including the process by which this was overcome.

Mr. A., a rather withdrawn, needy, intellectualizing man in his early forties, was in a very grim mood when I returned from my vacation. The treatment, which had lasted already far too long, was a general disappointment to him; he had changed as much as he would. Over the summer, he had learned to be independent, and he had taken the decision to stop. The anxiety and depression he was experiencing made him realize he would have to give up his perfectionistic expectations about himself and had better grit his teeth and accept reality. The patient went on in this vein, and I suddenly began to feel influenced by his way of thinking as though I had been failing him and should accept the responsibility for the imperfect result, feel bad and leave him to lead his independent life. My attempts at this point to interpret his mood and determination as a reaction to separation and the summer break were not really convincing to either of us, even though technically correct. In any case, the patient did not want to come during evening hours as this interfered with his wish to socialize with business associates—something he felt he had not been doing enough of and was jeopardizing his otherwise successful career.

After another hour, during which he reacted to my interpretive efforts as attempts to censure him, I began to question myself and realized the patient had struck a particular chord in my character—the tendency to feel guilt and accept responsibility for a situation that did not turn out as expected. This awareness allowed me to begin to distance myself from the countertransference web I had been caught in. A day later the patient made an allusion to childhood incidents involving his mother. The latter would come home in a very irritable or depressed mood and nonverbally convey to the patient that he was a bad son, that her mood was his total responsibility, whereupon he would resentfully try to make it up to her, please her, at the same time that he would feel desperately caught up and want to get away. Suddenly I understood that in the past few sessions he had enacted this scenario with me—he was in the position of the mother and I was in his role. The correct interpretation of this reenactment and its multiple motives put the analysis back on track. Only then could his complaints about his life be understood as violent reproaches for my absence.

This vignette shows the occurrence of a temporary "fit" between the transference of the patient and a "real" aspect of my character. The power of the resulting affects interfered temporarily with the working of the analyzing instrument. My own reaction had to become the focus of my interest. The earlier interpretation of the patient's reaction to my vacation could then be seen as an effort on my part to distance myself from more painful affect by an intellectualized interpretation of the transference instead of concentrating on what was the immediate dynamically active issue.

A similar issue was explored by Sandler (1981), who studied certain character traits which can best be understood as devices to evoke particular types of response in others, to actualize a wished-for relationship existing in fantasy. He states, "the analyst will often respond overtly to the patient in a way in which he feels indicates his own (the analyst's) problems … (But) very often the irrational response of the analyst … may … be usefully regarded as a compromise formation between his own tendencies and his *reflexive acceptance* of the role which his patient is forcing on him" (p. 698). The type of character traits most likely to evoke such responses in the analyst are the "sadomasochistic ones." It is in the nature of characterological behavior that it stimulates a specific reaction in the audience. This reaction is a combination of the demand that the behavior makes and the recipient's sensitivity and characteristic mode of functioning. Thus, a stubborn, procrastinating analysand might have the unconscious purpose of stimulating the wish to nag or take over as the mother was compelled to do. This is the principle of complementarity first written about by Helene Deutsch.

To a minimal degree, the activation of a character response in the analyst puts him at a crossroad in the paths of acting out vs. understanding. The analyst's ability to do the latter is a function of his inclination to anxiety, guilt, pathological defenses, and the like. There is, unfortunately, a possibility that certain of the analyst's character traits either block or distort his perception of the patient's communication of affects or in the instance just mentioned, that the analyst perceives correctly but that he can only react neurotically.

The question may be asked, "What motivates a particular character response in any person?" The answer has to be some aspect of the situation for which the character reaction is a solution. This is as true for the analyst as it is for the patient. One of my supervisees had developed certain passive compliant attitudes as a solution to an aggressive conflict with a dominating parent. Whenever a patient behaved in an aggressive, demanding fashion, the form of the supervisee's response would be clearly compliant regardless of its contents.

Character and Parameters. How does the analyst typically react when he feels attacked, criticized, loved, idealized, or stuck? Such issues are more often taken up in the personal analysis than the other categories because they lead to obvious conflict in the analyst. I shall have less to say about them as there is a vast literature on the topic. Glover (1955) refers to the silent resistances and counterresistances—the most dangerous—for obvious reasons. He gives a clue as to their appearance—when the analyst is tempted to or does actually depart from his usual way of doing things. Examples include the way patients are ushered in or out of the office, the way bills are handled, and so on. I shall take up one specific aspect, that of parameters. In what situations does an analyst feel the need to introduce a parameter in an ongoing analysis? There are at least two categories: in one, the patient's affective reactions cannot be managed by the usual method of abstinence and interpretation; in the other, the treatment appears stuck and interpretations are ineffective. In the first category one of the variables is the analyst's tolerance for affective storms. There are vast stylistic differences influenced by character, experience, background history, which will determine when an analyst believes he needs to introduce a change in the treatment whether it be medication, a shift to a more supportive stance, or some other departure from a strict analytic stance.

The second category—that of stalemated treatments, is as difficult to resolve. A well-known analyst, now deceased, once related to a group a most fascinating vignette about a very wealthy patient he had been treating in Europe in the early 'thirties. Money meant nothing to her. After some time, the treatment seemed stuck. All the interpretations of the patient's resistance, aggression, and contempt failed to resolve the impasse. One day, the analyst then announced to the patient that until further notice, he had decided not to charge her a fee! Surely, a very dramatic gesture, which, as he tells the story, had a dramatic impact. The patient was very much shaken and the treatment moved forward again after months of stalemate. It would seem to me to rob our understanding of this intervention if one failed to take into account certain "characteristic" attitudes of the analyst in question which became apparent as I came to know him over many years—his willingness to sacrifice himself, his capacity for *Le beau geste*, and many other traits, including his sensitivity to feminine charm. We can only imagine what he may have experienced prior to the introduction of the parameter—chagrin, anger, frustration, helplessness, or some variation of these affects according to his particular sensitivity and character structure, along with curiosity and puzzlement. His casual comments about the incident left no doubt that even in an informal setting he did not think it of much relevance to refer to his own personal attitudes in discussing either the crisis or its resolution, leaving his audience in an affective state combining awe, admiration, and envy! My point is not simply to identify character traits for their own sake, but to demonstrate what we lose in our explanatory and descriptive potential when we leave them out of our formulation. Consideration of character leads, of course, to thorny, perhaps unanswerable, questions that need to be asked. Was the above situation stuck because of the analyst's blind spot, and could one say that the dramatic gesture represented his (preconscious?) solution to his characterological problem in the treatment, involving his response to the patient's aggression and devaluation?

Analytic Failures and Limitations of the Analyst. Throughout the literature on transference and in case presentations, one often reads that "the transference could not be analyzed." Freud (1937), in "Analysis Terminable and Interminable," written in part as an answer to Sandor Ferenzci's reproach that he had failed to analyze the latent negative transference, defends himself by saying that when such transference is not active, the analyst can do little to bring it to the surface—acting unkindly would be artificial. While in principle we would all agree with Freud, the actual facts of the analysis of Ferenzci are far more complicated. To analyze even briefly a close collaborator whose psychic health left something to be desired, poses almost insuperable obstacles. One would not dream of doing this today and any analyst attempting this would be suspect of major countertransference complications—perhaps, in the case of Freud, a special response to the idealization by Ferenczi.

André Green once made the point that our narcissism tempts us to say that a given case is not analyzable, rather than to say that a case is not analyzable by a given analyst. In some cases, there is no question that the patient was unanalyzable; in others, there seems to have been a poor match between the patient and a prior analyst. It is possible to identify conflict areas not dealt with properly. It is more difficult to pinpoint the reasons for this omission. This would include lack of awareness on the analyst's part based on a combination of cognitive lack and emotional (i.e., personal) limitations.

It is not always easy to decide on the actual factors, even if the character of the prior analyst is known.

In trying to clarify for myself what is meant dynamically or structurally by a good match or a poor match, I experience considerable difficulty. Do we mean more than an intuitive sense that a given patient and a given analyst will "work" well together? Certain analysts acquire a given reputation (both positive and negative). Dr. A. is tough. Dr. B. is a bit more giving, works well with depressed patients. Dr. C. is a bit aloof, distant. Dr. D. has suffered a lot himself and can empathize better with similar patients. I am aware the above are extremely crude formulations. In terms of referring patients, we might have a sense that patient A. is particularly vulnerable to narcissistic injury or is not well armed against too intrusive or aggressive an approach, whereas, patient B. is a rather tough, arrogant, somewhat psychopathic individual who needs someone who will not be easily manipulated. In the absence of hard data about our colleagues, we rely on vague impressions in making referrals or even on deciding what a given patient requires. Such assessments take into consideration our evaluation of the analyst's character as much as they do his technique.

Another approach to the complex issues of matching is provided by the work of Emde (1988) who compares the dynamics of matching with the early mother/child fit as studied by the developmentalists; this allows a much more refined approach to the many components, such as affect attunements, vicissitudes of empathy, social referencing, caregiving, the capacity to operate in the zone of proximal development. The more difficult patients can be defined as those who have more stringent requirements in order to do some analytic work. They need just the right mix of support and demand in order to develop a trusting relationship. Sandler and Sandler (1978) have written about a related issue from the object-relations point of view: "what is... necessary for a real relationship of any significance to be established is the propensity of the second person towards whom the transference is directed, to react in a special way, and in the process of object choice he is subtly tested to see whether he will respond in a particular way or not.... The idea of testing out the role responsiveness of another person brings together the concepts of object choice and object relationship inasmuch as we make rapid trial relationships until we find someone who fits the role we want the 'other' to play and is prepared to allow himself to respond according to that role" (pp. 288–289).

An aspect of matching that has been controversial is the impact of the sex of the analyst on the treatment. It is commonly held that what matters most is the sensitivity and empathy of the analyst, except in cases where there has been frank abuse by one parent, or in certain cases of homosexuality, or if the patient is adamant in his request for a therapist of a particular sex. While male analysts can be the recipients of maternal transferences, I recently heard of a case of a male patient who had been well analyzed by a female analyst, yet needed a second analysis with a male therapist to work out the negative oedipal situation. The second analyst raised the possibility that for certain patients who tend toward the concrete, the absence of the penis in the female analyst impedes the reliving of the fantasy of the wish for a penis from the father. In other cases, this lack does not seem to matter as much; some other male person in the patient's environment serves as a displacement for this set of fantasies.

Apart from such gross considerations, there must be a way in which our own character structure facilitates or impedes the understanding and tackling of certain resistances. R. M. Loewenstein stated that the analyst should, in general, not rely on the same attitudes as those of the patient; thus, an analyst who tends to be flip or arrogant might have difficulty in analyzing similar attitudes in the patient. He gave an example of a patient relying on humor to relieve certain anxieties, and advised the analyst to be careful about introducing humor in his interpretations. A particular window we have on colleagues' styles is afforded us by patients who come for a second analysis.

I am well aware of the many caveats in such instances, particularly if the first treatment was less than successful. We must take what we hear with several grains of salt, nevertheless; in spite of transference distortions (and I might add, our own competitive wishes!), certain aspects of the previous therapist's style often emerge with surprising clarity.

In one case, there seemed to be a close fit between the therapist's unintended messages and a patient's fears and resistances. The therapist, attempting to be supportive, minimized his own importance to the patient; he told her that attitudes have a way of becoming self-fulfilling prophecies. He explained that if the patient anticipated she could not cope with his absence, she would be more likely to run into trouble. The patient understood such statements as a covert message not to reveal to the therapist her considerable dependence on him and to keep hidden certain fears and fantasies. In this way, she would be less likely to rock what she understood to be a very conditional acceptance. It turned out that the patient's secretiveness, unintentionally reinforced by the therapist's behavior, was a reenactment of the same attitude toward her mother, both intrusive and overly possessive. The patient idealized her former therapist. The latter failed to appreciate the patient's sensitivity to his message and overlooked crucial aspects of the transference.

I have made the following observations which I am sure are not unique. I work somewhat better with certain types of patients than with others. The cases with which I experience the most difficulty and which do not end satisfactorily seem to go wrong in predictable fashion. Discussion with friendly colleagues in small groups will often reveal transference paradigms that repeat themselves and cause me difficulty. There is little doubt that these involve certain aspects of my own character. For reasons I have studied in other writings, it is very difficult to become aware of one's character; the less pathological aspect may remain untouched and somewhat outside the future analyst's awareness.

This leads me to an important clinical question, "How is an analyst basically limited in his therapeutic endeavors by the way in which he has not resolved certain conflicts?" There need not be a simple correlation between therapeutic impairment and imperfect conflict resolution. There are many ego-syntonic traits or attitudes that color the way an unresolved conflict impairs the analyst's functioning. Thus, will an obsessional analyst be limited in the way he can help an obsessional patient deal with aggression? It is not difficult to imagine how this could occur. The analyst might either short-circuit the emergence of aggression in the transference prematurely, thus robbing the patient of an appropriate emotional experience and intellectualizing the work, or he might be blind to certain manifestations of aggression altogether; or, finally, he might, because of reaction formations of his own, be too permissive or not firm enough. Reich (1951), (1953) has written about this in her papers on countertransference. I do not believe there is an easy answer to this question, but certain typical configurations must recur. I have knowledge of patients with masochistic character formation whose analyses failed with analysts who had more than their fair share of non-neutralized aggression. My sense was that the analyst's character stance (an overly aggressive attitude) gratified the patient's masochism in the transference, thus making an interpretive resolution impossible. Here again, the critical issue was that the analyst did not perceive himself as aggressive, and thus chronically misunderstood the patient's complaints.

I suspect that on some level many of us are probably well aware of our limitations and either preconsciously or consciously fill our practice with the type of patients we can best work with. Further, we are well aware and take into account in some vague, often unformulated way, our colleagues' style when we make referrals and try to achieve a fit. Institute admission committees which still assign students to a specific training analyst operate on the same, often nonverbal tacit premises. The characteristics of the training analyst's style is talked about slightly uneasily or in humorous fashion, as if one were treading on dangerous territory.

What is the role of self-analysis and how helpful is it in dealing with the analyst's character pathology? My personal impression and experience is that it is of some value in dealing with acute manifestations of countertransference, but much less effective in countering the more chronic, subtle, disturbing character attitudes which I have been describing. Thus, if I find myself anxious or unwilling to raise certain thorny questions with a patient, a bit of self examination is more likely to be helpful than in instances dealing with the aforementioned transference difficulties. The analyst, just like the patient, is the victim of his own repetition compulsions—to reenact what he does not remember. There is a final arena where the problem of the analyst's character can be noted—that of supervision. However, for a multiplicity of reasons, some practical, some tactical, and some pedagogic, the supervisor rarely alludes to the character countertransferences of his supervisee. An examination of these important issues requires a separate paper.

REFERENCES

Darley, J. Fazio, R. (1980). Expectancy confirmation processes arising in the social interaction sequence. *Amer. Psychol.*35:867–881.

Day, M. (1988). Reality in the therapist. *Practical Rev. Psychiat.*125.

Deaux, K. (1984). From individual differences to social categories *Amer. Psychol.* 44:105–116.

Deutsch, H. (1926). Occult processes occurring during psychoanalysis In *Psychoanalysis and the Occulted*. G. Devereux. New York: Int. Univ. Press, 1953 pp. 133–146.

Emde, R. (1988). Development terminable and interminable, II. *Int. J. Psychoanal.* 69:283–297.

Fine, B. Moore, B. (1988). *A Glossary of Psychoanalytic Terms and Concepts*. New York: Amer. Psychoanal. Assn.

Freud, S. (1916). Some character types, met with in psycho-analytic work. *S.E.* 14

——— (1937). Analysis terminable and interminable. *S.E.* 23.

Gill, M.M. (1982). Analysis of transference Vol. 1 .*Psychol. Issues Monogr.* 53. New York: Int. Univ. Press.

Glover, E. (1955). *The Technique of Psychoanalysis*. New York: Int. Univ. Press.

Green, A. (1975). The analyst, symbolization and absence. *Int. J. Psychoanal.* 56:1–19.

Greenson, R.R. (1967). *The Technique and Practice of Psychoanalysis*. New York: Int. Univ. Press.

Lipton, S. (1977). The advantages of Freud's technique as shown in his analysis of the Rat Man. *Int. J. Psychoanal.*58:255–273.

Reich, A. (1951). On countertransference. *Int. J. Psychoanal.*32:25–31.

——— (1973). *Empathy and countertransference In Annie Reich: Psychoanalytic Contributions*. New York: Int. Univ. Press, pp. 344–361.

Sandler, J. (1981). Character traits and objects relationships *Psychoanal.* Q.50:696–708

——— & Sandler, A.M. (1978). On the development of object relationships and affects .*Int. J. Psychoanal.*59:285–297.

Stein, M.H. (1981). The unobjectionable part of the transference. *J. Am. Psychoanal. Assoc.* 29:869–893.

Ticho, E. (1966). The effect of the analyst's personality on psychoanalytic treatment *Psychoanal. Forum* 4:135–172.

CHAPTER 11

An Essay on Method in Applied Psychoanalysis

[(1984). *Psychoanal. Q.* (53):551–581.]

ABSTRACT: The author attempts to evaluate critically the application of psychoanalysis to literature by examining problems of method and the assumptions psychoanalysts unwittingly make about texts they are about to interpret. The special advantages of psychoanalysis over other interpretive systems are discussed, and several examples of the possible use of psychoanalysis in the study of literary texts are presented.

Psychoanalysis has been so misused in its application to other fields, such as literature, that a re-examination of the definition, limitations, and possible contributions of a psychoanalytic approach is in order. Some critics even go so far as to question whether the application of psychoanalysis to a literary text can be valid. There is now a considerable literature on the limitations of applied psychoanalysis (e.g., Kohut, 1960); (Skura, 1981); (Trilling, 1950); (Werman, 1979). Most papers dealing with the issue stress the difference between a live patient and a text—the lack of free association and patient response in the applied field—and urge caution in using psychoanalysis in other than the clinical realm.

In this paper, I will attempt to place the psychoanalytic concept of interpretation within the more general framework of a broad definition of interpretation and meaning. This will be followed by specific consideration of how analysis circumvents the absence of a live patient in its examination of a literary text. I will define four main approaches.

1. In the first approach, the analytic writer treats a novel, play, or poem as a case history, ignoring the as-if nature of the literary text and performing a type of character analysis.
2. The second approach relates the text to the mental life (both normal and abnormal) of the author. The text is viewed as a modified form of free association.
3. The third approach considers the text in its own right and carries out a thematic analysis identifying traces or derivatives of mental contents.
4. The fourth approach concerns itself with the reaction of the reader and the production of poetic and aesthetic effect.

Using a number of well-known literary texts, I will illustrate each of these approaches and discuss its validity. As an introduction to this, I will examine Freud's thinking on the relationship between psychoanalysis and literature.

Eissler (1968) described a personal bias of Freud's which shaped his attitude toward literature: his awe and admiration for the talents of the greater writers and their capacity to reach psychological insights intuitively. This led Freud to approach literary texts as organic, live, real. Said Eissler, "Shakespeare's creations may have been experienced by him, not as figments of the mind, or as artistic illusions, but rather as sectors of a live world that has to be analyzed in the same way as one analyzes the minds of live and really existing people" (pp. 152–153).

Freud's bias is apparent in his work on *Gradiva* (1907) and in the use he made of *Macbeth* (1916, pp. 318–324) in his attempt to explain the puzzling character type of "those wrecked by success." He searched for the hidden motivations of Lady Macbeth, who falls apart psychologically after achieving an external success. One gets the impression that Freud expected the playwright in his genius to furnish clues to explain the puzzling breakdown. In this case, Freud's attempt failed as he realized that a literary work was never designed for that purpose. In addition to examining literature and works of art as barely modified case studies, Freud was also interested in the psychology of the artist and in understanding the basis for his own reactions to great works. It is instructive for us to examine the sort of questions which served Freud as points of entry for applying psychoanalysis to other fields. In the "Leonardo" paper (1910), he started his inquiry by noting that something prevented Leonardo's personality from being understood by his contemporaries—particularly his attitude toward his art: Leonardo left many works unfinished and cared little about their ultimate fate. In the "Moses of Michelangelo" paper, Freud (1914) was drawn to analyze the inscrutability of the statue and its particularly powerful effect on him. In his paper on the uncanny (1919), he examined a feeling that is significant to the realm of aesthetic experience yet often neglected by experts in that field. In each case, then, Freud started by focusing on contradictions in the life or work of an artist, or on something unexplained by another discipline, which was of personal interest to him and which he believed could be clarified by using the psychoanalytic approach. The details Freud started with are often quite limited in scope, yet they afforded him an opening to discuss questions of wide interest.

Freud's theorizing about the creative product and its genesis was influenced by his self-analysis and by the exploitation of the richness of the dream. It is not an accident that Freud gave the dream a special position in its role as gatekeeper to the unconscious and as first model, by analogy, of the creative process.

In his early writings Freud overcame some of the obstacles in comparing dream states and waking thought by establishing intermediary way stations. The 1908 paper, "Creative Writers and Day-Dreaming," established an analogy: the poet is *like* a child at play. He creates for himself an imaginary world which he takes seriously, i.e., he endows it with considerable amounts of affect, all the while distinguishing it clearly from reality. Play is superseded by daydreams; these are followed by the novel, that is, by works of art with a narrative structure. Certain universal fantasies, such as the family romance or the Oedipus story, structure myths and certain novels. Dreams and poetry are tied together through a common element—the state of man dissatisfied and unhappy. Unfulfilled wishes are the motive forces of fantasies; all fantasies are wish fulfillments, serving to correct a frustrating reality. A much later work, *Beyond the Pleasure Principle* (1920), incorporated the skillful analysis of a child's play with a wooden reel, understood by Freud as an attempted mastery of loss. Many examples of works fueled by such a motive come to mind. Proust's *Remembrance of Things Past* is an apt illustration of this dynamic element.

In a little-known passage from the "Michelangelo" paper, Freud (1914) clarified beautifully his view of some of the specific contributions analysis can make to the study of art. He wrote:

In my opinion, what grips us so powerfully can only be the artist's intention, in so far as he has succeeded in expressing it in his work and in getting us to understand it. I realize that this cannot be merely a matter of intellectual comprehension; what he aims at is to awaken in us the same emotional attitude, the same mental constellation as that which in him produced the impetus to create. But why should the artist's intention not be capable of being communicated and comprehended in words, like any other fact of mental life? Perhaps where great works of art are concerned this would never be possible without the application of psycho-analysis. The product itself after all must admit of such an analysis, if it really is an effective expression of the intentions and emotional activities of the artist. To discover his intention, though, I must first find out the meaning and content of what is represented in his work; I must, in other words, be able to interpret it... I even venture to hope that the effect of the work will undergo no diminution after we have succeeded in thus analysing it (p. 212).

There is something very compelling about this succinct statement; it still has hints of the dream theory, with the concept of "identity of perception," which Freud utilized in Chapter VII of *The Interpretation of Dreams*. This passage of Freud's also provides a method for the application of analysis to works of art. Better than any other discipline, analysis can provide an understanding of the "meaning and content of what is represented" through the observation of small details often considered unimportant when judged by existing aesthetic standards. This is achieved through objective knowledge of symbolism, and through the understanding of fantasies and their means of representation as derived from the study of dreams. Also necessary is the capacity to understand what is represented in the work. This requires a process akin to empathy. Freud separated the intentions and the emotional activities of the artist, thus distinguishing motives from process. Finally, Freud saw a work of art as a particular type of representation of the artist's mental life. It is not a separate entity and is best appreciated by making constructions about the artist's mental life. There are some problems with the above formulation, however. It is by no means proven that the artist aims "to awaken in us the same emotional attribute, the same mental constellation as that which in him produced the impetus to create." A derivative of this theory was later espoused by Hanns Sachs (1942) who viewed the artist as the vehicle through which forbidden, guilt-laden unconscious fantasies may be given some form of expression. There is a resonance, then, between the author's unconscious and that of his audience. A common sharing results, and the audience is in a position to use the work as a vehicle to live out some of its personal fantasies. The successful work will allow a greater range of possibilities through the artistic skill and creative use of ambiguity. By using the word "intention," Freud was stressing the volitional aspect of creativity far more than is generally held to be true. Many artists, if not most, are unaware of what forces drive them to create and what meaning they intend the audience to find in their work. This is especially true in nonverbal art forms. In his writings, Freud was generally more interested in the psychology of the artist than in the nature of the literary text.

Freud's (1916) paper on "those wrecked by success" included a lengthy analysis of the play, *Macbeth*. It illustrates very well the process of Freud's thinking and is worthy of extended commentary. It is a peculiar paper, in that Freud saw fit to resort to a fictional character to help him solve some of the puzzling clinical features of a character type.37 The first level on which Freud examined the play was that of character, treating the personages as real and explaining their behavior as though they were live people interacting with one another. Such an approach can certainly yield new insights, such as the uncovering of hidden motives to explain behavior. In the case of *Macbeth*, the character approach failed at one critical point well described by Freud. How is one to account for Lady Macbeth's breakdown in view of the strength of that lady in the beginning of the play? If anyone should have shown signs of remorse or guilt, surely Macbeth would have been a more plausible candidate. He seems far less determined than Lady Macbeth to kill Duncan and is more aware of the ignominy of the act itself.

The attempt to understand Lady Macbeth's decompensation and suicide on this level can be pursued in terms of evidence within the play (i.e., the level of so called observable data). If this fails, as it does in the present instance, the depth psychologist can import explanations from outside of the text and not well supported by it, but still within the limits of plausibility—using the concept of self-directed aggression and reconstructing possible motives. Such formulations include Lady Macbeth's wish for self-punishment for having

---

37 Arlow (personal communication) has suggested the reverse possibility—that Freud wanted to use his understanding of the character type to try to unravel the mystery of Lady Macbeth.

wanted Duncan dead, or her interpreting her childlessness (whatever its causes) as a punishment. The latter explanation has an interesting structure; it is plausible, as imported from the historical origins of the legend, but it requires a span of time between the accession to the throne and the subsequent breakdown. It even has the unusual quality of being supported by evidence from within the play itself, yet it is unacceptable because of the short span of the action. In the original story ten years elapsed between the murder and the later events. However, Shakespeare's play condenses the action for the purposes of dramatic structure to a bit less than a week, thus making it impossible to resort to the historical truth. As Freud (1916) stated, "... the contradiction remains that though so many subtle interrelations in the plot, and between it and its occasion, point to a common origin of them in the theme of childlessness, nevertheless the economy of time in the tragedy expressly precludes a development of character from any motives but those inherent in the action itself" (p. 322). Freud wisely wrote: "We must, I think, give up any hope of penetrating the triple layer of obscurity into which the bad preservation of the text, the unknown intention of the dramatist, and the hidden purport of the legend have become condensed" (p. 323).

A third level abandons the search for psychological plausibility and turns to the study of aesthetic and tragic effects, i.e., looking at events not as psychologically motivated but included for other purposes—dramatic action, movement, and the like. In this approach, also pursued by Freud, a new hypothesis was constructed. Lady Macbeth's behavior is "understandable" if we see her conflicts and identity as displaced from Macbeth, that is, if we see the two characters as having been interchanged at least in their psychological reactions. This leads us to an important realization for the depth psychologist. The continuity of character is an illusion created by the playwright. In terms of the process of creation, we know that the author may identify with different characters as a play or novel proceeds. I have studied some aspects of this shift in some scenes of Flaubert's *Madame*

Bovary and have shown the shifting identification of the author, sometimes with one character and sometimes with the other (Baudry, 1979). Thus, the shifting evolution of guilt in *Macbeth*, seen first in one character, then made more evident in another, is consistent with what we know about the creative process. Of course, the skill of the playwright lies in combining elements of poetic necessity with those of psychological plausibility, or even of so overwhelming the audience that a question about plausibility is not raised because the affects aroused deaden the sense of critical judgment or make unnecessary a search for rational explanation. Until I read Freud's study of Lady Macbeth, I had never been troubled by the apparently unexplainable nature of Lady Macbeth's breakdown.

Having been frustrated in his attempt to solve the riddle of Lady Macbeth, Freud suggested one last approach. He looked for underlying themes to unify disparate characters and scenes—in the case of *Macbeth*, "fathers and sons."

Although he did not pursue this further, one could attempt to formulate various classes of hypotheses on the basis of this piece of data. One class would remain at the level of the text and bring to it certain psychoanalytic hypotheses about the relationship of fathers and sons to see whether the play illustrates their validity; or one could try to unify scattered bits of data and attempt to sketch out a clearer statement, perhaps an identifying theme of the play as a particular vicissitude of father-son relationships. It would be possible to examine other Shakespearean plays to test such a theme and to look for variations, *Hamlet* being a logical choice. There is a further level of *Macbeth* not addressed by Freud. As analysts, we might be interested in the study of dramatic effects and ask why and how such effects are produced. We are also curious about the nature and determinants of various audience reactions including the sense, "this is implausible."

Interpretation and Meaning

It is not possible to interpret a text without making some systematic, fundamental assumptions on which to base our interpretations. On the simplest level, to interpret is to reveal a new meaning which underlies the text—"a" really means "b." The interpretation can pertain to the structure or another version of "a," or it may demonstrate a new context which clarifies the original text. To interpret also means to take one set of facts and insert them into a more general system of thought. In this manner we might assert that a poem can have a religious, an allegorical, a historical, a Marxist, or a sociological interpretation. Within each system, different rules of evidence apply. An interpreter espousing a polemic theory might not be very concerned with scientific accuracy. A more encompassing concept of the meaning of a text includes a complex range of possibilities, from the most personal ones related to the author (conscious, preconscious, and unconscious), to those more impersonal sets of ideas related to the historical and cultural epoch and including the genre to which the text belongs. The possible range of meanings of a text is considerable; there is no *one* true meaning.

Some literary critics, notably Hirsch (1967), have argued for a separation of the concepts of meaning and significance. For these theorists, meaning refers to the author's intended meaning (on whatever level). What changes through the ages is not the meaning of a text but its significance—that is, the context in which a particular meaning is seen or understood, depending upon current social and cultural values. The advantage of this point of view is the separation of the "objective" search for meaning from the reader-related concept of significance. Some literary critics, such as Trilling (1950), have disagreed: "There is no single meaning to any work of art... changes in historical context and in personal mood change the meaning of a work and indicate that artistic understanding is not a question of fact but of value.

Even if the author's intention were, as it cannot be, precisely determinable, the meaning of a work cannot be in the author's intention alone. It must also lie in its effect" (p. 331).

Speaking as an analyst, I prefer to distinguish, as Hirsch does, the more objective readings of a text, from the more personal, subjective components. Yet, even an objective reading will still be largely a function of the system and assumptions of the interpreter. A college student, a literary critic, a novelist, and a psychoanalyst could start with the same text and arrive at very different readings of varying degrees of sophistication and scholarship. Some authors, notably Holland (1968), have taken the extreme position that the meaning of a text becomes little more than the projection of an individual's identity themes and conflicts. This view makes of meaning an entirely subjective endeavor and negates the entire field of scholarship. The danger of subjective intrusion is present in any interpretation and can lead to the disregard of other tools available to evaluate an interpretation from the point of view of scholarship and faithfulness to the text.

One of the questions I am raising is whether texts have properties independent of the author which could be called psychological. Language has its own sets of predetermined meanings, implications, and referents, independent of the wishes and purposes of an author. The latter simply borrows them for his own use. The same point was made by a contemporary French critic, Doubrovsky (1966), in a brilliant work on criticism in France: "Though the writer speaks a language, there is also a language speaking through the writer. The real meanings of the written word exceed in every direction the restricted meaning of the work meant. Or, more precisely, the framework of willed significations supports the fabric of the possible significations, of which some, by definition, must escape the author..." (p. 104). "Far from its signifying essence being frozen in an eternal present, the work of art is constantly projecting itself toward an indefinite and open future" (p. 105). The richness of meanings of a work of art is partly intentional, partly preconsciously and unconsciously determined, partly the result of the nature of language, and partly the result of the absence of a clear context which limits the range of possible meanings.

In the case of *Macbeth*, the poor preservation of the text adds its own contribution to obscurity and ambiguity. A simple example will illustrate the problem. In Act, I, Scene vii, there is a brief exchange between Macbeth and Lady Macbeth. Macbeth: "If we should fail,—." Lady Macbeth: "We fail!" This "we fail" is open to at least three interpretations because the punctuation in the original text is unclear. 1) We fail? (meaning we, fail—how can you imagine this?). 2) We fail! (meaning what is the matter with you? We shall have to accept whatever destiny fate has in store for us, and this should not deter us). 3) We fail (implying a more resigned and philosophic stance). Sometimes the author may deliberately resort to ambiguity for purposes of enriching the multiple meanings which reverberate. As analysts, we are interested in the purpose, development, and possible aims of motivational ambiguity. This ambiguity has to be differentiated from obscurity or meaninglessness. In general, great works such as *Macbeth* expose the blind spots of the explanatory devices which open them up to interpretation. The many literary meanings are contained within the text itself and not linked (as is the dream) to another level of discourse of which the text is a distorted symbolic expression.

Having so far examined some general concepts of interpretation and meaning, I will now turn to the arena of psychoanalysis. In contrast to the other systems and theories, what are the specific attributes, methods, and advantages of a psychoanalytic approach to a text and what special skills are required to carry out this task?

The basic approach of psychoanalysis is to look at all human behavior from the vantage point of conflicts, most often unconscious, and to lay bare their structure, their modes of representation, their development, genesis, transformations, and solutions, both adaptive and maladaptive.

Psychoanalysis was initially the science of the unconscious, of the hidden. It eventually extended itself to include functions such as memory and cognition, formerly the domain of academic psychology. With the advent of ego psychology and the study of character which focuses on the formal aspects of behavior, starting with surface descriptions, psychoanalysis moved closer to issues at the heart of literature—those of structure and narrative. As a discipline, psychoanalysis possesses certain very distinct advantages over other methods of literary interpretation, a fact that can be forgotten by excessively zealous critics.

Psychoanalysis, when properly applied, is not reductionistic. It combines several points of view. To arrive at a diagnosis of character, we do not rely on a catalogue of descriptive traits alone, but combine dynamic, structural, genetic, and adaptive approaches. Waelder (1929) described some of the advantages of an analytic approach, which is "characterized by the fact that it is continually divesting our knowledge of the mind of its subjective features and disguises, and which thus indeed conforms to the essence of the development of scientific thought in general, overcoming by an endlessly converging process its basic antimony, i.e. that its means of dealing with its subject are themselves part of this subject… " (p. 111). Psychoanalysis has led to the accumulation of vast stores of knowledge about the functioning of the human mind, particularly in the realm of defenses and the multiple, often unexpected, transformations of unconscious fantasies in both pathological and nonpathological areas. This allows analysts to pick up clear-cut derivatives which nonanalysts would ignore. They are in a position to focus on certain minute details which might strike the literary critic as irrelevant but which hold important clues to hidden meaning. Freud (1910) demonstrated this in the "Leonardo" paper by examining ledgers for expenses which Leonardo kept and then interpreting such ledgers as mini-obsessional devices that allowed the expression of warded-off affects which Freud reconstructed. In addition, analysts through their training

306

are sensitized to observing clues, often preconsciously, which reinforce impressions derived from other observations. The same message can be conveyed through many channels.

A brief comparison of dreams and literary texts will serve as a useful prelude to discussing the application of psychoanalysis to literary texts. The early approach of analysis to literature was based on making analogies to dreams and symbolism. However, the attempt to extend the understanding of the dream to that of waking mental products immediately raises the question of the difference between the two which an application of method must take into account. (1) We must reconcile the narcissistic regressive aspect of the dream with the process of waking thought consciously constructed. Dreams are automatic phenomena, whereas literary products are at least in part under conscious control. (2) There are certain functions of the dream, such as being the guardian of sleep, which cannot be easily applied to waking products. (3) A fundamental aspect of a successful work of art is the degree to which it is a creation; that is, not simply a projection of the unresolved conflicts of the artist but a new solution. This is the familiar concept of sublimation which implies more than a successful defense. It is possible, in theory, to reduce a dream to, and explain all its elements in terms of, the workings of the unconscious mind, its mechanisms (condensation, displacement), and its contents. A dream is nothing more than the workings of the mind during the condition of sleep. We might admire the elegance of a construction of a manifest dream, but we would not apply the label "creative" to the end product. I am using the word "creative" to refer to a complex synthesis of unconscious, preconscious, and conscious elements through the application of artistic technique resulting in an aesthetic effect.

The development of the theory of dream interpretation and the meaning of the interpretation of a dream can be contrasted with the application of interpretation to a literary text. Until the advent of psychoanalysis, dreams were interpreted, independent of the dreamer, as oracular or as special

THE BROAD SCOPE OF PSYCHOANALYSIS: CLINICAL, THEORETICAL AND APPLIED

communications from the gods. Only occasionally would some symbolic meaning coincide with the dreamer's psychology. It was one of Freud's great discoveries that dreams do not have significance except in relation to the dreamer. His method of interpreting dreams required consideration of the dreamer's associations. All previous methods of dream interpretation could then be seen as nonscientific, arbitrary, and subjective. The dream is an authored text. It cannot be understood without the cooperation of its author. A context is necessary. The meaning of a dream as determined by psychoanalysis is not arbitrary and can be discovered only by applying certain well-defined principles. As Freud (1900) defined it in *The Interpretation of Dreams*, "...interpreting a dream implies assigning a 'meaning' to it—that is, replacing it by something which fits into the chain of our mental acts as a link having a validity and importance equal to the rest" (p. 96). Ricoeur (1965) pointed out that dream interpretation leads from a less intelligible to a more intelligible meaning. The same does not hold true for a literary text. It has meanings in its own right, and even though it can be placed in the context of the author's life, this is not its primary value, except for the analyst who is specifically interested in understanding the process of transformation associated with creativity.

In analogy with dream interpretation some analysts refer to a literary text's latent content. This is a dangerous analogy as it suggests that there is a real or true meaning in another register and that the text is a deceptive surface which has to be deciphered. Trilling (1950) was critical of the search for hidden motives in a play such as *Hamlet*, which would imply "that there is a reality to which the play stands in the relation that a dream stands to the wish that generates it and from which it is separable. But *Hamlet* is not merely the product of Shakespeare's thought, it is the very instrument of his thought" (p. 333). The text offers itself for us to see. I prefer the terms "oblique" or "hidden" to indicate the effort and care required to tease out a certain meaning. When we do use the term latent, we are referring to the author and postulating that some hidden unconscious fantasy is acting as an organizer of the plot or story. Doubrovsky (1966) expressed the same idea: "The profundity of a work must therefore be understood in a perceptual sense as one speaks of the depth of a visual field in which the multiplication of viewpoints can never exhaust the material to be perceived ... so that there are indeed levels of signification, defined by the level of perceptual acuity; there are indeed 'depths' of meaning but not strata" (p. 99).

A text presents a different sort of compromise formation from that of a dream. Considerations of aesthetics or poetics, conscious intent, available models, and cultural factors in the broadest sense determine the end product in a way very different from that applicable to dream work. In contrast to a dream, a literary text does not require the author's associations to be understood. It is, of course, possible to use the text of a story written by a patient in analysis, much as one would use a dream, and to ask the patient to associate to various elements. In such a case, one would hope to gain an understanding of the personal relevance of the story to its author, and possibly of the ways in which the experience of the author finds its path in the story. Such an approach might also clarify some of the author's intentions. We generally use the term significance rather than meaning when we are interested in the personal ramifications of a text. This does not, however, exhaust the meanings of a literary text. To arrive at them, all we usually need is the manifest content. Our appreciation of the author's private or personal use of symbols is not a prerequisite for the reading of the text, although it may enrich our understanding and enable us to appreciate more subtle effects and ambiguities. It may also rule out certain interpretations as inconsistent with the author's intent. The power of a text often transcends the author's intended purposes. It is important to try to differentiate what an author intends from the full range of meanings which can be derived from a text.

Although I have used the term psychoanalytic interpretation as though it were uniform, there are in reality a number of different models which can be applied. They share certain common assumptions, to be sure (e.g., conflict, determinism, multiple function), but stress different aspects (symptom, dream, transference, fantasy, character) (see Skura [1981] for detailed discussions). Looking at a text as a symptom, for example, would emphasize the pathological aspect of the work either formally (e.g., looking at certain repetitions as obsessions) or by focusing on the conflicts expressed therein. Certain stories of Kafka lend themselves to this approach. As an example, the story entitled "Josephine the Singer, or the Mouse Folk" (Kafka, 1922) endlessly and repeatedly dwells on reasons for the audience's interest in the mouse's quite ordinary piping. Perhaps because of the rather clumsy and bland effect of the story, it is tempting to view the monotonous repetitions as a failed artistic effect which has in it components of an obsessional need to express some inner fantasy.

Looking at a text as a dream emphasizes the search for the latent content, the altered states of consciousness, and such concepts as condensation, displacement, and the hidden meaning behind a deceptive surface whose organization has to be disregarded in order to reach the true meaning. Certain art forms, such as poetry, lend themselves to this, particularly if the circumstances of their composition are associated with a dream or a dream-like state. An obvious example is "Kubla Khan" by Coleridge. A Keats poem, "La Belle Dame Sans Merci," the subject of a forthcoming paper by me, is another such example. In one instance, at an interdisciplinary colloquium on applied analysis, Dr. Donald Kaplan's conceptualizing a difficult and abstract poem, "Beyond the Alps" by Robert Lowell (1956), as an "association" to a brief autobiographical segment included in the book with the poem appeared to yield considerable meaning. The method he employed was to make an analogy between the poem and a dream, both being the result of condensation and displacement. The autobiographical segment held the key to decoding the poem by enabling him to connect obscure imagery to the personally meaningful details in the poet's life that were included in the same book. It was the factor of this inclusion that made the connection permissible.

Looking at a text from the vantage point of transference will emphasize the object relations aspect of the work, the attempt of the author to reach out to the audience (real or fantasized), and the search for the infantile objects. There is an aspect of object relations as organizer that is particularly applicable to theater and tragedy. Bennett Simon (1984) has examined tragedies from the point of view of the biased interpretation that a particular character makes about another character's motives or actions. For example, for reasons of revenge Iago is bent on poisoning Othello's mind and imposing a warped view of reality by playing on Othello's jealousy and gullibility. Simon has made use of the Kohutian concept of the unempathic mother and has tried to show how a character's reaction to being chronically misunderstood by another inexorably moves the play to its tragic ending.

Looking at a text as a fantasy would again emphasize certain aspects of unconscious mental functioning, the transformation of the infantile wishes, the defensive modes of operation, the universal themes and their vicissitudes which recur in humankind.

Looking at a text from the point of view of character would emphasize the formal aspects—its narrative structure in relation to the content. The structuralist school has developed this aspect. Character has also been used in another context, that is, the examination of a character of a fictitious personage such as Hamlet and its development throughout a play.

These approaches do not clash; sometimes they can be combined usefully.

Problems of Method in Applied Psychoanalysis

We arrive at meanings by a process of interpretation. Interpretations in the analytic sense are reconstructions of hypothetic mental processes, transformations, and implied meanings which the ambiguity of language allows. Where does the meaning reside? The text evokes hypotheses in the reader who shares certain common assumptions, fantasies, and experiences with the author. How is interpretation in applied psychoanalysis different from that in the clinical situation? In the clinical setting, interpretation refers to a method for revealing hidden meanings in the context of an ongoing process. Psychoanalysis has developed its own system of procedures and rules to uncover the multiple meanings of dreams, symptoms, and attitudes.

Again, using the dream for purposes of comparison, psychoanalysis allows us to reconstruct the latent dream text from the manifest dream by using the patient's free associations in the course of an ongoing treatment which provides a rich context. Psychoanalysis has both described the various mechanisms by which the manifest dream is created out of the latent content and has discovered a process by which we can recover the "seed" thoughts, so to speak. In practice, we do not exhaustively analyze the text of a dream; we are more interested in what the dream can tell us about the dreamer—his current preoccupations and hidden wishes. It is possible from certain dreams to reconstruct large segments of the determinants of the patient's neurosis. Such a reconstruction might be called the meaning of the dream (for the analyst). However, we would not interpret this to the patient; we would instead focus on the purpose of the dream. This refers to the author of the dream (whether consciously or unconsciously intended is a secondary matter).

We are unable to set up a similar method to reveal the intentions of the author of a piece of creative writing. The determinants (not causes, as the complexities are worked out retrospectively) are so numerous as to defy a dynamic ordering except in very extreme cases. We make the following assumptions about a work of art. It is a mental product, and, like all mental products, it follows certain basic psychological principles, such as the principle of multiple function. That is, we expect it to be a complicated compromise formation that includes drive derivatives, defenses, aspects of the superego, the repetition compulsion, and some adaptation to reality. As previously mentioned, the nature of this compromise formation is different from that of a symptom, dream, or character trait. Included in the art work are such factors as technical skill, talent, and sensitivity, which are not easily reducible to psychoanalytic formulations.

There is a further problem in the application of psychoanalysis to a text, due to the absence of the unconscious, defenses, or conflicts, which are attributes of persons (authors) not of fictional characters. In applying psychoanalysis to a text, we are confined to the descriptive level and must substitute other data for the missing points of view. This is the core problem of applied analysis; it is met in a variety of ways, none of them truly satisfactory.

As mentioned earlier, I will outline four main approaches.

The first approach is for the interpreter to enter the fictional world and attribute to the characters in a novel or play the conflicts, defenses, and attitudes of live people. Once this step is taken, then it becomes easy to use analytic concepts, ignoring the "as if" quality of the enterprise. In its extreme form the first approach, which was also the earliest form of applied analysis, claims to be able to explain a character's behavior through a "discovery" of his unconscious motives, treating the text as a case study. This way of proceeding overlooks the fact that characters are figments of the author's imagination; they have no past, no memory, and they "live" only for the duration of the play. The author of a play is often more concerned with theatrical or poetic effect than with the creation of real human beings. However, if one chooses to enter the fictional realm, cannot analysis "discover" traces consistent with the expression of motives and feelings normally kept out of awareness? Is not the author, who, after all, possesses an unconscious, able to convey some of its elements in his creative work without realizing the accuracy of his observations? If so, analysis is in a position to enrich the understanding of the work by demonstrating the existence of such evidence and its consistency with what we know from the clinical realm. Wangh (1950) did this in the case of *Othello* by demonstrating convincing "evidence" of Iago's hidden homosexual attachment to Othello.

In the second approach one uses the text as a portal of entry into the psychology of the author and sees the work as a form of modified free association. In order to interpret a text in this way, one must possess a set of assumptions and values similar to the author's or be aware in the greatest possible detail of the author's value and assumptions. This may help to avoid one of the pitfalls common to psychoanalytic interpretation—the inappropriate attribution of a personal meaning to an aspect of the work best explained by reference to the more impersonal elements. This does not negate the possibility of a combination of factors; that is, a cultural factor can also serve as the expression of more personal themes. The role and relevance of "unconscious" factors in explaining a character's behavior is a matter of considerable controversy. It is often not clear whether a given action requires the import of psychological theory or whether it may be "explained" by what is loosely termed poetic license. We are most often dealing not with an "either/or," but with an "and." Such a controversy is apparent in the discussion of Hamlet's procrastination by the literary scholar, G.L. Kittredge. He went out of his way to explain Hamlet's delay as due to doubts about the authenticity of the specter ("The spirit that I have seen may be the devil").

Kittredge (1939) wrote: "This doubt as to the ambiguous apparition accords with ancient doctrine and was perfectly intelligible to any Elizabethan audience. Disregard of Hamlet's dilemma has led to misinterpretation of his character, as if he were a procrastinator, a vain dreamer, an impulsive creature of feeble will. But Shakespeare has done his best to enforce the imperative scruple as to the apparition" (p. xv). Kittredge followed this with a number of specific references to similar reactions on the part of other characters (Horatio, Bernardo). There is the danger that the analyst, when faced with a puzzle in a text, will, as in the clinical situation, resort to various aspects of unconscious motivation, ignoring certain historical considerations relevant to the play. It is also possible, as in *Macbeth*, that the data might not be available to account for a particular bit of behavior. To explain certain senseless aspects of behavior as derived from "an unconscious need for punishment" in the absence of confirmatory evidence can be quite misleading, if not positively false.

Within a play, what are the limits of the explanatory value of unconscious motivation? Is it acceptable to explain certain aspects of the adult behavior of fictional characters by referring to their childhood, as some authors do in their interpretations? In my view, such interpretations stretch the limits of common sense. One can say that certain behaviors or actions of a real person would suggest certain childhood antecedents, but to refer to a fictional character's past is to add one's own fiction to that of the author. Yet one could make the counterargument that such concepts as the oedipus complex are, after all, based on what we know about childhood experience. Resorting to the oedipus complex as an explanatory hypothesis, however, will be valid only to the degree that the text supports it directly—for example, through the identification of triangular relationships or by the presence of loving statements about the mother in association with hostile attitudes toward the father. A truly enlightened psychoanalytic approach requires a thorough grounding in other disciplines to minimize causes of error. The text itself cannot directly answer questions about the mind of the author. It can, however, provide data which help us to formulate hypotheses. At a certain point it becomes necessary to go to other sources for more evidence (biography, letters, journals). As a brief example, much of Keats's poetry contains images of fusion and orality; much of it deals with themes of abandonment, and the mood is often depressed. It does not surprise those who are analytically trained to discover in Keats's early history multiple

315

object losses, an inability to mourn, and evidence of considerable depression. It is possible to reconstruct from the imagery and metaphors a number of likely unconscious fantasies and to show how Keats attempted to come to terms with his losses.

In the absence of such information, the general application of "psychoanalysis" to a text is not possible; or it will yield only some trivial aspect, such as the fact that the characters have oedipal conflicts. The most common pitfall is for the unwary interpreter to restate the text using psychoanalytic terminology and substituting general truths of little interest for the specific images and interactions of metaphors of the text. Proust's dread of going to sleep becomes an index of his fear of loss of identity.

A careful reading of a text and some knowledge about its composition may yield a particular point of view or a general organizer which is of heuristic value. For example, the statement made by Virginia Woolf (Bell, 1980, p. 208) to the effect that writing *To the Lighthouse* was a "necessary act" to rid her of her obsession with her dead parents suggests a particular organizer—the work of mourning. It is possible to compare the characters of the mother and the father at the beginning and at the end of the novel and to consider their various representations, the shift in affects, the quality of imagery, various metaphors of incorporation and introjection, and the degree of aggression, to mention but a few possibilities. In this way, the evolution of the novel can be seen as paralleling the author's own mourning; creativity is used in the service of both making possible and undoing the loss of the object. It is important not to "degrade" the text—that is, to use it for some purpose for which it was not "designed." By this, I mean that the questions asked of the text must have some relevance to its inner structure or to the intentions of the author.

Many of the writers in applied analysis fail in this kind of approach by carelessly equating the manifest content of a work with its intrapsychic equivalent, relying mainly on the mechanism of symbolic translation.

As an example, if a poem describes a rather transparent oedipal fantasy, the interpreter may all too quickly equate the manifest content of the work with the author's mental life, relying on a mechanical application of analogy, identification, and projection. Kings and queens become fathers and mothers, lances become the masculine attributes of power, and so on. The conflicts inferred as applying to the characters in the work are quickly transferred to the author, with the interpreter ignoring the transformations they may have undergone en route. In this approach the text is seen as a thinly veiled representation of the author's wishes, fears, and conflicts. Terms such as defense or primary process are, in my view, not applicable to a text, although a section may provide an illustration of what a defensive process would be if the text were spoken by a live person. Outside of a dynamic frame of reference, it is not easy to decide to what degree a text reflects its author's primary process mode of functioning, in contrast to a secondary process mode. We are interested in the influence of the author's defensive processes on the text. Such processes could influence either form or content, or both. How to determine which of the author's defenses are represented in a text has not been spelled out. Should we think of a text as analogous to a character trait—with the author imprisoned within the confines of its limitations? The question of the relationship between defenses and the outer limits of an author's creativity are not clear.

For many practical reasons it is sometimes neither possible nor methodologically sound to attempt to relate text to author. At times the data about the author are not available or not verifiable, or, even if available, they may be hard to assess.

This leads to the third approach of applied analysis. The text is examined as a self-contained structure, and aspects of its form or content are studied in analogy to some mental phenomenon or repetition of a family relationship. One searches for derivatives of typical universal fantasies or examines the metaphors, imagery, and form from a psychoanalytic perspective, with no attempt to infer dynamic relationships. The aim is to describe certain organizers and patterns in the text, using data which a nonanalyst might well overlook. Several works from the same author can be examined to further discover the common elements idiosyncratic to that author. The French structuralist school of Lacan and Derrida has pushed this approach to its limits. Arlow (1978) used this approach in the case of the Japanese writer, Mishima, demonstrating convincingly the role of the primal scene as an organizer of several of his novels. The identification of such an unconscious fantasy does not permit us to draw conclusions about its role in the author's mind without information outside the work itself. This is true of all constructions of a psychological nature drawn from a piece of literature: we are not able to relate our conclusions to the life of the author without further data.

A derivative of the structural approach to a text is the study of function rather than of meaning in the context of narrative structure. What is stressed here is the analysis of the formal aspects of the narrative. Thus, a particular character behaves in a certain way not because of inner motives, but rather because the author needed this behavior in order to reach a particular ending he had in mind.

When queried about the reasons for including a particular character molded after an acquaintance, a patient who was a creative writer replied that this inclusion best allowed him to develop certain traits and attributes of his main character. This approach is not, strictly speaking, "psychoanalytic," although it can generate interesting questions for the analyst. Robert Fitzgerald's (1981) Introduction to a collection of Flannery O'Connor's short stories illustrates the enrichment of analytic strategy, as details about the timing of the composition of different passages of a work of fiction are taken into consideration. He wrote: "In the summer of 1950, when [O'Connor] had reached an impasse with Hazel [a character in a novel] and didn't know how to finish him off, she read for the first time the Oedipus plays. She went on then to end her story with the self blinding of Motes, and she had to rework the body of the novel to prepare for it" (pp. xv–xvi). This passage can serve as a departure point for demonstrating the multiple factors that are relevant to psychoanalysis.

1. One could simply look at the novel as a text. Do the motivation and the characterization hold together, make sense, add anything to our understanding of the human mind? Are there weaknesses in the description? If so, where? This approach does not try to explain but simply to understand on a plane slightly above that of common sense, investigating the psychology of the characters as though they were real by using the tools of empathy and clinical judgment.

2. The second approach deals with the psychology of the author and her relation to the text. We might ask what kind of a person would write a novel of this sort, or we might be interested in the process of creativity—particularly if we were in possession of earlier versions of the novel. We could be interested in the nature of the inhibitions of the artist. Was the reading of the *Oedipus* tragedy fortuitous? That is, did O'Connor's revised ending fit with the previous draft? If so, did the author need to shield her own solution behind the cloak of Greek tragedy so as not to bear the psychological burden of the ending? Were the author's own oedipal conflicts involved in the act of writing itself? The list of questions should be limited only by the availability of the data to point the way in some direction.

3. The third approach, although focused on the narrative structure of the text and its various organizers, can also include a consideration of the function of various elements, particularly the above-mentioned facts about the timing of the composition. Within the process of creating the novel, the usual ordering of events in the sequence has to be reversed from that in real life situations. The end comes before the

middle and the middle had to be altered to lead to the end. Instead of asking what is the meaning, we look at the function of various segments. This method of dealing with the structure of the novel and issues of poetic license broadens the psychological understanding.

4.   The fourth and final approach of applied analysis focuses on reader reactions and examines the text to understand the means by which the author arouses feelings in the audience. This leads to the study of aesthetic and poetic effects. This last approach is congenial to psychoanalysis, as it reintroduces a dynamic system—that of the subject. The clinical analogy is the use of the therapist's reactions and state of mind to yield clues about the patient. Freud (1919) used this last approach in his well-known paper, "The 'Uncanny.'" According to Arlow (1969), "The aesthetic effectiveness of metaphor in literature is derived, in large measure, from the ability of metaphorical expression to stimulate the affects associated with widely entertained, communally shared unconscious fantasies" (p. 7). The greater the degree of ambiguity (as differentiated from obscurity or meaninglessness), the greater the possible aesthetic effect and resonance with multiply determined unconscious fantasies.

I will now turn to the difficult problem of validation in applied analysis. If psychoanalytic meanings of a text are not related to the intentions of the author, thus limiting the range of speculations, what avenues are open to the investigator devoted to textual interpretation who wishes to avoid wild analysis? Unfortunately, it is possible to take a great work such as *Hamlet*, apply to it almost any psychoanalytic theory—Kleinian, Kohutian, classical, object relations—and find in the text some "evidence" to support the approach. When we do not possess the biographical data to limit our speculations and rule out certain of the more far-fetched possibilities, we must rely on other criteria for the usefulness and validation of our interpretations. They must bring together assorted types of data (both form and content) hitherto unexplained. They must be parsimonious, possess inner logic, and be consistent with psychoanalytic knowledge. Finally, they should add to our understanding and possibly to our enjoyment of the work.

One of the criteria often used in validation of hypotheses is that of plausibility. Hartmann (1927), quoting Max Weber, reminded us that "no matter how meaningful a self-evident interpretation as such may appear to be, it cannot on this account alone claim to be a causally valid interpretation. In itself it may remain only an especially plausible hypothesis" (p. 388). Understandable connections are neither true nor false; they are a means of expression and description. They have to be the starting point of scientific work—not the goal. Unfortunately, in much of applied analysis such interpretations are the end point and are therefore taken for granted, with only minimal attention paid to the tedious work of validation.

In light of imprecise methodology, various interpretations of a play are best compared by asking how the authors arrived at their conclusions. In the absence of clear-cut guidelines, it is possible that a critic will select certain explanations in accordance with his private theories of motivation. Our erroneous expectation that plays should copy reality leads us to evaluate the work in terms of its plausibility. The stories of Kafka, in which the boundary of dream and reality are constantly called in question, are a good example of the artistic use of implausibility. Audiences have different expectations of degree of plausibility depending on the art form. We do not expect as much plausibility when it comes to opera as when we see a play. The theater of the absurd has toyed with the limits of implausibility and even with the irrelevance of character. It is useful to recall that analysis is the only system of meaning which, in its method, takes into account the properties of the text it is examining before making an interpretation. That is, it does not blindly translate the patient's manifest text by resorting to mechanical devices such as symbolism; rather it first searches out the proper context in order to determine which elements are dynamically significant. In the clinical situation this context is often the transference relationship to the analyst. In its absence one may end up with a reductive account of the text. It is possible, of course, for a sensitive clinician to take an isolated session from a patient's treatment and to derive from it a wealth of data about the major conflicts, the identity themes, the object relation scenarios which are being re-enacted in the present, the nature of the defenses, and the like. What is more difficult clinically is to derive technical maneuvers from this approach, in the absence of the context of the session. In the clinical setting, we validate our interpretations by noting shifts in affective or defensive reactions to them and the emergence of new material such as dreams and infantile memories.

In contrast, a text will not react to our interpretations. In the most favorable instance, an investigator would examine a novel or series of poems and make certain hypotheses about the biography or life of the author. If he could then turn to the life and retrieve some data previously unknown to him which would confirm his hypothesis, this would provide the most satisfactory type of validation. The purpose of our interpretations is to gather wide arrays of data in the most parsimonious fashion.

One of the best examples of the creative use of psychoanalysis in the study of character is Wangh's (1950) paper on *Othello*. As in Freud's paper on Leonardo, Wangh justified the introduction of psychoanalysis by noting that critics have been unable to account for Iago's hatred of Desdemona through recourse to apparent motivation. "The magic of the play lies in its hidden content, which speaks directly to the unconscious of every spectator" (p. 203). Wangh suggested that it is Iago, rather than Othello, who is the prime victim of delusional jealousy. In order to prove his point, he amassed an impressive amount of evidence ranging from a careful analysis of the circumstances surrounding the onset of the illness, historical material derived from the original story on which *Othello* was based, and evidence within the play itself, including the analysis of a dream of Cassio. In all the instances, Wangh stayed close to the data of observation and quoted from the play, allowing the reader to judge the evidence. He also moved back and forth from his knowledge of paranoid states derived from clinical work to the evolution of the character of Iago within the play.

Validation of the second approach in applied analysis—that which relates the work to the mental life of its author—is based on the assumption that the work is a *modified* form of free association. If one emphasizes the word modified, then it is possible to identify sensitively certain aspects of the author's mental life in his works. Knowledge of the context, careful attention to many possible transformations, and awareness of literary history are mandatory. The anchoring of the work to the mental life of the author makes this approach the most sympathetic to the basic assumptions of psychoanalysis.

The third approach, which is confined to the analysis of the text and its many themes, is the most difficult to validate (since there is no outside mind to serve as organizer or reference point), yet it is the most likely to probe the nature of the literary (since it deals with the text itself). In addition to analyzing the content, it is possible to enrich the method and increase its plausibility by a study of the form. As an example, one can see that a dream of the English poet, John Keats, which included considerable motion (whirling, floating) in its manifest content, found its way into a poem in the form of a ballad. The ballad lends itself to dancing. This third approach is a powerful and creative tool which allows the analyst to uncover organizers which a nonanalyst might miss. The knowledge of unconscious fantasies and their transformations in the clinical realm afford a bridge, through analogy, to the literary text. Other organizers in addition to universal fantasies can be various object relation scenarios, drive derivatives, developmental stages, affective states, reactions to trauma (e.g., object loss), various neurotic or psychotic phenomena, or even various normal phenomena (e.g., dream state or altered states of consciousness). The text is treated as if it were a single session or a series of sessions.

I have said the least about the fourth approach of applied analysis—that devoted to the investigation of aesthetic effect or the subjective reaction of the reader. It has been most studied by such writers as Kris (1952), Sachs (1942), and Arlow (1969). It is such a broad topic, particularly in the area of validation, that it deserves a separate paper in itself.

Before closing, I wish to emphasize that psychoanalysis has its limitations which are determined by its strategy—looking at human behavior from the vantage point of conflict and wish fulfillment. These limitations are not a defect but an inherent property of any theoretical system. In the case of psychoanalysis, one cannot criticize it for failing to explain some behavior or a work of art outside the framework it assigns itself. A truly psychoanalytic reading in the best sense is not simply reductionistic but rather a study in meanings, relationships, and transformations. This is an application of its developmental approach to human behavior.

REFERENCES

Arlow, J.A. (1969). Unconscious fantasy and disturbances of conscious experience. *Psychoanal. Q.38:1–27.*

——— (1978). Pyromania and the primal scene: a psychoanalytic comment on the work of Yukio Mishima. *Psychoanal. Q.47:24–51.*

Baudry, F. (1979). On the problem of inference in applied psychoanalysis: Flaubert's 'Madame Bovary.' *Psychoanal. Study Society8331–358.*

Bell, A.O. Editor (1980). *The Diary of Virginia Woolf, Vol. 3: 1925.–1930.* New York/ London: Harcourt Brace Jovanovich.

Doubrovsky, S. (1966). *The New Criticism in France.* Translated by D. Coltman. Chicago: Univ. Chicago Press, 1973.

Eissler, K.R. (1968). The relation of explaining and understanding in psychoanalysis: demonstrated by one aspect of Freud's approach to literature. *Psychoanal. Study Child*23:141–177.

Fitzgerald, R. (1981). Introduction In *Everything That Rises Must Converge* by Flannery O'Connor. New York: Farrar, Straus Giroux, pp. *vii–xxxiv*.

Freud, S. (1900). The interpretation of dreams. *S.E.* 4/5.

——— (1907). Delusions and dreams in Jensen's Gradiva. *S.E.* 9.

——— (1908). Creative writers and day-dreaming. *S.E.* 9.

——— (1910). Leonardo da Vinci and a memory of his childhood. *S.E.* 11.

——— (1914). The Moses of Michelangelo. *S.E.* 13..

——— (1916). Some character-types met with in psycho-analytic work. *S.E.* 14.

——— (1919). The 'uncanny.' *S.E.* 17.

——— (1920). Beyond the pleasure principle. *S.E.* 18.

Hartmann, H. (1927). Understanding and explanation In *Essays on Ego Psychology. Selected Problems in Psychoanalytic Theory.* New York: Int. Univ. Press, 1964 pp. *369–403*.

Hirsch, S.D. (1967). *Validity in Interpretation*. New Haven: Yale Univ. Press.

Holland, N.N. (1968). *The Dynamics of Literary Response.* New York: Oxford Univ. Press.

Kafka, F. (1922). Josephine the singer, or the mouse folk In *The Penal Colony; Stories and Short Pieces..* New York: Schocken, 1976 pp. *256–277*.

Kittredge, G.L. Editor (1939). *The Kittredge Shakespeare's Hamlet* .New York: John Wiley Sons, 1967.

Kohut, H. (1960). Beyond the bounds of the basic rule. Some recent contributions to applied psychoanalysis.. *J. Am. Psychoanal. Assoc.*8: 567–586.

Kris, E. (1952). *Psychoanalytic Explorations in Art.* New York: Int. Univ. Press.

Lowell, R. (1956). *Life Studies: Beyond the Alps.* New York: Noonday Press,

Ricoeur, P. (1965). De *l'interprtation: essai sur Freud.* Paris: editions du Seuil.

Sachs, H. (1942). *The Creative Unconscious. Studies in the Psychoanalysis of Art.* Cambridge, MA.: Sci-Art.

Simon, B. (1984). With cunning delays and ever-mounting excitement, or what thickens the plot in tragedy and psychoanalysis in psychoanalysis. *Vital Issues* 2:385–432.

Skura, M.A. (1981). *The Literary Use of the Psychoanalytic Process.* New Haven: Yale Univ. Press.

Trilling, L. (1950). Freud and literature. In *Readings in Psychoanalytic Psychology,* ed. M. Levitt. New York: Appleton-Century-Crofts, 1959 pp. 321–337.

Waelder, R. (1929). Review of Freud's Hemmung, Symptom und Angst. *Int. J. Psychoanal.*10:103–111.

Wangh, H. (1950). Othello: the tragedy of Iago. *Psychoanal. Q.*19:202–212.

Werman, D. (1979). Methodological problems in the psychoanalytic interpretation of literature: a review of studies in Sophocles' *Antigone. J. Am. Psychoanal. Assoc.* 27:451–479.

CHAPTER 12

A Dream, a Sonnet, and a Ballad:
The Path to Keats's "La Belle Dame Sans Merci"

[(1986). *Psychoanal. Q.,* (55):69–98.]

ABSTRACT: This paper explores the relationship between Keats's ballad, "La Belle Dame sans Merci," and some of its precursors, including one of the poet's dreams and a sonnet titled "On a Dream." The process of creativity is examined.

> *Here are the poems, they will explain themselves as all poems*
> *should do—without comment.*
> —Keats, February 12, 1819, in letter to his brother and sister-in-law

INTRODUCTION

While researching the background of one of the greatest ballads in the English language, "La Belle Dame sans Merci" by John Keats, I uncovered a remarkable sequence of texts which help us to reconstruct certain intermediary steps in the process of creativity and writing.

A personal journal which the English poet Keats kept as a lengthy letter to his brother and sister-in-law, over a period of several months, includes a report of a dream and shortly thereafter a sonnet entitled "On a Dream," and then a poem which has been called the most beautiful ballad in the English language, "La Belle Dame sans Merci." The ballad includes a dream in its content. My interest was aroused in this sequence by the fact that a dream appears to be a "seed" in three different aspects of John Keats's literary output within a very brief period of time. A dream is mentioned in the correspondence; then the same manifest dream is barely transformed as the last lines of a sonnet titled "On a Dream," and finally, a few days later, the great ballad, "La Belle Dame sans Merci," includes a literary dream.

I will consider the flow of material from correspondence to dream, to sonnet, and to ballad as though it were an extended analytic hour. One of my hypotheses is that the sequence—dream, sonnet, ballad—allows for the gradual expression of warded-off depressive affects as though the poems were an "interpretation" of the dream—with the difference that the poet may not have listened to or even been interested in the content of the interpretation. This approach to the poems permits us to make certain hypotheses which would not be possible if the poems were simply considered as separate texts unrelated to each other or to elements in the author's life.

I will first try to reconstruct the meaning of the dream experience from information about it in the journal and from its subsequent fate in the poems. The study of meaning will include how the dream is used (its function) in each different fragment—correspondence, sonnet, ballad.

Second, the detailed description of the transformation which the dream experience undergoes as it is incorporated into the poetry will provide a microscopic view of the evolution of the creative process. I will try to show how the various aspects of the dream—its affect, imagery, and probable latent content—emerge and become clarified as the poet's imagination transforms the raw material into verse. I will suggest that the more successful of several poems allows much freer expression of forbidden, threatening, and painful ideas and feelings. It would be tempting to postulate that this free emergence of unconscious elements is a precondition of all great art. Too defensive a stance leads to stilted or less interesting imagery. This is certainly true in the case of the Keats sonnet which I will consider.

In a final section, I will discuss problems of method and validation in applied analysis.

HISTORY

A very few words about Keats's brief and tragic life are in order. Born on October 31, 1795, he was the oldest of four, followed by George (1797), Tom (1799), and Edward (1801); the latter died in infancy. The youngest, Fanny, was born in 1803. The father died as the result of a fall from a horse when John was only nine. At this point the family was thrown into chaos. The mother, unable to manage the family affairs, quickly succumbed to the pleas of a minor clerk in a banking firm, William Rawlings, marrying him in desperation less than four months after her husband's death. The grandmother, who disapproved of the hasty marriage, took over the care of the children who went to live with her. While in boarding school, at age fifteen, Keats lost his mother to tuberculosis, the dreaded disease that was to fell his brother Tom and himself as well. The grandfather had also died by then. The grandmother gave over the care of the boys to a guardian, Abbey, a suspicious and uneducated man who interrupted John's schooling in 1811, having decided he should learn to support himself. The grandmother died in 1814, leaving the children without a home.

After spending several unhappy years in apothecary training, John moved into his brother George's house in 1816, but a stable family life was not destined for him. George, who had played both a fraternal and paternal role in the poet's life, married Georgiana Wylie and moved to Kentucky in 1818. There is no doubt that Keats experienced a severe loss at the marriage and departure of his beloved brother and his wife. George had been a stabilizing influence in Keats's life. His marriage had recreated a stable family unit, something Keats had not experienced since the death of his parents. In

December 1818, the younger brother, Tom, died of tuberculosis and a few weeks later, shortly before the composition of the poem, Keats developed a sore throat which he correctly diagnosed as an early stage of tuberculosis, the disease that would kill him two years later. During this same period, he first confessed his love to a young woman, Fanny Brawne, a passion that in all likelihood was never consummated even though Keats became engaged to her for a brief period later in the year 1819. Clearly, Keats had many doubts about the wisdom of such a choice. He was beset by persistent financial problems and was encountering poor reviews. He sensed his failing health, and he worried that he might have to give up writing for Fanny Brawne's sake. He was known to suffer chronically from recurrent mood swings and severe depressions.

DATA

I will now turn to Keats's journal[38] to outline the events preceding the dream. In order to maintain a bond with his beloved brother and sister-in-law, now pregnant, he kept this journal from which he sent them passages. The correspondence serves as the backdrop for the works I will consider in detail and for some others I will mention in passing.

The correspondence to George, often addressed to Georgiana, is full of reminiscences, longings, and open expressions of love, as the following excerpt dated March 12, 1819, shows: "I hope you are both now in that sweet sleep which no two beings deserve more than you do. I much fancy you and please myself in the fancy of speaking a prayer and a blessing over you and your lives. God bless you. I whisper good night in your ears and you will

---

38 Page numbers for all quotations from Keats's journal are from Volume 2 of the edition of his letters edited by Rollins (1958).

dream of me!" (pp. 73–74).[39] An entry dated April 5 informs us that Keats has found a lock of Georgiana's hair in a letter addressed from Georgiana to George and that he intends to put it in a miniature case of George's. On April 11, Keats discovers a prank which affects him deeply: some love letters written by an alleged Amena Bellefilla addressed to the now deceased Tom turn out to have been written by a common acquaintance, Wells. Keats is furious and swears vengeance.

On April 15, Keats includes in his correspondence a curious bit of writing, an extempore piece entitled "When They Were Come unto the Faeries' Court." Obscure in meaning both comic and nightmarish, this piece deals with the story of a princess lured into fairyland in spite of the warning of her three servants who are three transformed princes. W. Jackson Bate (1963), in his excellent biography of Keats, mentions that the piece could be seen as related to the situation in the strangely beautiful ballad, "La Belle Dame," that Keats was to write five days later. Here is the plot. A fretful princess travels to a fairy court with an ape, a dwarf, and a fool. Finding no one at home, she flies into a rage; the dwarf trembles, the ape stares, the fool does nothing. The princess takes her whip in order to turn on her three attendants, and the dwarf with piteous face begins to rhyme in order to distract her. While the princess is within, her only means of transportation—a mule—manages to get rid of its saddle and escapes. The princess is never seen again. In spite of the comical effect, an eerie sense of warning pervades the piece: after the princess entered the door, "it closed and there was nothing seen but the mule grazing on the herbage green." This anticipates the theme of disappearance in the Belle Dame ballad.

On April 16, having to stay home because of the rain, Keats describes a recent walk with Coleridge and sees fit to list the topics discussed. These

---

39 I mention this entry because of its similarity to the theme of the poem, "The Eve of St. Agnes," which contains the first direct allusion to the "Belle Dame" story.

include different species of dreams, nightmares, dreams accompanied by a sense of touch, single and double touch, a dream related, and a ghost story (p. 89).

The April 16 entry starts out with a passage stressing Keats's wish for revenge against Wells,

I will hang over his head like a sword by a hair, I will be opium to his vanity. If I cannot injure his interests—he is a rat and he shall have rats bane to his vanity. I will harm him if I possibly can. I have no doubt I shall be able to do so, let us leave him to his misery; alone except when we can throw in a little more (p. 91).

This passage seems to stress Keats's helplessness in the face of Wells's trickery. Then without transition Keats continues:

The Fifth Canto of Dante pleases me more and more, it is that one in which he meets with Paolo and Francesca—I had passed many days in rather a low state of mind, and in the midst of them I dreamt of being in that region of Hell. The dream was one of the most delightful enjoyments I ever had in my life—I floated about the whirling atmosphere as it is described with a beautiful figure to whose lips mine were joined [as] it seemed for an age—and in the midst of all this cold and darkness I was warm—even flowery tree tops sprung up and we rested on them sometimes with the lightness of a cloud till the wind blew us away again—I tried a Sonnet upon it—there are fourteen lines but *nothing of what I felt in it—O that I could dream it every night* (p. 91, italics added).

We do not know the exact date of the dream, save that it was recent. There is little reason to doubt that the dream recorded by Keats was genuine and not made up; it occurs naturally in the context of the passage preceding it and seems an apt commentary on Dante's Fifth Canto—the clear day residue.

The affects aroused by the dream apparently drove the poet to try to capture something of its pleasure by writing a poem on it. "I tried a Sonnet upon it—there are fourteen lines but nothing of what I felt in it." Clearly, an uncontrollable shift in affects intervenes. Here is the sonnet:

ON A DREAM

As Hermes once took to his feathers light,
When lullèd Argus, baffled, swooned and slept,
So on a Delphic reed, my idle spright
So played, so charmed, so conquered, so bereft
The dragon-world of all its hundred eyes;
And, seeing it asleep, so fled away—
Not to pure Ida with its snow-cold skies,
Nor unto Tempe where Jove grieved that day;
But to that second circle of sad hell,
Where in the gust, the whirlwind, and the flaw
Of rain and hail-stones, lovers need not tell
Their sorrows. Pale were the sweet lips I saw,
Pale were the lips I kissed, and fair the form
I floated with, about that melancholy storm.

The sonnet is immediately followed in the correspondence by more personal passages addressed to Georgiana. "I want very much a little of your wit my dear sister.... Are there any flowers in bloom like any beautiful heaths— any street full of corset makers? What sort of shoes have you to fit those pretty feet of yours?... Do you ride on horseback? What do you have for breakfast, dinner and supper? Without mentioning lunch and bever and wet and snack and a bit to stay one's stomach" (p. 92). In a later section Keats amuses himself by giving directions on how Georgiana could employ her day: "While you are hovering with your dinner in prospect you may do a thousand things—put on a hedgehog into George's hat—pour a little water in his rifle, soak his boots in a pail of water, cut his jacket round in shreds like a Roman kilt or the back of my grandmother's stays—sow off his buttons" (p. 93). The mood of these remarks, their jocularity, suggests the pranks a young child would like to play on his father—to make a fool out of him and perhaps reverse the roles.

The next day, April 21, Keats writes, "I stopped at Taylor with Woodhouse and passed a quiet sort of pleasant day. I have been very much pleased with the panorama of the ships at the north pole with the icebergs, the mountains, the bears, the walrus, the seals, the penguins and a large whale floating [its] back above water. It is impossible to describe the place" (p. 94). This passage again contains an allusion to floating—a favorite image in Keats's poetry. That evening Keats included in the letter the well-known ballad, "La Belle Dame sans Merci," which ushered in one of his most creative periods, during which he produced odes, sonnets, and a philosophical treatise, "The Vale of Soul Making." The ballad, to which I now turn, was probably written April 19:

LA BELLE DAME SANS MERCI
O what can ail thee, knight-at-arms, Alone and palely loitering?
The sedge has withered from the lake, And no birds sing.

O what can ail thee, knight-at-arms, So haggard and so woe-begone?
The squirrel's granary is full, And the harvest's done.

I see a lily on thy brow,
With anguish moist and fever-dew,

334

And on thy cheeks a fading rose
Fast withereth too.

I met a lady in the meads,
Full beautiful—a faery's child,
Her hair was long, her foot was light,
And her eyes were wild.

I made a garland for her head,
And bracelets too, and fragrant zone;
She looked at me as she did love,
And made sweet moan.

I set her on my pacing steed,
And nothing else saw all day long,
For sidelong would she bend, and sing
A faery's song.

She found me roots of relish sweet,
And honey wild, and manna-dew,
And sure in language strange she said—
'I love thee true'.

She took me to her elfin grot,
And there she wept and sighed full sore,
And there I shut her wild wild eyes
With kisses four.

And there she lullèd me asleep
And there I dreamed—Ah! woe betide!—

The latest dream I ever dreamt
On the cold hill side.

I saw pale kings and princes too,
Pale warriors, death-pale were they all;
They cried—'La Belle Dame sans Merci
Thee hath in thrall!'

I saw their starved lips in the gloam,
With horrid warning gapèd wide,
And I awoke and found me here,
On the cold hill's side.

And this is why I sojourn here
Alone and palely loitering,
Though the sedge is withered from the lake,
And no birds sing.

In the correspondence following the ballad, Keats adds an amusing lighthearted commentary on one aspect of the poem, selecting one of the more irrelevant details. "Why four kisses—you will say—why four because I wish to restrain the headlong impetuosity of my muse—she would have fain said score without hurting the rhyme—but we must temper the imagination as the critics say with judgment. I was obliged to choose an even number that both eyes might have fair play: and to speak truly, I think two a piece quite sufficient. Suppose I had said seven, there would have been three and a half a piece—a very awkward affair and well got out on my side" (letter of April 19 to Georgiana Keats, p. 98). This is the same chatty, jocular mood we find right after the sonnet—a distancing from the gloom of the poetry.

There follows in the correspondence a poem titled "A Chorus of Fairies." In the third stanza, titled "Zephyr," we find a reminiscence of the imagery of the dream—perhaps a last lingering. Zephyr addresses gentle Brema and beckons her to accompany him "over the tops of trees to my fragrant palace where they ever floating are—beneath the cherish of a star called Vesper— who with silver veil hides his brillace pale" (p. 98).

INTERPRETATION

The setting of the works of Keats that I have just described is not typical of most literary texts. In many ways it fulfills the ideal requirements for analytic interpretation. We are in possession of the author's manifest dream, the context in which it occurred, some of his reactions, and the various creative products which he himself relates to it. To have the correspondence, the dream, and the author's comments as data allows us to approximate more closely his intentions and his states of mind.

From the perspective of an analyst, all the written material presented so far— correspondence, dream, comments on the dream, and the several poems—are to be understood as compromise formations. To be sure, poems are more likely to be influenced by issues of form, they will contain more imagery and metaphors, and they will have been subject to more conscious elaboration than the dream. Similarly, the correspondence will be governed by Keats's style and by his sense of what is appropriate. It should nevertheless be seen as a creative product which will contain seeds of conflicts similar to those found in the dream or in the poetry.

I will begin my interpretation with a close examination of the obvious day residue of the dream, Dante's Fifth Canto. Here are excerpts:

After I had heard my teacher name the olden dames and cavaliers,
pity came over me, and I was as if bewildered\

I began: "Poet, willingly would I speak with those two that
go together, and seem so light upon the wind."

And he to me: "Thou shalt see when they are nearer to us;
and do thou then entreat them by that love which leads them;
and they will come."

Then I turned again to them; and I spoke, and began:
Francesca, thy torments make me weep with grief and pity.

But tell me: in the time of the sweet sighs, by what and how \
love granted you to know the dubious desires?

And she to me: "There is no greater pain than to recall a
happy time in wretchedness; and this thy teacher knows.

"But if thou hast such desire to learn the first root of our love,
I will do like one who weeps and tells.

"One day, for pastime, we read of Lancelot, how love
constrained him; we were alone and without all suspicion.

"Several times that reading urged our eyes to meet, and
changed the colour of our faces; but one moment alone it was that
overcame us.

"When we read how the fond smile was kissed by such a lover,
he, who shall never be divided from me,

"kissed my mouth all trembling: the book, and he who wrote
it, was a Galeotto. That day we read in it no farther."

A brief synopsis of the story of Paolo and Francesca as recounted by Dante is relevant to the dream. Francesca was married to a deformed man, Gianciotto of Rimini, and had fallen in love with his brother, Paolo, while reading together the tale of Lancelot. They were discovered by Gianciotto who, in jealous fury, slew them both. The lovers eventually found themselves in the second circle of Hell, reserved for adulterous lovers eternally condemned to swirl about in unending storms.

The relation between the dream and the manifest imagery of the Dante canto is compelling. Dante begins, "Poet, willingly would I speak with those two that go together, and seem so light upon the wind." A bit later, "Then I turned again to them; and I spoke, and began: 'Francesca, thy torments make me weep with grief and pity.'" In the latter part of the canto which describes the kiss, the last two lines are explicit. "When we read how the fond smile was kissed by such a lover, he, who shall never be divided from me, kissed my mouth all trembling.... That day we read in it no farther." I am making the assumption that the dreamer borrowed the imagery of the canto because it resonated with or reflected some of his unconscious wishes or fantasies. What do we find in the canto?

Francesca alludes to the book she and Paolo were reading: "One day, for pastime, we read of Lancelot, how love constrained him; we were alone and without all suspicion." The story of Lancelot is doubly relevant. Lancelot is in love with Guinevere, wife of King Arthur, but he does not dare confess his love to the queen. One day when she is smiling at his embarrassment, Galehaut, her friend and confidant, begs Guinevere to grant Lancelot the forgiveness of a kiss, and the queen kisses Lancelot. Thus, it does not seem farfetched to assume that Galehaut played the kind of role for Guinevere and her knight that the story of Lancelot played for Francesca and Paolo. More important, the Fifth Canto and the written text of the dream and journal may have played such a part for Keats and Georgiana in Keats's fantasy. There is considerable evidence for this in the imagery of the dream, directly borrowed, as it were, from Dante, and in the details in Keats's correspondence referring to Georgiana. The kiss in the dream could then express both the forbidden impulse and its forgiveness—as the queen's kiss is granted in forgiveness. It is likely, then, that the reading of Dante stimulated in the poet the wish to seduce his sister-in-law as Paolo had seduced Francesca; the consequence of the seduction, represented as a kiss, is a sojourn in hell which reawakens in Keats thoughts of the death of his loved ones and associated depressive affect and mourning [40]

Pederson-Krag (1951) has referred to the identification of Keats with Francesca and to the poet's guilty love for Georgiana. I would endorse her comment that Keats was, on some level, attempting to seduce his sister-in-law in his correspondence. On the simplest level one could imagine one of the core dream thoughts to be, "If only I could be kissed by Georgiana the way Francesca was kissed by Paolo, I would find it an ecstasy and would be willing to sojourn in Dante's second circle of Hell."

Although I have so far focused on the erotic aspects, there is another implication of the Dante canto: its location is hell, and so the role of death has to be considered. We do not know why the canto "pleases" Keats "more and more," but it is conceivable that the poet is primarily concerned about

---

[40] I shall not concern myself in this paper with the deeper meanings of the dream, including the nature of the wish expressed toward Georgiana, now pregnant. There are additional complexities; for example, there is some evidence that Keats has also identified both with Francesca, thus expressing longings for his brother, and with the jealous husband who murders the guilty lovers. The further day residue of rage at Wells who wrote the fake love letters to Tom must also be kept in mind.

death and illness and thus may be mourning both his brother, buried four months previously, and his mother, felled by tuberculosis. Keats may have had a premonition that he would join them in the not too distant future. The theme of love may be a defense against the anticipation of death, or there may be various complicated relationships between the two—for example, "Since I will soon die, I might as well enjoy myself," or "Why worry about death? I will be reunited with my mother." There are several plausible hypotheses which we cannot effectively prove or disprove because of the paucity of evidence.

I will now turn to the function of the dream for Keats and as used by him in the correspondence with George and Georgiana. This will preface a similar examination of the function of the dream in the sonnet and in the ballad. On a simple level, we can postulate that one function of the dream is to minimize Keats's unhappiness and foreboding of death ("it is not true") and to present as fulfilled certain wishes both current and infantile. But what of the fate of the warded-off affects? They reveal themselves ever so briefly in the manifest content—"in the midst of all this cold and darkness"—and are replaced by their opposites in the line, "O that I could dream it every night." What about the function of the dream in the letter, the first creative product? I have already suggested that the dream serves as a veiled (or not so veiled) hint of Keats's guilty attachment to Georgiana. It allows a clear expression of his wish in such a way that it does not take an objectionable form. The dream, as it is used in the correspondence then, is a solution to a conflict arising in Keats's relation to George and Georgiana. Keats can use the manifest dream as a carrier of his secret (or not so secret) longings, expressed with sufficient ambiguity to free him from taking direct responsibility for the affects that are revealed. He may have also used the sharing of the dream and what we see as its day residue to communicate, in an ambiguous manner, his concerns about death to those he loved the most. This use of the dream may be quite secondary to the conflicts which ended up in dream form, or to the purpose of the dream.

Next, I will turn to the sonnet, "On a Dream." Keats was right to be dissatisfied with it. It has a contrived quality. The manifest, barely altered dream is appended in the last six lines, and the first eight lines, full of mythological allusions, are largely intellectual and stilted. A reader with no knowledge of the occurrence of the dream would have no way of understanding the title or of appreciating that the last six lines are the almost literal representation of the poet's personal experience. As we are in possession of the day residue, however, a closer examination of the symbolism and allusions contained in the first eight lines will enrich the examination of the fate of the original dream. I will consider these as modified associations.

The first line, "As Hermes once took to his feathers light," clearly mirrors the sensations of floating and flying in the dream. The next line, "When lullèd Argus, baffled, swooned and slept," is explained by Pederson-Krag (1951) as follows: "The hundred eyed Argus servant by Juno was guarding Io from Jove's attention when Hermes, Jove's messenger, played so sweetly to him that all his hundred eyes closed at once, at which point Hermes murdered him" (p. 275). Keats makes an analogy between Hermes and his own spirit which, unlike Jove, is not interested in Io. Note the implied negation which recurs more forcefully in the next two lines: Keats's idle spright fled away, "Not to pure Ida with its snow-cold skies" (Ida was the mountain where the page Ganymede had been raped by Jove), "Nor unto Tempe where Jove grieved that day" (Tempe was the valley in which Apollo was frustrated by the transformation of Daphne, daughter of a river God; fleeing from the amorous Apollo. She escaped by being changed into a laurel).

As analysts, we might see the "Not" as an attempted escape from the cold (snow-cold skies) and from grief (Jove grieved that day). Indeed, this view is strengthened by a consideration of the last six lines. Keats has implied that he is not tempted even in sleep (or fantasy) to relive scenes of masculine love, or rape, but rather he is drawn back to return to the scene of his dream—now transformed in several ways. In contrast to the original dream's oceanic, manic-like quality, here the grief, depression, sadness, and death break through—"sad" hell, "lovers need not tell their sorrows." The adjective "pale," clearly an allusion to death, occurs twice, and the heaviness is again emphasized by the word "melancholy" describing the storm. Thus, the first poetic "associations" to the dream reveal, perhaps in spite of the poet's wishes, his depressive affect; the form Keats's "spright" floats with is no longer a beautiful figure but a barely disguised representation of death. In the sonnet, Keats tells us, there was "nothing of what I felt in [the dream]." On a manifest level Keats was unable to convey the ecstatic quality of the dream in his poem. From the point of view of defensive operations, we could say that the poet could not maintain the cheerful mood that was initiated by the dream and that interrupted a depressed mood of some days' duration.

I will now examine the ballad in some detail. There is a lengthy tradition associated with La Belle Dame starting in the middle ages and re-emerging with particular strength in the German Romantic movement. Keats's title itself is ambiguous. It can signify "the fairy's lack of pity for the mortal she lures from the world or her own deprivation since she exists without hope of divine grace" (Fass, 1979, p. 43). Keats made prior use of the title of the ballad, derived from a poem by the French medieval writer, Alain Chartier. A month before the dream, Keats wrote the lovely ode, "The Eve of St. Agnes." In the poem an ardent lover, Porphyro, introduces himself by a stratagem into the bedroom of the sleeping Madeleine on the eve of St. Agnes. Madeleine, according to an old tradition, was waiting for a dream to show her the features of her future betrothed. In effect, Porphyro is able to seduce Madeleine while she is still half asleep while singing to her "an ancient ditty, long since mute,/ In Provence called, 'La belle dame sans merci.'" The main themes deal with love awakened and seen in a dream. Love and death are intertwined. Sleep, dream, and awakening are confused, blurring the reality of vision. "Her eyes were open, but she still beheld,/ Now wide awake, the vision of her sleep."[41] It is perhaps no accident, then, that Keats should have seized upon "La Belle Dame" as an extraordinary means of representation of the complicated feelings associated with his own dream in which, like Madeleine, he had a vision. "How changed thou art! How pallid, chill, and drear! / Give me that voice again, my Porphyro, / Those looks immortal, those complainings dear! / O leave me not in this eternal woe, / For if thou diest, my Love, I know not where to go" ("The Eve of St. Agnes," Stanza XXV).

The ballad, in contrast to the earlier sonnet, is full of ambiguity. There is a dreamlike quality to the entire poem. This is consonant with the idea that the form of the ballad could have been stimulated in part by the dream—and represents a return of the original form after the distancing of the sonnet. The first three stanzas are spoken by an unidentified narrator, which suggests an analogy with an inner voice. The fourth stanza, starting with "I met a lady in the Meads," is in all likelihood spoken by the knight at arms. There is a complex shift from waking to sleeping which is then interrupted by the knight as narrator telling his dream to an unidentified audience. He then awakens either as a result of the horrible dream or simply after it is ended. The last stanza, purporting to be an explanation ("this is why I sojourn here"), explains nothing. Its form is reminiscent of the activity of the mind during the process of secondary revision.

There are multiple levels of confusion in both content and form, which are perhaps associated with the unclear boundary between fantasy and reality. There is confusion about what ails the knight, though the issue is clearly one of bondage. Does he remain on the hillside because of the dream or because of the experience, and why should such a poetic encounter, full of love, be followed by the warning dream? Is the fairy equated with La

---

41 Note the similarity with the earlier correspondence with George and Georgiana.

Belle Dame? There is confusion regarding the nature of the fairy. Does she represent an "evil fantasy, luring the hero away from the real world or does she represent the sinful world—materialism, keeping the hero away from the path to his real home—heaven in this instance"? (Fass 1979, p. 27).

It is tempting to see the fairy as the transformed figures from the original dream. From a blissful oceanic fusion emerges a being whose identity is still obscure but who is now both comforter and comforted in the dual role of mother and child. No words are exchanged between the Knight and the fairy, which adds to the sense of mystery and other-worldliness. There seems to be a willed obscurity in the lines, "And there I dreamed—Ah! woe betide!—/ The latest dream I ever dreamt/ On the cold hill side." It is not clear whether latest should be understood as "last" or whether it should be taken literally, meaning that the knight at arms had had many previous dreams in the location. There is a puzzling use of time in this sequence—"latest" refers to past and "ever" refers to future in a strange juxtaposition, from the vantage point of the present observer standing outside of the narrative time.

Although the ballad is full of ambiguity concerning the characters and their motives, one aspect is not ambiguous: its somber, almost unrelieved depressed quality, with themes of starvation, cold, desolation, illness, and death. The eruption of the depressive affects clearly continues the process initiated by the sonnet but in a much richer, more poetic vein. In the ballad, love is alluded to but the fairy, without explanation, "wept and sighed full sore." It is not clear who is the comforter and who the comforted. In the rough draft of the ballad the poet clearly struggled (either for poetic or for personal motives) against too direct an expression of the theme of death.

The first draft of the third stanza ran thus:

I see death on thy brow
With anguish moist and fever dew
And on thy cheek's death a fading rose
Fast withereth too.

In the printed version, death is omitted in each case. Thus, "I see a lily on thy brow... / And on thy cheeks a fading rose."[42]

I will now turn to a closer examination of the "dream" contained in the latter part of the ballad. In contrast to the sonnet which included the original dream imagery without clearly identifying its source, in the ballad we now find a literary dream. As in the sonnet, the dream occurs toward the latter part of the work. It is no longer a "beautiful dream" but more a nightmarish vision, a spoken warning, oracular in nature, of death, bondage, starvation, and cold. It is integrated in the poem and clearly marked off as a literary dream. And yet it flows smoothly, connected both to what precedes it and to what follows it. As Bate (1963) puts it, "He [the knight] does not actually witness the horrid warning of starvation that this attempted union may bring. That anticipation, which may be genuine or primarily the expression of his own uneasiness, has come to him only in a dream—a dream that has also banished 'la Belle Dame.' And if the dream is now proving to be prophetic, it is again through his own divided nature, his own act, his persistence in continuing to loiter on the cold hillside even though the autumn is about to become winter" (p. 481).

It is expedient to study the separate transformation of the content of the original dream by tracing the fate of the affects and of the complex imagery. In the original dream experience the dreamer found ecstasy and hoped that

---

42 It should be mentioned that there are two versions of the ballad included in Keats's collected works. Keats undertook relatively minor revisions in some four of the stanzas at the suggestion of Hunt, at a time when he was quite ill. It is difficult to attribute psychological significance to these changes.

he could dream it every night—that is, return in fantasy to the experience. In the sonnet the poet's "idle spright" fled away to the second circle of Hell, the scene of the dream. In the ballad the situation is reversed; the knight for unclear reasons cannot or will not escape from the desolate scene including the dream. The core image portrays the union between the dreamer and the beautiful figure. Though the sex of the figure is not identified in the original dream, it makes sense to assume it is female. The dream is unchanged in the sonnet but is expanded in the ballad into a story from the fourth to the ninth stanza. The form is that of a dreamlike fantasy which expands the original imagery and etches out a more complete, if somewhat mysterious portrait, giving it the identity of a fairy. The tableau, "I floated about the whirling atmosphere… with a beautiful figure to whose lips mine were joined," is transformed into "I set her on my pacing steed / And nothing else saw all day long / For sidelong would she bend and sing." The oral imagery of the dream is expanded to being fed "roots of relish sweet" and being told "sure in language strange … / 'I love thee true'"; it is expanded to being taken to "her elfin grot / …. And there I shut her wild wild eyes / With kisses four." The other part of the manifest dream indicating depression and death finds its own representation but is split off from the tale—in the introductory three stanzas—and projected onto the fairy in one line, "And there she wept and sighed full sore." It emerges encapsulated in the literary dream. This lengthy elaboration can be contrasted to the condensation achieved in the form of the real dream.

Can we say anything about the function of "the dream" in the ballad? This literary dream encapsulates the dreaded inner voice of conscience, doom, and foreboding of death. Yet the poet is able is able to convey these affects while still preserving the ambiguity of the characters' reactions, thus enriching the multiple meanings and displaying his ambivalence. The function of the dream in the ballad could be considered analogous to that of a dream within a dream. The ballad represents a poetic fantasy on the original dream. The literary dream could be seen in the nature of a superego injection, until then warded off by the dreamer and poet. In the above I am blurring the distinction between "real dream" and "literary dream," which, of course, oversimplifies the issue. We are not sure why Keats included a literary dream as part of the ballad, or whether it was in any way related to the original dream experience. We do know, however, that dreams had profound significance for Keats. As I will show later, Keats contrasted dreams (which he mistrusted) with poetic vision (which was equated with true insight). On this level, then, a literary dream is an ambiguous product and might reflect the author's wish that the nightmarish vision be "only a dream."

There is still another level of possible interpretation of the ballad which I have carefully avoided up to this point because it is so fraught with danger—the symbolic area. However, a certain transparency and fitting together of the themes of the ballad suggests the following.[43] If we heard a patient tell us about a dream with a similar manifest content, how many of us would almost preconsciously formulate the story of the ballad as the encounter between a lover and his lady's more private anatomy (the grotto) with dreaded consequences following consummation. The image of "starved lips... / With horrid warning gapèd wide" sounds very much like a castration threat. This reading suggests that the lips in the original dream represented a multiple condensation and that in the ballad death and castration are fused—a not uncommon clinical finding. The dream within the ballad then contains the most repressed level—that of castration at the hands of the lover which becomes fused with the representation of the mother. From the point of view of method, this last interpretation is consistent with the previous formal interpretation. Indeed, a professor of literature, Vera Jiji, reading the poem, commented spontaneously that some of the truncated lines ("And no birds sing") could represent the theme of castration in a formal way. There is

---

43 This reading was suggested by Harry Trosman.

support for the existence in the poet of castration anxiety in his avoidance of women as sexual objects and in his selection of an unavailable woman with whom to share at a distance his most personal outpourings.

The lure of symbolic interpretation is evident in Williams's (1966) treatment of the ballad. His paper, subtitled "The Bad-Breast Mother," is more an example of the application of Kleinian concepts than a clarification of the poem. Williams states that "the turning of the idealized breast into 'La Belle Dame sans Merci,' the daemonified breast mother, may well have been felt unconsciously to have been due to [Keats's] own devouring greed, complicated and intensified by its being mixed with envy" (p. 70). The evidence Williams offers to buttress such conclusions is rather flimsy. "We can see that a greedy component of his personality existed by the frequency of his allusions to and preoccupation with food and drink and their pervasiveness in his imagery and in his letters. The envy may be linked with his very considerable ambition" (p. 71). Williams made even more fanciful use of the theory in stating that the word "'Garland' ... would refer to the halo of idealization or, alternatively, could represent the arms of the babe Keats twined round his mother's neck, imprisoning her in his embrace and trying to keep her for himself" (p. 71). Such reductionism does justice neither to the theory nor to the poem.

DISCUSSION

My efforts at a psychoanalytic interpretation of the poem led me first to rely on the more traditional method of relating the poem to the mental life of its author. I accumulated as much relevant outside information about the author as possible to try to recreate a context and to insert the personal and poetic products within a fictional mind. This makes it possible to reconstruct some of the more plausible connections and meanings. However, such an effort has its obvious limitations, since the valence of any particular element is hard to assess.

I then pursued a second line of investigation, a type of structural analysis, limiting myself largely to a description of the manifest content, particularly the stated affects, the imagery, and the metaphors. This approach initially avoids any dynamic formulations. As there were three different products, I examined the shift and transformations from the dream to the sonnet and finally to the ballad. From such a description one hopes to be in a position to draw some inferences about the meaning of the transformations and their psychological underpinnings.

Finally, I alluded to the reader's reaction to the sonnet and the ballad as additional data on which to base inferences about the creative process.

We are faced with an interesting issue in the case of the sonnet and the ballad. The stimulus for their composition is the dream and its lingering effect upon the poet. We cannot view this stimulus as ordinary day residue, to be sure, as it includes both the manifest content and imagery of the dream and its reverberations in the unconscious. Hamilton (1969) has suggested that "object loss leads to a regressive fusion with the lost object and that the dream becomes an integral part of this process, having originally been utilized by the infant to cope with the loss of direct oral gratification from the mother during sleep.... Keats resorted to poetry in an attempt to complete the mourning process and to make restitution for the lost object, most importantly his mother, by externalizing his dreams in the forms of poems" (p. 529).

In the material I have discussed here the role of the dream is complex. In addition to the potent stimulus of the content, the form of the dream becomes a carrier of the lost past. The conflicts which gave rise to the dream involve a struggle against awareness of depressive affects; because of their painful nature, these affects found only marginal expression in the dream. The same defensive stance, however, need no longer be maintained in the poem. It is not clear whether Keats was conscious of the intrusion of the depressive affects in his work and whether his humorous gloss in the correspondence following the ballad ("Why four kisses") reflected a defensive stance made necessary by the poem's depressive affects, or whether the depression expressed in the poem was cathartic and allowed the poet to regain distance from what was, after all, a rather dismal set of circumstances. The gloss is a healthy reminder for us to be extremely cautious in our reconstruction of the author's conscious state of mind. It is conceivable that Keats wrote the ballad without being at all interested in or even aware of its personal meaning or its connection with the dream.

I noted earlier that the ecstatic mood of the dream could not be maintained in the sonnet, being replaced by a depressive mood like the one that had plagued the poet for some days prior to the dream. Perhaps the inability to maintain the ecstasy can be viewed as a failure of defense, which interfered with the poet's creativity and led to a stilted, uninteresting poem. Indeed, the inclusion of the barely transformed manifest dream might then represent a failed attempt to recapture the ecstatic mood of the dream. Thus, the reader's reaction to this poem might be an indicator of the incomplete assimilation by the poet of the conflicts aroused by the dream.

Something must be said about the several hypotheses suggested by the data and their varying levels of plausibility. The description of the process of transformation from dream to sonnet and ballad does not initially require the importation of psychological hypotheses. This last step is necessary at the point at which I compared the process with dreamwork and alluded to defensiveness, implying the presence of conflict. The affect of depression is mentioned by the poet and is clearly more evident in the ballad than in the sonnet or the dream. In comparison to the ballad, the sonnet appears to be too close to the original dream experience. It has not yet been integrated by the poet, and defensive needs have the upper hand. The sonnet incorporates the real content of the manifest dream without identifying it as such,

351

representing it instead as a flight of imagination. It is hardly transformed and the subtle shifts from waking to sleeping which lend an aura of mystery and beauty to the ballad are missing. Three days later, Keats's creative imagination had a chance to play with both the form and content of the experience, and he produced a haunting work of art.

If we compare the contents and affects of the dream passages, we find remarkable shifts. In the "real" reported dream, there is barely an allusion to death except indirectly, via the words "in the midst of all this cold and darkness." In the sonnet, we move closer to depression and to hints of death, first in the form of denial: Keats's idle sprite does not flee to "pure Ida" with its snow-cold skies or to Tempe where Jove grieved. The imagery of the last four lines refers to lovers not needing to tell their sorrows. The lips of the figure are referred to twice as "pale" and the storm is "melancholy." It is as though the sonnet begins the process of undoing of the manic-like defense of the real dream.

In the process of transformation, then, the poet had first to distance himself from too personal an intrusion; he finds a proper poetic mode in order to give free rein to the expression of his feelings in a different register. However, the defense against the depressive affects is still partly maintained in the ballad, through the use of ambiguity, the attribution of weeping to the fairy, and finally the encapsulation of the frightening warning in a literary dream. Perhaps we could consider these devices as successful (formal) defenses allowing the emergence of a creative solution. Finally, the ballad amplifies the theme of death through the emergence of one of its childhood antecedents—castration —which is absent from the manifest dream.

Concerning the personal meaning of the various products—dream, sonnet, ballad—in the context of the author's life situation, some hypotheses are better supported by data than others. From the point of view of the study of creativity, this is clearly the less interesting part of my discussion as we discover once more the everyday conflicts, frustrations, and anxieties which take their toll of even the most gifted. The themes of love and death are intertwined. The attachment of the poet to Georgiana—his guilt about it and his identification with Paolo—do not require much speculation. The similarity between the manifest content of the dream and the Dante canto suggest that an analogy on some other level is present. The reconstruction of the parallels between Lancelot/Guinevere/Galehaut, Paolo/Francesca/Lancelot, and Keats/Georgiana/journal allows the reconstruction of the nature of Keats's attachment to his sister-in-law. The identification of the fairy with the lost mother is commonplace in fairy tales. What I termed the symbolic interpretation dealing with castration is less well supported by the data. The relationship between object loss and creativity is not a new concept. Certainly, Keats had more than his share of losses and setbacks.

Even though the data are rich, there are a number of unexplained features. It is not clear why certain affectively laden episodes do not obviously find their way into the poetry or the dream. To take but one example, Keats's discovery of the prank played on his deceased brother aroused in him very strong feelings, yet I could detect no obvious representation of that incident. Here I am in disagreement with Pederson-Krag (1951), who felt that the slaying of Argus by Hermes in the sonnet was sufficient evidence for Keats's murderous wishes. The dead brother, Tom, is most likely represented in the third stanza of the ballad, starting with "I see a lily on thy brow." The absence of data hampers our inquiry about the more general meaning of Dante to Keats, surely an interesting aspect.

An issue that needs to be considered is whether the imagery in the poetry following the dream is necessarily dynamically related to it, or whether it could be explained on some other basis—e.g., it is simply characteristic of Keats's fondness for images of floating. I think the inclusion of the dream in the sonnet and the indication by Keats that he wrote the sonnet with the dream in mind is clear evidence. None of Keats's other poems have detailed dreams as content (as does the ballad), although images of sleep and dreaming are frequent throughout his sonnets and other poems. His poetry is full of allusions to fusion with a loved woman, breast imagery, and references to states of dreaming, sleeping, dying, and transition to waking (Hamilton, 1969). The imagery contained in the ballad and other poems examined here cannot, of course, be attributed only to the effects of the dream. It is in many ways typical of Keats's style, including the style of his correspondence, which I will illustrate briefly. The central image in the dream—the two figures floating in the air—is not unrelated to one of Keats's favorite themes, "indolence," the power of passivity. "If I had teeth of pearl and the breath of lilies, I should call it languor, but as I am I must call it laziness. In this state of effeminacy, the fibers of the brain are relaxed in common with the rest of the body and to such a happy degree that pleasure has no show of enticement and pain, no unbearable frown" (p. 78). The association of love and death takes this form in a letter to Fanny Brawne in July 1819: "I have two luxuries to brood over in my walks—your loveliness and the hour of my death. O, that I could have possession of them both in the same minute. I hate the world: it batters too much the wings of my self-will and would I could take a sweet poison from your lips to send me out of it. From no others would I take it" (Baker, 1962, p. 71).

This passage returns to the original image of the dream, which can then be seen to express not only a fantasy of love but also of *Liebestodt*, of dying together, or at least of the lover being the beloved executioner. Dying together in the act of love may also have been charged with other meanings for the poet. It should be noted that Georgiana was pregnant during all of this time. Keats, very much concerned with surviving and immortality, may have yearned for a child.

I have said relatively little about the cultural setting of Keats's works. It would be reductionistic to imply that "La Belle Dame" and the sonnet are nothing but elaborations of the dream thoughts and imagery. Many of their elements need to be placed in the context of the Romantic movement and its various favorite clichés and their particular expression in the poetry of Keats. To take one example, a recurrent theme in Keats's poetry is the abandonment of the narrator/hero by a woman who leaves him perhaps while he was asleep. A famous example[44] of this theme is to be found in the long narrative poem, *Endymion* (composed April–November 1817), where a pair of winged horses carry Endymion and his Indian bride aloft, but as he turns to her she dissolves, Eurydice-like, in the moonlight leaving him alone: "...I have clung/To nothing, loved a nothing, nothing seen/Or felt but a great dream!"

The blurring of distinction between dreaming and reality is a recurrent theme of Keats. The last two lines of the "Ode to a Nightingale" express this.

Was it a vision, or a waking dream?
Fled is that music—Do I wake or sleep?

The related concern with the potential disappearance of the loved one is expressed in its negative in the "Ode on a Grecian Urn":

Bold Lover, never, never canst thou kiss,
Though winning near the goal—yet, do not grieve:
She cannot fade, though thou hast not thy bliss,
For ever will thou love, and she be fair!

The dread of awakening, which is related to the knight's loitering, is a common theme. The poem "On Death" contains many other themes of the Belle Dame ballad:

---

44 I am grateful to M. Frank Alweis for this example.

Can death be sleep, when life is but a dream,
And scenes of bliss as a phantom by?
The transient pleasures as a vision seem,
And yet we think the greatest pain's to die.
How strange it is that man on earth should roam,
And lead a life of woe, but not forsake
His rugged path; nor dare he view alone
His future doom which is but to awake.

The relation between dreaming, waking, sleeping, and poetry always fascinated Keats. In an early work, "Sleep and Poetry," written in 1816, Keats explored the relation between dreams and artistic insight. Sleep is presented as a motherly comforter!

Soft closer of our eyes!
Low murmur of tender lullabies!
Light hoverer around our happy pillows!

Some of the same functions are attributed to poesy: it should be a friend to soothe the cares and lift the thought of man.

In his "reworking" of the poem "Hyperion" into the "Fall of Hyperion—A Dream" shortly before his death, Keats differentiates escapist dreams from the imaginative vision of the poet:

The Poet and dreamer are distinct,
Diverse, sheer opposites, antipodes.
The one pours out a balm upon the world, The other vexes it.

In the same poem he came back to the issue.

> For Poesy alone can tell her dreams,
> ...Who alive can say,
> 'Thou art no Poet—may'st not tell thy dreams'?
> Since every man whose soul is not a clod
> Hath visions, and would speak, if he had loved,
> And been well nurtured in his mother tongue.
> Whether the dream now purposed to rehearse
> Be Poet's or Fanatic's will be known
> When this warm scribe my hand is in the grave.

Thus, it seems that Keats was concerned with the survival of his works after his death but also doubted his right to consider himself a creator. Are his visions those of the "fanatic"? Is he deceiving himself? In this light he might have taken particular delight in trying to transform the "fanatic's dream" into a poetic vision. That it took him more than one attempt is understandable. This same concern was expressed in the lovely "Ode to a Nightingale" in the line quoted earlier: "Was it a vision [i.e., a true discovery worthy of being conveyed, a real insight], or a waking dream?" [i.e., a personal product of no value].

In addition to being interested in the relation between dreams and poetry, Keats took great pains to elaborate his own theories about creativity. These have been studied by Leavy (1970). His paper, however, fails to go beyond the manifest content of the poet's statements. Leavy says that the "use of Keats's ideas on creativity depends on our willingness to concede that the poet possessed an exceptional access to the workings of his own mind permitting him to know what he was doing and how he did it. I am therefore quite deliberately using Keats's ideas as if they were themselves, so to speak, 'psychoanalytic interpretations' of the data of experience. I am making almost no attempt to 'analyze' Keats by uncovering the unconscious intentions of his ideas" (p. 176). While we may admire the ability of the poet to share with us his experience, I believe we do not do him justice to treat him as a theoretician without understanding the many meanings of the terms he uses.

My efforts have been in the direction of a limited descriptive approach to the transformation of imagery and affects. This may be disappointing to readers looking for explanations of creativity. It is, however, in line with my belief that applied psychoanalysis is far too burdened with speculations and too devoid of data close to observation. Ideally, such data as I have provided could generate further hypotheses capable of testing. What emerges is a greater respect for the complex process leading to the selection of a title in a foreign language to express the myriad of meanings contained in a very brief dream which closely mirrors a few lines in an acknowledged master's poem.

Before closing, I wish to remind you of Keats's discontent with the sonnet's failure to capture the mood of the dream. Was he any more satisfied with the ballad? Perhaps the above analysis will help answer this question. If Keats was still trying to recapture the ecstatic quality of the original dream, the answer would have to be an unqualified "no"; if the poet were to judge the result in terms of the poetic effect and beauty of the ballad, the answer would have to be an unqualified "yes!" Finally, what would Keats's reaction have been to the above analysis if I could have sent him my paper, as Freud did with Jensen? Could the answer be found in the quotation I have put at the beginning of my article? It is relevant, as it is included in the letter to George and Georgiana: "Here are the poems, they will explain themselves as all poems should do—without comment" (p. 58). In light of my reconstructions about the possible meaning of their content I can well sympathize with Keats's emphatic statement.

REFERENCES

Baker, C., Editor (1962). *Keats' Poems and Selected Letters*. New York: Scribner Sons.

Bate, W. J. (1963). *John Keats*. Cambridge: Harvard Univ. Press.

Dante (1314). *The Divine Comedy*. Translated by M. B. Anderson. New York: Heritage Press, 1944.

Fass, B. (1979). *La Belle Dame sans Merci: The Aesthetics of Romanticism*. Detroit: Wayne State Univ. Press.

Hamilton, J.W. (1969). Object loss, dreaming and creativity. The poetry of John Keats *Psychoanal. Study Child* 24:488–531.

Leavy, S.A. (1970). John Keats's psychology of creative imagination. *Psychoanal. Q.* 39:173–197.

Pederson-Krag, G. (1951). The genesis of a sonnet. *Psychoanal. Soc. Sci.* 3:263–276.

Rollins, H.E., Editor (1958). *The Letters of John Keats 1814–1821 Vol. 2*. Cambridge: Harvard Univ. Press. Williams, A H. (1966). Keats' "La belle dame sans merci": the bad-breast mother *Amer. Imago* 2:363–381.

CHAPTER 13

Faulkner's *As I Lay Dying*: Issues of Method in Applied Analysis

[(1992). *Psychoanal. Q.* (61):65–83).]

ABSTRACT: This paper seeks to illustrate several possible approaches in the application of psychoanalysis to Faulkner's novel, *As I Lay Dying*. In applied analysis, the specific form and content of the work in question must be considered in order to determine which aspect of psychoanalysis will be most relevant in creating a meaningful context and in increasing our understanding.

Psychoanalysis as a theory was not devised to deal with nonliving subjects, yet many apply the tools of analysis to literary characters as if they could be treated the same as patients on the couch. In a previous paper on this topic (Baudry, 1984) I described four possible psychoanalytic approaches to a novel: 1) the story of the characters in a novel as case history; 2) the novel as an aesthetic structure (including form and style); 3) the novel as a reflection of the life of the author; and 4) reader reaction as a point of entry into the novel.[45] I would like to apply these approaches to Faulkner's novel, *As I Lay Dying*, and try to determine which approaches are most successful as a point of entry into the work and its relation to the author.

This paper is written from the viewpoint of a practicing analyst using the data of his clinical and supervisory experience as phenomena analogous to

---

45 For a more literary approach to the same question, see Skura (1981).

the unfolding of the novel. As my paper concerns itself with issues of method in applied analysis,[46] it cannot do justice to the many complex layers of plot, structure, and style in Faulkner's novel. Hence, I will neglect certain aspects of the narrative and will have little to say about many of the characters. This is not because I do not consider them important or relevant, but rather because I have assigned myself a limited aim—to deal with methodology. This topic is often neglected in both literary and psychoanalytic writings.

The attempt to apply analysis in a general way to a work of art can only result in uninteresting conclusions or in the refinding of some bit of analytic theory. This is the well-known problem of reductionism relating to issues of boundary. How can one discipline relate to another without appropriating it? The first task lies in the search for an organizer or a point of entry into the work. What are the questions which analysis, in contrast to other systems of literary criticism, is in a position to answer in regard to a specific work?

A prerequisite is a thorough and sensitive reading which will serve as a manifest text and provide a basis for evaluation. This reading must be understandable and able to be challenged by informed readers. Only then are we in a position to select a point of entry into the work. If an attempt is made to relate the novel to the author, a detailed knowledge of the author's life, including his or her particular circumstances around the time of the composition of the work in question, is required. If I may be allowed an analogy, the work can be seen both as a symptom and as a character trait. As a symptom, it might be said to express some particular state the author is in at the time of its composition—as the result of a loss, for example, or of a major developmental step, such as marriage. As a character trait, it might reveal the author's customary habits and the unconscious fantasies which

---

46 An interdisciplinary group made up of analysts and literary scholars has been meeting monthly since 1975 at the New York Psychoanalytic Institute and struggling with issues of method in the application of psychoanalysis to literature. Much of my work is heavily influenced by the deliberations of this group.

inform them. These would permeate typical narrative sequences and shape stylistic and formal aspects of the work. The possibility that there is no demonstrable relation between the life and the work is not really tenable in a literary piece. Klee (see Thomas, 1990) has suggested that an artist's work is related to his life in much the same way that a tree's branches are related to its roots. In both instances, there is an obvious causal connection, which is nevertheless difficult to analyze.

The length of *As I Lay Dying* precludes my being able to give in detail an account of the aforementioned "sensitive reading." I will instead briefly summarize those aspects of the plot necessary for the arguments to be made later.

The narrative concerns the events following the death of Addie Bundren and the conflicts and difficulties posed by her request to be buried with her family of origin rather than with her husband's. (I am excluding for the moment the one chapter in which she is still alive.) Her family is forcibly brought together for the trip, which becomes an odyssey of suffering, with multiple tragedies. The narrative is frequently interrupted by passages in an authorial voice dealing with problems of identity, death, fatality, and time, and the relationship between something and nothing. Sentences are often broken off in the middle, the subject is not always clear, and pronouns are purposely confused. The text includes a few concrete illustrations—a line drawing of a coffin, for example, and a blank space in the middle of a sentence. Some passages are in italics, reflecting the speech or musings of another character, not always specified, but generally from the recent past. There are occasional references to characters from previous novels, including horses which play a major role in both mirroring and expanding a character's mood or state of mind. The chapters, varying in length from one sentence to several pages, are assigned to different narrators, including members of the Bundren family and some neighbors.

I will now turn to my first category, "the case history approach." The characters belong to lower-class hill people with very limited capacity for introspection, or for communicating emotions. Their reliability as narrators is often questionable. There is no development of character as a result of the action, and the interaction between the family members is at a bare minimum—often at a nonverbal level. Thus, the critic's traditional pursuit of character development bogs down because of the fragmented nature of the work. Perhaps we can better enter the novel by asking how and by what means the author has succeeded in involving us in an intensely human and moving experience, one in which we empathize with the tragic fate of the family. This would involve a consideration of my second approach.

I believe this can best be done through an examination of some aspects of the author's style. In a beautiful passage, the adolescent daughter, Dewey Dell, has made love with Lafe at the end of a cotton row in the field, and she describes her realization that her brother, Darl, was aware of the event.

> It was then, and then I saw Darl and he knew. He said he knew without the words like he told me that ma is going to die without words, and I knew he knew because if he had said he knew with the words I would not have believed that he had been there and saw us. But he said he did know and I said "Are you going to tell Pa are you going to kill him?" without the words I said it and he said "Why?" without the words. And that's why I can talk to him with knowing with hating because he knows (p. 24).

The repetition of "he knew" and of "without the words," like a musical refrain, intensifies the nonverbal dialogue; although there is no mention of facial expressions, one senses gazing and a barely restrained affect of a primitive sort. The special quasi-incestuous closeness between brother and sister is obvious. The emphasis of the nonverbal over the verbal channel of communication poses a special challenge for the application of analysis, which relies so heavily on spoken dialogue.

The text itself does not yield its meaning readily. In fact, one aspect of Faulkner's style here, as elsewhere in his work, is the deliberate withholding of meaning: Faulkner tends to delay disclosure and to cultivate ambiguity and obscurity. The narrative action often remains fluid, ill defined. He uses repetitions to create a special language (reminiscent of Gertrude Stein's work), as in his rendering of Vardaman's consciousness. After learning of his mother's death, the little boy, Vardaman, is overtaken by a combination of feelings, including helplessness and rage. His universe is fragmenting. In a semi-dream state, he relives his version of the death. "I can hear the bed and her face and them and I can feel the floor shake when he walks on it that came and did it. That came and did it when she was all right but he came and did it" (p. 49). Vardaman runs to the barn: "Then I can breathe again, in the warm smelling. I enter the stall, trying to touch him, and then I can cry then I vomit the crying. As soon as he gets through kicking I can and then I can cry, the crying can" (p. 49).

Clearly, no eight-year-old boy would speak this way. Some critics, taking a very concrete stance toward the text, have even suggested that the boy is slightly retarded. Through poetic repetition Faulkner is able to evoke the sorrow of a latency child full of rage and tears, so agitated and yearning so for his lost mother that he cries and vomits at the same time. It is not immediately clear whether the breaking up of the syntax in this passage is primarily an aspect of the author's experimental style, or whether it is meant to convey psychological significance—for example, the graphic portrayal of the distraught state of a child so disorganized by grief that he can only play with words as objects rather than as conveyors of meaning.

To continue with the examination of Faulkner's style, I would like to give an example of an extreme use of condensation. This mechanism is typical of dream formation and is related to what Freud called the primary process, a mode of functioning of the unconscious. In the final part of the same "Vardaman" chapter, Faulkner writes:

> It is dark. I can hear wood, silence: I know them. But not living sounds, not even him. It is as though the dark were resolving him out of his integrity, into an unrelated scattering of components— snuffings and stampings; smells of cooling flesh and ammoniac hair; an illusion of a co-ordinated whole of splotched hide and strong bones within which, detached and secret and familiar, and is different from my is (p. 52).

Vardaman as character is abruptly replaced by the author/narrator interpreting Vardaman's experience for the reader. This section ends by returning to Vardaman, who says, "I am not afraid. Cooked and et. Cooked and et." Let us stay with this remarkable condensation, repeated twice for emphasis after the reassuring presence of the horse and the statement, "I am not afraid."

What is Faulkner conveying here? On a manifest level it refers to the fish which Vardaman caught and brought home in an earlier chapter, just before his mother died. Instead of being praised for his catch, he was told by his angry father to take it out and clean it. The fish was described by Vardaman as "cut up into pieces of not-fish now, not-blood on my hands and overalls. Then it wasn't so. It hadn't happened then. And now she is getting so far ahead I cannot catch her" (p. 49). The fish becomes a concrete representation of the lost mother. This is confirmed in the shortest chapter, which runs "My mother is a fish" (p. 74). The little boy feels in some way responsible for his mother's death. Vardaman describes the mysterious process wherein something becomes nothing, denying the blood on his hands. Full of love for his mother, he wants nothing more than to catch up with her, be with her, and find comfort in her. But "cooked and et" also conveys an image of incorporation consistent with the little boy's desperate clinging to some aspect of the mother who has just left him. While the manipulation of viewpoint does violence to our concept of reality, the effect produced is one of utmost emotional reality and immediacy. On an allegorical level, some critics have suggested a link between the fish and the early symbol of Christ as a fish. Both are killed and ritualistically ingested to prevent the death of the believer. This religious meaning is psychologically consistent with fantasies of incorporation which Vardaman demonstrates in his childish conception of grief. Other religious symbols in the novel include the three days during which Addie Bundren lies in the coffin before the beginning of her final journey.

At this point I have not addressed the core person in the novel—Addie Bundren, whose failure to control her own fate while living is compensated for by her capacity to bring her family together after her death. In the central chapter of the book, in which she is the narrator, time is reversed, creating an uncanny feeling in the reader. What is most impressive is the recurrent theme of the inability of words to convey the richness of intended meaning, a central idea in this book, expressed in one way or another by each character. A related idea is the aloneness of each member of the clan, an aloneness totally unbridgeable except by such concrete means as physical violence— for example, switching. When Addie finds herself pregnant with Cash, she says to herself: "That was when I learned that words are no good; that words don't ever fit even what they are trying to say at" (p. 157). And a bit later, she continues, in an obscure passage: "I knew that it had been, not that they had dirty noses, but that we had had to use one another by words like spiders dangling by their mouths from a beam, swinging and twisting and never touching, and that only through the blows of the switch could my blood and their blood flow as one stream" (p. 158). This last sentence is confusing. "Dirty noses" is a brief flashback to the children in her class who received the blows of her switch, but the metaphor of the spiders condenses images of isolation, of prey, and of the role of hatred in fostering contact. The concreteness of Addie's conception of identity is remarkably conveyed in the following monologue about her husband:

> Why are you Anse. I would think about his name until after a while I could see the word as a shape, a vessel, and I would watch him liquify and flow into it like cold molasses flowing out of the darkness into the vessel, until the jar stood full and motionless: a significant shape profoundly without life like an empty door frame; and then I would find that I had forgotten the name of the jar. I would think: The shape of my body where I used to be a virgin is in the shape of a and I couldn't think Anse, couldn't remember Anse (p. 159).

If a patient were talking this way, we would surely be struck by the sequence of associations—first, the concrete representation of Anse's name as a vessel, the man represented as filling the vessel, yet lifeless and empty, his identity denied; then a sudden move to thinking about herself as a container, and the state of virginity graphically represented in the text by an empty space. What is the relevance for the author of such primitive-sounding imagery? Does it represent a product of regression in the service of the ego during creativity? Or does it indicate some pathologic state in his mental economy, with a too ready availability of unconscious mental processes? Or are we to see it primarily as a meticulously planned passage echoing the style of Joyce without any special psychologic significance? It was Greenacre's opinion that artists have a greater capacity to be in touch with the more primitive aspects of their mental life than do other people. Another remark can be made about this central passage: the novel dwells insistently on the limits of language, and here the author resorts to an empty space to convey meaning. The reader is compelled to fill the space by naming it and is thus in the position of enacting what the function of Anse is for Addie—a space filler.

If the recurrence of questions about identity expressed on a concrete level by all characters is a consistent aspect of Faulkner's novels, we may be in touch with a matter of keen concern to the author. It is known that he changed the spelling of his name from Falkner to Faulkner, which may reflect, among other things, a concern about changing identity.

This leads me to the examination of some aspects of the relation of the novel to the author's life, starting with his circumstances during its composition. We are told that the novel was written in forty-six days. Faulkner had recently returned from his honeymoon with Estelle Franklin and had settled in Oxford, Mississippi.[47] The book was written mostly at night during his shift as supervisor in the university's power plant. The honeymoon had nearly ended in total disaster: both participants drank heavily, and Estelle had made an unsuccessful suicide attempt by walking into the Gulf of Mexico. She was saved by the intervention of a neighbor. A fragile young woman, Estelle soon realized that she came second to her husband's interest in his writing. At the time he wrote *As I Lay Dying*, Faulkner had already achieved some success with his previous novel, *The Sound and the Fury*. Every morning, he would walk to his mother's house and have coffee with her, which some critics see as a sign of excessive closeness, a characteristic of all the Faulkner boys that is felt by some critics to be responsible for the animosity found in Faulkner toward women in general.

Any attempt to penetrate the author's private life is hindered by Faulkner's secretiveness. Jay Martin (1983) tells us that Faulkner did everything he could to hide his real interior life from the scrutiny of others. Choosing to write about a family whose members were unable to express their feelings in words and who related to each other only in limited ways is consistent with Faulkner's passion for secrecy. His own pronouncements about his work are,

---

47 Most of these details about Faulkner's life are drawn from the recent biography by Frederick R. Karl (1989).

for the most part, not helpful to an interpretation of them. His opinions are often ambiguous and conflicting. When Malcolm Cowley asked Faulkner about the genesis of his stories, he received little help. Faulkner was evasive; he said they were not his own: "I listen to the voices; sometimes I don't like what they say but I don't change it" (Martin, 1983, p. 300).

This disowning of responsibility for one's own activity is typical of a number of characters in the novel, Anse and Dewey Dell in particular. Faulkner seems to have feared that his literary work might expose him, and so he claimed that he was not really connected to it. However, such pronouncements need not spell the end of our endeavor as analysts. We know that the unconscious cannot be silenced; all we need is to develop the necessary technique to read how an author's unconscious mind betrays itself in his or her work. Like any other mental product, a work of art is a compromise formation, though the laws governing its genesis are, of course, different from those that apply to symptom formation or to the genesis of a character trait. A work of art is more influenced by conscious choice, aesthetic considerations, and cultural factors than are mental structures. This is why we cannot assume that a particular trait or attitude found in a novel simply reflects a similar attribute of the author or of anyone close to the author.

As Blotner (1974) informs us, *As I Lay Dying* was started on October 25, 1929, the day after panic broke out on Wall Street. Faulkner stated, "I set out deliberately to write a tour de force. Before I ever put pen to paper, and set down the first word, I knew what the last word would be" (Blotner, 1974, p. 215). This suggests that the book may have been written to justify a particular ending, rather than to delineate the development of character.

This book was especially significant for Faulkner, judging by a letter to his editor: "By this book I will stand or fall" (p. 216). Blotner raises the question of whether the rapidity of the writing—unusual for Faulkner—was due to the fact that there existed earlier versions of most of the story. This does not appear to be the case, however. The episode of the spotted horse is found in two short stories: one is titled "Father Abraham," and the second appears to be a fragment (a 17-page surviving segment of 203 lost pages), titled "As I Lay Dying." Why this title, based on a line from Homer's *Odyssey*, was chosen for the brief segments is even more obscure than in the case of the novel. In one possible connection with Homer, Mrs. Armstid's eyes were described as dog's eyes—a clear if indirect reference to Homer, but scarcely enough to explain the use of this title. There may be some flimsy narrative connection between the short stories and the novel. The short story, "As I Lay Dying," ends as follows: "...she descended the steps and went down the road: a figure that progressed without motion like a blasted tree trunk moving somehow upright upon a flood" (McHaney, 1987, p. 38). In any event, the title was obviously already in the author's mind, available for use in the future.

What can be learned from the literary origin of the title? It comes from the section of Homer's *Odyssey* that deals with Odysseus' trip to the Underworld. The dead Agamemnon complains that his cruel wife would not close his eyes as he descended into Hades. He says: "As I lay dying the woman with the dog's eyes would not close my eyelids for me as I descended into Hades" (see Karl, 1989, p. 386). Could the title refer to the privileged vision of the poet as he penetrated the dark confines of a domain both awesome and fearful, a descent into his own underworld of fantasy and fears? Is there a personal meaning to Faulkner of the murder of Agamemnon, a man killed by a woman? Of possible relevance is the fact that in a brawl Faulkner's father, Murry, was shot in the middle body, face, and back; as Karl (1989, p. 50) informs us, "Murry lay in this state—not dying, but not really in a position to live." He was rescued by his own father and nursed by his mother. Also, Faulkner suffered a near fatal attack of scarlet fever at age four, according to a local paper.

To consider another approach to the meaning of this title, Bleikasten (1990) studied the grammatical and textual significance of the words. He pointed out that this title is from another text; intertextuality is already at work. The wording contains a riddle; the sentence is incomplete. Who is the "I"? Is it Addie, or the author, or even the reader? If Addie, does the novel serve as a kind of Scheherazade series of tales? Since some of the chapters are very brief, is the title from the first chapter? Why the use of this particular tense? Bleikasten aptly concludes that "what the novel is concerned with is not so much death as the process of dying… *As I Lay Dying* works from the start with the double paradox of a dying life and a living death" (p. 164).

Continuing the relation of the novel to its author, can we demonstrate a connection between Faulkner's personality and that of his characters? One of his attributes deserving special mention is that of imposture, which is well illustrated in his behavior following rejection at the hands of Estelle, whom he later married. He had gone as far as to give her a ring. When she announced that she no longer loved him and was planning to marry an officer (this was apparently done under pressure from her family, which disapproved very much of the marital plans), Faulkner determined he would become an officer himself. He hoped for some feats of glory and heroism. Unfortunately, the end of World War I interrupted the air force training he had initiated some four months before. Faulkner returned home with a limp and began to make up stories which became more elaborate with each new telling, about a plane crash and a near fatal injury. The limp disappeared after some time, only to reappear under stress or when Faulkner was trying to impress women. He made up stories about war exploits, and he wore unearned pilot's wings. His life was thus colored by the enactment of certain fictive elements. Other traits attributed to Faulkner by those who have written about him include passivity, dishonesty, and a certain slipperiness of identity and morality. All of these can be found in the Bundren family, including Anse. Could we imagine what the author's personal attitude is toward those very undesirable traits he so successfully caricatured in Anse?

There is another trait of Faulkner which may be of relevance to the form of the novel. Martin (1983) tells us that Faulkner "seems to have wanted to deny that he was a single person because he wanted to express his impulses but he also wanted to keep himself blameless for dealing with the primitive stuff of his unconscious mind" (p. 301). What better way to do this than to split the narrators into many fragments and to interrupt the narrative at frequent intervals.

Can we possibly discover which of the many narrators in the novel the author feels most in sympathy with? Can our own reaction to the text be of help? This question will allow me to develop the relevance of the reader's reaction as an aid to the analysis of the novel (my fourth approach). This resembles the role that the analyst's affects may play in providing clues about what is going on in the patient's mind.

I would like to focus on a character whose identification with Faulkner has not been emphasized, at least in the critical literature I have consulted. While reading the reactions of the little boy, Vardaman, to his mother's death, I found myself very moved by the boy's experience, and I hypothesized that the author's aesthetic distance from Vardaman was much less than in the case of the other characters. I sensed a closeness and a sympathy between the author and the little boy, particularly during the scene in which Dewey Dell discovers him in the stall. The odors of the horse, the warmth of the semi-dark place, and certain unusually vivid descriptions of the animal suggest a special significance to the author. In this chapter about the horse, Faulkner writes: "The life in him runs under the skin, under my hand, running through the splotches, smelling up into my nose where the sickness is beginning to cry, vomiting the crying, and then I can breathe, vomiting it" (p. 50). Does it make sense to assume that Faulkner has projected some of the more primitive and personal elements of himself onto that unhappy little boy? To flesh this out, one would have to come up with evidence, such as an especially meaningful image of the author's childhood connected with Vardaman, perhaps a secret known only to him.

I believe I may have stumbled upon such an element by chance. While reading the Martin (1983) article on Faulkner, I came across the following: "While William was growing up, his father owned and managed a livery stable—messy, fragrant, full of filth" (p. 313). Although we are told that, by and large, William adopted his mother's rather negative picture of his father, could it be that the imagery of the horse and stall encapsulates the author's secret love and search for a father who did not make it easy for a little boy to approach him, being either cold, hostile, or conspicuously drunk, passive, and disorderly? Near the end of the same Vardaman chapter is the obscure sentence, "I can see hearing coil toward him, caressing, shaping his hard shape—fetlock, hip, shoulder and head; smell and sound." And then, "I am not afraid" (p. 52). Is it plausible that the touch and smell of the horse, so comforting to the frightened child, reflects the author's personal experience with or fantasy about objects associated with his father? Thus, rather than being markers of anal imagery, as some authors with a psychoanalytic bent emphasize, such episodes may encode Faulkner's secret closeness to his father. That the images are expressed in the language of odors and filth is of secondary importance.

Is it possible that Faulkner is disturbed by the outpouring of emotions in this chapter? I was struck by the sudden interruption of the Vardaman narrative by the narrator's intruding himself in what seemed a jarring and aesthetically inappropriate fashion to "explain" what was happening to Vardaman. "It is as though the dark were resolving him out of his integrity, into an unrelated scattering of components—snuffings and stampings…" (p. 52). While reading this passage, I was reminded of certain supervisees who suddenly shift from describing a session with a patient to very technical jargon; almost invariably this shift denotes some uneasiness or conflict in the supervisee. Should my observation about this passage be agreed upon, we could raise the same question about Faulkner. One possible objection to my argument might be that such interruptions in the course of the narrative are frequent in this novel; however, the break in mood and rapid shift in point of view remain striking and possibly deserving of a psychological explanation.

Before concluding, I would like to turn to one other approach which may reveal a great deal about the meaning of a text. A colleague, Dr. Theodore Cherbuliez, and I have been collaborating on examining in great detail the first five minutes of patient hours, including what we have come to call the static—i.e., all the words which are not essential to the conveying of meaning. We have discovered that what we choose to call "static" is purely arbitrary and that the nonessential words can become the focus of attention and be very revealing about the structure and meaning of the patient's narrative. In similar fashion I have chosen to examine the first chapter of *As I Lay Dying*. It presents the reader with a number of problems and challenges. To a naïve reader, the author says a great deal which will be understandable only later, in retrospect. Freud once believed that the first dream in an analysis often encapsulated the core aspects of the patient's neurosis. Could the same be true of a novel's first chapter? With this in mind, let us turn briefly to a close look at the structure and content of this first chapter, given over to Darl as narrator (see Appendix for text).

At first glance the content of the chapter appears sparse, with few unnecessary words. We see two people coming up a path single file to a cottonhouse. One goes through a window and out the other side. The other comes around. They pass a wagon and drink; beyond it one hears someone named Cash making a box which turns out to be a coffin for someone called Addie Bundren. Several readings are required to detect a number of features. Not a word is exchanged between the participants, yet the chapter is full of sensory modalities—visual, kinesthetic, and auditory. There is no obvious leader. The choreography is quasi-military in its precision. This is reinforced by references such as "straight as a plumb-line," "square," "right angles." The behavior of Jewel and Darl is remarkable in its well-defined distance keeping—their stride is unchanging, in perfect synchrony though they do not speak to each other. A relationship of close watching exists. A mood is created of repetition, monotony, and aridity; no emotions are displayed on the surface. The atmosphere changes dramatically as Darl sees Cash, whose planks have a human quality ("soft gold, bearing on their flanks... "). Cash is completely and single-mindedly involved in his task with loving concern. The rhythm of life alluded to by the path "worn so by feet in fading precision" (a strange, ambiguous image: are the feet in fading precision or is the path?) is echoed by the concrete representation of the sound of the adze, chuck-chuck-chuck, following Darl as a reminder of the coming death of Addie. The theme of comfort and confidence is expressed with muted sarcasm. This final sentence is choreographed in the text, reinforcing the continuing yet diminishing sound.

Death is introduced casually, without fanfare or emotion. This aspect is reflected in the description of objects which have had much use (the hat, the cottonhouse). Their state of breakdown is described factually as though this is their destiny. Jewel, who appears dead in the upper part of his body, is endowed with life from the hips down. This includes the genitals and brings me to the primal scene imagery and scenes of generativity, often sadistic in nature, which abound in the novel and in which the reader finds sexual innuendoes unexpectedly thrust upon him or her by the author.

The relation between life and death is entwined in the imagery of wood which recurs several times in unexpected settings. First, the cottonhouse made of logs "leans in empty and shimmering dilapidation," suggesting a dreamlike quality; then we see Jewel, "his pale eyes like wood set into his wooden face." Later we are told of the planks of the coffin, "yellow as gold, like soft gold, bearing on their flanks in smooth undulation the marks of the adze blade." Wood is an image of decay, but also of life, including a necrophilic fantasy: the mother will be carried in comfort and confidence inside a living thing of flesh (flanks).

Still other elements can be singled out. The first paragraph introduces two different perspectives, a precursor of the multiple narrators of the work. A contrast also emerges between structure and looseness, fragmentation and synthesis. The author introduces details, withholding their significance until much later. In one example, mention is made of Jewel's stopping at the spring to take a gourd from the willow tree and drinking. Much later, in the Addie chapter, we learn about Jewel's special relation to his mother and the role that a spring had for her: "In the afternoon … instead of going home I would go down the hill to the spring where I could be quiet and hate them. It would be quiet there then, with the water bubbling up and away …" (p. 155). In another example the image of Jewel starting behind Darl and coming out several feet ahead of him is consistent with the fate of the two brothers at the end of the novel. Jewel, the half crazy and violent wild one, remains part of the family as Darl is carried away in a psychotic state. The void in inner life is compensated for by minute description of body posture, movements, and inanimate objects. The lack of narrative does not interfere with the poetic evocation of powerful themes of fate, life, and death. By juxtaposing rich and unexpected adjectives and metaphors, Faulkner creates a halo effect—the evocation of new meanings through suggestion. This may be one of the most powerful stylistic devices of the novel.

The first chapter also introduces the core of the novel, its preoccupation with death and the conflict about burying and not burying Addie. Anna Burton (personal communication) has suggested that the entire saga of the family's encountering one obstacle after another in its ill-planned efforts to return Addie to her father's burial grounds was reminiscent of certain dreams which present a task that is sought after but then delayed by one obstacle after another. This reflects the dreamer's ambivalence about the task at hand. The Bundren family has an unusual capacity to delay the mother's burial and deny the stench, decay, and suffering thereby engendered. Yet, Addie's death is not mourned for a long time, as Anse somewhat sheepishly introduces the new Mrs. Bundren to the assembled clan.

To summarize, psychoanalysis is the study of mental life from the point of view of conflict, development, and transformation of psychic structures. Although it is not designed primarily for the study of literary texts, I have tried to illustrate its value by combining a number of complementary approaches which do not do violence to the literary aspect of the work yet provide some additional insights which can increase our understanding and our pleasure. When utilized together, these approaches do provide mutual checks and balances, help create a fuller context, and increase our chances of discovering meaningful organizers so that our endeavors will enrich our appreciation of great works such as *As I Lay Dying*.

APPENDIX

CHAPTER ONE, "DARL," FROM AS I LAY DYING, BY WILLIAM FAULKNER[48]

Jewel and I come up from the field, following the path in single file. Although I am fifteen feet ahead of him, anyone watching us from the cottonhouse can see Jewel's frayed and broken straw hat a full head above my own.

The path runs straight as a plumb-line, worn smooth by feet and baked brick-hard by July, between the green rows of laid by cotton, to the cottonhouse in the center of the field, where it turns and circles the

---

48 Copyright 1930 and renewed 1958 by William Faulkner. Reprinted by permission of Random House, Inc.

cottonhouse at four soft right angles and goes on across the field again, worn so by feet in fading precision.

The cottonhouse is of rough logs, from between which the chinking has long fallen. Square, with a broken roof set at a single pitch, it leans in empty and shimmering dilapidation in the sunlight, a single broad window in two opposite walls giving onto the approaches of the path. When we reach it I turn and follow the path which circles the house. Jewel, fifteen feet behind me, looking straight ahead, steps in a single stride through the window. Still staring straight ahead, his pale eyes like wood set into his wooden face, he crosses the floor in four strides with the rigid gravity of a cigar store Indian dressed in patched overalls and endued with life from the hips down, and steps in a single stride through the opposite window and into the path again just as I come around the corner. In single file and five feet apart and Jewel now in front, we go on up the path toward the foot of the bluff.

Tull's wagon stands beside the spring, hitched to the rail, the reins wrapped about the seat stanchion. In the wagon bed are two chairs. Jewel stops at the spring and takes a gourd from the willow branch and drinks. I pass him and mount the path, beginning to hear Cash's saw. When I reach the top he has quit sawing. Standing in a litter of chips, he is fitting two of the boards together. Between the shadow spaces they are yellow as gold, like soft gold, bearing on their flanks in smooth undulations the marks of the adze blade: a good carpenter, Cash is. He holds the two planks on the trestle, fitted along the edges in a quarter of the finished box. He kneels and squints along the edge of them, then he lowers them and takes up the adze. A good carpenter. Addie Bundren could not want a better one, a better box to lie in. It will give her confidence and comfort. I go on to the house, followed by the Chuck. Chuck. Chuck. of the adze.

REFERENCES

Baudry, F. (1984). An essay on method in applied analysis. *Psychoanal. Q.*51: *551–581*

Bleikasten, A. (1990). *The Ink of Melancholy. Faulkner's Novels from "The Sound and the Fury" to "Light in August."* Bloomington/Indianapolis: Indiana Univ. Press.

Blotner, J. (1974). *Faulkner: A Biography.* Two volumes. New York: Random House.

Faulkner, W. (1930). *As I Lay Dying.* New York: Vintage, 1987.

Karl, F. R. (1989). *William Faulkner: American Writer.* New York: Weidenfeld Nicolson.

Martin, J. (1983). William Faulkner: construction and reconstruction in biography and psychoanalysis. *Psychoanal. Inquiry* 3:295–340

Mchaney, T., Editor (1987). Manuscript 7 *As I Lay Dying* In *William Faulkner Manuscript Series,* Noel Polk, General Editor. New York/London: Garland Publishing.

Skura, M. (1981). *The Literary Use of the Psychoanalytic Process.* .New Haven: Yale Univ. Press.

Thomas, W. (1990). Karl's Darl. *London Review of Books,* January 11.

CHAPTER 14

Flaubert and Madame Bovary:
An Intimate Courtship

[(2002). *J. Amer. Psychoanal. Assn.* (50)(4):1283–297.]

The process by which Gustave Flaubert created the character of Emma Bovary is examined, as are various of the author's sources for the heroine and their transformation in the course of composing the novel. Certain aspects of the author's psychic makeup, including his bisexuality, are discussed in this light, as are Flaubert's early traumatic losses and their influence on his way of working. Finally, it is suggested that writing had multiple functions for the author and that the creation of Emma Bovary served as a partial solution to unmet needs.

In Emma Bovary, Gustave Flaubert created one of the most striking portraits of the human heart: a young woman imbued with all the romantic clichés about life, who suffers the disappointments of married life, has a number of affairs, and tries in various ways to take fearsome revenge on her husband for failing to live up to her romantic expectations. She spends his money recklessly, acquiring in the process material goods for which she has no use, and, after bringing him to financial ruin, finally commits suicide.

It may well be, as Freud indicated, that his case histories read like novels, but the opposite is certainly not true. A novel should be more than a case history. There has to be a degree of universality. A great novel has to be able to stir us passionately, even disturb us. We need to feel that what we are reading is only a surface beneath which lie complex and rich themes. To create a portrait with universal appeal it is necessary to get away from the individual, and for this a considerable amount of synthesis is required. When someone asked who the model for Emma was, Flaubert replied: "No, Monsieur, no model posed for me. Madame Bovary is a pure invention. If I copied anyone, my portraits would be less lifelike; for in that case I should have kept my eyes on individuals, whereas my desire was to portray types" (Steegmuller 1939, p. 239).

The overall topic can be broken down into two lines of inquiry: (1) What capacities and special talents allowed the author such insight into the feminine mind? and (2) How did his imagination enable him to transform the material thus available to him into a work of art? The first question, to which this paper is devoted, centers on the capacity of a male author to imagine himself in the persona of a woman and requires that we examine the mechanisms of this process. It is of course related to such well-known qualities as empathy, identification, curiosity, psychological-mindedness, and self-observation. I will argue, however, that Flaubert's unusual capacity to describe the soul of a woman went beyond innate constitutional tendencies in the area of acuteness of perception, self-observation, and language development (interestingly enough, he was a late talker, as was Sartre, who idolized him and wrote about him an almost unreadable four-volume study) and was in part rooted in very profound bisexual characteristics.

A wealth of biographical material about Flaubert is available, but perhaps none as revealing as the nine volumes of his letters, which some consider on a par with his best novels. After a hard day's work, Flaubert loved nothing more than to sit down late at night and pour out his turmoil and share with his friends his random thoughts about the work he was engaged in at the moment, or about literary theory, creativity, life, women in general, or the political situation in France. These letters, which were not meant for publication, are a kind of literary autobiography. They offer a rich opportunity to plumb the depths of the author's mind during his prolonged labor. Almost half of these letters were written to Louise Colet, a minor poet with whom he carried on an episodic and stormy liaison during the mid-1840s and then, after a three-year hiatus, during most of the time it took to compose the novel. The relationship was carried on mostly through correspondence, as Flaubert was extremely reluctant to leave his study in Croisset to meet Louise, who lived in Paris, or to meet in Mantes, a neighboring city. Nor did he want her to come to his home, giving as a reason that this would disturb his elderly mother. The letters to Louise offer a mixture of tenderness, deception, rationalization, seduction, poetry, and profound insight into the psychology of the man whose nickname was "the bear of Croisset." Of course, their content cannot be taken at face value but instead must be evaluated as any manifest content we might obtain from a patient. Many of these letters are cannily crafted. Flaubert, fearful of any intrusion, was terrified that too frequent meetings with his lover—indeed, any more than once every few months—would drain his mind and deplete his creativity. He sought excuse after excuse to delay their next meeting, at the same time convincing her of his profound attachment to her without giving her false hopes. At times, as in a letter written in January 1847, he could be painfully blunt: "You want to know if I love you? Well, as much as I am able to, yes; that is, that for me love is not the most important thing, only the second. It is like a bed where you put your heart to relax it in. One does not spend the whole day in bed" (Flaubert 1927, vol. 2, p. 1).

Flaubert's Psychological Situation in 1851

A few comments about Flaubert's character and psychological situation in 1851, the year he started on his novel, will set the stage for what is to follow. Flaubert was the second of three children of a successful surgeon who lived and practiced in Rouen, the provincial capital of Normandy. The oldest sibling, Achille, became a physician like his father. Two other children died soon after birth. Gustave was born in 1821. Another infant lived only a brief time, and the youngest, Caroline, was born in 1824. She idolized her three-years-older brother, and the two were unusually close. Flaubert reacted very deeply to her untimely death shortly after giving birth, when he was in his early thirties. He devoted the rest of his life to bringing up the child, also named Caroline, together with his elderly mother. The sister's husband, a ne'er-do-well, disappeared from the scene and was ostracized by the family.

Flaubert remained very tied to his mother. In some ways he never separated from her. She was the most important figure in his life. Depressed, shadowy, and solemn, she suffered from migraine and insomnia, and Flaubert was extremely sensitive to any possibility of offending her. She controlled him through her weakness. Flaubert's relationships with other women were clearly colored by his continuing involvement with her. In an amusing letter written to Louise Colet on August 4, 1846, shortly after the first week they spent together in Paris, Flaubert wrote: "my mother was waiting for me at the railroad station. She cried when she saw me come home. You cried when I left. Our misfortune is such that we cannot go anywhere without causing tears on both ends!" (Flaubert 1927, vol. 1, p. 212).

Indeed, Flaubert was himself very sensitive to loss, influenced in part by his mother's obsessional inability to tolerate separation from him. She managed the house for the three of them and catered to his desire to be in complete control of his environment, keeping away all visitors and making sure there was no noise in the house until Flaubert rang a small bell upon awakening around ten or eleven in the morning, thereby giving permission for normal household activities to resume. She idolized him, even though he never shared any aspect of his work with her. Flaubert's attempt to read part of his novel to his father failed miserably when the latter fell asleep during the proceedings. As the relation between the two men had always been rather stormy, this incident created an even wider gulf between them.

Flaubert had been destined for the legal profession, which he abhorred. Fortunately for his future career, he suffered a number of epileptic attacks in his early twenties, which he attributed to stress. He used his illness to convince his father to allow him to pursue a literary career. He was very much shaken by the illness, and even in later life, after the fits had abated, he was always fearful that tension might cause a recurrence. He dreaded being alone. Yet he never married and shunned any real commitment to a woman. More than once during his travels away from home, he would write loving letters to his mother reassuring her that she never needed to fear that a rival would displace her in his affections. He could most be himself in the company of prostitutes, whom he idealized. In an early novel he wrote the story of one of them, whom he named Marie. The choice of name was not accidental, since for him there was a close connection between prostitutes and the Virgin. He wrote the following about their occupation: "The idea of prostitution is a meeting point of so many elements: lust, bitterness, complete absence of human contact, muscular frenzy, the clink of gold, so that to peer into it deeply makes one reel. One learns so many things in a brothel, and feels such sadness and dreams so longingly of love!" (Steegmuller 1939, p. 284). Flaubert was convinced that happiness in any case was a total illusion. To explain his keeping his distance from women he once wrote to a friend: "The beautiful breast which had the capacity of arousing such passion could contain a malignancy which would soon destroy it" (p. 295). His capacity to admire feminine beauty had in all likelihood been traumatically damaged by his witnessing, through holes in the hospital fence and alongside his beloved sister, their surgeon father performing autopsies on women while resting his cigar between their toes. This experience of the morgue had a profound impact on him. He would write to Louise, "How striking it is that I invented ferocious dramas in the setting of the morgue, to which I felt powerfully compelled to return. I believe I have a special propensity to elaborate unhealthy scenarios" (Flaubert 1927, vol 3., p. 268; July 7–8, 1853). Flaubert's fantasy life, which found outlets in masturbation with sadomasochistic themes, led him to fear his own capacity to hate and to destroy. These urges were also projected outward. His own fears of losing control, his desires to withdraw from the world, all favored a literary career. Writing became the center of Flaubert's life. Since *Madame Bovary* centers around the character of its heroine, Emma, it might be useful to examine in some detail the story of Flaubert's relation to the women in his life.

Flaubert's Relations to Women, Real and Fantasied

Flaubert's relation to women included his real experiences as colored by aspects of the internal images making up his inner world. I will begin with his early objects. The first type is represented by his mother, a dour, angry, depressed, nervous, and controlling woman who suffered from severe migraines. Once Flaubert became a writer, she completely altered her behavior toward her son, particularly after her husband's death in January 1846, barely three months before Caroline's death. From that point on she adopted a subservient, childlike devotion to him and catered to his every need. Flaubert, for his part, seemed to use her as a buffer against entanglements with women as sexual objects. He replaced her husband, and the two of them served as parents for his niece Caroline.

His bond with his beloved sister combined elements of idealization and excessive closeness. He used special terms of endearment in his letters to her, referring to her as *mon petit raton* (the literal English translation, "my little rat," fails to capture the affectionate and intimate flavor of the French).

The bond he established with women as sexual objects fell into three categories. The first and most intense was a powerful adolescent love lived out mostly in fantasy. While spending the summer of his fourteenth year in

Trouville, a seaside resort in Normandy, the youth happened upon a red cape about to be overtaken by the rising tide. The gallant young man rescued the garment. Later that day, at the pension where he was staying, the owner of the cape, a young woman nursing an infant, thanked him profusely. He was struck by her beauty, her melodious voice, her long black hair, and her full bosom. The young French-woman, Elisa Schlesinger, was vacationing with her infant and the man Flaubert assumed to be her husband. This incident and its repercussions became the nidus for a lifelong passion toward the young woman and her husband. The scene and its variations found outlets both in Flaubert's early writings (see Baudry 1980) and, I believe, in his depiction of Emma Bovary's most passionate experiences with her lover Rodolphe.

The second type of women in Flaubert's life were prostitutes. Curiously, he managed to idealize their lot, projecting his own unmet needs and identifying with them and pitying them. Flaubert attributed to them his own loneliness, his always disappointed yearnings for happiness, and his desire for an intense, short-lived connection with no aftermath. He looked upon them almost as high priestesses fulfilling a quasi-religious role, totally misunderstood and unappreciated by their clients. In Flaubert's case, the traditional Madonna/ prostitute split became also a fusion. Yet in real life, Steegmuller (1939 p. 33) reports, when Flaubert went to a brothel he always ostentatiously chose the ugliest and made love without even removing the cigar from his mouth.

Flaubert's lifelong fear of commitment to a woman was related to his dread of being encroached upon, controlled, and invaded. Also crucial was his terror of becoming a father. The third type of relation was represented by Louise Colet, a difficult, demanding would-be writer, married at the time Flaubert met her. The stormy affair lasted for several years and after an interruption of about three years resumed during the time Flaubert was writing his novel. Like his other liaisons, the affair was carried out largely in fantasy, through an extensive correspondence including erotic letters as a substitute for their all-too-rare meetings (perhaps a dozen or so during the course of four years). At one point during his liaison with Louise, he went through all the tortures of hell when the latter missed a period. Fortunately for both, the scare did not materialize.

Starting the Novel

Early in September 1851, a grumpy Flaubert, dressed in his bathrobe and smoking his pipe, sat down at his desk in the family home in Croisset, a small village in Normandy on the banks of the Seine. Having recently returned from an eighteen-month trip to Egypt with one of his closest friends, Maxime Du Camp, he was quite unsure about his literary future. Both Du Camp and another of his closest friends, the poet Louis Bouilhet, whose professional judgment he trusted implicitly, had roundly criticized his most recent effort, *La Tentation de Saint Antoine*, as being bombastic, romantic, and overloaded with metaphor and stilted imagery. In an effort to curb his runaway style, the little group of friends had finally convinced Flaubert to undertake a very banal and low-key subject: the life of a young woman in a small village in the Normandy he knew best. An article in a provincial paper provided the outlines of the story, and it was rumored that the medical officer, the husband of Eugenie, the young woman whose story was the basis for the plot Flaubert would develop, had studied with Flaubert's father in Rouen.

Writing the novel would drain Flaubert's energies beyond even his wildest imagination. For over four years it dragged on. But the very month he began it, he wrote to Louise, who had contacted him again after the hiatus in their stormy relationship: "I started my novel last night. I anticipate stylistic difficulties which terrify me. It is no easy matter to write simply" (Flaubert 1927, vol. 2, p. 316; Sept. 1851). A month later he wrote, "I am tormented, I scratch myself. It is difficult to get my novel going. I have stylistic abscesses and the phrases itch me without accomplishing anything" (p. 326; Oct. 1851). Several months later, the same mood seemed to prevail: "In writing this book I am like a man playing the piano with lead weights tied to each phalanx" (vol. 3, p. 3; July 27, 1852). I hope to show how writing about a woman helped Flaubert find an adaptive solution to his conflicts with women. First, however, I will describe some components that entered his synthesis of the novel's heroine, Emma Bovary.

The Synthesis of a Literary Character

In a study of Flaubert, the critic Victor Brombert (1965) notes "a curious symbiotic relationship... between Flaubert and his heroine. The novelist, despite his practice of a double perspective, draws his fictional creature toward himself and discovers himself in Emma even more than he projects himself into her. This complex relationship, in which the writer is to some extent playing hide-and-seek with himself, in which he punishes himself while granting himself a perspective that transcends the limits of his own temperament, makes it extremely difficult to assess the exact measure of personal involvement and to come to grips with the nature of this tragic experience" (p. 183; see also Bart 1966, pp. 73–106). How did Flaubert accomplish his tour de force and create Emma from the deepest layers of his imagination?

In "Character in Fiction and Fiction in Character" (Baudry, 1990), I wrote the following about the synthesis of Emma as a fictional character: "The end result is a complex combination, a compromise formation—a composite in the sense of a conscious and preconscious amalgam by the author of things seen, heard, experienced, and imagined—and some autobiographical projections and aspects of himself. Finally, there are some determinants derived from the function of Emma within the novel and esthetic requirements of narrative and plot" (pp. 382–383). I will now describe some of the components that went into Emma, starting with some of the sources Flaubert tapped in order to put together such a coherent, convincing, and powerful portrait of a young woman's struggles against the constraints of her sex, a character both idealistic and crass, desperately unhappy, self-involved, and struggling constantly to attain ideals that always eluded her except for very brief periods.

The character of the woman he portrayed can hardly be considered normal. Narcissistic, impulsive, acquisitive, vengeful, and sadistic traits are found side by side with a naively desperate romantic facade to render a complex and conflicted human being desperately striving for a degree of happiness the reader knows cannot be ever attained (for a description of the role of revenge in Emma's character, see Arlow and Baudry 2002). Despite her obvious flaws, she has some likable traits: she is idealistic and lacks neither courage nor a vision. There is something tragic about her character quite similar in important aspects to that of Flaubert.

A good starting point for my inquiry would be the well-known utterance, "*Madame Bovary, c'est moi*," a response Flaubert is reputed to have made out of exasperation to an interviewer who attempted to get him to reveal the identity of his real-life models for the character. In fact, there is no proof that Flaubert ever made the remark. It is recorded nowhere is his correspondence or in the many interviews he gave at the time of the novel's publication. For my purposes, however, this hardly matters, since it happens to be true and serves as a convenient springboard into my topic.

The quip, of course, is a bit simplistic, since a careful reading of the novel reveals that Flaubert projected parts of himself into most of the other characters in the novel as well, whether the psychopathic Rodolphe, who did not even remove the cigar from his mouth as he made love to women, or the shy Leon, terrified for so long of even hinting to Emma how much he loved her, or even the bumbling Charles, who in his bovine manner had no inkling that he was utterly unable to satisfy a woman (for reasons, it is true, very different from Flaubert's).

The close connection between Flaubert and Emma was first divined by Baudelaire, who wrote the following in one of the earliest reviews of the novel: "To accomplish his tour de force, [Flaubert] had to divest himself as much as possible of his sex and to become a woman. The result is a marvel; for despite all his zeal as an actor he was unable to keep from infusing his male blood into the veins of his creation, and Madame Bovary in the most forceful and ambitious sides of her character and . . . remains a man." Having read his review, Flaubert wrote to Baudelaire: "Your article has given me the greatest possible pleasure. You have entered into the secrets of the book as though my brain were yours. It is understood and felt to its deepest confines" (Steegmuller 1939, p. 340).

Both Flaubert and Emma had their share of qualities of the other gender. In a loving tribute to Flaubert, the Peruvian writer Mario Vargas Llosa (1986) wrote, "it is thus more than by chance that in the visit to her lover's home she plays at being a man—she combed her hair with his comb and looked at herself in his shaving mirror and even falls into the habit of clenching between her teeth the stem of a large pipe of Rodolphe's. . . . Her biography abounds in details that make her wish to be a man, a constant from her adolescence to her death. One of them is her manner of dress. Emma often adds a masculine touch to her attire and takes to wearing men's clothes; what is more, the men in her life find this attractive. When Charles meets her for the first time at Les Bertaux, he observes that 'a pince-nez framed in tortoise shell, like a man's, was tucked between two buttons of her bodice.' This propensity of Emma's to take over characteristics of the other sex goes beyond the physical: it is implicit in her dominating nature, in the swiftness with which, the moment she notices any sign of weakness on the part of the male, she immediately takes over from him and forces him to assume female attitudes" (p. 143).

Vargas Llosa reminds us that the novel's narrator emphasizes Leon's passivity toward Emma: "He never disputed any of her ideas; he went along with all her tastes; he was becoming her mistress more than she was his. Leon is also described as incapable of heroism, weak, common and more spineless than a woman. Flaubert was intuitively familiar with the female's potential capacity to castrate her mate. In Emma's case, masculinity is not only a function she assumes in order to fill a place left empty, but also a striving for freedom, a way of fighting against the miseries of the feminine condition" (p. 146).

There is little doubt that for Flaubert Emma functioned in the nature of a double. Flaubert's bisexual tendencies were not something he was ashamed of; quite the contrary. In his correspondence he wrote openly about such tendencies. He also possessed character traits of a profoundly narcissistic and exhibitionistic quality. We know that in adolescence he would look at himself in a mirror and fantasy that he was a woman. He wrote in his correspondence: "I would have wanted to be a woman, for the beauty, to be able to admire myself, see myself naked, let my long hair down to the heels and look at my reflection in the brooks. I let my thoughts wander in daydreams like these" (Flaubert 1927, vol. 2, p. 327; Nov. 1851). Another similarity between the two deserves mention. Through Emma, Flaubert could give voice to his tendencies to lose himself in daydreams: "Each morning when I awoke it seemed to me that some great event was going to take place that day; my heart was filled with hope as though I were waiting for some shipload of happiness to arrive from some distant land; but as the day wore on, I lost all courage; especially at dusk I realized nothing would happen.... I recall often having scratched the green dust on copper coins to poison myself, tried to swallow pins and approach open attic windows to throw myself in the street" (vol. 3, p. 63; Dec. 1852). Even allowing for some exaggeration, we are reminded of similar events in the novel as Emma contemplated suicide.

The tendency of Flaubert to project part of himself into his fictional characters was occasionally the cause for an amusing bit of mischief. Our author was confused when he wrote about Emma's poisoning herself with a dose of arsenic. In fact, some of the signs Flaubert attributes to the effect of this substance are not those of arsenic poisoning (for example, the black substance coming out of her mouth) but are instead the toxic consequences of mercury—a drug Flaubert was taking himself at the time to control a syphilitic infection he had contracted during his recent trip to Egypt. While writing the powerful scene, Flaubert, as was usual for him, lived through the event vicariously: "When I was describing the poisoning of Emma Bovary, I had such a taste of arsenic in my mouth and was poisoned so effectively myself, that I had two attacks of indigestion, one after the other—two very real attacks, for I vomited my entire dinner" (Steegmuller 1939, p. 308).

Another important source drawn on in creating the character of Emma was Flaubert's liaison with Louise Colet, details of which he incorporated in the novel, at times to her considerable dismay. For example, she gave Flaubert a bejeweled cigar holder inscribed with the motto "*Amor nel cor*" inside. This same motto turns up on a signet ring Emma gives to Rodolphe. Needless to say, Louise was more than a little agitated at what she saw as a betrayal of intimacies: "Imagine my indignation, you who have a righteous soul," she wrote to a friend (Steegmuller 1939, p. 337). Other features of their affair also found their way into the novel. When Flaubert first met Louise in 1846, she was still married, and his excitement at having an adulterous liaison—the most enduring sexual relationship of his life—certainly was mirrored in Emma's excitement during the initial stages of her affair with Rodolphe, the wealthy landowner who seduced and eventually abandoned her, much as Flaubert abandoned Louise in August 1848 and again, and finally, in 1855. Flaubert also questioned Louise closely about her activities as an adolescent—her daydreams, readings, and the like.

In an even more personal vein, he imported events and feelings from the circumstances of his sister's death into his description of Emma's final hours. Planning to attend the funeral of a friend's mother, Flaubert writes in a letter to Louise about his friend's grief and then adds, abruptly, that "since it is necessary to put everything to good use," he hopes that the funeral atmosphere and Pouchet's bereavement will provide him material for the novel (Vargas Llosa 1986, p. 87).

Flaubert could become very personal when writing on a topic close to his heart. Such was the case when he came to the section of the novel dealing with adultery. In a very moving passage, he describes Emma's reaction to her first act of adultery, having perhaps for the first time truly given herself to a man. He writes that "her blood was flowing in her flesh like a river of milk" (Flaubert 1857, p. 181). I suggest that the imagery of milk is consistent with a reworking of the powerful adolescent love of Flaubert for the nursing mother. That there are even earlier determinants for this image is likely but not easy to substantiate.

Writing, a Solitary Profession

There is a clear division in Flaubert's life between his first twenty years, during which he lived a relatively normal life, studying, traveling, enjoying the company of women and friends, and his later years, when he cut himself off from most contacts, retreated to the solitude of his study, and devoted himself entirely to his profession. Writing served Flaubert both as justification for a much-needed retreat from the world and as a monastic shield against instinctual temptations he both feared and despised. Indeed, Flaubert had described an impulse to castrate himself during the peak of his adolescent rebellion. He had campaigned against the demands of the flesh, stating proudly that he had managed to stay away from women for a period of two years. But as might be expected, writing also served as an outlet for pent-up instinctual strivings. Flaubert spoke of writing in terms both phallic ("an ejaculation of the soul") and anal (writers were "sewers of humanity"). Through writing he could recapture and re-create the powerful adolescent passion he felt for Elisa Schlesinger. "I once knew a friend," he wrote, "who at fifteen adored a young woman breast feeding her child. This image was fixed in his mind. As time passed I loved her more and more—with the fury one has for unattainable things—I made up stories to find her again. I made up our encounter. I saw her eyes again in the blue swirls of rivers and the color of her face in the maple trees in the fall" (Flaubert 1927, vol. 3, p. 142; March 1853). Thus, writing allowed him to re-create the image of his lost love. The way the passage is written reveals a failed attempt to maintain distance from himself, a stance later to become the linchpin of his theory of creativity. "I once knew a friend," he begins, and takes up the third person; then, in the very next sentence, he abandons this distancing device and shifts to the first person.

Writing also enabled Flaubert to access feelings that would otherwise be suppressed. After his sister's death he wrote to Du Camp: "My own eyes are dry: it is strange how sorrow remains hard and bitter in my heart" (Flaubert 1927, vol. 1, p. 196; March 23–24, 1846). Yet in his novels he could write touchingly of loss and sorrow. Writing also helped in warding off the fear of death, disintegration, and forgetting. Once, at the side of his sister's coffin, he was reading Montaigne. "My eyes kept turning from the book to the corpse," he wrote his friend, "and I told myself that forms pass, that only ideas remain. Her husband and the priest were snoozing. Occasionally I felt a thrill at some turn of phrase in the Montaigne and reflected that writers too pass away." I would add that a great writer's capacity to arouse readers of later generations remains intact.

But writing entailed sacrifices, and Flaubert had to justify to himself the choices he made. "If I keep inside myself a warm hearth," he wrote Louise, "it is because I shut off all outlets. Everything I did not spend may be useful now. I have enough vitality to feed all my works. No, I regret nothing about my youth. I was dreadfully bored, I contemplated suicide" (Flaubert 1927 vol. 3, p. 146; March 31, 1853). Despite all this, Flaubert achieved a wonderful mastery over his craft and put it to good use, as the next section demonstrates.

DISCUSSION

Though I have emphasized the similarities between Flaubert and Emma, there are important differences between the them. Unlike Emma, Flaubert never left home, instead remaining in Croisset with his mother and his niece. I believe that for him *Madame Bovary* functioned as a cautionary tale. Flaubert understood that Emma's quest for love and happiness could end only in disaster. In his real life, the author must have sensed the danger of active involvement with the type of women who attracted him—the glittering, narcissistic, demanding glory-seekers like Louise or the prostitutes, neither of whom could love a man. Thus, the novel spells out the dangers of attempting to realize one's fondest dreams. This may account for Flaubert's deep sympathy for Emma and also for the aspects of himself he projected onto her. The novel served as a *raison d'etre,* a buffer from real relationships, but it also allowed the writer to express and gratify the daydreams that haunted him. His way of writing certain powerful scenes in which he becomes totally immersed, to the point of merging with his characters and experiencing their physical sensations, makes this very clear. Yet the safety of his writing chamber allowed him to justify a form of severe self-control. Thus, in a letter to Louise dated October 7, 1853, he wrote: "I have many wishes and inclinations which I resist. One has to deprive oneself when one wants to accomplish something. Ah what vices I would have if I did not write! The pipe and the pen are the two safeguards of my morality—a virtue which turns to smoke via both tubes. Art thus became a demanding religion requiring personal sacrifices: if you are looking for both happiness and beauty, you will reach neither, for the second can only be gotten through sacrifices" (Flaubert 1927, vol. 3, p. 362).

Finally, creating a novel about a woman he could more or less control must have given Flaubert deep satisfaction and a sense of mastery, at least in fantasy. He could sculpt a woman according to his deepest wishes and mold her—something Louise resisted fiercely. As he told her in a letter dated March 27, 1853, expressing his grandiose omnipotent side, "A woman is a creation of man—God created the female and man has made woman" (Flaubert 1927, vol.3, p. 138).

Eventually, then, if we attend carefully to its many layers of themes and messages, the character of Emma can be seen as a rich symphonic confession of the drama of its author: Emma as a naive, hopeless idealistic dreamer and romantic, easily hurt; Emma as yearning for happiness; Emma as full of illusions; Emma as a misunderstood young woman; Emma as a passionate lover; Emma as a vengeful and controlling destructive force. These can easily be seen as separate strands of the character of that most complex and conflicted man, Gustave Flaubert.

REFERENCES

Arlow, J., & Baudry, F. (2002). Flaubert's Madame Bovary: A study in envy and revenge. *Psychoanal. Q.71:213–233.*

Bart, B.F. (1966). *Art, energy and aesthetic distance. In Madame Bovary and the Critics: A Collection of Essays*, ed. B.F. Bart. New York: New York

University Press, pp. *173–206*.

Baudry, F. (1980). Adolescent love and self-analysis as contributors to Flaubert's creativity. *Psychoanal. St. Child* 35:377–416.

Baudry, F. (1990). Character in fiction and fiction in character. *Psychoanal. Q.* 59:370–397.

Brombert, V. (1966). *The Novels of Flaubert: A Study of Themes and Techniques.* Princeton: Princeton University Press.

Flaubert, G. (1857). *Madame Bovary, Patterns of Provincial Life,* transl. F. Steegmuller. New York: Modern Library, 1950.

Flaubert, G. (1927). *Oeuvres Completes de Gustave Flaubert,* ed. L. Conard. 9 vols. Paris: Conard.

Steegmuller, F. (1939). *Flaubert and Madame Bovary, a Double Portrait. New* York: Farrar, Straus & Giroux, 1966.

Vargas Llosa, M. (1986). *The Perpetual Orgy: Flaubert and Madame Bovary.* Transl. H. Lane. New York: Farrar, Straus & Giroux.

CHAPTER 15

The Myths of the Virgin: A Psychoanalytic Review

[previously unpublished.]

I. Introduction

Fantasy, myths, dreams, and their relation to reality have occupied psychoanalysis since its start. The end of 2024 and Christmastime is as good a time as any to re-examine, from a psychoanalytic point of view, the nature and motives of the material available about the lives of the Virgin Mary, Jesus Christ with his virgin birth, and the associated myths. My goal in using psychoanalytic understanding is to try to deepen the connection between religious systems, the legends they created that were taken for truth, and their connection with mostly unconscious structures—powerful systems with very personal aspects. The creation of myths is not limited to religious systems.

It permeates much of our great literature. In an example, the existence of Romeo and Juliet as actual living people is unlikely even though the existence of the Montague and Capulet families in Verona is definitely true.

Even what we term history is open to questions about its authenticity. It has been said that history is written by the victors. It is important to state that in this paper I am in no way disparaging or questioning the meaning and powerful impact, nor the value, that the belief in Christ, or in God, or the Virgin has for the believing person. The belief needs to be respected.

Belief is beyond reason and, therefore, cannot be scientifically studied and proven or denied. This issue was studied in great detail by Pascal, a 16th-century philosopher whom I discussed in a recent paper.

In my work, I will not be concerned with the historical accuracy of the religious legends—which is impossible to determine and is irrelevant to my purpose. Instead, I will try to relate the rich metaphors and symbolic language used in religious writings to our inner preconscious and unconscious beliefs and psychological developmental stages.

Because the created myths were so rich and visually arresting, episodes from the life of the Virgin occupied much of religious painting, starting in the Byzantine period, and moving on to the Middle Ages, and the rich work of the Renaissance.

II. The Nature of Myth-Making

The word myth comes from ancient Greek meaning speech, narrative, or fiction. I consider myth as a language which has a definite form, depending on the nature of the group which created it, and the nature of the beliefs during the time of its creation.

Myth can be considered as a product of a societal dream with components similar to those found in unconscious products, namely condensation, displacements, and symbolization, and it is therefore amenable to psychoanalytic understanding. It uses imagination, not rational explanation.

III. The Myth of the Virgin

Before addressing the story of the Virgin, a few historical antecedents must be addressed. Fraser (1959) in *The New Golden Bough,* mentions that:

The custom of marrying gods, either to images or to human beings, was widespread amongst the nations of antiquity. In an Indian village in Peru, a 14-year-old-girl would be selected. The girl thereafter remained a virgin and was sacrificed to the idol for the people. They showed her the utmost reverence and deemed her divine [p. 94].

In Babylon, there was a temple with a magnificently decorated bed in it. No human being spent the night there except for one woman chosen by the gods. It was said that the deity himself came into the temple at night and slept in the great bed, and that the woman, as a consort of the god, might have no intercourse with mortal men. The same thing took place in Thebes in Egypt, in the temple of Ammon. The woman is referred to as the divine consort, and she was considered as important as the Queen of Egypt.

The life of the Virgin Mary occupies only a few scattered paragraphs in the Bible, mostly in Matthew. They are sometimes contradictory to other writings in Luke and Marc. As a result, Mary's life is full of uncertainties. This made it possible to weave an extensive cloth of legends which were fused with the few real facts without being concerned with their veracity. Voragine mentions in passing that:

such indeed was Mary's innocence that it shone forth outside of her and quelled any urgency of the flesh in others. Thus, the Jews tell us that although Mary was surpassing fair, no man could ever look on her with desire [p.152].

Many additional details exist about the lives of Mary, and of the Christ, in writings beyond the usual gospels. These apocryphal texts have been excluded at various times from acceptable biblical texts. Voragine (1941) in *The Golden Legend,* originally called *Legenda Sanctorum* and written about 1270 A.D., has added valuable material on the thinking at this time. He states that the Virgin Mary dwelt in the temple with the other virgins from her third to her fourteenth year; this text focuses on God and the salvation of the human race. It includes many details of doubtful historical veracity, but of great symbolic significance. For example, the wood of the tree whence Adam ate becomes the wood of the cross. Everything is given meaning relating to God. At the time, creation of legends were not required to relate to objective reality. Most spectacular is the creation of the Virgin as both an incomplete woman, yet also symbolizing the most passionate, caring, and loving woman who ever existed. One cannot deny the appeal she has, particularly for the poorer or disadvantaged populations of our world, offering them a route to salvation, charity, and love. The vision that this part of our population had for her, if it could be written down, would have to be quite different from the evolving picture of the description of Mary in the church dogma. This may suggest a wishful transformation of the image of Mary to meet the most unsatisfied needs of the less-advantaged population.

The Virgin's pregnancy by the intermission of the Holy Spirit is a good example of the exclusion of a sexual encounter. To further the virginal aspect of Mary, her parturition requires the total absence of pain at birth and the uselessness of a midwife. There exists a mythical story about a midwife named Salome who wanted to confirm Christ's normal birth by examining Mary's genitals. As she began her examination, her hand suddenly became paralyzed. This frightening event continued until she repented. It was said that her hand regained movement after she touched the Christ Child's body.

There is one other important factor leading to the popularity of the Virgin. In contrast to God, who could never be represented, the repressed need to visualize the leaders in order to make them more real and accessible burst forth with intensity when it came time to portray the Virgin and the multiple components of her femininity. Also, there was much less material, mostly legendary, to illustrate the life of Christ.

There is an additional frequent aspect of her appearance which might connect with many of the experiences of the viewer. It is her periodic profound sadness, purposefully shown to illustrate her very early anticipatory knowledge of the inevitable ordained loss of her child early in his adult life. With the uncertainty of duration of life, especially in the Middle Ages, along with the primitive aspect of medicine, the loss of children or parents early in life must have been a frequent and unwelcome accompaniment of life for a long time.

All of this justifies the explosion of images of the Virgin starting with Byzantine times. There is also a crucial factor to explain her popularity, namely that she was human before being divine, something which fostered the development of what came to be called Mariolatry. This fueled the profound departure from Catholic beliefs of the Protestant movement concerning the role of the Virgin relating to God. The ensuing reformation led to the destruction of any images of her, and also of other saints, in many churches, for being seen as interfering with true faith.

In contrast with the above, I will now turn to Mary's so-called real life and its basic uncertainties. For example, Mary's age at the birth of Christ is unknown. It is assumed to be somewhere between twelve and seventeen. This was the median age for Roman girls to get married at that time. It is unclear where she spent her time between ages three and thirteen. Did she reside with other virgins in the temple as Voragine states? Or did she stay with her parents? Kristof (2024) states in an article, that Jesus was called "Son of Mary," and that in this intensely patriarchal society, this suggested that Jesus had no certain earthly father, alive or deceased, that anyone could identify. Yet even without a partner, it is suggested, but again not proven, that Mary had lots of children: in Mark, Jesus had four other brothers and some sisters with no recognized father, and no genealogy. Likewise, little is known about the duration of her life after the crucifixion. It is as though her earthly usefulness to the Church ended after she gave birth. Nowhere is it stated how long she lived after the crucifixion. At that point, she might have been around forty, some five years beyond the average duration of life which was about thirty-five in Roman times. Voragine mentions two possible ages at death, one around forty, and the other around seventy-two. It is also uncertain where she died. Like her son, she would have been one of the few who led a double life, one earthly and the other heavenly, including her body residing in both places. Her assumption to Heaven allowed a complex fusion of imagery. In one painting the Virgin is lying in death, and the Christ is holding a baby in his arms, representing her soul. This is a reversal, as though Jesus allows the Virgin to give birth to her soul which will be taken to Heaven, leaving the body behind. In another legend, the Virgin's body is also miraculously resuscitated, as happened to Christ. The latter eventually comes back to Earth with his physical body. What more beautiful stories could we construct which allow us to deny the final disintegration of our bodies upon death?

The Virgin's assumption to Heaven, called by God, did not require any proofs on her part beyond the fact that she gave birth to someone who, as a result, became the son of God—that is having two fathers, an earthly one and a second celestial one much more powerful and responsive than the earthly one, except in one instance. This Heavenly Father gave a deaf ear to his earthly son's appeal for help during his crucifixion, saying the very moving words: "My God, my God Why hast thou forsaken me?" Perhaps the most important not-sufficiently-included factor in the importance of Mary is that Christ only attained the human body and form through his birth and his connection with Mary as his mother.

Yet in spite of the rare facts about the real Mary, in contrast with the rich historical material about Christ, there are many more churches and cathedrals named after the Virgin, rather than after Christ. This is, in part, due to the fact that she is closer to the human plane and more approachable than Christ or God. Most of the great Romanesque and Gothic churches of the late Middle Ages (for example, *Notre Dame de Paris*, recently reopened Chartres or Reims) and the paintings of the 1300s to 1500s are devoted to the Virgin often caring for the infant Christ; the latter is never shown circumcised. I will develop some of the possible reasons for this explosion of the role of the image of the Virgin in a later section.

In the art world, there are many more paintings showing the Virgin Mary than the adult Christ. It seems most of the great painters dwelt on just a few themes about Mary: her motherliness, including breast-feeding, her sorrow, and her humility. After her rise in Heaven, multiple aspects and qualities were devoted to her, in contrast to those very few assigned to Christ. Marina Warner (1976) details six attributes to Mary: (1) details of her real life, (2) the Queen, (3) the Bride, (4) the Mother, and (5) the Intercessor. Each attribute is given predominance depending on the social, political, and religious climate at the time. For example, being the Queen of Heaven combined both the setting up of a court in Heaven resembling the one on Earth, and also satisfies the role of courtly love.

IV. The Nature of Religion

The Central Role of Soul

It is necessary at this point to introduce the word *soul* as playing an essential role in religion. It is part of common language, and has a meaning which is felt but cannot be proven. It is defined in the Webster dictionary as an entity regarded as the immortal or spiritual part of the person. It has an existence on its own. It enables the individual to establish a relation to God and Christ's teachings in complete freedom of any intrusion of the body, including lust, sexuality, and sin.

Sometimes this freedom seems to exceed normal limits This will be evident when I examine a bit later the use of the Songs of Songs, one of the most openly erotic passages in the Bible, which became the center of over thirty sermons around 1130 A.D. by Bernard De Clairvaux, a priest who was also a mystic. Clairvaux and others seemed to be comfortable using carnal language as applying to the soul, and suggesting that the intensity of pure love for God and the Christ is so much more intense than anything the body can feel, so that the same language can be shamelessly adapted to this new use.

Because of the general attitudes of the people at the time of the writing of the gospels, and the existence of many texts written without the need for scientific accuracy, the Church was obliged, at various times, to decide on a complex basis, which texts could be included in the acceptable gospels, and which had to be excluded, often being considered as heretical. It is not clear to me what criterion were used by the Church to decide on this matter. Did it have to do with acceptable dogma and/or connected with historical accuracy? I am not sure, but I suspect more the former than the latter.

For its own purposes, the Church included Bible stories of doubtful origin. For example, historians question the veracity of the story of the three Magi kings even given specific names, such as Melchior and Balthazar, who come from the East to adore the infant Christ, bringing three specific gifts: gold, myrrh, and frankincense. Research has suggested that these three kings were only given royal status in the third century. Some scholars believe that they were a literary invention of Matthew. They were valuable to the Church because they represented gentile kings who came to pay homage to the new king. But thinking about the reality of the story, it does not make sense that three important kings would travel hundreds of miles bringing expensive gifts for a recently born baby in a very poor setting with a humble carpenter father. and about whom rumors claimed him to be a messiah, with no tangible proof of his godly nature whatsoever.

Also, history was not a separate scientific discipline. Instead, it was considered part of rhetoric. It was not yet a science devoted to accuracy and search for truth. Cicero wrote that: "it is permitted to rhetors to falsify somewhat in their histories in order to make their point more forcibly." As a result, in Jacobus' time, the impact of the story on the mind of his hearers is of much greater importance than historical accuracy. The richness of these religious legends inspired the many stained-glass representations of the saints and other religious figures meant to teach churchgoers the lives of religious figures in a concrete way, more powerful than a written text which, in many cases, many could not read. It also fueled the great painters, from the Byzantine world on to Giotto in the West, to find their inspiration in the rich symbols of these legends.

Religion and Marriage

There is a complicated history as to how religion implicated itself in the ceremony of marriage. We have to go back to the year 1100 A.D., and the history of the troubadours as recounted in Warner (2005). At that time, marriages were often arranged marriages when both partners were still children. The Church really believed, from very early on, that carnal love led to sinfulness. Yet it was not until 1563 that a church ceremony became an indispensable condition of validity for marriage

The Management of Sexuality in Religion[49]

It is important to realize that, in the beginning of Christianity, sexuality was not banned. Priests and Bishops *could* have wives. The gradual exclusion and banning of sexuality took several centuries to become firmly established (Brown, 1988). Christianity remained scattered and disorganized until the year 350 A.D. when it became the official religion of the Romans.

In the 4th Century, Saint Augustine developed the concept of Original Sin as connected with Adam and Eve's disobedience. Armstrong (2005) explains that:

> The inherited guilt was passed to all of Adam's descendants through the sexual act which was polluted by concupiscence, the irrational desire to take pleasure in mere creatures rather than in God. As a result, God is forgotten and creatures revel shamelessly in one another. [p. 113].

The first written mandate requiring priests to be chaste was in 304 A.D., at the Council of Elvira, stating that: "All Bishops Presbyters and Deacons were to abstain completely from their wives and not have children."

The negative role of sexuality may be related to a generally misogynist attitude of the male clergy towards women. It could also lead to the creation of an essentially asexual woman, except for her breasts

---

49 In some ancient civilizations in the Near East, certain high priestesses of fertility goddesses would engage in ritual sexual acts with worshippers or rulers as a way of symbolizing unity with the divine promoting fertility. In similar temples, there would be Hierodules who were slave women or female priests who would engage in sexual acts at the request of visitors.

Still another example of this negation is the insemination by the Holy Spirit. Depending on the period, and its portrayal by painters, it can take place through the eyes or through the ears.

As it is difficult to erase sexuality in life, religion has adopted various means of defusing its presence. It managed to keep its language by displacing it from the body to the soul. Terms commonly associated with marriage, such as bride and bridegroom, are often used, but not always displacing it to the soul. Sometimes marriage is used to describe the relation between Christ and the Church. Marriage is an important aspect of the life of nuns, who may be given a ring to proudly display their marriage to Christ.

One important consequence and advantage of Mary remaining a virgin is that she does not belong to the man who deflowered her, as was typical in early Christian times. God or his envoy, the Holy Spirit, are the representatives of a fatherly figure. Freud (1918) mentions this in his paper "The Taboo of Virginity." A sexual woman is seen as dangerous to a man during sex, which can release enormous amounts of aggression on her part. It is for this reason that in some primitive societies, the defloration of the woman is performed by a friend of the husband-to-be. Is this in any way represented in the Bible where the Virgin, even though never deflowered, is rendered pregnant first by the Holy Spirit, before being handed over for marriage to her earthly husband Joseph? Other instances of suggested union or marriage refer to Christ and the Church, or God and Israel. In still other references, the marriage ceremony refers to the Virgin when she arrives to Heaven and becomes the Queen, and marries the Christ symbolically

The Song of Songs

This piece is perhaps the most erotic poem in the Bible. It has been attributed to Solomon but the evidence for this is lacking. This song describes the union between a woman and her lover, anticipating her marriage. The language is unambiguous:

> "*Let my beloved come into this garden and taste its choice fruits'*
> *'May your breasts be like clusters on a grapevine."*

It is noteworthy that Bernard de Clairvaux used this piece as a central organizer for over forty-three of his sermons, in around 1130 A.D. Clairvaux and others seem to be comfortable using carnal language and applying it to the soul as though the nature of its feelings is, if anything, more intense than that of the body, and therefore can benefit from the same language which can then be shamelessly adapted to this new use. Clairvaux lived a very ascetic life, and had lost his mother while a youth. He was a very astute politician who helped found more than160 abbeys in Europe, and frequently visited the Pope in Rome. He was so admired that Dante made extensive use of his sermons, and used him as an intermediary between Beatrice and the Virgin Mary in his *Divine Comedy*. In his *Golden Legend*, Voragine devotes several pages to Bernard's life. As mentioned before, one cannot ascertain their historical accuracy. Voragine writes:

> Once when he had fixed his gaze on a certain woman for some little time, he suddenly blushed for himself, and as a stern avenger of his own default, he rose up and lept into a pool of frigid water, remaining there until he was almost bloodless and wholly cooled of the heat of fleshy desire by the grace of God.

So strong was the danger of lust, that Voragine gives us three more examples. This time it is a woman who is attracted to him and either slips naked into his bed when he was sleeping, and begins to stroke him, though he remains shameless, and finally, when he remains unmoved, shameless though she was, she blushed and, "being filled with a great horror and admiration, arose and fled."

In a third incident, a woman came unbidden to his bed, impudently, and without a sound. When he saw her, he, at once, cried, "Robbers, thieves!" At this cry the woman fled. We are reminded of the stories of Christ's temptation by the Devil

It was not by accident that I chose the two quotes from the poem as referring to women's breasts, as two of Clairvaux's sermons deal specifically with breasts, and I will describe some of his arguments.

In Sermon 9, titled 1"On the Breasts of the Bride and the Bridegroom," he makes the following points:

He immediately identifies the longing of the bride with dryness of the soul. He shifts the words "Your breasts are better than wine," as spoken by the bride, and referring to the bridegroom.

The breast, (1) refers to his native kindness and, (2) to promptness to forgive.

But now the forgiver is God.

But Clairvaux asserts that he needs to show he is correct. In (2), he continues to say that say that the bridegroom fulfills the bride's desire by giving her a kiss. This echoes the psalm's statement: "You have granted him his heart's desire, not denied him what his lips entreated." He then makes the extraordinary statement:

> The filling of her breasts is proof of this. For so great is the potency of that holy kiss that no sooner has the bride received it that she conceives and her breasts grow rounded with the fruitfulness of conception.

In other words, Clairvaux sees this passage as illustrating the Virgin Mary's pregnancy. The reception of the kiss is a reward for having conceived.

411

Breasts are seen as being better than wine, which is equated with carnal pleasure. So the grape, once pressed, is desiccated, whereas the breast can be endlessly replenished, In this sermon, Clairvaux skillfully transforms an openly erotic theme by displacing it to a virgin's breast, and her conception through the nonerotic kiss of the bridegroom copying Mary's conception, and all the gifts she is giving to the thirsty souls of men. I find it puzzling that he is ready to identify the fullness of breasts with conception. This seems like an unwarranted conclusion difficult to justify.

It is interesting that the holy nature of breast milk also permeated the contents of a painting. In the Middle Ages, there is a 1356 painting showing the Virgin holding the child Christ on her lap, and at the same time a stream of milk is issuing from her breast and reaches Clairvaux who is standing nearby. Warner suggests that there is another version of the poem in which Christ is the speaker complaining of man's cruelty to him, and addresses the human soul as his sister and his spouse, for whom he has prepared a bed in Heaven.

V. Limits of the Psychoanalytic Approach.

Before using psychoanalysis to approach the story of the Virgin, a cautionary note has to be stated. Both the Christ and the Virgin are real people in the sense that both lived on this earth as human beings for a period of time, although there is uncertainty about how long Mary lived before her assumption to Heaven. Unfortunately, the only record we have is a combination of events witnessed by the disciples and considerably altered by the Church, and heavily associated with the creation of legends. Hence, we are at the borderland between real people and characters molded by complicated forces beyond their control, a bit like characters in a play who seem so real that we talk about them as living individuals in spite of their being gifted creations of a great writer like Shakespeare.

How can we bring psychoanalysis to deal with this experience and its religious accompaniments without reducing it to abstract and empty formulations? I am not sure.

A danger about using psychoanalytic theory as an explanatory structure is to make clear that I am not reducing religious stories to be products of unconscious phenomenon, but rather aim to deepen our understanding of these phenomena by showing the connection with unconscious concepts without implying any causality.

I will first mention the vocabulary used in Heaven to describe the relation of the Virgin to God and to Christ. It is pure incest with both bride and bridegroom. The Queen of Heaven is sitting next to her son with both arms connecting with him, and finally, the fusion of Son/Father. The nature of gross denial to accept the implication of these words is simply amazing (see Daniel Rancour-Laferriere, 2018). Finally, we have the pure virginal state after birth to contend with, in order to keep the Virgin safe from the above, especially in Heaven.

The development of the rich legends around a human Mary make sense as fulfilling a very personal need, if one considers that the original Trinity of God, the Son, and the Holy Ghost were primarily of masculine origin. God the Father induced a mixture of awe, fear, and the great expectation of Salvation. But God the Father also aroused guilt, shame, punishment, and hope for Grace and Salvation depending both on the nature of the sin the person confessed, or on some unknown failure he was guilty of. All the above were clearly related to the functioning of the Superego and the Ego ideal. The Holy Spirit was seen as the way God could communicate with the devout but also seen as the way the Virgin could be made pregnant by the Father while still remaining a virgin. The Church remained very uneasy about allowing a full woman to occupy such a central role.

There is one other advantage to the virginal state of Mary, namely that Christ could be devoid of filial rivalry with his true father since the latter never deflowered his mother. So there may be complex psychological reasons for the existence of the Holy Spirit. Freud mentions, in his paper, "The Taboo of Virginity" (1918), that in some tribes, another man besides the husband initiated the first intercourse with the bride-to-be. So in the case of God, he sent a second agent in order not to have to deflower the Virgin himself, and he was able to succeed on two counts, first to avoid sex altogether, and second to achieve a state of pregnancy without intercourse or penetration taking place. There are rumors that have circulated that a Roman soldier named Pantera was actually the man who impregnated the Virgin. Whether the Virgin actually had sex with her husband is, in reality, quite probable, unless her not having been deflowered implies that in reality she does not belong to him but instead remains tied to her Father in Heaven but not on Earth.

Voragine wonders why our Lord wished his mother to be espoused:

For this St Bernard gives three reasons. It was necessary for Mary to be espoused to Joseph in order that by this means, the mystery might be hidden from the demons, her virginity might be confirmed by her spouse, and her modesty and good renown preserved.

Another reason was that the espousal of Mary would take away the curse from every degree of womankind, namely from virgin, wife, and widow, whence the Virgin herself was all of these. [p. 205].

A word must be said in favor of Joseph, Mary's earthly husband, who is often made fun of. In contrast, it is possible to see him as a remarkable husband who, out of pure love of the pregnant Mary, is willing to marry her and accept her word that she knows no man. He is a virginal father, but a real paternal presence to *Word being made Flesh.* He is the shadow of God the

Father, and the man nearest to Christ, and he cooperates in God's plan to create the holy family.

At this point I will not discuss the life course of the Virgin but will focus instead on two episodes which lend themselves a bit better to analytic thinking.

First, the management and significance of the soul and the body as they ascend to Heaven, and second, the role of the lactating virgin and her breasts the *"Maria Lactans."*

VI. The Significance of Heaven

Its existence allows all sorts of complicated incestuous-like relationships, since the soul encounters no physical obstacles in Heaven, and can experience the most intense love, free of bodily equivalents. It is the preferred connection between mortal beings and our deities. For example, The Virgin Queen can become the Bride of Christ, her son, or even his daughter, without violating any rules, in addition to being his mother. In another case, St. Catherine of Siena asked the Virgin to allow her to marry the infant Christ, and the Virgin, in response, gave Catherine a ring to express her permission (Meiss 1951, p.11). It is possible that Catherine saw some paintings with this theme before her vision.

As a result of the above, our unconscious can be gratified by multiple instinctual satisfactions on an oedipal level without having to suffer any accompanying guilt feelings. Carroll (1986) points out that the exclusion of the father can satisfy men's wish to possess their mother alone, whose virginity protects them from the conscious intrusion of guilt-ridden sexuality. On the other hand, women can be satisfied, through identification with the Virgin, to have guiltless sex with the father, and to receive a baby from him. As Arlow (1975) indicates, any conflict over id-impulses can further be resolved by the ego through renunciation, sublimation, and character transformation. These changed impulses can also be further gratified by the group during religious ceremonies.

Heaven can also invite us to accept the anxiety of death, knowing that a powerful mother is ready to greet us in the next world. We shall not be alone. Earth and mother have often been equated, so that death is not a total abandonment but a return to where the human being came from. Did not the Virgin and her son make it to Heaven without having to give up their bodies which were miraculously resuscitated? However, the separation of Heaven and Earth sometimes was detrimental to the arguments made by the Pope. A mosaic in Rome in 707 A.D. includes Pope John VII prostrating at the feet of the Virgin (Warner, p. 107), thus reinforcing the power of the Pope in dealing with earthly emperors, and with his subjects. Subsequently, many other popes portrayed themselves in close contact with the Virgin. Eventually, some earthly kings adopted the same double representation. The power of the Church was clearly demonstrated when an Archbishop was able to make a requirement that French kings be crowned in the cathedral of Reims before assuming their regal role. The first crowning took place for *Louis le Pieux,* in 836 A.D., in an earlier church in Reims, some 500 years before the current cathedral which was built in the 13th century.

Accompanying the development of the queenly role of the Virgin, her statues and crowns were richly adorned with diamonds and other precious stones, thus contradicting earlier themes of Christ praising humility and restraint.

VII. Maria Lactans

I will now turn to the theme of the Virgin breastfeeding. It rapidly became associated with mercifulness and benevolence, leading to her need and duty to protect her followers. The Virgin became the Mother of All Mankind. This began to open the door to humility and sublimity.

From an analytic point of view, we have to give meaning to the importance of her motherliness. In early Roman times, it is likely that infant mortality was very high, and the value of motherly love and breastfeeding, holding on to life, was one of the most valuable gifts which could be given to an infant. This image of the nursing mother has other psychological implications. In early Renaissance Florence, it was customary for a bourgeois mother to give her child away to a wet nurse for the first two years of his life, and then take him back after that.

Rancour Laferriere (2018) makes the point that this second separation from a woman he considers his mother might have been quite traumatic for the child, and also for the biological mother who was a stranger. In this socioeconomic setting, where giving up the newborn was an accepted custom, and not considered an error, the image of the happy contented breastfeeding ideal mother must have aroused complicated feelings in the biological mother, a mixture of guilt and envy, plus idealization of the suckling Virgin.

Like the soul distinguished from the body, the milk of the Virgin became an emanation from Heaven, thus confusing the spiritual and the physical. This was apparent in the commentary on the *Song of Songs* by Clairvaux The milk of the Virgin took on a life of its own. Beyond symbolizing the gift of life, milk also symbolized the intercession of the Virgin. Warner (1976) points out that from the 13th century, "phials in which her milk was preserved were venerated all over Christendom in shrines that attracted

417

pilgrims by the thousands" (p. 200), and that sometimes, "it liquefies on certain feast days as if it were fresh."

After the late Renaissance, prudery and modesty seem to have taken over, so that the nursing Virgin showing her breast was no longer acceptable as a subject.

VIII. Conclusion

What stands out from the examination of the myth of the Virgin Mary is its power to evoke and communicate powerful emotions amongst huge segments of the population, and its ability to arouse multiple channels of creativity, starting with the construction, throughout Europe, of over 100 churches and abbeys and monasteries, including the decoration of some churches with beautiful stained-glass windows such as *la Sainte Chapelle* in Paris or the Rose of the facade of *Notre Dame.* It is amazing that the intensity of the devotion to the Virgin has been communicated across multiple sensory channels, whether musical, literary, or poetical, from the simplest of the troubadour songs and poems to the many *Ave Marias* composed over ten centuries by great composers such as, Josquin des Prez, Luis de Victoria, Schubert, or Leo Delibes, or some popular songs of famous groups such as "Let it Be" by the Beatles.[50] Finally, even the Virgin had to succumb to commercialization in Germany, as the name of her milk was given to a particular wine *Liebfraumilch.*

The condemnation of carnal sexuality by the Church, in part motivated by some unacceptable behavior by early priests, have created an insoluble dilemma. Namely, the establishment of an ideal woman to be loved, admired,

---

50 In this case, it turns out that Mary was also the name of Paul McCartney's mother who died of breast cancer when he was only 14 years old. Thus, his mother and the Virgin were fused for him.

and idealized whilst an essential part of her identity is obliterated. And the continuation of families through sex and childbirth is also abolished or pushed into the background, and not dealt with, as it cannot be integrated into the dogma established by the Church. This seems to be acceptable to the true believer. Such is the complexity of the mind as it struggles to integrate religion and the continuation of the species. The best ending of the Virgin's story is a statement from Freud's (1937) *Moses and Monotheism:* "Our intellect very easily goes astray without any warning, and that nothing is more easily believed by us, than what without reference to the truth comes to meet our wishful illusions" (p. 129).

REFERENCES

Arlow J. (1975). *The Madonna's Conception through the Eyes Psychoanalytic Study of Society,* vol. III. Madison, CT: Int. Univ. Press.

Armstrong, K. (2005) *A Short History of Myth.* Edinburgh, Scotland: Canongate Books Ltd.

Barthes, R. (1957). *Mythologies.* Paris: Editions du Seuil.

Brown, P. (1988). *The Body and Society.* New York: Columbia Univ. Press.

Carroll, M. (1986). *The Cult of the Virgin Mary: Psychological Origins.* Princeton : Princeton Univ. Press.

Frazer, J. (1959). *The New Golden Bough.* New York: Criterion Books.

Freud, S. (1918 [1917]). The Taboo of Virginity. *Standard Edition,* vol. XI., pp. 193–208.

——. (1937). Moses and Monotheism. *Standard Edition,* vol. XXIII.

Jung, C. (1938). *Psychology and Religion.* New Haven & London: Yale Univ. Press.

Kristof, N. (2024). *New York Times* Opinion 12/21/2024/Virgin-birth-jesus-html.

Kristeva, J. (1997). *The Portable Kristeva.* Kelly Oliver ed., New York: Columbia Univ. Press.

Meiss, M. (1951). *Painting in Florence and Sienna after the Black Death.* Princeton: Princeton Univ. Press.

Rancour-Laferriere, D. (2018). *A Psychoanalytic Perspective on Devotion to the Virgin.* London: Routledge.

Voragine, J. (1941). *The Golden Legend of Jacobus de Voragine.* London: Longmans Green & Co.

Warner Marina (1976). *Alone of All Her Sex: The Myth and the Cult of the Virgin Mary.* London: Weidenfeld and Nicolson.

CHAPTER 16

Freud and Marie Bonaparte's Correspondence (1925–1939): An Intimate Relationship.

[(2024). *American Imago* (81):189–211.]

I. Introduction.

We are extremely fortunate to be able to study a recently discovered trove[51] of correspondence between two extremely erudite and candid writers, Sigmund Freud and Marie Bonaparte, a princess of Greek origin so proud of her connection with the great Napoleon[52]. Reviewing the correspondence of almost 1000 pages between 1925 and 1939 gives us a window into the personality of two fascinating individuals as well as the deteriorating situation in Europe. Finally, we witness the birth of the French psychoanalytic movement which was heavily dependent on the influence and financial help of Marie Bonaparte. We should also be very grateful to the author of this French translation, because many of the hastily scribbled letters of both participants (there are many pictures of the documents in the book) are

---

51 Actually, Anna Freud had deposited the correspondence with the Library of Congress with the stipulation it could not be opened until 2032 . However, the grandchildren of Marie Bonaparte decided to allow publication in German in 2020. It is not clear why the Library of Congress did not adhere to Anna Freud's stated desires. The book was translated into French in 2022.

52 There is a previous biography of Marie by Celia Bertin who spent 5 years of her life interviewing many witnesses. See Baudry (1985).

almost illegible and nearly impossible to understand. Bonaparte would have enjoyed publication of this book as she was avid of fame, and publicity. She wrote endless correspondence with the conscious hope it would be published.

From a historical point of view this book gives us a unique and uncensored view of Freud's developing thinking about the psychoanalytic process as well as a continuing insight into how Freud managed a relationship with one of his analysands, being mostly comfortable in detaching his analytic work from his deepening personal involvement. The two, in his view at the time, were clearly split off from each other with no leakage in any direction. This resembles a bit the relationship he established with his daughter Anna whom he analyzed briefly. Indeed, the comparison is appropriate as Marie in many ways considered Freud as a substitute for her beloved father who had passed away two years before. She had no difficulty in very soon starting all her letters with *Mon cher pere* (my dear father). As taken as he was by this extraordinary patient Freud became slowly aware that his patient also had an unconscious motivating even during her most open disclosures. On 21 May 1927, he wrote to her "I love your sincerity even if it also is in the service of resistance."

It is crucial to clarify what the life of a Greek princess would have been like in the late 1920"s: multiple ceremonies, dinners, endless social occasions meeting with other royalties and politicians. There was no room for independent intellectual pursuits and certainly even less acceptance for Marie to delve in this new unknown field of psychoanalysis. Thus, she writes on 23 April 1926 that "I have to sneak into work like a thief because my absurd social rank forbids this, considering it a crime." She is forced to hide under false names to pursue her researches which Freud knows[53] about. A very gifted writer, she composed over 15 books during her lifetime including

---

53 This refers to her use of the name Narjani to cover her alleged work on her view of female frigidity.

some books for children and another book inspired by the death of her father two years previously. Most interesting for the analytic reader she put together *Five Copy Books Written by a Little Girl between Ages of Seven and a Half and Ten with Commentaries*.[54] Engaging in these literary activities required a degree of conviction and assertion not typical at this time especially for a woman.

A few words about her early life are in order. She nearly died at birth after a forceps delivery. Her mother died one month later[55] and Marie was always a sickly child being brought up with the image of being an invalid .The threat of death pervaded her life and was the source of many phobias and anxieties which were partially alleviated during her many analytic visits to Vienna.

It would be possible to look at the evolving stages of letters exchanged between the two participants through a variety of lenses: first student to idealized professor, then analysand to analyst, then developing friendship, then relation between two equal participants, then complex involvement in the profession including very different views on female sexuality, finally a helper and maternal care and love for a very sick Freud. Each stage can be looked analytically as having complex conscious, preconscious, and unconscious components in both participants with evolving transference and countertransference components complicated by a variety of enactments both in and out of treatment.[56] As Freud was comfortable with his evolving technique at the time, he did not seem to be troubled by the variety of intense feelings aroused by the patient analyst contact. It is important not to adopt a judgmental attitude because of our current understanding of what we would

---

54 Apparently according to Nellie Thompson (2003) these notebooks had been forgotten by her and only discovered in her father's papers after his death. Rereading these documents prompted her to seek an analysis with Freud.

55 It is most likely that on some unconscious level Marie felt responsible for her mother's death.

56 At one point Marie's biographer Celia Bertin reports that she showed Freud her breast.

consider proper technique, some one hundred years later. Let us see what we can discover, while maintaining a relatively benevolent attitude.

II. Early Letters July–1925 to February 1926[57]

In this section I will study the exchange of letters during the first two stages of the analysis each lasting about six weeks as they offer considerable insight into the developing relationship without the intrusion of external factors including Bonaparte's actually working on the French translation of Freud's essay on Leonardo, the first paper she felt comfortable tackling as it did not deal with an actual analytic encounter which she was only beginning to experience. She also quickly organized a French analytic movement very early on in her relation to Freud.

The very first letters focused on a problem: Marie wanted to come to be analyzed but she could only stay for 3 months as she had to be back in Paris for her son. Freud replied he did not want to accept a time limit for the treatment. The letters do not describe the actual treatment which started in October 1925 and were in part focused on Marie's sexual frigidity. In spite of her attachment to analytic ideas she never gave up the belief that her frigidity was based on an anatomical dysfunction, namely too great a distance between the clitoris and the urinary meatus. She never explained the basis for this belief. She even wrote papers and also made up data to back up this belief using the name Narjani.

The next letter from Marie is dated 19 December 1925 suggesting she had had her way and was back in Paris. During this first time in Vienna she consulted a friend of Freud who was a gynecologist (he had delivered his 3

---

57 Although I will generally proceed by dates I will occasionally insert a quote from a later date if it seems appropriate to the topic discussed.

children) and hoping to convince him to perform the intervention she had in mind which would clear her frigidity. She seemed guilt free in describing her sexual appetite and the many affairs she had with important politicians in France including Aristide Briand. In many ways she was an ideal patient, completely trusting towards Freud, very open and sincere, and finally both curious about her inner life and very able to free associate. She also shared with Freud important journals she had kept as early as her adolescence. These were suggestive of certain early exposures to primal scene experiences which Freud reconstructed and were later confirmed by the still living early participants. Unfortunately, this correspondence did not reveal any actual details of the sessions.[58]

This first letter after her return to Paris is chatty friendly as though Freud already became a loved confidant. She refers to him in her first letter (Dec 19th) as *mon maitre et mon ami,* shifting to *mon maitre aime* (my beloved master) a few days later. In this first letter she tells Freud how sad she is to be without him! She looks at the clock and when it is 5:00 pm something inside her feels cold.[59] She writes in her last sentence: "You are more powerful than the pope or the 'King Solomon' And I venerate you and love you." In a letter written on Dec. 25th Christmas day, she narrates a dream in which she was the "conductor of a train penetrating a tunnel going beyond all obstacles even seeing a sign 'danger of death' Everyone on the train admired my courage and all the obstacles dissolved in smoke as soon as they were encountered."[60] [61] Finally, in her next letter dated 27 December she explains that people in

---

58 The few details which we possess can be found in Celia Bertin's biography(1982) which I previously reviewed for *JAPA in* 1985.

59 I assume this must have been the time of her session.

60 It happened that a local train passed near Marie's house in St Cloud, a suburb of Paris.

61 It also turns out that in the cahiers she wrote as a child, she referred to "le Serqinte as a train monster which is alive and can kill through its penetrating glance" (p. viii in introduction of letters).

her entourage are very suspicious of her recurring trips to Vienna, claiming she is rejoining her lover, others claim she is fleeing from her home duties and still others that she is preparing her divorce. I suspect that on some preconscious level all these suppositions had more than a grain of truth. She was overflowing with excitement as she shared with her entourage details of the analytic encounter she had with Freud. It was easy for her to explain to Freud that most of her dreams deal with some form of penis envy confirming his view of feminine development.

In her Dec 27th letter two days later, she eagerly anticipates her coming return to Vienna describing her state: she has reassembled her strength to better confront her next visit "something like leopards or tigers do, when before lunging they lean on their hind legs." The hidden aggression is hard to avoid! But even this image of the animals is also derived from a childhood fear of a hyena connected with the image of her father carrying her on his back on the way to her bed at night (17 May 1926). For the child Marie the hyena was also a devourer of cadavers! In her associations she is both. The cadaver is the child in bed. Marie is continually hungry; she only feels fulfilled when she is next to Freud. A letter of 22 May reads like an analytic session with childhood memories followed by connections with both current and past anxieties with a quality of genuine insights. I am not sure to what degree they affected her basic character organization.

Marie's acceptance by Freud, the master of analysis, an ideal strong man allowed her to attain the masculine brain she so much sought after by a complex process of identification. Freud became a self object for her.

Very quickly Marie tells Freud that she is jealous of his other patients, referring to them as "my brothers," even though she knew that some of Freud's patients were women. In a later letter she also complains she is jealous of Freud's affection for "Wolf," the dog he gave to his daughter Anna, and from whom he was separated during his stay in a rehabilitation center. She is so quickly able to enmesh herself with his family that she becomes included normally in their routine. In March 1926 she thanked Freud for the lovely basket of goodies brought to her by Mrs. Freud at the railroad station on the way back to Paris. In the same letter she comments on the warm and affectionate letter Freud's daughter, Anna, wrote to her. She ends with: "I love you dearly." With the passage of time Marie's letters become more personal. She shares her entire world, her anxieties, her self analytic understandings, and most importantly very concrete details of all her sexual encounters without exception, including detailed drawings of her anatomy and the respective positions of the participants. Writing letters several pages long the correspondence becomes a substitute for being continually present with Freud. She has no idea of how much she is burdening him. She compensates for this in part by becoming actively involved in the translation of his works in French and putting together the French analytic organization somewhat against the resistance of some colleagues who seem to resent the fact she was not a physician[62] and also that she was a woman!

Before moving on it is time to examine how Freud responded to this deluge and outpouring of love and affection. First, he writes far fewer letters. Between December 1925 and the end of March 1926 Marie wrote 20 letters and telegrams in contrast to Freud's 6 responses.[63] Second, he shifts from first addressing her as *Votre altesse royale* to *Ma Chere Princesse*, and finally on 14 March to "dearest poor body ink," a reference to the way her father called her as a child when she spilt ink on her fingers. It is only in May 1926 that he shifts to "Ma Chere Marie" and then "Mimi" in June 1926 alternating with "my dear Marie" in the majority of correspondence till 1939. In his letter of 2 March 1926 after the initial "my dear princess" he writes "I do not use the

---

62 The issue of lay analysts was a source of major contention in Paris for many years. In addition Marie suffered from not being a physician and even considered going to medical school.

63 This will change later as Freud has comments about her translations and at times respond to her insights with additional interpretations.

language of transference, I do not write 'Marie' or even more 'Mimi' but I do not expect to hide my cordial feelings towards you because I believe that our relation can comfortably exist independently of the transference even though it is true that it would not have been installed without it."

Marie's involvement with Freud leads to more enactments. In Paris she meets an analyst from Poland, Rudolph Loewenstein who later became one of the leading figures of ego psychology in New York. After serving as one of the translators of Freud's work into French, Loewenstein later became her lover then analyzed her son, and later became her analyst.[64] He eventually sent her his sister for analysis. Marie shared with Freud details of all of her patient's sexual life.

III. Deepening relationship 1926–1927

On her return to Paris at the end of February she hears from Freud about his health issues. He informs her about the appearance of chest pain indicating some cardiac insufficiency. The cardiologist is trying to get him without success to cut down on his smoking. He asks Marie not to regret him too much, as though he is imagining a severe slowdown in his activities, maybe even preparing her for his eventual demise. Terrified of losing him, Marie responds that the presence of the sublime father she found in Freud cannot be taken away from her and that she will hold on to it as long as she lives, as long as her mind "while in good health is still able to understand you" (p. 31). Freud answers the next day that he is spending some time in a cardiac of a rehabilitation center and that his three patients come for their sessions with him. In the next room his wife and his daughter Anna keep him company. He is clearly concerned about Marie's excessive attachment to him. Apparently

---

64 I am not sure I have the right order.

he had warned her during her first stay in Vienna not to get too attached to him. "I will not live long. I am old. I am ill" (fn 4, p. 33). A bit reluctantly in a letter of 3 April 1926 he shares with her that he understands how much Marie has become an important part of his life and of all our lives.

For Marie, Freud was the open door to the fulfillment of all her unmet wishes and need for a father to replace the father she lost and whom she blamed for her deficiencies. After some self analytic work, Marie becomes aware that since childhood her father was seen like a thief. "He stole my money; he prevented me from having a penis. He was the architect of my body; I held him responsible for my anatomical construction" (4 March 1928). For Marie, Freud undid all these damages as a beloved father. She deluged him with almost daily letters.

Eventually, Freud complained that the nearly daily letters were just too much to contend with. Nevertheless, Marie was not easily put off and, disregarding his request, she continued like an express train to send him long almost daily correspondence. Depressed at times, she refinds courage by reading a letter from Freud (18 March) and she writes back immediately that she "noticed a sense of pride (penis) returning to her that Freud would consider her worthy of receiving such a letter."

However, her enthusiasm for the findings of analysis and its very newly coined vocabulary met with a substantial opposition by French psychiatrists. For instance, Pichon, one of the translators wanted to omit the word "libido" and substitute the French word *aimance* in spite of Marie's objections. As a result, Marie then began to take more active charge, doing some of the translations herself and hiring others to help her including Loewenstein. Being very accurate in the work of translation was very demanding and required extreme attention to details. Marie occasionally asks very probing questions. For example, when she later is translating Little Hans in French she asks Freud how to translate *Wiwimacher* or *lumpf* into French. *"Fait pipi"*? Freud replies that she could contact a child's maid to find out what the Latin genius relies on for these words!

IV. Topsy and the dogs: another powerful bond.

Dogs were an important part of Freud's life. They were often present during his hours with patients. Freud also was very involved with Wolf the Alsatian Hound given to Anna in 1925 to accompany her on her solitary walks. On one occasion in 1927 Wolf bit Ernest Jones on the thigh and Freud indicates in a letter to Eitingon that he had to reluctantly punish Wolf although he— Jones—deserved it (Freud,[65] written at the onset of WWII). Topsy developed cancer of the mouth, an illness similar to Freud's. Marie's father had also died of cancer two years previously. Freud acquired two dogs named Tattoun after the dog Marie had gotten her daughter Eugenie whilst she recovered from her tuberculosis.

V. Continuing personal closeness

The next several hundred pages detail the personal and professional bond of great intensity. Ruth Mack Bunswick, an American analyst in treatment with Freud, becomes an intimate part of the growing circle of friends and patients. She shuttles back and forth from Paris to Vienna sharing intimate details of both participant's lives. Marie continues her self analytic efforts and assures Freud (10 April 1926) that her love for him, if it survives the evolution of the transference, is completely apart and independent from the

---

65 Most of the details are to be found in the detailed introduction to the book published in 1994 by Gary Genosco, a professor in social sciences and humanities at the university of Toronto.

result of the analysis, The result of the latter she tells him is to understand the origins of irrational guilt feelings which then melt like *moisissures au soleil.* Two issues will dominate much of the content of the rest of the book: the understanding of Marie's frigidity and then impact of her adolescent daughter's tuberculosis.

From Marie's point of view. Freud has become the most important person in her world. She continues on 21 March "There is nothing in my life but solitude—or you." She explains that she is like a snail retreating into her shell when wounded. This behavior worked for everybody except her father. She could never withdraw her love for him no matter what the circumstances.

Freud responds to her letters revealing some of his personal reactions. He says: "When someone insults me I can defend myself but when someone praises me I am defenseless!" (p. 81). In response to the flow of letters he sometimes sends her a poem. At other times, aware of her potential inability to control herself, he tries to warn her against giving in to her overwhelming sexual impulses including some directed towards the analysts she came in contact with.

Unfortunately, because of her fixation on the penis and castration anxiety which she believes is the explanation of the baby's reaction to losing the breast, she is furious with those French analysts who see in the oral phase a true developmental phase in its own right, in spite of Freuds' counsel to the contrary. She also has difficulty in seeing Freud in the transference as a feminine counterpart to the mother! Her contempt for the maternal continues as she adds that nature is the mother, the full stupid breast which feeds! She also showers Freud with gifts for his birthday including some Greek honey which she had shipped to him from Greece. He is not entirely happy and responds by saying that he would begin to suspect that she may well consider his 70th year like the beginning of his second childhood (21 April 1926). Yet, he thanks her for the gifts for his birthday by sending her a telegram; 'All your charming presents remind me of you. Stop. none

431

equal in value to who you are (7 May 1926). Freud comments on the funds gathered for him for his birthday and states he was told that there were almost no donations from America. He adds "I am not surprised, but what are they worth if they do not contribute any funds!" (10 May 1926). He did acknowledge a tribute from Albert Einstein. It is hard to convey the richness of this celebration. Many analysts including some from London made a special trip to Vienna for the occasion.

Marie's letters continue to be a mixture of her fantasies, her dreams, and her attempt to master them. She is very involved in doing self analytic work. She is capable of and shares her almost daily insights with Freud. The latter, impressed by her insights, writes 3 days later, "How is it possible that you can see through a human being so quickly and so infallibly. How can you discover so quickly the motives which others cannot fathom? It must be that you possess the inborn capacity of a genius!" (10 May 1926).

However, Marie continues to be very troubled. She also behaves like an obedient, but cunning and defiant child under a cover of complete submission; a child vis à vis Freud, who counsels her not to read Edgar Allen Poe before seeing him, as the reading so frightened her in the past. She asks him in the next letter, what she should be permitted to read? She will follow his suggestion. In addition, does he wish for her not to read any of his papers? She continues "if I am obliged to read nothing, I will obey but if I am allowed to read something what do you advise? Gradiva, The case of Dora, or Little Hans, or the Wolfman? Am I permitted access to these texts?" (27 May 1926). "It does not matter. I will deliver myself to you with wrists and feet bound. Until then, I will write nothing, read nothing, prepare nothing. I will live like an insect on leaves or on the small sunflowers! I think of you and love you. I love you more than ever" (22 May 1926). She continues to confide that the name Marie (also referred to as Mimi) was also that of her mother but also that of the Virgin, of the woman god, and also the wife of God the father! The latter three words underlined. There is here a not so subtle allusion to Freud as her God. But in the same letter Marie also reminds Freud that her mother died soon after having given birth to her.

In a letter of 31 May she mentions to Freud her intention of attending a concert by Yvette Guilbert[66] and talking to her about Freud. The latter knew Marie's father. Freud tells Marie that the latter's portrait is next to hers (i.e., Marie's) in Freuds' home.

Soon afterwards Marie tells Freud about the crucial conversation she had with Pascal,[67] a Corsican man who worked in her parent's stables and who had slept with Marie's nursemaid in the same room as the supposedly sleeping child. He confirmed all of Freud's reconstructions. Marie was so excited by the accuracy of her work with Freud that she ends her letter: "I have a burning desire to see you again. I would now allow analysis to cut me into pieces even to turn me into a *bouillie* (semi liquid substance) I love you, I love you!." Freud is very delighted to hear from Marie the confirmation of all his early reconstructions involving Pascal, and ends his letter in French: "It is really very beautiful. *Je vous embrasse*" (I kiss you) (2 June 1926).

In his answer Freud seems to take seriously her questions about which of his works she might read, including Dora, Little Hans, and the Wolfman. Freud adds that the latter is now a poor refugee in Vienna and that he (Freud) gives him a small monthly sum to enable him to send his sick wife to the country. He also tells her that she is under no obligation to send him some money.

In response Marie obviously very excited continues her own analytic reconstruction of her past. She is eagerly looking forward to her sessions with Freud and asks him whether if she were delayed in Paris because of her son's oral exam, she could stay an extra week in August as three weeks analysis feels a bit short (7 June).

---

66 This artist was very much appreciated by Freud.

67 There are rumors that he might have been a distant family member of Marie's father.

Again, there is an interruption between 7 July and 9 august suggesting she visited Freud during this interval, shortly after her return to Paris.

In her first letter (August 9 1926) she writes: "one thing that consoles me is the analytic situation. It allows me to reestablish some closeness with you." She tells Freud he should call her Mimi, obviously recreating the childhood intimacy she so missed with her father

Marie's letters are an unending continual conversation with Freud about her inner world, her associations and her discoveries about herself, occasionally revealing some detail of her early life. For example, coming back from Dieppe some time aged 4 and 3 months she developed severe illness with coughing blood. "The doctor told my parents I might not survive the night. A telegram was sent to her father in Bulgaria traveling for work to rush back. When he arrived, I had survived" (14 August 1926).

Finally, after more endless letters sent, without thinking of the burden they might have posed for Freud to read the lengthy associations dreams and reconstructions they contained, Freud finally responds "you are not saying a word about the teasing audacity (impertinence taquine) you have to attribute to me the merit of all your discoveries" (18 August 1926). He continues to share with Marie some highly personal details of his life, including the not longer hidden intimate relationship between his daughter Anna and Mrs. Burlingham. In her next letter Marie raises the question of what going to medical school would entail. Having to submit her will to mediocre people would be noxious in contrast to "trying to please a father like you which elevates the spirit" (9 September 1926). She wants to write a letter to Mrs. Freud but is unsure how to address her *"Chere Madame le Professeur"* yet continues to remark to Freud how much she appreciates her "maternal" caring such as the strawberries she gives her. She remembers to send the Freuds a telegram in German to celebrate their 40th year of marriage but soon worries she had the wrong date! She describes her horror of earthworms as they represent the animals which eat cadavers in contrast to snakes which she finds adorable as they represent a living phallus (10 September 1926). Marie's desire for masculinity continues invading many aspects of her life. She will drive her motor car having obtained the required permit, with the driver sitting next to her. However, soon afterwards on her way to Chartres, she manages to drive the car on the sidewalk, crushing several fruit trees and breaking the car's front windshield!

VI. A family tragedy for Marie

Marie is struck by a tragedy. The doctors, taking care of her 18 year old daughter suffering from pleurisy and a 104F fever, fear she may have been infected by tuberculosis The only likely suspect at first would be the a priest whom the husband had hired against Marie's wishes to teach her Greek and religion.68 Marie rages against herself with guilt: How could she have allowed herself to become a mother against her will, against her nature! and twice! And what if her daughter's options were to live or to die. No, that's not it, maybe to be condemned to be ill for years (11 December 1926). At first overcome, Marie is able to do some self reflection of a very insightful nature. She realizes that the intensity of her reaction to the danger her daughter might be in is a repetition of the intense feelings she had as a child when she was thinking of the death of her mother who also likely suffered from tuberculosis with hemoptysis. A compassion mixed with guilt because behind this was the thought "Detach yourself for this woman." And the hatred of the Greek priest could be a projection when I so quickly accuse him. Since I came to this realization I feel calmer and can wait. I also understood I will also have to die like my mother when giving birth. All of this taking place in the very house my mother died in (13 December 1926). Freud answered two

---

68 This later turned out not to be the case.

days later with a very reassuring letter. From the details Marie gives him, he is not at all certain the illness is TB. He adds "You know, the mother who is the best caretaker is not the most tender one but the one who understands the best. For that calmness (*du sang froid*) is required. I am sure your next letter will most likely display a different mood." He adds "even though it is unnecessary I cannot avoid telling you how aggrieved I am for what you and your beloved daughter are going through" (15 December).

Unfortunately, the diagnosis of TB is confirmed but in a strange fashion namely by ruling out other diagnostic possibilities (16 December). Though calmer Marie worries about the marriage prospects for her daughter. But all of this will have to wait a few months to see how the disease evolves. It turns out that the daughter also had jaundice.[69] It may be relevant that at the same time Marie was working on an article to be published in a French analytic journal concerning her examination of Mrs. Lefevre, a French criminal who assassinated her pregnant daughter in law! (20 December).

Marie's daughter continues to improve without a firm diagnosis. On 28 December she writes to Freud how appreciative she is toward the *Frau Professor* for having sent a bookstand (*liseuse*) to her daughter Eugenie who has to remain in bed several more weeks. Marie also tells Freud that she was asked to give a conference on "Freud the man" She reassures him she will not be indiscreet, she will only give obvious details such as the fact that he has 5 sisters and a brother that he are an excellent family man… etc. things of this nature! (31 December 1926). Unfortunately, in addition to TB Eugenie will develop some painful full of liquid cysts in her hip which will have to be evaluated and also turn out to be tubercular infections (June 1929). For the next years the poor child will require a number of operations behind a leg bone to drain these recurrent cysts. By early 1927, Freud writes to Marie

---

69 Actually Eugenie's condition worsens with episodes of hemoptysis as she is sent to a number of sanatoriums in Italy.

that he is working on nothing because the adaptation to a new prosthesis was very difficult. Being very incapacitated and experiencing a lot of pain do not favor intellectual pursuits (January 1927). He adds in the same letter that while in Berlin he spent two hours with Einstein[70] the famous physicist. Freud found him quite friendly and spontaneous, adding that as Einstein is as familiar in psychology as Freud is in physics. "We had a very agreeable conversation. The latter has a much easier task in his work as he could rely on a long series of predecessors whereas I had to make my way alone in an inextricable dense patch ('un maquis inextricable')."

In her next letter (13 January 1927) Marie tells Freud that the "young lion is tamed." This refers to Loewenstein the analyst with whom she had had an intimate relation at the same time she was also with other men. Knowing her reputation, the latter told her of other women he had seduced. Marie adds that the liaison is happening in spite of the fact that Loew. is 15 years younger than her and that also he is rather ugly.

VII. Narjani and Marie's unproven ideas about female frigidity[71]

In spite of her analytic work with Freud, Marie remains convinced with no outside evidence that female frigidity is due to an anatomical issue which can be corrected by operation: too much distance between the clitoris and the urethra. Under the name Narjani, she publishes a number of mostly fictitious articles describing this problem and its cure. She also claims that women over 1 meter and 68 centimeters are generally frigid. It turns out that her daughter reached this problematic size. Marie wanted her operated on!

---

70 It turns out that Einstein had sent Freud a congratulatory letter for his 70th birthday.

71 See Narjani 1924 for an article Marie published under this fake name pretending to be the surgeon Halian who operated on her in Vienna.

Sometime during her stay in Vienna in April 1926 Marie was able to convince Freud's family's gynecologist, to whom she was referred, that he should operate on her genitals according to her unproven ideas to decrease the distance of the clitoris to the urethra. Perhaps ashamed or embarrassed she wants to hide her real identity. She used a false name ("Marie Madol") to register herself at the hospital, hiding her true identity. When the administration asked for her passport, her real identity was discovered revealing her lie. The head doctor graciously accepted this attempt at a fake identity. In his next letter Freud addresses her as "Chere Marie Madol," using her fake name and reminds her that if she claimed not to have a passport she could have been taken to the police station.(24 April 1927). To soften this point, he kindly adds that if there were a real improvement after the operation things would change. He also tells her that a novel she had written (probably *Vaga*) and sent him hoping for his praise, is not publishable because of its contents and fails to evoke any empathy in the reader. In her next letter Marie expresses her disappointment that a story she wrote with her blood and her tears could not find a way to his heart (28 April 1927).

Two weeks later after her return to Paris after the intervention she writes to Freud (May 8th) that the second conversation she had with him was the hardest she ever had in her life; you held a mirror in front of my eyes and I saw myself as not beautiful. She confides in Freud that after her operation she was in a manic almost psychotic state accompanied by an overflow of tenderness for her son and her husband who did not understand and sent a priest to see her in the hope of converting her. She writes further that what she was experiencing was like an erotic hypomania. Actually, she confessed to Freud that she was in such state of confusion that she gave in to the insistent demands of Halban (the gynecologist) who said to her after her recovery from the operation: "Shall we try and see?" It seems that Freud's reaction was intense and extremely critical. He accused her of an immoral act and "un crime de lese science" (a crime against the very nature of science)

Marie seems to realize that her behavior was not a sin but an example of stupidity. Did she actually do it on purpose and in full awareness? She writes to Freud that the need to revenge against her friend, and also him, was actually mostly directed against herself. She is hoping but also fearing that the surgeon would not want to publicize the operation (which she invented) in his writings. Halban had first suggested publishing it with the name Narjani.[72] Marie is obviously hoping, probably unrealistically, that he would operate on other women and that the two of them would publish their work. Actually, the operation was mentioned briefly in Halban's gynecologic writings! In her letter to Halban she writes of this work as the most beautiful of her entire life and she appreciates his having collaborated with her (27 May 1927). In spite of his doubts, Halban agrees to operate on women specifically referred to him by Marie who would travel to Vienna. Marie also becomes interested in the stories of African women who are subjected, as a rite of passage, to clitorectomy. Marie continues writing to Freud that although she is aware he doesn't love her as one of his children, she still needs him. She adds at the end that if she indeed were his daughter, he would have made her into soup and given it to Wolf[73] (8 May 1927).

Back in Paris she tells Loewenstein the entire story . The latter is quite horrified and Marie finds his reaction "interesting." In the same letter she tells Freud that the operation was a success! (12 May 1927).

Freud answers her very thoughtfully. He advises against too quick a conclusion and tells her she is neglecting the vagina in the role of pleasure.

---

72 The name Bonaparte had invented to write about her ideas of the operation and its value. She is convinced that Halban does not want to steal her ideas but that he may be a bit embarrassed to add his name to this operation. She actually thinks he could publicize the operation and make a lot of money creating envy in his colleagues! She adds that Halban asked that she be very cautious about discussing the operation and certainly not tell Freud nor any friends in Paris she adds that he is behaving like a little boy who has stolen a pot of jam..

73 The name of his dog.

He also writes that in her case the goal of the analysis as a liberator of impulses worked very well[74] but that she still has a long way to go in the second goal which is to master them. Freud also confronts Marie with the complication of the paradox of her giving her own impulses completely free rein, whereas with her patients (she was about to start an analytic practice as it seems without his permission being mentioned in their letters), she would have to submit their impulses to reason. Furthermore, others will know about her lifestyle and this could cause her severe problems undermining her authority and may derail her in her work. Around this time she is referred one of her first analytic patients (21 March 1928). In the next letter Freud informs her that as her analysis was not finished she is transgressing the rules by accepting an analytic patient. At the same time, he is also encouraging her to do so (3 April 1928). By then she had of course carried out some analytic work in supervision with him. Surprisingly he is also suggesting to her that one of her patients could also accompany her on her next trip to Vienna[75] so Freud could examine him.

Marie continues to argue with Freud that she did not understand that as an analyst you had to control your impulses. She reassures him that she considers her clients as inferior and that she would never want to be intimate with inferior people. She explains that she cannot change her character and she wonders whether Freud does not think she should be an analyst if she cannot control her impulses. This is something she never promised. Perhaps Freud sees her as inferior because she is a woman but actually nature and life have given her a male brain and male erotic impulses which she should be entitled to express.[76] She also becomes aware in a later period that in the

---

74 I am not sure he is right as her erotic life was unusually active even before she met Freud.

75 I assume Freud has in mind than he would see this patient also.

76 There is here a hidden reproach to Freud whom she fears considers her as a woman with all the limitations appropriate for that sex.

transference Freud the analyst would be seen as an enemy of her sexuality (15 June 1929). Freud reassures her that he does not intend to inhibit her sexuality even though the role of father had led him to adopt such attitudes (19 June 1929).

Finally in the next very long letter, (21 May) a frustrated Freud, realizing her stubbornness, tries to correct all her mistakes and misunderstandings about sexuality and also his views about boundary violations between patients and analysts and what he thinks is proper behavior for a respectable analyst. He includes a reference to Napoleon Bonaparte who had a probable liaison with a washer woman in Montmartre before his marriage to Marie-Louise of Austria. In another letter Marie delights in telling Freud that the woman Loewenstein wanted to marry rejected him because he impregnated her and she had to undergo an abortion! (23 March 1928).

Continuing her correspondence Marie tries to get back on the good side of Freud and tells him how Eugenie, normally very agitated, was dramatically calmed and delighted in reading the case of Little Hans. She could not put the book down once started. It was a relief for Marie to see her quiet.

Freud's receipt of the proof of the first issue of the first French psychoanalytic journal arouses a lot of anger in him. Pichon for unclear reasons wrote "under the patronage of Prof. Freud" instead of directed by Freud. This difference is seen as an insult by Freud who would like to change this error before publication but it is too late! Marie feels in part responsible for this error. Freud explains further that even the notion of patronage which is found only on the cover will disappear once the volume is bound. Freud sees this as a gesture of unfriendliness or rivalry by the French analytic movement.

We don't hear about Marie's stay after 25 August . The next letter is from Paris on 21 December 2027. Somewhat surprisingly her reputation has deteriorated, partly because of the mixed reception of analysis in France because of its origin in Austria, plus her standing as a woman and a nonphysician. The medical profession wants to prevent non MD's from practicing it. They are worried that nontrained lay analysts will play a role and will not be excluded. Eventually there will be some legal trials on this matter in 1950. The medical profession continues to see analysis carried out by nonanalysts as an illegal violation of medical practice

Eugenie, Marie's daughter, also becomes quite interested in analysis and reveals to her mother a fear she had as a child, namely when she went to the bathroom as a child, she feared that a snake would come out of the toilet and penetrate her insides! Marie shares these details with Freud but expresses guilt at having revealed the highly private world of Eugenie without her permission.

Freud has no difficulties in reverse asking Marie whether she could receive his daughter Anna for an afternoon in Paris as the latter would otherwise feel quite lost in Paris (22 February 1928). Marie is delighted but somewhat guilty in not sharing Anna's visit with the analytic group (25 February 1928). She goes beyond Freud's requests hosting her for several days and accompanying her to visit some of the great sights. A bit later she also hosted Freud's son and his wife.

Probably suffering a mixture of guilt associated with some defiance and willful assertion of her right to live out her impulses, Marie wrote the following to Freud, her adopted father: "During a walk in the spring forest with Loewenstein: he became tender, took my hand and kissed it. We were seated on a bench and I let him kiss my cheek and even a breast but not my lips. This is because he has his girlfriend and I have my boyfriend." Marie adds a bit later that it would be very shaming to confess it to you (28 May 1928.) She states she does not want her senses to take over but in the next paragraph she adds that next summer both she and Loewenstein would be in Switzerland and they both "could try" for two weeks to see what happens. This implies that sex at that time would be a willful affair not an explosion of uncontrolled desire. What does Freud think of this option?

In the same letter she gives a detailed description of her sexual encounter with her boyfriend including a drawing of their respective position during sex and the manner she masturbates! It sounds almost as if she wants Freud to be included in her affairs. Furthermore, she does not seem to realize that in her obsessive search for orgasm she is completely neglecting the role of real love and intimacy which was causing her real difficulties. The mixture of personal revelations and analytic efforts become hopelessly entwined. In a coming issue of the French analytic journal Marie intends to publish a part of her own self analysis and life as a child (8 August 1928). Before her next visit Freud expresses the concern that if he could not speak as because of his prosthesis, the analysis could not take place. The next letter dated 21 November after an interval of 2 months suggests that Marie's treatment perhaps could be continued in Berlin. In late November Freud writes that he cannot treat Marie while she is in a sanatorium[77] because his own schedule does not give him the extra time needed. She tells Freud that her son Pierre opened by mistake a love letter written to her by Loewenstein. (29 November 1928). She has no shame in telling Freud she is continuing her sexual encounter with Loewenstein. Even while in Vienna or Berlin she manages to have endless affairs with men she does not even love. On 3 April 1929, she writes to Freud that on her next trip for analysis she will devote herself entirely to this task and not have affairs the way she had done last time. Without asking Freud she is taking on more analytic cases. Here too there is a lot of variation about where analysis takes place in a garden or in winter on her balcony with blankets being provided to the satisfaction of Marie's patients. In a recent letter Freud suggests to her that if she feels the need for more analysis she could also consult Ferenczi or Eitingon (14 December 1930). Marie is obviously hurt and suggests that maybe Freud

---

77 It is not clear what made the stay necessary. She had serious problem with the bladder and bleeding, probably the result of extensive masturbation and manipulation of her internal organs. She was willing to even pay him travel time to the sanatorium!

is fed up with her. In any case if she were to see anyone but her beloved father she would consult a woman! (31 December 1930). As Marie is more involved in all aspects of the analytic community Freud responds much more frequently to her almost daily letters and treats her as a valuable colleague.

Worrying about her daughter's neurotic symptoms, Marie hopes that Freud could also take her in analysis on the next joint trip to Vienna (11 April 1929).

In his return letter Freud raises some interesting objections to this idea. For an analysis, especially cut in segments, to work in a young adult a certain maturation is needed which Eugenie has not yet attained. Also, Vienna in the cold of winter is not a great place for someone having just recovered from TB. Freud also suggests that Marie might help her achieve some of the same results through discussion with her, behaving like an analyst (18 April 1929).

The way she writes suggest that she sees her letters as a highly accurate portrait of her life and that they would be useful for a genuine biography of her person particularly should she become a celebrated person, which is very likely! (25 April 1929). We do not hear about Marie's stay and brief analysis except that Freud apparently gave her the special ring reserved for his most faithful disciples and Marie feels in spirit like the "husband of the father" (3 December 1929).

The lack of boundaries is somewhat extreme .On 1 April 1930, Marie tells Freud that her son Pierre, following a disappointment in a relation with an American girl, will start analysis with Loewenstein even though he had discovered by mistake a love letter written by Loewenstein to Marie. A bit later in November 1930, Lowenstein sends his sister to Marie for a didactic analysis. There is another surprising discovery. In a letter to Freud (28 April 1932) Marie tells Freud that her son Pierre recalled a memory he recovered.[78] He tells Marie that at an uncertain age, but possibly 11, that mother and son

---

78 It looks like Marie had forgotten this real event.

were lying down in the forest and that he started to touch his mother's breast under her clothes and she did not stop him; he even had an erection and he said to himself. "Wow she lets me do this." When Pierre told his mother of this memory they talked in the night for a long time and Marie realized he was sexually excited and she also realized she was also anxiously aroused. Later she told the entire incident to Loewenstein who seemed embarrassed by this revelation (same letter). In his reply (30 April 1932), Freud says nothing about Marie's role but only comments about the lack of barrier against incest in her son. Marie confesses to Freud that her son had a more powerful barrier against incest; and that she they took together in spite of Freud's warning that this might not be a good idea.

Marie continues brief visits to Vienna in late April 1930.

A bit later she develops some uterine tumors and because of a combination of her wealth and of her mistrust of gynecologists who would not share her view of female sexuality she pays for the trip of Halban, the Viennese gynecologist, who had first operated on her to come to Paris at the American hospital, to do the required operation late in May 1930.

By early 1932 Freud's problems with the prosthesis augment and deplete his finances. He writes to Marie that a number of colleagues have helped him financially including one of his patients, Edith Jackson, an American child psychiatrist (5 February 1932). Surprisingly Freud shares with Marie that by April 1932 he only has 3 patients in analysis (to Marie's 5!) and that he has not received any new demands. He adds that people are of course right; he is too old and the work with him is too uncertain (14 April 1932).

On a recent visit to Vienna Marie acquired a certain psychic independence from Freud claiming he was not admitting the right of women to express their impulses freely. The discussion could have no solution, since for Marie it became a political issue on the rights of women to express their sexuality, focusing on this rather than her personal conflicts in this area.

THE BROAD SCOPE OF PSYCHOANALYSIS: CLINICAL, THEORETICAL AND APPLIED

Marie is frustrated that she has to wait weeks before resuming her analysis with Freud. She then dares to ask his permission to enter into analysis properly with Loewenstein. It is clear that both her liaison with him (and her desire to be analyzed by him) are an expression of vengeance against Freud the father. She discovers also her ability to have an orgasm with Loew was because he was the best available substitute for the man she really wanted (22 January 1933). She is aware that her intimate liaison with him might be a problem but she assumes that Loew. could be objective as he understands her so well.(4 October 1932). She is also aware that she would have to share with him and of her infidelity towards him, which he does not yet know about! (24 October1932). Her main worry at the time is that Freud would at some time see this as a betrayal of him or at least infidelity and Marie states she is so fearful of losing Freud's love that she would be willing to remain frigid in order not to lose the love of her father (11 November 1932). She also states that Lowenstein was the only lover she had had whom satisfied her fully twice! (15 November 1932).. In his thoughtful answer Freud states that he gives her full authorization to go ahead but it is his judgment that she does not need it, i.e., that her desire to go ahead and work with Lowenstein is an acting out of some unconscious need to act out an infidelity and revenge against the father (13 November 1932). Further, he would not want her to maintain her frigidity out of loyalty towards him. She will keep Freud apprised of her ongoing analysis with Loew. and informs him she will not pay the latter but simply take money out of the loan she made to Loew. in Berlin some time before.. But she does not stay long because on 10 December i.e., barely 3 weeks later, she leaves for Denmark to celebrate the silver anniversary of 25 years of marriage.

Adultery continues with her children. When they visit some royalties in Denmark Eugenie is very attracted to Axel age 44, the husband of Margaretha who is Marie's cousin. She may have had an affair with him. His wife of the same age is not jealous because at night she slips into Pierres' room (29 January 1933). Meanwhile Marie writes to Freud that her analysis is progressing well as she is analyzing her sexual encounters 'in vivo!' She writes a bit later that when she comes to Vienna in July she could resume a few weeks analysis with Freud. It looks like Marie is able to change analysts as readily as she is able to change lovers! (25 February 1933). There seems to be a transgenerational transmission of issues. When Eugenie is visited in the hospital (because of her leg operation) Marie complains to Freud that for eight or nine hours Eugenie discusses the details of her sexual life exhaustively (including her anatomy) with her mother who acts as her analyst.

VIII. The last Five years 1933–1938

In early 1933 Freud writes to Marie about the growth of antisemitism and of the third Reich with Hitler, which may spread to Austria. He wonders whether he should follow the advice of friends and go to Switzerland; or perhaps it might make sense to stay here and just die (26 March 1933). Because of the worsening situation in Berlin, Eitingon is forced to close the institute and Marie hopes to create a similar one in Paris (May 1933). Around the same time Marie has a spectacular trip to Corsica[79] and finds another lover there.

In a letter to Freud (16 May 1933) she refers to the first time to his possible emigration to Paris. She would be glad to give him temporary abode in her house. The situation worsens. There is an attempted assassination of the chancellor Dreyfus in Vienna by some Nazis in October 1933.

---

79 It should be mentioned that Napoleon came from Corsica and that any Bonaparte descendant is greeted with great enthusiasm like a hero. Marie had had in the past several encounters with Corsicans.

Interestingly enough, the Arabs in Palestine are starting to complain about the massive immigration of Jews fleeing the Nazi persecution (3 November 1933). Before her next trip to Africa with her lover Marie sends Freud a sweater she has knitted herself. Freud, increasingly disabled, is very pleased to wear it (8 November 1933). He also writes to her how delighted he is that she considers herself one of his children. He could be proud of her (7 December 1933). A bit later he compliments her on her work on women's sexuality, adding that in this area he is lacking reference points (8 February 1934). Unrealistically, Freud hopes there could be a benign fascism in Austria and in any case he feels unknown by the authorities and therefore safe! (19 February 1934). Yet on 28 July 1934, the Austrian chancellor was assassinated by invading Nazis. By chance Marie discovers that Solange, a maid she had kept for many years, had undetected TB for many years and that she was likely responsible for Eugenie's infection, provoking much guilt on Marie's part (15 November 1934). Finally, in December 1934 Marie begins to realize the problem that her acting out has created. She believes that Loew. should not have taken her as a patient after their affair in Berlin. Also, the discovery of the amorous letter by Pierre should have dissuaded him from choosing Loew as analyst. As a result, his analysis did not end well.

Towards the end of 1936 Freud was clearly near the end of his productivity. He writes to Marie (8 December) that he is torn between the wish for rest and the fear of new sufferings tied to the continuation of life plus the anticipation of suffering connected by the separation of everything you still care for. This is followed by days when he can no longer eat or even drink in addition to the pain of his lesions.

Marie continues to be devoted to Freud's interests including buying the correspondence with Fliess which Freud feared could fall into the wrong hands, revealing some very personal details of his early life, including some self analytic discoveries. Fliess's wife who owns these letters is seen by Freud as having evil intents (3 January 1937). Marie writes to Freud that he is part of the history of human thought like Plato and Goethe (7 January 1937). On her trips to Greece Marie continues to send Freud more spectacular Greeks artifacts which give him a great deal of pleasure being located in his office.

In May 1937, Marie tells Freud that Loew. had sent her a patient he had in analysis but had to interrupt because his own first wife Marilise had just passed away during a complicated pregnancy requiring a C section. The transference and counter transference are too much for Loew[80] to contend with (31 May 1937). Marie suspects that Loew was also in love with this patient.

In a letter dated 18 February Marie mentions that she would pay Freud for the analytic hours that Eugenie did not take. It seems that she went to Vienna for 2 months of analysis. At the end Eugenie interrupted her troubled relation with Axel, the 44 year old man, and selected instead a young Polish prince which Marie approved of readily. She also mentions that Eugenie plans to take her future husband to Vienna so he could meet Freud. In December 1937. We hear that Freud is seeing Eugenie again for analysis and that she is referring to him angrily as an old Jew (19 December 1937). Freud also writes to Marie about details of this treatment of her.

In the early months of the 1937 Marie is preoccupied by the difficulties of Eugenie, her daughter, who is having some second thoughts about an impending marriage. We hear in passing that she had spent three months in Vienna in analysis with Freud and was planning to return there with her fiancé so that Freud could meet him and give Eugenie his unbiased opinion about him! Eugenie changes her mind and desperately seeks a new mate. Freud wisely writes that it is usually when you don't seek that you find! (10 September 1937).

The situation deteriorates rapidly. On 11 March the German chancellor resigned to be replaced by Hitler. On 12 March Austria was annexed to

---

80 This abbreviation is one way Marie refers to Loewenstein.

Germany and Hitler arrived in Vienna on 14 March. On 17 March Marie arrived in Vienna and remained there till 10 April. On 22 March Anna Freud was interrogated by the gestapo. Freud has no other choice but to leave. He is taxed about 20% of all his assets plus 30,000 marks for his antiquities. Unfortunately, the Germans have confiscated all his assets and Freud cannot afford the requested funds. Marie helps him out financially. At the same time Freud suffered some fever after the last surgical operation he had to undergo. On April 10th Freud sends to Marie a letter including the list of family members he hope could accompany him, in all 16 people including his physician Max Shur, and his family, and his faithful servant Paula Fichtl.

The book describes no further correspondence until a brief note on 5 June. The day before, Freud and a small number of his family boarded the Orient Express train for Paris and a few hours later went to Calais and arrived in London on 6 June 1938. Freud lived there until his passing in September 1939.

He resumes his correspondence on June 8th. He thanks her for the loving and caring 12 hours spent in St Cloud on the way to Calais and narrates the enthusiastic reception he received on the arrival to Victoria station.

In order not to prolong this paper I will not deal with the rest of the correspondence . The last letter by Marie is dated 23 September 1939. The day Freud died. He did not have a chance to read it!

IX. Discussion

A few comments are necessary to review the dramatic events in my paper. First, beyond the very beautiful trust which developed between the two participants the most difficult issue to confront is the mixture of the personal and the analytic, the lack of boundaries between the two, and the willingness for Freud to accept having a carnal relation between analyst and patient.

Second is the distressing discovery of the unacceptable behavior of some experienced analysts, most obviously Rudolph Loewenstein, who behaved in a totally immoral fashion on many levels, even at this early stages of principles and rules concerning appropriate behavior in an analytic setting. Reading about the sexual encounters between Marie and Loewenstein was like a cold shower for me. How could the analyst I so admired be capable of such abominable behavior with no sense of remorse or guilt? Noteworthy is that during my own training I had a very cordial and friendly relation with Rudolph Loewenstein, speaking French as one of the few analysts in New York born in France. I had several enjoyable dinners in his house and often drove him in my car to Princeton for many years as he was an invited guest at our bi yearly CAPS meetings. I also used some of his early papers on ego psychology in my teaching students.

At no time did Loewenstein reveal any details of his life in Paris even though we conversed in French. The one exception very late in his life was to share with me his unfortunate encounters with Lacan who was briefly in analysis with him.

The last unusual feature of the letters reveals the willingness of all analysts including Freud to share details of their analysands' progress with their families.

There is no question that the analytic process was corrupted and invaded by this mixture of the personal and the professional. What is not clear is how much the interpretations given were tainted and required a sort of implied unspoken splitting between analytic and personal. The latter would have to be left outside the consulting room. This may explain the initial very rigid rules of analysis after the war, at least in the US. This was true for most of the European analysts who emigrated to the US. They never wrote about their experiences in Europe. The analytic community in the 30's was indeed very troubled.

The other point of interest beyond the cut up nature of the analytic process is Marie's obsession with orgasm and her unproven theories about its anatomical causes. She never gave up on her views, publishing a number of papers with false data. Nevertheless, she forces Freud to confront some of his beliefs about female sexuality which were rooted in the existing prejudices at the time. Thus, the very basic psychological topic became complicated by socio political issues. As a result, disagreements could not be confronted in a useful fashion.

Finally in the last few years, Freuds' cancer of the palate occupied center stage from him. In spite of his courage, he was under almost constant pain needing many operations impeding both his speech and eventually his capacity to think and to write. As an incidental finding, most of the participants of the above analytic community (as did the entire population) suffered from frequent and multiple infections—both respiratory, bladder and genital—for which no real treatment existed, requiring long stays in bed or even in a sanatorium. Much of the correspondence described in detail the profound impact of these events forcing many cancellations of trips, meals, and gatherings

REFERENCES

Baudry F. (1985). La Derniere Bonaparte *J. Amer. Psychoanal. Assn.,* 33:214–224 and this volume, Chapter 15.

Bonaparte, M. (1940). *Topsy, History of a Golden-Haired Chow.* New Brunswick and London: Transaction Publishers.

——— (1953). *Female Sexuality.* Madison CT: International Universities Press.

——— (1958). *Derriere les vitres closes. Les souvenirs d'enfance de Marie Bonaparte.* Courtenay: Librairie Françoise Causse.

——— & Freud, S. (2022). *Correspondence Integrale.* 1925–1939. Paris: Flammarion.

Narjani. A.E. (1924). Considerations sur les Causes Anatomiques de la Frigidite chez la Femme. *Bruxelles Medical* 27:768–778.

Thompson, N. (2003). Marie Bonaparte's Theory of Female Sexuality: Fantasy and Biology. *American Imago* 60(3):343–378.

CHAPTER 17

Montaigne: A Precursor to Freud

[previously unpublished.]

I. Introduction

Philosopher c'est apprendre à mourir '(Socrates)[81]

Montaigne (1533–1595) was a man full of paradox, a most modern thinker under the garb of one of the greatest 16th century philosophers (see also Masud Khan,1975). Reading his essays, I was impressed, like others, by his psychological mindedness, and also that some 320 years before Freud, he had intuitively discovered many of the findings of psychoanalysis and the activity of the unconscious. This paper aims at acquainting an analytically-minded audience with the scope of Montaigne's discoveries as there are very few papers written about the essays by mental health professionals. I discovered that there are over 300 references to his work in the *PEP-web,* either in papers written which mention him in passing, or in articles quoting from his writings. Yet there are only a handful of analytic papers devoted to his work, mostly in the French analytic journals, and only two articles in the English psychoanalytic literature (Canestri, 2009) and Wolf and Gedo (1975) though there are, of course, many books written about him in the classical

---

81 This means that to philosophize is to detach the soul from the body, and to teach us not to be afraid of dying. The usefulness of life lies not in its duration but in what you make of it.

literature section. One of the most famous is *Montaigne en Mouvement* by Jean Starobinski (1982), which has been translated into English.

As an important figure, his life and essays were studied extensively by two literary scholars: Bakewell and Starobinski. I will quote the latter during the course of this paper but will indicate some of the main lines of Bakewell as an introduction. She writes accurately that the "*Essays* has no great meaning, no point to make no argument to advance. It does not have designs on you; you can do as you please with it" (Bakewell 2010, p. 7). These essays have no great meaning. Hence, writing about it is a challenge. Bakewell deals with this by giving a question about life, and 20 answers describing how Montaigne dealt with these throughout his complicated life.

I will first give a summary of his complex and rich life which he narrates so beautifully in his essays. This will also acquaint the reader with Montaigne's style, so central to the appeal that the reader experiences while strolling through the nearly 1200 pages of the volume. I will next describe some of his essays, including the process of writing. After this necessary long introduction, I will spell out, specifically, many discoveries of Montaigne which seem to anticipate those of Freud. Some of these have been described in a book of essays written by literary scholars *Psychoanalytic Approaches to Montaigne* (1997), and also in Wolf and Gedo's paper.

II. Montaigne's plan

Like the great Greek authors who wrote plays with great psychological insight, Montaigne was able to spell out many of the nuances of our unconscious, and origins of certain defense mechanisms, including the role of sexuality in amazing detail. This was in part due to an acute capacity for honest self-observation and his emphasis on the process of writing as a tool to discovery, a bit similar to free association. The only weak point, from a psychoanalytic perspective, is his view of women, rather characteristic of the 16th century and its several limitations.

Montaigne was the first Renaissance author to create a literary genre out of self revelation and self exploration. It was based partly on the belief that each man carries within him the entirety of the human condition. The writing of his essays also suggests that human observation is a worthwhile aspect of study, first for personal pleasure, and eventually evolving to the scientific. Philosophy became transformed into psychology, aided in the late 1600s by the work of Descartes.

Montaigne is cautious about embarking on this road. He writes:

Custom has made it a vice to talk about oneself and obstinately prohibits it; hating the boasting which always seems to be attached to any testimony about oneself. Instead of wiping the child's nose you cut it off [II, 6, p. 424].

He justifies his efforts further:

Here you have not my teaching but my study: the lesson is not for others, it is for me. Yet for all that, you should not be ungrateful to me for publishing it. What helps me can perhaps help somebody else meanwhile I am not spoiling anything: I am only using what is mine. And if I play the fool it is at my own expense and does no harm to anybody. Such foolishness as I am engaged in dies with me: there are no consequences [II, 6, p. 424].

That Montaigne achieved his goal is due to the fact that he does not consciously try to reach himself by an effort but rather avoids artificiality by simply observing what emerges without censoring. It is a prelude to free association The only prior example in trying to attain a view of the self would be St. Augustine in his confessions, which, apparently, Montaigne did not read.

In his introduction to the reader, he is both openly self-confident and hidden under a seductive openness, skillfully warning the reader not to waste his time in reading him!

> You have here reader a book whose faith can be trusted, a book which warns you from the start that I have set myself no other end but a private family one.... Here I want to be seen in my simple, natural everyday fashion without striving or artifice, for it is my own self I am painting. Here drawn from life you will read of my defects.

He ends his preface as follows:

> And therefore, Reader, I am the subject of my book: it is not reasonable that you should employ your leisure on a topic so frivolous and so vain, March 1st, 1580 [Screech, p. lxiii].

We would have to wait nearly 400 years before another author, Jean Jacques Rousseau, in his *Confessions,* would make himself the subject of a book. In contrast to Montaigne, Rousseau was an angry and rather bitter man who had had a most unhappy childhood.

III. What is an essay?

It is not easy to translate the French word *essai* into English. The closest I can come to is "trial effort" which suggests a degree of tentative uncertainty, an incomplete first stage, waiting to see what the result might be before proceeding further (Telle,1968). The scope of his *Essays* is truly amazing.

The English edition of his works totals 1283 pages. This includes 94 separate essays which were composed over a 20-year period. Reading the essays is a bit like traveling inside the mind of a very knowledgeable, cultured man, very familiar with great Greek and Latin authors such as Lucretius, Tacitus, Cicero, Heraclitus, Plato, and many other important historical figures, including several kings. At least one great author from the past is quoted in every essay. In search for truth, Montaigne justifies his reliance on the past; "I think it is less risky to write about the past than the present"[82] since the author has only to account for borrowed truth.

The essay, "On Schoolmaster's Learning" (1:25), reveals the ambivalence he felt towards his father's strict controlling behavior in overwhelming him with Latin and Greek literature. He was caught between his admiration of schoolmasters selected by his father and the frequent ridicule they were subject to in comedies, being seen as pedantic—having knowledge but unable to use it in any way. Montaigne stated that our minds are swamped by too much study and by too much matter, just as plants are swamped by too much water (p. 151).

It should be added that Montaigne had a purpose in writing in French rather than Latin. In an essay, "On Some Lines of Virgil's" (3, 5, p. 97), dealing very openly with sexuality in both genders, including all its organs and actions, he makes it clear that he thought many of his favorite readers would be women, and that they would not be well versed in Latin. He assumed they would take this essay in their private chambers. I will deal with this essay a bit later.

---

82 By "the present" Montaigne means contemporary external events, not his own thoughts or opinions.

IV. Montaigne's Life and Character

Montaigne's life itself is a mixture of paradoxes not usually associated with the life of a great writer. Prior to a literary career, Montaigne had a government job for many years. He was first a Conseiller in the parliament in Bordeaux, and eventually became mayor of Bordeaux for two successive terms during one of the most bloody and disturbed periods in the history of France, the period of the massacre of St. Barthelemy and of the religious wars which tore the country apart.

Following in the footsteps of his father, Montaigne first became a devoted public servant. He helped negotiate between opposed religious factions, and he gave frequent counsel to Henri III and later Henri de Navarre, the future king Henry the IV. He went to the court in Paris and traveled widely. In 1581, after having finished the first two volumes of his essays, Montaigne found himself traveling to Germany for a political trip. He was obviously held in high esteem and was elected mayor of Bordeaux, and reelected in 1583 for two more years.

As a political figure, Montaigne tells us that "my voice is so strong and booming that when I have needed to have a word in the ear of the great on a matter of some gravity, I have often put them to the embarrassment of asking me to lower it" (3, 13, p. 1235).

It is amazing how Montaigne was aware of the psychology of using his voice, and his capacity for self-humor; he continues:

> Volume and intonation contribute to the expression of meaning. It is for me to control them so that I can make myself understood. There is a voice for instructing, a voice for pleasing, or for reproving... when I am barking at my footman with a rough and harsh voice, a fine thing it would be if he came to me and said: Speak more softly. Master, I can hear you quite well [3, 13, p. 1235].

Montaigne clearly enjoyed alternating banter and seriousness.

His father, from a devout Catholic family, was also in the government, in the town of Perigueux, and became the mayor of Bordeaux. His mother (Antoinette de Lopez) of Spanish origin, came from a Morrano well-to-do family from Aragon. Her family lived in Toulouse, and his father was a business associate of the Eyquems. She played an obscure role in his life. She is only mentioned twice in the essays. Wolf and Gedo (1975) suggest that the castle of Eyquem, the dowry she brought to the marriage, did not afford her the respect she deserved, and that in her old age she bitterly complained about having been victimized by both her husband and her son. It was inferred she was rather cold and self centered.[83]

Montaigne was born the third child of 11 children and the oldest to survive. For the first 3 years of his life, he was sent to live with a peasant family, supposedly to develop close bonds with ordinary people. Montaigne writes about this unusual event:

> God gave me a good father (who got nothing from me apart from my acknowledgement of his goodness—one cheerfully given); from the cradle he sent me to be suckled in some poor village of his, keeping me there until I was weaned—longer in fact—training for the lowliest of lives among the people. He adds that his father hoped boys brought up in this manner would become accustomed to frugal and severely simple fares that they have to clamber down from austerity rather than scrambling up to it [3, 13, p. 1249].

As if Montaigne feels he needs to justify this behavior, he further adds:

---

83 I could not find data on which the above speculations were based. There is a brief passage I will quote which expands a bit on this way of upbringing. Both Wolf and Gedo are self psychologists.

My father's humor had yet another goal: to bring me closer to the common-folk and to the sort of men who need our help; he reckoned that *he should be brought to look kindly on the man who holds out his hand to me* rather than on one who turns his back on me and snubs me Montaigne adds that "the reason why he gave me godparents at baptism drawn from people of the most abject poverty was to bind me and join me to them.

On his return home he was completely taken in hand by his devoted and strict father. The latter hired Latin speaking servants who spoke to him only in Latin and a German tutor to speak to him only in that language. He purposely was not taught French for several years. His father died when Montaigne was 35 in 1568 and his mother amazingly outlived Montaigne. She lived most of her life close to him.

A bit like Don Juan he began to pursue women very early:

There is indeed some worry and wonder in confessing at what tender age I happened to fall first into Cupid's power—happened is indeed right for it was long before the age of discretion and awareness so long ago that I cannot remember anything about myself then. You can wed my fortune to that of Quartilla who could not remember ever having been a virgin [3, 13, p. 1234].

Montaigne was married in 1565 to Francoise de la Chassagne from a noble family, and had six daughters, only one of whom survived infancy. The first, Toinette died in 1570 at age 3 months. Montaigne obviously missed not having sons as this deprived him from reliving with his sons the sort of relationship he had enjoyed with his father. In 1571, Montaigne returned to his estates and started writing his essays, but he continued his political career at the same time traveling widely. His relationship with his wife was amicable but calm. Montaigne felt that passionate love was detrimental to freedom. He wrote that he was unsure whether he would not prefer "having produced a perfectly well formed product with the acquaintance of the muses rather than the acquaintance with his wife!" As Montaigne enjoyed joking, it is not clear whether such statements should be taken at face value. This rather misogynist attitude towards women is, however, often exemplified throughout his work. In his last essay, Montaigne quotes Alcibiades as:

> asking in amusement how Socrates could put up with the sound of his wife's perpetual nagging he replied, "just like those who get use to the constant grating of wheels drawing water from a well [3,13, p.1128].

In his adult life, Montaigne first became an important political figure in Bordeaux, where, in 1557, he met the true love of his life, the writer La Boetie, who died 5 years later (I will come back to the importance of La Boetie a bit later).

Later in life, he was plagued by a number of illnesses, including renal stones, starting at age 40, which at times caused him much pain. As a result, he wrote extensively about the importance of coming to terms with illnesses you could not control:

> I am of Crantor's opinion that we should neither resist illnesses stubbornly and rashly nor succumb to them out of weakness but yield to them naturally, according to our own mode of being and to theirs. We must afford them right-of-passage and I find that they stay less long with me who let them go their way [3, 13, p. 1235].

One of Montaigne's most endearing traits was his honesty and his desire not to hide something contrary to be discovered after his death. In the essay (1,

7) entitled "That Our Deeds are Judged by our Intentions," and completed just before he died, he wrote: 'If I can, I will prevent my death from saying anything not first said by my life" (p. 29).

As one proceeds, many characteristics of Montaigne's personality become evident: his equilibrium, his calm demeanor. He does not appear to have grudges or grievances. He seems happy, at peace with himself, and willing to share whatever comes down his path without attempting to hide or cover up any aspect of his personality, including his faults and weaknesses. He describes without shame, in almost a detached manner, his transitory impotence, including some psychological antecedents, and arrives at interesting views about the relation of his body to his mind. He is not stubborn, rather quite humble, at the same time that there is a hidden narcissistic streak feeding his urge to write which he skillfully hides via the opposite attitude. He also warns us that he is *mal forme* (poorly put together), and it is too late for him to be able to change, so we should not take him as a model! His motto was *Que Scay-je* ("What do I know") accompanied by the portrayal of a scale. He was clearly influenced by Socrates *connais toi toi meme*. He portrays himself as a man welcoming the ideas of others, not insisting he must be right, open to dialogue and willing to admit he was wrong without shame or anger. He respects the truth even when spoken by someone he dislikes.

I will first describe one rich essay as it is unusually revealing about Montaigne's character and attitude towards life. It is the sixth essay in the second book titled "On Practice," written in 1569. My reason for dwelling on this essay is that it contains the detailed narrative of Montaigne's most frightening encounter with death. This will demonstrate Montaigne's unusual capacity for insightful description of his slow recovery, Including the re-emergence of self-awareness and of returning memory. In a brilliant first section, he first describes how we can approach the experience of death through sleep:

Our ability to fall asleep which deprives us of all action and sensation is useless and unnatural were it not that Nature by sleep teaches us that she has made us up as much for dying as for living and already in this life shows us that everlasting state which she is keeping for us when life is over to get us accustomed to it and to take away our terror [p. 417–418].

He continues that it is not the moment of death which is frightening since it is so brief, it is the approaches to death which fill us with terror. It is "the power of imagination which makes the true essence factual sickness bigger by half" (p. 418). This certainly predates Freud's discovery of the role of fantasy in mental life.

Without any forewarning Montaigne then turns to what could have been an uneventful horseback ride in his estate. Suddenly, seemingly out of nowhere, one of his servants who wanted to show off and get ahead of his companions, came barreling by on a huge farm horse, crashing into Montaigne, causing his horse to topple over. Montaigne fell, lost consciousness for a few hours, and was feared dead by his terrified servants who carried him back to the chateau. This incident, in which he could almost have died, further aroused his anxiety about the fragility of life. It could be taken away at any moment. Yet, as though a dispassionate observer, he gave his narrative of the event: the huge brown colored stallion barreling into him, falling over his face, bleeding cuts over his body several feet from his horse, and his sword several meters away. Of course, he could not remember what happened after he fell, but he obviously gathered the details from his domestics and constructed the narrative afterwards. When his servants straightened him up, he said, "I threw up bucketfuls of pure clotted blood and I had to do the same several times on the way" (II, 6, p. 419). The closeness he came to death itself deeply impressed him. It could happen anytime. His sensations were closer to death than to life. One of the first things he did, even in a preconscious state, was:

> to order a horse to be provided for my wife whom I saw struggling and stumbling along the road which is difficult and steep. It might appear that such thoughts must have risen from a soul which is awake: nevertheless, I played no part in them. They were empty acts of apparent thinking provoked by sensations in my eyes and ears.

This again is a good prelude to the concept of splitting, in part precipitated by the trauma of the fall.

As he describes his slow recovery, he becomes aware of the power of his unconscious. He writes:

> "Everyman knows from his own experience that he has a part of his body which often stirs erect and lies down again without his leave. Now such passive movements which only touch our outside, cannot be called ours" [II, 6, p. 422].

This is an obvious reference to his erectile issues.

He obviously suffered from a concussion. Semiconscious, he saw his house but did not recognize it. He felt no affliction for himself or others, rather a kind of lassitude and utter weakness without pain. Clearly in an altered state he writes (later): "I was offered several medicines: I would not take any of them, being convinced I was fatally wounded in the head. It would have been—no lying—a very happy way to die" (II, 6, p. 423).

Montaigne then gives us a very accurate description of his slow recovery:

> When I began to come back to life and regained my strength which was two or three hours later. Only then did I feel myself all at once

linked with pain again having all my limbs bruised and battered by the fall; and I felt so ill two or three nights later that I nearly died a second time but of a livelier death! [LL, 6, p. 423].

Montaigne then shares with us the slow regaining of memory:

The last thing I could recover was my memory of the accident itself; before I could grasp it I got them to repeat several times where I was going, where I was coming from, what time it happened. As for the manner of my fall, they hid it from me for the sake of the man who had caused it and made up other explanations. But some time later, the following day when my memory happened to open up and recall to me the circumstances which I found myself honed in on that instant when I was aware of that horse coming at me. (For I had seen it at my heels and already thought I was dead, but that perception had been so sudden that fear had no time to engendered by it.) It appeared to me that lightning had struck my soul with a jolt and that I was coming back from the other world [II, 6, p. 423].

What does Montaigne tell us of what he learned from this terrifying incident: "In truth to inure yourself to death, all you have to do is to draw nigh to it" (II, 6 p. 424). It is significant that nowhere in his recounting of this terrifying incident does he blame his foolish servant for crashing into him. He does not express anger nor ever the wish to punish this man for his irresponsible behavior which nearly killed him.

V. Montaigne and La Boetie[84]

As mentioned before, the relationship with La Boetie was central to many aspects of Montaigne's psychology, and very much a factor in his deciding to write his essays. A bit like Freud and Fliess, he developed an intense erotic attachment to his friend saying, in explaining the relationship the famous line *Parce que c'était lu, par ce que c'était mo* (Because it was him, because it was me). This suggests an unexplainable necessity having little to do with external reality, more like a *coup de foudre*, an unexplained intense explosive love like a union between two souls. Early in their relationship La Boetie chided him for his many amorous escapades in his young adulthood.

His grief over the latter's death stimulated him to write his essays, partly in memory of his friend, but also as an identification with his friend, and also as a way of continuing a dialogue with him after death, especially since La Boetie gave Montaigne his entire library. Montaigne's desire to retreat in his tower was for him a way of dealing with his melancholy over the loss of his friend, and also of his father who died a few years after La Boetie. His loss fostered his creativity. He began writing his essays in 1570 while still continuing his political life. He tells us: "Recently I retired to my estate, determined to devote myself as far as I could to spending what little life I have left quietly and privately" (1, 8, 31).

We do not know if the relationship was ever consummated but I suspect it was not. Montaigne emphasizes the importance of soul love as a basis for "Amitie" (I, 28), in contrast with sexual union which is intense but vanishes after it is carried out, leaving no trace. He downgrades licentiousness in contrast to the loving relationship which needs to be sacred and revered. "He shared the platonic theory of mutual love that by kissing each other, lovers

---

84 See also Charpentier Francoise(1988) Figure de la Boetie dans les Essais de Montaigne; Rev. fr .psychanal (52,(1):175–189).

exchange souls and so literally 'live' in each other" (3, 5 p. 996). He makes clear that for him, "women are incapable of responding to such familiarity (i.e., loving friendship) and mutual confidence to sustain that holy bond of friendship nor do their souls seem firm enough to withstand the clasp of a knots lasting and so tightly drawn" (I, 28, p. 210). The essay on "Affectionate Relationships" (I, 28) was to have been followed by 29 sonnets from La Boetie but it was later decided by Montaigne to delete them from the final version. It may be relevant that Montaigne did not marry until three years after his friend's death. It will not be a surprise that mourning and death became a major topic in the essays to which I will return.

As his friend was also a writer, composing his essays allowed Montaigne another path to identify with him. Montaigne also quoted from La Boetie's works in his *Essays* and devotes one full essay to his sonnets. It is significant that the second essay "On Sadness" allows us to come closer to the man. Knowing that Montaigne was deeply involved in the mourning of his friend, we are surprised to read that he considers himself among those who are most free of this emotion. Only in the course of reading do we discover that what he defined as sadness is an exhibitionistic display of emotions which he contrasts with the genuine deeply felt grief of melancholy such as occurred with the death of La Boetie.

VI. Organization of the essays

One has to give up the idea that the title of each essay will be followed consistently or even broached except for the opening lines. His titles themselves can be even disorganized or, or sometimes playful *Comme nous pleurons et rions d'une même chose* (book I, 38) or "On a Monster Child" (book II, 30) or "One is Punished For Defending a Fort Without a Good Reason" (1, 14).

He does not follow a well defined course. Rather like a bee going from one flower to another he interrupts himself, changes topicsj, and drops the subject entirely, or more likely, will show how the ancient Latins or even Asiatic kings illustrated the point he wants to write about.

Until one gets used to it you get the impression of penetrating in the room of a messy teenager with clothing and books all over the place wondering "How did your mom allow you to get away with all this disorder?" But wait— in his own way we are led to discover an extraordinary mind.

In some ways he is quite proud of not reaching for perfection. He writes (3, 5, p. 989): "I may correct an accidental slip (I am full of them, since I run on regardless), but it would be an act of treachery to remove such imperfections as are commonly and always in me."

What stands out most when you immerse yourself in his pages is his sensitivity to the world around him, his acute perception of himself and his willingness to be open with all his faults, including those he is ashamed of, adding a touch of humor. He wrote in his last essay; "I am past the age of elementary schooling, old age has no other concern than to look after itself" (3,13,1231). Here are some of the titles of his essays to convey the breadth of his interests: from book 1: "Our Emotions Get Carried Away Beyond Us." "On Liars," "On Idleness," "On Fear," "1One Man's Profit Is Another Man's Loss," "On Cannibals," and "On Smells." In book 2: 1"How Our Mind Tangles Itself Up," and "On Not Pretending to Be Ill."

The essays were written during two periods; the first, which included books 1 and 2, were composed between roughly 1572 and1580, and sent for publication. Book 3 was finished around 1588. Montaigne also made many changes and additions as he matured and became more confident in his purpose. As he made progress the tone of his work changed, becoming more self-revealing and less abstract.

He states very plainly in the last essay he ever wrote that, in contrast with some kings who use their death as a permission to their followers to punish someone they did not dare kill when they were alive, "If I can, I will prevent my death from saying anything not first said by my life" (1, 7, p. 29)[85]

VII. Freud and Montaigne

Before tackling Montaigne's anticipation of psychoanalytic findings, it is necessary to review how and when psychoanalytically-minded writers were drawn to this extraordinary set of writings. I was surprised to see only two articles written by analysts on Montaigne. One, by Canestri, examines the psychology of old age and the use of diversion to manage getting old. The other, by Wolf and Gedo (1975), also examines in detail some of the connections between Montaigne's discoveries and those of Freud. As mentioned before, some essays using psychoanalytic theory were written by literary scholars. I will mention one close to my thinking: *Lire outre ce que l'auteur y a mis* by Gisele Matthieu-Castelani (p. 5–17) in Montaigne Studies (1997).

It should be said first that there are aspects of Montagne's life where he parallelled Freud. One most obvious example is the nature and function of deep male friendship: Montaigne and La Boetie, versus Freud and Fliess. In each case the fantasies around the relationship provided emotional support, an important paternal transference, and an outlet for passionate, noncarnal, homoerotic feelings, and finally a role as a selfobject, in the Kohutian mode, also fostering meaningful creativity.

Perhaps Montaigne's greatest discovery was to observe calmly his mind in action, a prelude to free association.

---

85 See Canestri (2009) for a consideration of the significance of old age in in Montaigne and in literature.

It seemed to me that the greatest favor I could do for my mind was to leave it in total idleness, caring for itself, concerned only with itself, and calmly thinking of itself. I hoped it could do that more easily since with the passage of time it had grown mature and put on weight[86] (1, 8, 31).

But to his surprise, what he discovers instead is a prelude to free associations:

On the contrary [my mind] it bolted off like a runaway horse[87], taking far more trouble over itself than it ever did over anyone else; it gives birth to so many chimeras and fantastic monstrosities one after another without order or fitness, that, so as to contemplate at my ease their oddness and their strangeness, I began to keep a record of them hoping in time to make my mind ashamed of itself [p. 31].

He labels his effort as *farouche and extravagant* (fearsome and excessive). He writes further:

But what displeases me about my soul is that she usually gives birth quite unexpectedly, when I am least on the lookout for them, to her profoundest, her maddest ravings which please me the most. Then they quickly vanish away because then and there I have nothing to jot them down on; it happens when I am on my horse, or at table or in bed—especially when on my horse, the seat of my wildest musings [3, 5, p. 961].

---

86 It is not entirely clear what Montaigne is expressing in his comparison of his mind with an overweight body.

87 It is likely that the metaphor of the horse is a reminder of the horse which nearly killed him earlier.

By describing in great detail the workings of his mind, Montaigne antedates the discoveries about the self (Grossman 1962), including the split between the experiencing self and the observing self. But the self is also defined as the true being which remains eternally one and unchanging. What is most admirable is that Montaigne understood the great value of what would have been considered as garbage by traditional philosophy.

One of the most significant discoveries of Montaigne is to discover three different levels to his productions: first, the clear and distinct ideas of reason (mirroring Freud's concept of the descriptive conscious of the topographic theory), second, the level of more subtle ideas and emotions less accessible and detached from the first layer, including dream images which can disappear (Freud's preconscious). The third layer is what is discovered by the work of self-observation, clearly related to Freud's level of the descriptive unconscious (see also Mathieu-Castellani, 1997). It includes ideas, images, sensations not apparently connected to what Montaigne sees as his functioning mind, and suddenly emerging unbidden in a disorderly fashion, sometimes with no apparent meaning. Montaigne emphasizes here the power of instincts to bring to the surface another that he at times does not recognize.

Without meaning to, he also foresaw some analytic concepts such as displacement as the following essay suggests: "How our soul discharges its emotions against false objects when lacking real ones" (vol 1, 4). He quotes Plutarch saying: "of those who dote over pet monkeys or little dogs, that the faculty for loving which is in all of us, rather than remaining useless, forges a false and frivolous object for want of a legitimate one" (p.19).

In another essay (3, 11, p. 1161) he beautifully describes rationalization:

I realize that if you ask people to account for "facts" they usually spend more time finding reasons for them than finding out whether they are true. They ignore the "whats" and expatriate on the "whys."

Anticipating Freud, he understands intuitively the value of free associations including paying attention to his dreams. He says:

> I do not dream much: when I do it is of grotesque things and of chimeras usually produced by pleasant thoughts, more laughable than sad. And although I maintain that dreams are loyal interpreters of our inclinations, there is skill in classifying them and understanding them [3, 13 p. 1247].

He is astute in understanding human emotions, anticipating Freud. For example, he writes, ahead of Shakespeare's Othello:[88] "Of all the spiritual illnesses jealousy is the one which has more things to feed it and fewer things which cure it" (3, 5, p. 977).

He is also aware of the advantage of fantasy over reality. He writes:

> And was Luna's humor not clearly lunatic when being unable to enjoy her beloved Endymion she went and put him to sleep for several months, feasting herself on the enjoyment of a boy who never stirred but in her dreams (3, 5, p. 99).

Like Freud, he notes "the fact that our delights and our waste matters are lodged higgedly-piggedly together; and that its highest pleasure has something of the groanings and destruction of pain" (3, 5, p. 992).

---

88 After finishing this paper, I came across the book "Shakespeare's Montaigne" (2014) in which the editor Stephen Greenblatt pointed out that, in all likelihood, Shakespeare read The Florio translation of Montaigne, and actually used two of his essays in his plays. This includes "On the affection of Fathers for their Children" for King Lear and "On the Cannibals" in The Tempest, where there are a number of references, including the name of the character Caliban, clearly derived from the word cannibal.

VIII. Montaigne and Sexuality

There are two essays in which Montaigne deals openly with sexuality and its different manifestations in men and women: "1On the Power of Imagination" and "On Some Lines of Virgil," in which he stresses the danger of women's sexuality for men, and the failures of sexual union to satisfy some of the soul's desires.

There is perhaps no other topic which preoccupied Montaigne as much throughout his life. This is based on a number of reasons combining biological, psychological, and relational issues. First, Montaigne suffered his whole lifetime from a feeling of inferiority because his penis was far too small and inadequate to fulfill his needs. He suffered from periodic impotence and attempted to compensate for this insufficiency in a variety of ways. Writing became a pleasurable substitute for his deficient sexuality. He delighted in quoting from famous Greek and Latin authors on this topic, reassuring himself that he was in good company. He feared that women could not love him properly.

He quoted Horace writing: "I am ashamed to find myself amid this green and ardent youth, whose member firmer stands in its undaunted pride, than a young tree upon a mountain side" (2, 18 p. 666).

His persistent feeling of sexual inadequacy found two outlets. Montaigne used ancient poetry, as Starobinski puts it, "as a prosthesis to make up for a deficit in the French language and for its taboos" (Starobinski 1982, p. 206). This is reminiscent of Freud who used Latin to express, sensorially, certain feelings which German could not.

In one example, Freud recommended the following treatment for one of his neurotically troubled female patients: *"Penis normalis dosim repetatur!"* Here is Montaigne referring instead to the impact of having sex on a man:

It is health bringing and appropriate for loosening up a sluggish mind and body; as a doctor I would order it for a man of my mold and disposition as readily as any other prescription, so as to liven him upland, keep him in trim until he is well on in years and to postpone the onset of old age [3, 5, p. 1009].

The essay on some lines of Virgil deserves some closer attention as it reveals some of Montaigne's most personal views on sexuality. In this essay, Montaigne does not quote the lines from Virgil which inspire him until 12 pages of this over-60-pages-long essay: in fact, one of the longest he composed. The lines from the *Aeneid VIII* describe an erotic moment between Venus and one of her lovers. Not until this point in his essays does Montaigne broach the topic of sexuality and the difference between men and women in as great detail, including the most intimate aspects of their relation including disturbances in his own sexual functioning. What would motivate him to do this? Shame, guilt, or the wish to tease the reader or, more on the surface, a disinterest in orderliness and the wish to proceed in his own personal style of disordered order? Montaigne introduces the lines from Virgil by saying: "Poetry can show us love with an air more loving than love itself. Venus is never as beautiful, stark naked, quick and panting as she is here in Virgil."

This suggests that Montaigne put greater value in the fantasy, spiritual aspects of love, as was typical of the renaissance, rather than on the purely carnal enactments. He adds that few men have married their mistresses without repenting of it. In general, he does not see women as able to prefer the more spiritual aspects. He writes: "When Socrates was asked whether it was more appropriate to take or not to take a wife he replied, 'whatever you do you will be sorry'(3, 5, p. 9610).

He adds: "By my own design I would have fled from marrying wisdom herself if she would have had me." And a bit later: "Most of my doings are governed by example, not by choice [3, 5, p. 962].

This essay openly confronts gender-change, sexuality, penis envy, and impotence due to castration anxiety, and its management in men, again anticipating Freud's discoveries. On one of his trips passing through Vitry le Francois, Montaigne met an old man who, until age 22, was known as a girl called Marie. He said that Marie had been straining to jump at this time, and his male organs suddenly appeared. He was named Germain and remained unmarried, developing a full beard. Was this a case of transgender rather than hermaphroditism?

Montaigne then quotes a song from girls in the village, warning each other not to take great strides, lest they become boys like Marie Germain (I am not sure whether this is a fear or a wish!). Montaigne adds that:

It is not surprising that this sort of occurrence happens frequently. For if the imagination does have power in these matters, in girls it dwells so constantly and so forcefully on sex that it can (in order to avoid the necessity of so frequently recurring to the same thoughts and harsh yearnings) more easily make that male organ into a part of their body [1, 21, p. 121].

Montaigne dwells at length on the general fragility of male members (particularly vulnerable on the first encounter), anticipating Freud's discovery of castration anxiety: He writes:

Married men have time at their disposal: if they are not ready they shouldn't try to rush things. Rather than fall into perpetual wretchedness, by being struck with despair at a first rejection, it is

477

better to fail to make it properly on the marriage-couch, full as it is of feverish agitation, and to wait for an opportune moment more private and less challenging.

He adds that women are wrong to greet us with those affected provocative appearances of unwillingness which snuff out our ardor just as they kindle it [p. 114]. In another passage he refers to the power of the male member to become erect when it is not desired. This suggests two possibilities: either Montaigne was embarrassed to be aroused by other women or second that he was embarrassed by the intrusion of sexual arousal with La Boetie. We shall never know which or both are accurate.

In the same essay Montaigne gives vent to rather misogynistic attitudes towards women along with fearsome power. He mentions that: "In antiquity it was held that certain Scythian women were animated by anger against anybody; they could kill him simply by looking at him."[89]

A bit later he gives an accurate description of what Freud would later describe as the unconscious:

Our members have emotions proper to themselves which arouse them or quiet them down without leave from us. How often do compelling facial movements bear witness to thoughts which we were keeping secret so betraying us to those who are with us? (p. 117).

He describes the close stitching of mind to body, each communicating its fortunes to the other (p. 118). As an astute observer of projection, he states:

---

89 This may be related to the power of the Medusa who could turn men who looked at her into stone

It has angered me to see husbands hate their wives precisely because they are doing them wrong. At the very least we should not love them less when the fault is ours; at the very least they ought to be made dearer to us by our regrets and our sympathy [3, 5, p. 962].

He is also aware of the trauma that angry parents may impose on future generations. He writes of certain women:

I know of some who sincerely complain that before the age of discretion they were dedicated to debauchery. Vicious parents may be the cause, or the force of necessity which is a cruel counsellor [3, 5, p. 981].

In the latter part of this essay Montaigne highlights what he sees as the difference between men and women. The passage I am quoting was added after the essay was finished, as an addendum. I am not sure whether the attitudes he ascribes to men are more than a projection of his own views! He writes again using the ancients as a screen:

A young Greek called Thraconides was so in love with love that having won his lady's heart he refused to enjoy her so as not to weaken glut and deaden by the joy of lying with her that unquiet ardor in which he gloried and on which he fed [3, 5, p. 997].

He continues:

Foods are better when they are dear. Think how far kisses, the form of greeting peculiar to our nation, have had their grace cheapened by their availability.

Montaigne is horrified by the thought of a body giving itself to him but lacking love. He is following the ideal of platonic love. He warns the danger women represent for men: He feels the role of women should be to "accept, obey and consent."

> He adds: "this is why nature has made them able to do it at any time: we men are only able to do it occasionally and unreliably'" (3, 5, p. 1001). Montaigne sees women as: suffering from a base disorder which drives them to change so frequently and which impedes them from settling their affections firmly on one person whatsoever as we can see in that goddess Venus to whom is attributed so many changes of lovers (3, 5, p. 1001).

It seems in his view that the danger of being unable to satisfy a woman is ever present. Women seem to seek more carnal satisfaction than real love. Montaigne was also untrusting of women's capacity for deep love. In an essay; "On three good wives" (2, 35, p. 842) he wrote:

> It is no good widows tearing their and clawing their faces. I go and whisper straight in the ear of their chambermaid or private secretary "How did they get on? What were they like when living together?" I always remember that proverbial saying: *Jactantius moerent qua minus dolent*[90] [women who weep most ostentatiously grieve least].

I believe that the last paragraph of the essay deserves full attention as it reveals Montaigne's deepest wishes and fears. The entire process of writing becomes a substitute sexual outlet. Montaigne may feel a bit embarrassed

---

90 Tacitus Annals II.

in dealing so openly with the topic of impotence that he apologizes near the end referring to "these infamous jottings which I have loosed in a diarrhea of babble—a violent and at times morbid diarrhea. Embarrassed by the almost uncontrollable flow of words" (This essay is one of the longest, almost 71 pages.) Montaigne then quotes some lines from Catullus:

> As when an apple secretly given by her admirer breaks loose from the chaste bosom of a maiden as she starts to her feet on hearing her mother's footstep, forgetting she had concealed it beneath her flowing robes; it lies there on the ground while a blush suffuses her face and betrays her fault [3, 5 p. 1016].

Starobinski analyzes this poetic quote:

> The analogy has to do with making visible what is hidden. The passage casts Montaigne in the role of a young maiden whose love is revealed by the token she is incapable of hiding.... The power of poetry manifests itself one last time: it is rejuvenating, feminizing. It evokes the contact between the ripe fruit and the young breast in all its red heat [Starobinski, p. 212].

The apple then is clearly the gift Montaigne like a young maiden bestows upon us through his essays, a hidden love prize, warm and erotic, which also leads to the author's rejuvenation and transformation into a young blushing maiden. The apple is also a reminder of the apple Eve gave to Adam combining the awakening of knowledge with that of guilty sexuality.

IX. Last Essay: On Experience

This last essay could not be completed as Montaigne died before actually finishing it. It summarizes many of Montaigne's ideas about how to live one's life and deal with bodily ailments and concerns about his declining health.[91] Based on Epicure's philosophy his basic tenet was to take the time to live, to enjoy the current moment, and not to rush *Festina lente* (rush slowly) as Erasmus said. The opening sentence of this last essay explains the title, and is a quote from Aristotle's beginning of Metaphysics: "No desire is more natural than the desire for knowledge. We assay all the means that can lead us to it. When reason fails us we make use of experience."

It is very central to Montaigne that priority is given to feeling rather than pure intellectual knowledge. "In this universe of things, I ignorantly and negligently let myself be guided by the general laws of the world. I shall know it well enough when I feel it" (2, 6, 379). Does this not anticipate the emphasis Freud placed on the role of feelings and the defensive possibility of intellectualization?

Montaigne's curiosity and search for more is endless:

It is only our individual weaknesses which make us satisfied with what has been discovered by others or by ourselves in this hunt for knowledge: an able man will not be satisfied with it." [3,13 p. 1211].

His technique is well defined: I study myself more than any other subject. That is my metaphysics that is my physics [3,13, p. 1217].

---

91 From 1578 on Montaigne suffered from frequent bouts of renal colic due to stones causing almost unbearable symptoms of severe pain.

Montaigne is very astute in how we don't like to hear criticism (3, 13, p. 1222):

> You need good strong ears to hear yourself frankly judged; and since there are few who can undergo it without being hurt those who risk undertaking it do us a singular act of love, for it is to love soundly to wound and vex a man in the interests of his improvement.

Dealing with his increasing renal colic occupied much of his preoccupations. He wrote:

> But is there anything so delightful as that sudden revolution when I pass from the extreme pain of voiding my stone and recover in a flash the beautious light of health full and free as happens when our paroxysms of colic are at their sharpest and most sudden (3,13, p. 1241).

Montaigne devised the best way to deal with his pain; "Just put up with it. That's all you need. No other prescription: enjoy your sport, dine, ride, do anything at all if you can your indulgences will do you more good than harm" (3, 13, p.1242).

He adds a bit later:

> Anyone who is afraid of suffering suffers already of being afraid. We must learn to suffer whatever we cannot avoid. Our life is composed, like the harmony of the world of discords, as well as of different tones sweet and harsh, sharp and flat, soft and loud. If a musician liked only some of them, what could he sing?

As expected death preoccupies him throughout this last essay: "You are not dying because you are ill, you are dying because you are alive. Death can kill you well enough without illness to help her" [3, 13, p. 1239].

One of the ways he manages his preoccupation with death is to focus on the immediate present:

> When I dance, I dance. When I sleep, I sleep; and when I am strolling alone through a beautiful orchard, although part of the time my thoughts are occupied by other things, for part of the time too I bring them back to the walk, to the orchard, to the delight of being alone there and to me [3, 13, p. 1258].

As he ponders the course his life has taken, he comes to terms with the best way to look at his trajectory:

> Our duty is to bring order to our morals not to the material for a book not to win provinces in battle but order and tranquility for the conduct of our life. Our most great and glorious achievement is to live our life fittingly. Everything else—reigning, building, laying up treasure—are at most tiny props and small accessories.

In one of the latter pages, he clarifies how he comes to accept the inevitability of death:

> That is why I so order my ways that I can lose my life without regret, not however because it is troublesome or importunate but because one of its attributes is that it must be lost ... Above all now when I see my span so short, I want to give it more ballast; I want to arrest the swiftness of its passing by the swiftness of my capture, compensating for the speed with which it drains away by the intensity

of my enjoyment. The shorter my lease of it the deeper and fuller I must make it.

X. Conclusions

I can find no better way to conclude my paper than with a quote from Voltaire who wrote about Montaigne in a letter from Paris to *Comte de Tressan* in August 1746:

> He bases his thoughts on those of the celebrated figures of antiquity; he weighs them up; he wrestles with them. He converses with them, with his reader and with himself. Always original in the presentation of his objects, always full of imagination, always a painter and what appeals to me is that he was always capable of doubt.

In a sense we profited from Montaigne's sexual inadequacy, as it prodded him to write one of the richest and detailed descriptions of one of the greatest minds of the 16th century as enriched by an encyclopedic knowledge of the greatest Greek and Latin authors.[92]

---

92 After I finished the paper a colleague told me about a Florida State University thesis by Jennifer Countryman (2012) with the title. Two ways to think or Montaigne and Freud on the Human Paradox. Although the topic relates to my work it is written in a very abstract manner and is not well related to my approach. I also was informed by an editor of the existence in Montaigne Studies of an issue titled "Psychoanalytic Approaches to Montaigne." I quote one article which was relevant by Mathieu-Castellani.

REFERENCES

Bakewell, S. (2010). *How to Live or a Life of Montaigne.* London: Chatto and Windus.

Canestri, J. (2009). Les figures du temps dans la vieillesse et la méthode de la diversion chez Montaigne. *Revue française de psychanalyse.* (73)(5):1457–1463.

Charpentier, F. (1988). figure de La Boetie dans les essais de Montaigne. *Rev Fr Psychanal.* (52)(1):175–189.

Greenblatt, S. & Platt, P. (2014). *Shakespeare's Montaigne, The Florio Translation of the Essays.* New York: New York Review of Books.

Grossman, W.I. (1982). The Self as Fantasy: Fantasy as Theory. *JAPA* 30:919–937.

Kritzman, L. (1997). Psychoanalytic Approaches to Montaigne, Preface in *Montaigne Studies* 9(1).

Masud Khan, M. (1975). Freud and the crisis of responsibility in modern psychotherapeutics. *International review of Psychoanal.* 20:25–31.

Mathieu-Castellani, G. (1997). Lire "outre ce que l'auteur y a mis." *Montaigne Studies* (9)(2):5–17.

Montaigne, M, de. (2003). *The Complete Essays, ed* Screech, M.A. London: Penguin Books.

Starobinski, J. (1985). *Montaigne in Motion.* Chicago: Univ of Chicago Press.

Telle, E. V. (1968). A propos du mot «essai» chez Montaigne. *Bibliothèque d'humanisme et Renaissance* 30(2):225–247.

Wolf, E.S. & Gedo, J.E. (1975). The last introspective psychologist before Freud. *Annual. Psychoanal.* (3):297–310.

CHAPTER 18

Pascal: Vacuum, Void, and Emptiness
[previously unpublished.]

ABSTRACT: Based on limited biographical information, this paper tried to formulate some hypotheses concerning Pascal's fascination with vacuum and dread of void and emptiness. Anzieu's paper on Pascal's phobia and early traumata including the death of his mother at age three could be further studied based on Green's notion of the negative and the Botella's study of figurability.

INTRODUCTION

Why would you want to spend an hour of your time talking about Blaise Pascal (1623–1662), a 17th century French philosopher about 50 years younger than Montaigne? His issues and thinking are so up-to-date and relevant to our current political issues that he is worthy of a conference. It turns out this man had a brilliant career in 3 separate fields, and was considered as gifted as Mozart in the first field which captivated him: geometry and calculus, which he discovered at age 12. He solved some problems which had remained unsolved since Euclid. He was always in search of explanations for whatever problems he came across. For example, in early adolescence he noticed that a fork hitting a valuable porcelain would produce a musical sound. This stimulated him to write a complex paper on the nature of musical sound.

After mathematics, his second field of interest was philosophy, mostly centered on his *Pensees* (translated as thoughts or better: "Reflections") where, in addition to religion, he discussed issues about the dual nature of man, his humanity and his connection with the universe, both big and small, which he could explore with his mind always in search of "La Verite" (the truth).

The last area of his work centered primarily on religion, to which he devoted most of his energy during the last 10 years of his life, writing a series of letters, *les Provinciales*, devoted in part to clarifying the struggle between the Jesuits and the Jansenists.

France in the 17th century

A few words about 17th-century France will give us a frame for his life. Pascal lived during the end of the reign of Louis XIII, and at the beginning of the reign of Louis XIV, nicknamed the "Sun King." At that time France was a very troubled country recovering from endless wars of religion between Catholics, the main religion, and the Huguenots. Although theoretically a unified country, France was divided in a number of "Duchies." You may recall that in 1430, Joan of Arc, the liberator of France from the English, and beloved by the Armagnacs, was captured by the Burgundians and sold to the English who burned her at the stake in Rouen after a mock trial. France was also struggling with armed private groups which stole grains and supplies, raped women, and destroyed entire villages without any possible retaliations. Cities were also fortified to keep out invaders, and some Huguenots cities, such as La Rochelle, sometimes asked the British for help to fight the Catholic government troops which tried unsuccessfully to lay siege and capture the city and its port.

Paris was also the seat of considerable unrest in spite of prime minister Richelieu's attempt to restore order. For him the greatest danger was the nobility which was intriguing against him. The most recent unrest was labeled: "La Fronde," a violent fight between the government and nobility, largely over taxes imposed by the government to fund endless wars with Spain and the Habsburg monarchies. Also at that time, witchcraft was in the air and very much feared, and medicine was at a frighteningly primitive state.

There is an amusing story involving Blaise's father, Etienne, and his relation to the powerful prime minister, Richelieu. The latter banished him over a disagreement the two had about some taxes Richelieu wanted to impose on the population. Pascal's father had to flee Paris and return to Clermont Ferrand, his native city. Purely by chance Pascal's younger sister Marguerite was asked in 1639 at age 14 to perform in a children's play in front of Richelieu. She so captivated him that he immediately pardoned Pascal's father and appointed him commissioner of taxes in Rouen, a city where the tax codes were in chaos because of recent uprisings.

Early Life

In contrast to Montaigne we have unusually rich details about Pascal's early life because of two biographies, one written by Gilberte, his older sister, and a much more detailed one written by his niece Marguerite with the same name as his younger sister. It is not possible to verify the accuracy of these, the only two documents we have concerning his early life.

Born in 1622 in Clermont Ferrand, a large city in Auvergne, Pascal lost his mother at age three, shortly after she gave birth to his sister. They had hired a woman to breast-feed him in addition to a nurse who came into the household after the mother's death. According to the niece's biography, Pascal developed, at age two, an undiagnosed, unusually severe, and puzzling illness which, according to his niece, lasted almost the entire year. At one point he felt cold, appeared dead for several days, with no pulse, no breathing. His grandfather thought he had died but the family delayed burying him. According to the story told by the niece in her biography, Pascal's mother allowed very poor women to enter their home and she would give them a small amount of money. Apparently one of these women had the reputation of being a sorceress. Pascal's parents did not believe in sorceresses but they continued to allow the woman free entry. Eventually Pascal's grandfather confronted and threatened this woman who then confessed that she had indeed cast a spell on the baby, and that another life would have to be given up to save the child. The family eventually threw a cat out of the window which died upon hitting the ground. The rest is hard to believe but the sorceress said she required a certain cataplasm of three different plants to be administered on the infant's belly. The apothecary carried out this request and the cataplasm was placed as ordered. As the family anxiously waited, nothing happened, and as the woman was about to leave, she said she had forgotten to say that the child would only recover that same day after midnight passed. Apparently by one a.m. Pascal did return to life and could drink wine and water first, and then milk.

From earliest childhood Pascal suffered from severe anxieties. He could not tolerate seeing running water without breaking down, nor could he tolerate seeing his parents fondle each other even though he loved being fondled by either. This is suggestive of very early primitive scene anxieties.[93]

During his entire life he suffered from severe chronic intestinal pain, diarrhea, and debilitating headaches due to an incompletely closed fontanelle. He also had periodic paralysis of his legs. For unclear reasons, at age 24 he

---

93 *I will return to these anxieties so well described by Greenacre (1941) in the second part of her paper on "The Predisposition to Anxiety."*

could no longer swallow liquids except if warm, and only drop by drop. He died at age 39 of a burst infected colon. Pascal's attitude towards his frequent pains was that this was a just punishment from God which brought him closer to Christ's sufferings. In a masochistic fashion he also wore a special shirt with pins and spines.

In some of his writings he includes some amusing passages anticipating Moliere (#82, 107–108). This must have been personally relevant for both Pascal and Moliere as the medical profession at that time was abysmally ignorant, relying on bleeding or enemas or herbs to mismanage most illnesses.

Pascal's father, a tax collector unusually knowledgeable in mathematics, never remarried and, unusually impressed with the brightness of his children, decided he would educate them himself. As a result, they never attended school, and were participants in the father's connection with well-known mathematicians.

Before turning to his enormous productions, I will give you a few more details about his life as a young adult. Initially he was very much involved in the world and its pleasures. It is not clear whether he ever engaged in sexual intercourse. Following a few religious episodes which I will describe, he decided after age 30 to turn away from the world and lead an ascetic life. Shortly afterwards, to the surprise of his friends and relatives, he turned down an offer of marriage to a young woman, *Mademoiselle de Mesmes,* whom he was actually quite fond of and had, in earlier times, actually hoped to marry when reaching a proper age. He also befriended Charlotte, the daughter of one of his friends, M. de Roannez. She apparently suffered from severe physical pains. Between September and December 1656, he exchanged 12 letters advising her how to deal with this problem, offering many suggestions of biblical passages he felt might be helpful in accepting her fate. It is likely that he was also in love with her, otherwise why would he exchange so many letters with a young unmarried woman in such a short period of time? Pascal denounced marriage saying that it is the most dangerous and the lowest of Christian conditions. He felt it was necessary to break the power of sensual desire in order to connect with true faith.

Following his growing interests in religion, he adopted a very ascetic life, to the extreme in the last few years of his life, getting rid of any ornaments or tapestries in his house, letting his domestics go, and eating very simple foods in the kitchen with the cook, and also cleaning and washing his dishes and making his own bed.

The Pleiade volume dedicated to his works includes a piece labeled *Discours sur les passions de l'amour* (Discourse on the Passions of Love); but raises some concerns about whether Pascal actually wrote it. It includes the following paragraph (translated by me): "Can I convey the delight one experiences when one shapes all of our behavior with the goal of pleasing a person one holds in high esteem? . . . You strive to find means to reveal yourself, spending as much time on this project as though you were confronting the woman you love."

Scientific writings

I will now turn to a serious consideration of his writings, first scientific, then philosophical, and finally religious.

As early as age 16, he focused on geometry dealing with conic sections. He formulated what became known as Pascal's theorem, stating that if a hexagon is inserted in a circle the three interaction points of opposite sides lie on a straight line. This work was so skilled that Descartes was convinced that his father, rather than Blaise had devised this solution. It also turned out that Pascal's ideas were so complex that a computer program was named after him in the last century. At age 19 he was the first to invent a complicated adding machine called *a Pascaline* which could help his father verify tax accounts.

In 1647, at age 25, Pascal became fascinated by the problem of the existence of vacuum. He tried to disprove the belief that both Aristotle and Pascal's contemporary, Descartes, maintained: that nature abhors a vacuum. He devised an ingenious method to tackle this problem. He filled a long glass tube, closed at one end, with mercury, and inverted the filled tube over a pool of liquid mercury; the tube emptied itself partially, due to air pressure leaving a void at the top. He also repeated this experiment at various altitude levels, having some friends and relatives of his climbing with him the *Puy de Dome,* the extinct volcano in Auvergne, showing how the mercury became lower as one climbed the mountain with the gradually decreasing air pressure. The question remained: What was left at the top of the inverted tube once the column of mercury settled down, emptied of mercury once the tube was inverted? Was it some ethereal substance as Descartes insisted, or just a complete void? His adversaries were stunned by his experiments.

Philosophic works

I will now turn to the meat of my presentations; the section of his writings entitled *les Pensees* or in English "Thoughts" or "Reflections." This part of Pascal's literary production, in contrast to Montaigne's essays, were never meant for publication. These were brought together after his death by his nephews and other relatives, including his niece Marguerite. As a result, a solid interpretation of this work is very problematic. Unlike Montaigne, Pascal did not write delineated essays but rather scribbled on pieces of paper, often haphazardly, and even, on one instance, for an especially important thought, had the piece of paper actually sewn into his clothing, and carefully taking it to a new piece of clothing when appropriate. Time allowing, I will read a few samples of his works. Here are some of its main themes:

1. The two natures of man: beast-like, carnal versus the thinking person able to reason and govern himself.
2. The relation of man to the universe.
3. The problem of probability and the theory of the wager concerning the existence of God.
4. The role of what Pascal describes as our emotions and how they will most of the time lead us astray.

Here is one of the key thoughts (#347):

Man is but a reed, but the most feeble thing in nature; but he is a thinking reed. The entire universe need not arm itself to create him. A vapor, a drop of water suffices to kill him. But if the universe were to crush him man would still be more noble than that which killed him, because he knows that he dies and the advantage which the universe has over him; the universe knows nothing of this. All our dignity consists, then, in thought. By it we must elevate ourselves, and not by space and time which we cannot fill. Let us endeavor, then to think well; that is the principle of morality.

There is no doubt that this idealization of thinking was in part an assist to mastering early trauma. Thinking allowed Pascal to master his feelings of defect, physical inferiority, and chronic physical suffering. He wrote very beautifully two passages illustrating the contrast between the infinitely large and the infinitely small, which from a slightly different perspective could be seen as infinitely large. Read #72 pages 100 and 101. His fascination between the infinitely large and the infinitely small can also be found in many passages by Leonardo da Vinci.

Later, in the *Pensees,* there is a long section labeled "Emotions." This section will contain many crucial concepts which would not be clarified until the work of Freud. By the term emotions he includes a number of concepts ranging from fantasies to irrational unchallenged beliefs and biases sometimes utilized by authorities to fool us and make us accept their authority. He writes: "*le coeur a ses raisons que la raison ne connait pas.*" This could be translated as: "The heart has its reasons which our reasonable self is unaware of." By this he means that our instinctive emotional self is unaware or unconscious about what can motivate us. This is an early description of the power of our unconscious in affecting our feelings. There is another well-known passage where Pascal laments the human being who cannot be at peace with himself alone in a room.

I will now turn to the role of the "Pari," in English, the "Bet," or the gamble with a point of entry into Pascal's religious thinking. Perhaps his most famous discovery along with the help of Fermat, one of the great mathematicians of the period was to devise the concept of "Probability." In 1654 Pascal developed a system to predict mathematical futures using all available data.

As an example, he wondered how many throws would be required if you played with two dice to assure the possibility of having a double six. Using a complex mathematical equation which would form the basis of what would become risk management, he concluded that 24 shots would likely end badly whereas 25 throws would vastly increase your chance of winning. He invented the Pascal triangle to figure out the multiple possibilities available and thus to accurately calculate the risk or chance for an event to happen.

Since then, the concept of risk management has permeated our modern life including economics, the stock market, social sciences, insurance companies and in a broader sense the ability to predict the safety of cars and planes. Pascal also used the concept of wager concerning the existence of God to be discussed in the next section devoted to his religious writings.

Religious writings

Very early in his life Pascal saw God and religion as a true rescue from the pettiness and distortions created by our imagination as described above. After having extensively devoted himself to geometry, he concluded that basic axioms which are the basis of mathematical reasoning cannot be proven through human methods. These principles, he asserted, can only be grasped through intuition. For him this underscores the necessity for submitting to God in search for truths. As early as 1638 he composed an introduction to geometry written for children brought up at Port Royal, the Jansenist convent which came to occupy the center of his life during his last 10 years . He was fascinated by the method of approaching problems of geometry as an example of genuine search for truth. As an introduction to this book, he wrote the following:

> "There are three principal objects in the study of truth; The first is to discover it when seeking after it, the second is to demonstrate it when you possess it, and the third is to distinguish it from the false when you examine it." (p. 359).

In 1646 when Pascal was 24, his father broke his hip and was taken care of by two physicians who were Jansenists and following the work of Augustus introduced Pascal to their view of God and grace. These were still a small group separate from the bulk of the Catholic church and criticized by the Pope.

In addition to the above, three incidents influenced Pascal in his adhesion to this group. His younger sister Marguerite her face disfigured by smallpox, chose a religious life in Port Royal in 1652 against the strong opposition of Pascal who was rather emotionally lonely and also very attached to her, feeling that because of his poor health he needed her as much as she needed him. By then his older sister had married and moved away. Some time later, his niece named Marguerite developed a lacrimal infection which the doctors could not cure. She went to a church which owned a relic: a spine from Christ's crown of thorns. She then touched the relic to her infected part. She then asserted she was completely cured after this incident. This had a profound effect on Pascal who wrote a number of pensées on miracles. On another occasion Pascal listened to a sermon which connected deeply with his soul and determined him to devote himself entirely to the religious cause. He was so impressed by this sermon that he wrote a note to himself concluding: "I will not forget thy word. Amen." He seems to have sewn this note to his clothes and always transferred it when he changed them.

Relevant to these two events there are a few scattered thoughts about the phenomena of miracles. Pascal is torn between relying on the miracles to prove his faith versus being unable to explain them through reason! He writes (my translation, #423) "The miracles and the proofs of our religions are not of such a nature that one could say that they are absolutely convincing but they are of such a nature that one cannot say that it is unreasonable to believe in them! They are fueled by conviction."

Pascal is the man who could say: "I own a truth, this is all my strength, if I lose it, I am lost." But this truth which he possesses is neither abstract nor impersonal as he described early in his career: It is a truth which connects with the heart and fills it after having emptied it of everything else including self love. It provides joy, faith and love including a fusion with God who comes to govern it. The connection with God is eternal and is fueled by the spirit of charity which is always to be renewed and never ceases. It becomes clear that the truth which Pascal arrives at is beyond reason and cannot be questioned by reason the way a geometric problem could be. One could say that for Pascal, religion and the solid belief in God helped him manage the existence of void and emptiness which played such a big role in his life. It also enabled him to put aside the key role of reason and thought which earlier he praised as distinguishing men from animals. Pascal adds in another piece (#425): "Our world is not founded on truth. Truth wanders unknown amongst humanity. God has covered it with a veil which prevents those who do not hear its voice to recognize its existence."

I will now turn to his religious writings in the last 8 years of his life, after these miracles which had so impressed him. His father had died three years before in 1651, affecting him deeply.

The Provincial Letters

This work consists of nearly two dozen very long letters which are not easy to read and are overburdened with religious arguments. Because of the explosive nature of their main argument, they were published under the name Louis de Montalte. In a humorous fashion, Pascal explained that he was in the habit of writing long letters because he did not have the time to write a short one. Struggling with religious differences, pretending to take them seriously, Pascal loved to poke fun at the priests, and sarcastically describes his journey as he wanders from one to the other trying to understand the meaning of *au pouvoir prochain* difficult to translate in English, to capture the subtle nuance of the indeterminate transfer of power. ("The ambiguity of the unnamed power to come next.")

He refers sarcastically to endless discussions by groups of professors in the Sorbonne who seem unable to agree about the meaning of key words including also "grace." This series roundly criticized the Jesuits who believed that all men receive all the grace they need and, therefore, can behave as they wish and obtain forgiveness of their sins by buying with their money the goodwill and forgiveness of the church. In contrast, the Jansenists believed that grace can only be obtained through proper religious behavior and the belief that it is only God who has the capacity to judge us. They also believed that only a small portion of men would be predestined to be saved by God. Pascal correctly condemned the Jesuits as guilty of casuistry, justifying lax behavior. This profound disagreement reached the king, Louis the XIV, who ordered that Pascal's book be shredded and burned. In 1661, Port Royal was condemned and closed. Pascal's younger sister died this same year. The dispute went to pope Alexander VII who first sided with the Jesuits but came to change his mind and was persuaded by a long letter Pascal wrote to him.

I will now turn to the concept of the wager meant to affect those people who were uncertain about the existence of God.

The Wager

This piece was meant for the libertines, those who in the 17th century do not believe in God, and placed their personal freedom above everything. Pascal started by pointing out that reason alone cannot prove or disprove the existence of God but that life forces us to make a choice by its very nature. In a somewhat disingenuous manner Pascal analyzes the choices open to us:

1. you must wager (no choice)
2. If you side with God existing, you can gain all, including an eternal life, and lose nothing.

3. If God does not exist, you have lost nothing.

4. So then wager without hesitation.

5. Merely by existing in a state of uncertainty, we are forced to choose for practical purposes.

What Pascal does not consider is that according to his wager, belief in God is not based on true love or faith but is based on a very calculating process of figuring out which is more advantageous. Also, if the libertine chooses to believe in God and he does not exist, he has actually given up earthly pleasures, including sexuality, and gotten nothing in return.

A century later, Voltaire regarded the wager as indecent and childish. It also assumes that if the person sides with the positive existence of God, he will honor the bet and reward him.

Interestingly, after his sister's death in 1661—a year before his own death—Pascal inaugurated the first-ever bus line, called the *Carosse a cinq sols,* which would travel a predestined route whether or not there were passengers, thus initiating the idea of public transportation. For unclear reasons this idea did not work out and the line had to be discontinued. Shortly afterwards, Pascal's health took a turn for the worse, and he died in August 1662.

DISCUSSION

A French analyst Didier Anzieu, basing himself largely on Marguerite's memoir, wrote a very complex paper weaving in the very early traumas of his life and suggesting that Pascal suffered from the eight month's anaclitic depression described by Spitz, and was also saddled by anxieties and phobias about void and emptiness. Anzieu felt that Pascal was able to soothe his inner turmoil by displacing it outside. Because of his precocious intelligence, he could focus on the scientific study of the external world, which could be controlled and mastered, in contrast to the inner world's unmanageability. Anzieu concluded his paper with the proposition that Pascal's ability to prove the existence of an external vacuum helped him to preconsciously formulate the idea that psychic reality could tolerate a void. That is, unconscious beliefs and fantasies feed our efforts to find meaning in external reality. Once identified, this allows us to put together mental and verbal means to locate the unconscious fantasy in its proper psychic reality.

The degree and content of Pascal's anxieties and preoccupations suggests that many of his concerns were far beyond the neurotic level. One could assume that early in life Pascal did not have the presence of a good enough external object and, therefore, could not tolerate the physical absence of those he loved.

Recent developments in psychoanalysis, including Andre Green's work on the negative, and the work on figurability in France, plus the exploration of the void as being related to very early non-representation, allow us to deepen our understanding of Pascal's mind. It would have been helpful to have more data about the emotional connection between Pascal and his father. We know about the intense involvement of Etienne in his children's intellectual growth but, unfortunately, the details of his emotional connection with them is lacking. Did the father in some way compensate for the psychic loss and death of the mother? We shall never know!

In his contribution Levine (2013, p. 43) he assumes, along with Bion, that the original Experience, i.e., an unformulated unrepresented state, is in itself traumatic because it cannot be transformed into a represented experience. It is prepsychic and pathological. In her paper on the "Predisposition to Anxiety" (1941), Greenacre accurately describes characterological anxieties so similar to those Pacal suffered from, that I am including a lengthy quote. She suggests that:

suffering and frustration occurring during the antenatal and early postnatal months especially in the period preceding speech development leaves a heightened organic stamp on the makeup of the child.... It includes a kind of increased indelibility of reaction to experience which heightens the anxiety potential and gives greater resonance to the anxieties of later life.... It also includes the increased mirroring tendency arising partly from the imperfect developing sense of reality.... This is the antecedent towards over facile identification of neurotic individuals and in psychotics towards easy projection [p. 610].

Green has pursued similar ideas in his work on the negative and wit, his concept of decathexis. I believe that a considerable aspect of Pascal's pathology resides at this primitive level of non-representation.

In their book, *The Work of Psychic Figurability,* (Botellas, C. & Botellas, S. 2005), I found a quote (Ch 1, p. 17) by Isaac Newton (1642–1726) who lived during part of Pascal's period. In their book, this quote seems to mirror Pascal's view of the universe. Here is the quote: "The universe is an infinite vacuum of which only an infinite small part is filled by objects, objects that move across the limitless and bottomless void...."

The Botellas comment that Newton's intuition "implies the boldness and subtlety of a movement of thought transforming all the data of the moment into one single unity, bridling the immensity of the unrepresentable Vacuum." They add that this work of figuration is independent of reason (p. 18). I do not know whether Pascal ever read Newton, or whether the Botellas ever read Pascal, although they do include one reference to him (p. 109) in the book. A bit late, the Botellas state: "like primitive man who accepts the inevitability of death, acknowledging it and disavowing in the same magical act, memory acknowledges and disavows the reality of loss." In this context I believe that for Pascal, the faith in God served multiple personal essential unconscious functions: (1) create a meaning which replaces a psychic void including absence of memory and capacity for representation. (2) the assuaging of the anxiety about emptiness (3) reassurance concerning the anxiety about death and the void that follows.

(4) the relief that God, a fantasized person-parent, would look after him in the next world. (5) a compensation for the suffering in this world (6) the belief in miracles emphasizes the power of God and make helplessness more tolerable (7) the fulfillment of the idea that the heart has its reasons unknown to reason. Faith cannot be proved by rational mechanisms. This is important as it assuages Pascal's fear that although faith is irrational, its validity is not open to question. This allows Pascal to bypass the key concepts of reason and self-awareness which earlier were valued as such a powerful tool in the psychology of a human being, distinguishing him from the animal kingdom.

It would be possible to generalize about the role of Catholicism and most other religious systems as fulfilling similar needs in the life of human beings. Freud (1927) has developed these ideas in his paper "On the Future of an Illusion" stressing the role of God as an ambivalent replacement for the absent father to deal with unmanageable anxieties about life.

There is one core issue that our field is not able to tackle; that is the nature and development of genius. We can describe its growth, as in Mozart, but what makes it possible in the case of Pascal is simply beyond our understanding.

REFERENCES

Anzieu, D. (1975). Naissance du concept du vide chez Pascal. *Nouvelle Revue de Psychanalyse* 11,195–203 Gallimard Paris.

Beardsley M. (1960). *The European Philosophers from Descartes to Nietzsche.* New York: Modern Library, 1992.

Botella, C. & Botella, S. (2004). *The Work of Psychic Figurability.* London: The New Library of Psychoanalysis.

Chevalier J. (1950). *L'oeuvre de Pascal.* Bruges: Bibliothèque de la Pleiade, Gallimard.

Freud, S. (1927). The Future of an Illusion. *Standard Edition* 21:3–56.

Green, A. (1993). *The Work of the Negative.* London: Free Association Books, 1999.

Greenacre, P. (1941). The Predisposition to Anxiety Part II. *Psychanal. Q.* 10:610–648

Levine, H.B., Reed, G.S., & Scarfone, D. (2013). *Unrepresented States and the Construction of Meaning.* London: Karnac.

Pascal, B. (1656–1658). *Les Provinciales Ou Les Lettres Écrites Par Louis De Montalte À Un Provincial De Ses Amis Et Aux Révérends Pères Jésuites. ý* Neuilly sur Seine: Ulan Press, 2012.

——— (1670). *Pensées and Other Writings.* Oxford: Oxford University Press, 2006.

Saint-Chevron, J. (2023). *Voila ce qu'est la foi.* Paris: Salvator.

www.ingramcontent.com/pod-product-compliance
Lightning Source LLC
Chambersburg PA
CBHW062109020426

42335CB00013B/905